ATMOSPHERES OF
BREATHING

ATMOSPHERES OF
BREATHING

edited by

Lenart Škof and Petri Berndtson

Cover art: Maja Bjelica, "LUNGTREE VI," LUNGTREE Series (2016)

Published by State University of New York Press, Albany

For information, contact State University of New York Press, Albany, NY
www.sunypress.edu

Library of Congress Cataloging-in-Publication Data

Names: Škof, Lenart, editor | Berndtson, Petri, editor
Title: Atmospheres of breathing / Lenart Škof and Petri Berndtson, editors.
Description: Albany : State University of New York Press, 2018 | Includes
    bibliographical references and index.
Identifiers: LCCN 2017029912 | ISBN 9781438469737 (hardcover : alk. paper) |
    ISBN 9781438469744 (pbk. : alk. paper) | ISBN 9781438469751 (ebook)
Subjects: LCSH: Philosophy and science. | Respiration.
Classification: LCC B67 .A75 2018 | DDC 128/.6—dc23
LC record available at https://lccn.loc.gov/2017029912.

10 9 8 7 6 5 4 3 2 1

Contents

Acknowledgments

Some chapters of this book have been previously published in the following journals and edited collections.

A shorter version of Lenart Škof's "Breath as a Way of Self-Affection: On New Topologies of Transcendence and Self-Transcendence" was first published in *Bogoslovni vestnik* 77, no. 3/4 (2017): 577–588. Reprinted with permission.

An earlier version of David Kleinberg-Levin's essay "Logos and Psyche: A Hermeneutics of Breathing" was published in *Research in Phenomenology* 15 (1984): 121–147. Reprinted with permission of Brill Publishers.

An earlier version of James Morley's chapter "Inspiration and Expiration: Yoga Practice through Merleau-Ponty's Phenomenology of the Body" was first published in *Philosophy East and West* 51, no. 1 (January 2001): 73–82. Reprinted with permission of University of Hawai'i Press.

Silvia Benso's essay "The Breathing of the Air: Pre-Socratic Echoes in Levinas" was originally published in *Levinas and the Ancients*, ed. Brian Schroeder and Silvia Benso (Bloomington and Indianapolis: Indiana University Press, 2008), 9–23. Reprinted with permission of Indiana University Press.

David Abram's essay "The Commonwealth of Breath" was originally a part of *Material Ecocriticism*, ed. Serenella Iovino and Serpil Oppermann (Bloomington and Indianapolis: Indiana University Press, 2014), 301–314. Reprinted with permission of Indiana University Press.

We would like to thank our SUNY Press editors Andrew Kenyon and Chelsea Miller for their continuing support in proposing and publishing this book. We are also grateful to all our anonymous reviewers as well as SUNY editorial board members for their comments and insightful suggestions.

We wish to express our special thanks to Professor Emeritus David Kleinberg-Levin for helping us to reissue his essay. Finally, we want to deeply thank Maja Bjelica for all the help she has offered to us during the whole process of editing this book and preparing it for publication, as well as for providing her beautiful photo titled "LUNGTREE VI" for the cover of this book.

—Lenart Škof and Petri Berndtson

Introduction

LENART ŠKOF AND PETRI BERNDTSON

What then, in today's world, can we do in philosophy with the breath? It is our wish in this volume to present the readers with a new genre in philosophy—namely, a respiratory philosophy[1]—as an archeology of breath, and think of respiratory philosophers as spiritual archaeologists excavating its hidden ontological, epistemological, ethical, religious, and political layers. According to Luce Irigaray, it is our future task to become awakened to a new ethical constellation in which we will be "making awareness of the breath essential for an embodied ethics of difference in our globalized, ecological age."[2] This future age is called by Irigaray in her more recent writings the Age of the Breath or, within Christianity (in sense of its fulfillment), the Age of the Spirit. Since Anaximenes's famous sentence on breath as "aer" and "pneuma," Western tradition has entered an age of oblivion of the breath as a philosophical topic or principle. Analogously to Irigaray's designation of Heidegger's philosophy as one forgetting the breath,[3] we could depict Western tradition since Plato as being a part of the long process of forgetting this ever original of spirit in many traditions of philosophical and religious thinking of the world (we think of ancient notions of a *breath-spirit* substance, called in different traditions *lil, ku, ruah, pneuma, aer, spiritus, prana, ki, qi, ik', mana, orenda* . . .). Analogously, we can trace in Judeo-Christian tradition the similar process of forgetting of the breath in its originary biologico-spiritual sense. In the Hebrew Bible, we still can understand *ruah* as identifying "breath" of men and women with the "Breath" of God and, as Škof and Holmes point out in their introduction to *Breathing with Luce Irigaray*, also in the New Testament (cf. Rom 8:26), the life of prayer "brings spirit back to the body and back to the breath"[4] and thus nurtures and preserves, as it were, an ancient and archaic pneumatic covenant in the hearts of men and women. But despite some exceptions (as for example of the role of *pneuma* in the contexts of ancient Greek medicine) in the philosophical tradition of the West, breath as one of the key epistemological foundations of both our biological and spiritual life has quickly been abandoned and has instead become only one of many immaterial and disembodied substances, now being available only to specialists in one or another regional ontological disciplines (soul, spirit, ego, subject).

One of the *great breathers*[5] of the twentieth century and Nobel literature prize winner Elias Canetti warned us of the thinkers who have not breathed enough, as he wrote: "It is not enough to think, one also has to breathe. Dangerous are the thinkers who have not breathed enough."[6] Another great breather of the twentieth century, Hazrat Inayat Khan gave his own warning related to the breath: "My spiritual teacher, my Murshid, once said, 'People say that there are many sins and virtues, but I think there is only one sin.' I asked him what it was, and he said, 'To let one breath go without being conscious of it.'"[7] The meaning of the word "sin" must be understood here as "fundamental error," "wrongdoing," or "misdeed." Khan also says of the relation between breathing and philosophy the following: "the subject of breath is the deepest of all the subjects with which [. . .] philosophy is concerned, because breath is the most important thing"[8] as "in it is hidden the secret of life."[9] Would this not mean that from the perspective of the great breathers the sin of philosophy, that is, the fundamental error of philosophy is its constant "forgetting of breathing"?[10] What would be the connection between this possible sin of philosophy and dangerousness of the thinkers who have not breathed enough? A third great breather of the twentieth century, Japanese Aikido master Shinichi Suzuki, who emphasizes in his work the fundamental importance of the "world of nothing but breathing,"[11] sings along with Khan in harmony as he airs with confidence: "nothing is more important than breathing, breathing, breathing."[12] If we would take these words of Canetti, Khan, and Suzuki very seriously, it would challenge us with a new task of thinking. This task would be to create systematically a new philosophy of breathing that we could call by the name of *respiratory philosophy, breathing philosophy,* or *breathful philosophy*. What kind of philosophy would this new respiratory, or breathful, philosophy be? What it would think? How it would think? How would it understand the relations between thinking and breathing, philosophy and respiration? How would it differ from any other kind of philosophy or way of thinking? What could, perhaps, be the starting point of this new respiratory philosophy? These are all essential questions regarding this new respiratory philosophy.

According to Maurice Merleau-Ponty, "Philosophy will find help in poetry, art, etc.; in a closer relationship with them, it will be reborn."[13] Similarly, we suggest that philosophy could find help and guidance from the great breathers like Canetti, Khan, and Suzuki, as well as many other great breathers who will appear on the pages of this volume, and thus in a closer relationship with all them it could be reborn as a new respiratory philosophy. We have already received from Canetti, Khan, and Suzuki important guidance and warnings. Let us take these guiding words as the starting point from which we could perhaps begin to develop systematically this respiratory philosophy as an absolutely new way of thinking. So, what we have already learned from these great breathers is that it is not enough to think—one must also breathe. What would be, then, the relationship between thinking and breathing? Would the relationship be parallel, in which the thinker as a respiratory philosopher investigates breathing from a distance, or would it be a chiasmic relation in which the thinker and the experience of breathing somehow constantly intertwine in an essential manner, perpetually inspiring each other? The latter option sounds more plausible, as otherwise Canetti's warning that those thinkers who *have not breathed enough* are dangerous would not make much sense. Why would the thinkers who have not breathed enough be dangerous if the relation between thinking and breathing is merely parallel and distant? The relationship is not parallel as, for example, by holding his or her breath, the thinker can quickly influence experientially the ability to think and lose his or her illusionary idea of distance and dualism between thinking and breathing. This idea of distance can be kept only in a certain kind of breathing, and it is this certain way of breathing that allows one, in the first place, to have that kind of illusionary idea. So, if breathing and thinking are essentially intertwined, even if we are normally quite oblivious of this crossing, it is important to ask what this really means. How do they intertwine? How do they influence each other? Is there still some kind of distance between thinking and breathing, since we can speak of them separately, or is this separation only separation at a conceptual, linguistic level? Would this mean that every thought, even those we barely notice, is at some fundamental level already in a hidden and latent manner a respiratory thought—that is, a thought somehow inspired by the breath?

Let us here take one important example from the history of philosophy. René Descartes begins the third meditation of *Meditations on First Philosophy* with these famous words:

> I will now close my eyes, block my ears and shut down all my senses. I will erase from my thought all images of physical things or, since this is almost impossible, I will regard them as nothing, as false and empty, addressing only myself and looking more deeply into myself. I will try to make myself gradually better known and more familiar to myself. I am a thinking thing, that is, something which is doubting, affirming, denying, understanding a few things, not knowing many, willing, not willing, even imagining and sensing. As I already mentioned, even if the things that I sense or imagine happened not to exist, I am still certain that the modes of thinking that I call sensations and imaginings, insofar as they are simply certain modes of thinking, are in me. And in these few things I have listed everything that I know or, at least, what I have so far noticed that I know.[14]

If we truly take our initial guidance from Canetti and Khan in our efforts to think in a respiratory manner, we can say that the cardinal sin of philosophy, or the fundamental error of thinking, is in play with these words of Descartes.[15]

He forgets breathing completely, and as he forgets breathing he is not at all truthful in what he writes. As this major example from Western philosophy is investigated within the atmosphere of breathing, it reveals itself in a completely different manner to us than we are traditionally used to. Let us follow what Descartes does in this famous example, which has played such an important role in the whole of modern philosophy. What Descartes wants to do is to address only himself by looking deeper and deeper into himself. This means that he tries to make himself gradually better known and more familiar to himself. This path to self-knowledge as indubitable knowledge goes through various steps of withdrawal from the world. To be able to gain this indubitable and absolutely certain knowledge, one must withdraw from the world of senses, as the senses often deceive us. The first step in achieving this epistemological goal is to close one's eyes, thereby withdrawing from the visual world. After this, Descartes says that he blocks his ears, withdrawing also from the auditory world. He does not tell us how he does it. In order to make this epistemological move, he perhaps puts his fingers in his ear canals or blocks them with some fabric. After these two steps of perceptual withdrawal from the world, he states: "I [. . .] shut down all my senses." This must also mean that he somehow blocks his nostrils so as not to smell any odors of the world, either by holding his nose or by blocking both of his nostrils with fabric. But in order to shut down all his senses, he must also ensure that he does not accidentally taste anything. This means he must close his mouth, which is as easy as closing one's eyes. Now he is truly ready to address *only himself* with no distractions or deceptions from the outside world. He can truly begin to look deeper and deeper into himself and try to arrive at genuine self-knowledge. But the problem here is that he is not being truthful at all. There are two possibilities. Either he did not do what he said he would do, or he did not truthfully describe the experience of totally shutting down all of his senses. How do we know this for certain? If he did what he said he would do, he would have blocked his respiratory openings (both his mouth and his nostrils) and could no longer breathe in air. Thus, quite quickly, his task of addressing *only himself* and looking more deeply into himself to gain pure and indubitable self-knowledge would have manifested itself as a gradual sense of discomfort, leading ultimately to a dreadful experience of anxiety. This also means that Descartes would not have had the chance to state in a calm fashion the famous words, "I am a thinking thing"—rather, his sole thought would have been *I am feeling terrible. How long can I hold my breath? I really need to breathe.* With this train of thought, the Cartesian philosophy would have been an absolutely different philosophy. From Descartes's own description of his withdrawal from the world, we can easily infer that he did *not* shut down all of his senses as he said he would. He might have come close, opening either his mouth or his nostrils once in a while during his exploration of himself. In any case, it is clear that Descartes's "thinking thing" is from the very beginning tarnished by the breath, by the atmosphere of breathing.

This is an important example of what could be the meaning of the sin of philosophy from the perspective of respiratory philosophy. In his description, Descartes is not at all conscious of every breath he takes during the process of thinking. His cardinal sin of "forgetting of breathing" leads to a completely fictitious philosophical description. Following Canetti, could we say here that Descartes is indeed dangerous for philosophy because he has not breathed enough? If he would have breathed enough, he would have never been oblivious to breathing and would have never arrived at his dualistic philosophy in the way he that did. In respiratory philosophy, we can also conceive of a self separate from the world, but that self is an anxious self that has a constant urge to reconnect with our original way of being as breathing-in-the-world. Within the Western tradition, the almost universal forgetting of breathing made it possible for the dangerous idea of dualism to become a paradigm of modern philosophy.[16] It could be argued that modern philosophy's dualism is impossible if the starting principle of philosophizing is the experience of breathing, as breathing perpetually intertwines the self, the body, and the world.

If Descartes and most of the Western tradition have not breathed enough, then who could have breathed enough not to be dangerous? Perhaps we get a clue from the following aphorism from Canetti: "Philosophers one gets entangled in: Aristotle. Philosophers to hold others down with: Hegel. Philosophers for inflation: Nietzsche. For breathing: Zhuangzi."[17] In his autobiography, Canetti names Zhuangzi as the one "who for me has been the most intimate of all the philosophers."[18] So the Daoist philosopher Zhuangzi, according to Canetti, as his most intimate companion of all the philosophers, is *the* philosopher for breathing. If this is the case, we must be quite confident, even if we do not know this for absolute certainty, that Zhuangzi is a thinker, a philosopher, who has, in Canetti's view, breathed enough not to be dangerous. Would this make Zhuangzi, perhaps, the respiratory philosopher *par excellence*—even if we do not yet know in any explicit manner what that really means? Canetti does not tell us why he thinks Zhuangzi is the philosopher for breathing. Before we investigate why Canetti *perhaps* understands Zhuangzi as the philosopher for breathing, we should consider the other great thinkers he mentions in his aphorism. Does Canetti mean that Aristotle, Hegel, and Nietzsche, despite being some of the greatest thinkers of all time, remain dangerous if they did not breathe enough? Again, Canetti provides no answer. These thinkers would require similar kinds of respiratory investigations to those just described for Descartes in his *Meditations on First Philosophy*. One of the important tasks of anew respiratory philosophy will be to reread the great thinkers in a respiratory key to examine their relation to the phenomenon of breath.

So why choose Zhuangzi as the philosopher for breathing and a potential guide toward a new respiratory philosophy? The clue perhaps can be found in the following words: "The True Man [zhenren] [. . .] breathing deep breaths. The

True Man breathes with his heels; the mass of men breathe with their throats."[19] In these words of Zhuangzi we can first notice that he makes a distinction between the "True Man" and the "mass of men," and the difference between them is the way they breathe. First of all, let us briefly investigate Zhuangzi's Chinese term *zhenren*, which is often translated as "true man." The Chinese *ren* means "Man, a man, a person." The meaning of *zhen* is more complex, as it means "true, real, authentic." So, in addition to "true man," *zhenren* might be translated as "real man," "authentic man," or "true person." But why do many of the translations capitalize Zhuangzi's *zhenren* as a "True Man"? This is because, in his usage, "true man," or "authentic person," derives a special meaning—"Daoist spiritual master"—that is, a person who has undergone a spiritual transformation and thus has become perfected as a human being, that is, has realized his true or authentic nature as a human being. In achieving this spiritual transformation, the practice of breathing, or the cultivation of breathing, is essential. Thus, in this quotation from Zhuangzi it is highly important that this difference between the "True Man" and the "mass of men" is not in the first place at the level of thinking, and especially not at the level of knowledge, but at the level of breathing. Would this mean that, according to Zhuangzi, the difference of breathing is a more fundamental difference between people than the difference in their way of thinking? Yes, it would. So, there is *a fundamental difference of breathing.* The True Man breathes deeply. He "breathes with his heels." This expression can be understood in the sense that he breathes so deeply that his breath reaches his heels. His expanded breath, cultivated through breathing practices reaches his uttermost depths. He breathes from head to toe. So, it could be said that to breathe with his heels means to breathe with his whole being. In comparison to this, "the mass of men breathe with their throats," which means they breathe superficially and are thus hardly at all consciously connected with their breathing.[20] As they do not breathe at all deeply they do not reach the depth dimensions of breathing. They do not experience the vastness of the breath in all of its spiritual and ontological possibilities and atmospheres.

So, let us return to the heart of the matter: "It is not enough to think, one also has to breathe. Dangerous are the thinkers who have not breathed enough." First of all, most of the thinkers belong to "the mass of men [who] breathe with their throats" and thus "have not breathed enough." This makes them dangerous in Canetti's respiratory view. It is extremely rare to find a thinker who has breathed enough, that is, who breathes with his heels, with his whole being. In Zhuangzi, Canetti saw this rarity of the meeting of a great thinker and a great breather, and for this reason it could be very well said that this philosopher "for breathing" was for him "the most intimate of all the philosophers."

In this, our initial explorative journey of respiratory philosophy, it can be said that Canetti's respiratory view of the dangerousness of thinkers who have not breathed enough matches well with Khan's view of the real sinners who are not conscious of the breath. So, in Khan's respiratory view, as mentioned earlier, "there is only one sin" and that is "to let one breath go without being conscious of it." This is the only true error or fundamental wrongdoing in human life. Everything else is secondary in comparison. Shinichi Suzuki's phrase that "nothing is more important than breathing, breathing, breathing" states perfectly Khan's view: "breath is the most important thing." For this reason, to miss this most important thing in life is to sin, and sin we do, as most of the time we human beings are eminently unaware of the phenomenon of breathing and its manifold mysteries. The only antidote against this cardinal sin, according to Khan, is to become a "master of breath" who "*always* consults his breath" and is "*always* conscious of the breath."[21] But this is of course extremely difficult, as anyone who has tried even for short moments to be as conscious of the breath as possible knows. But the more one practices and cultivates the art of conscious breathing, the more possible the impossible begins to appear in one's experience.

According to Khan, breath is "the deepest of all the subjects with which [. . .] philosophy is concerned." If according to Martin Heidegger, "Being is the proper and sole theme of philosophy,"[22] then—from Khan's point of view—we could say the same thing about the breath. Khan could, thus, perhaps say: *the breath is the proper and sole theme of philosophy*. He writes: "People ordinarily think of breath as that little air they feel coming and going through the nostrils, but they do not think of it as that *vast current which goes through everything*, that current which comes from our consciousness and goes as far as the external being, the physical world."[23] So as for Heidegger, Being as the clearing is that open space within which everything appears and disappears, for Khan the atmosphere of breath is that "vast current" that surrounds, intermediates, and flows "through everything." In another instance, Khan says that "to an average person it seems as if [in breath just] some air goes out and comes in. But the mystics [as the masters of breath] follow this chain of breath in the pursuit of the Infinite."[24] In these quotations Khan makes a very similar distinction to that of Zhuangzi. Whereas Zhuangzi speaks of the "mass of men," Khan speaks of the ordinary or average people. And when Zhuangzi speaks of the "True Man" as a spiritual master, Khan speaks of the mystic as the master of breath. For Khan, a mystic is a person who has devoted his or her life to the study of the "*mystery* of breath."[25] The respiratory content is very similar to that of Zhuangzi, as also in Khan's view the ordinary, or average, people experience their breathing only as "little air [. . .] coming and going through the nostrils." This average person's experience of breathing is superficial and misses completely the vast depth dimensions of the breath and the immense atmospheres of breathing, that is, all the possibilities of breathing. On the other hand, the mystic as the master of breath or as the great breather experiences the breath as "that vast current which goes through everything." For the great breathers, "everything breathes again."[26] From these great breathers, or masters of breath, the new respiratory philosophy takes its inspiration as it tries to learn to re-experience all the questions of philosophy as questions concerning the atmospheres of breathing.

So, what could this completely new philosophy as respiratory philosophy be? That remains mostly an open question, as our respiratory journey has just begun. We could perhaps say that this question is as open as breathing itself. Breathing is openness, that is, respiratory openness, a perpetual opening to the atmosphere of air. The air itself is also pure openness as in itself it obstructs nothing. Things around us obstruct as, for example, they block our vision, movement, or speech, but the atmosphere of air is pure open freedom, free from any obstruction. In this respiratory and aerial openness, all questions, problems, and subjects of philosophy appear as questions, problems, and subjects of respiratory philosophy. Their appearance takes place within this respiratory openness as the atmosphere of breathing.

The basic insight of this new philosophy of breathing as respiratory philosophy is that there is a *respiratory difference* that makes this new way of thinking possible. What is this respiratory difference? It is what we have previously referred to with the help of the great breathers. It is the difference between breathing consciously and thoughtfully and not breathing consciously and thoughtfully. It is the difference between thinking breathfully and not thinking breathfully, and the difference between cultivating breathing and not cultivating breathing. It is the difference between the breath of the "True Man" and the breath of the "mass of men." This respiratory difference is a perpetual choice that we face each and every moment with each and every breath. The understanding of this difference in thinking is the fundamental principle of respiratory philosophy.

We can offer here one possible idea of what this respiratory difference in thinking could mean. In *Phenomenology of Perception*, Maurice Merleau-Ponty defines "true philosophy" as the task of "learning to see the world anew."[27] What might this mean if interpreted through the insights of respiratory philosophy? What would this *new way* of seeing the world entail? Let us take our lead from Canetti again, who once pondered "If eyes could breathe."[28] Could we learn to see the world anew with eyes that breathe? And if we would listen to Khan on this matter, what could we learn from him? Khan would advise that the vision would always consult with the breath. How would one learn to see in collaboration with the breath? Perhaps we could simply say that the meaning of this new way to see the world would be to see the world in *a respiratory way*. To see the world in a respiratory way would mean to see it within the atmosphere of breathing, and perhaps to see it according to the breath or to see it in collaboration with breathing. The respiratory philosophy would then be to relearn to see the world perpetually within the atmosphere of breathing. This would mean that whatever we are looking at, we must always be conscious of the atmosphere of breathing and strive to see our subject within it. In this way of seeing the world, the philosopher takes into account that his or her vision always takes place within the atmosphere of breathing and, similarly, that the object at which he or she gazes also appears within this respiratory atmosphere. There is no vision and no visual object without the respiratory atmosphere that surrounds and mediates them. Thus, through this new way of seeing the world, all the questions of life, including all philosophical questions, are transformed into respiratory questions. All questions of philosophy become *respiratory questions of philosophy*. They are seen perpetually from the perspective of breathing. A good example of what this means in practice is how *we looked* earlier *at* Descartes's words of *Meditations on First Philosophy* from the perspective of breathing. Our respiratory interrogation showed that if Descartes would have remembered breathing, his examination would have had a completely different outcome. This means that forgetting of breathing can have very serious consequences, and for this reason the great breathers like Canetti and Khan warned us of the thinkers who have not breathed enough.

Notably, the history of Western philosophy is a history of masculine domination in philosophical thought. It is thus no coincidence that as a thinker of sexual difference, it was precisely a woman philosopher, Luce Irigaray, who *as philosopher* has for the first time in the history of philosophy breathed through her entire philosophy. In her short but beautiful piece "Ethical Gestures Toward the Other" (Irigaray 2010), Irigaray devotes thoughts to breath/ing and warns us that we too often forget our breath as being the first autonomous gesture of our lives. She writes: "No doubt, we breathe on pain of death, but we breathe poorly, and we worry little about our first food of life: air."[29] Even more importantly, Irigaray links the cultivation of breathing to the cultivation of ethics in ourselves and in our intersubjective relations. Let us, nearing the end of this introduction, look at her words:

> Not only does our culture not teach us how to cultivate breathing to assure our existence in an autonomous way, but it does not make known to us that becoming spiritual amounts to transforming our elemental vital breath into a more subtle breath at the service of loving, of speaking and hearing, of thinking. Too often we confuse cultivation and spirituality with the learning of words, of knowledge, of competences. We have forgotten that to be cultivated amounts to being able to breathe, not only in order to survive, but in order to constitute a reserve of breath as a soul that helps us to transform our natural life into a spiritual life.[30]

Finally, it was Luce Irigaray, who in *The Forgetting of Air in Martin Heidegger*,[31] again for the first time in the history of Western thought, devoted an entire book to a criticism of a major Western thinker (Heidegger) for the forgetting of breath in his philosophical oeuvre.

In each chapter of this volume the questions of philosophy are investigated from the perspective of breathing, and thus these questions are transformed into respiratory questions. These philosophical questions include, for example, questions of ontology, ethics, aesthetics, hermeneutics, phenomenology, politics, and environment. Throughout the pages of this volume these different philosophical questions are changed into respiratory questions of ontology, ethics, aesthetics, politics, and so forth. Through this process of exploration, these phenomena can be understood as new depth dimensions or atmospheres of breathing. If the task of respiratory philosophy is to perpetually relearn to see the world in a respiratory way, that is, as a respiratory revision, this means that everything within our lifeworld needs to be re-thought, re-examined, and re-experienced within these atmospheres of breathing. The respiratory philosophy as the revision of the world is a cultivation of breathing. The thinker inspired by this respiratory revision, to borrow from Canetti, "no longer wants thoughts that bite. He wants thoughts that make it easier to breathe."[32] This volume is one of the first attempts in this task of relearning to see the world in a respiratory way as it offers to the readers so many in-depth variations and rich modulations of this world where "everything breathes again."

David Kleinberg-Levin's chapter on hermeneutics of breathing is without doubt one of the key elaborations on breath in the entire history of philosophy. In this chapter the phenomenon of breathing is articulated and interpreted in its vastness as the most open openness of human existence as well as the most fundamental openness to the world. This expansive openness gives Kleinberg-Levin space, time, and freedom to breathe in such an inspiring manner that it breathes room for any attentive reader to see immense possibilities and potentialities of new connections and intertwinings in respiratory terms. In this seminal text, Kleinberg-Levin presents—with the help of Heidegger, Merleau-Ponty ("respiratory body"), Heraclitus ("psyche" and "logos"), Kierkegaard, Rilke, and a few others—a completely new atmosphere: a respiratory atmosphere to think and explore questions of ontology, psychology, psychoanalysis, hermeneutics, poetry, speech, spirituality, communication, embodiment, religion, and more. Respiratory philosophy researchers of the future will benefit from this opening overture in which Kleinberg-Levin has laid out for us to understand how any theme can be investigated via the most fundamental openness of the breath. Further, his chapter suggests how breathing might constitute the whole of our life—from space to time, from speech to poetry, from anxiety to self-development. It is the challenge for future respiratory thinkers to develop further the multiple philosophical implications that can be articulated within this most fundamental openness of respiratory atmosphere that Kleinberg-Levin has offered to all of us.

Petri Berndtson explores in his chapter the possible relations between respiration and ontology. The leading question of the chapter asks if the experience of respiration can teach us an ontology that it alone can reveal to us? If so, what kind of ontology would this respiratory ontology be, and how would the phenomenon of breathing redefine the question of Being? With the help of Maurice Merleau-Ponty, this question of Being will be redefined as the question concerning "inspiration and expiration of Being." This notion of "inspiration and expiration of Being" comes from Merleau-Ponty's work "Eye and Mind." In this chapter, Berndtson's ontological investigation of "inspiration and expiration of Being, respiration within Being" will find help especially from Merleau-Ponty's and Martin Heidegger's ontological thinking of Being. In his investigation, the question of Being is understood as the question of ontological difference—the question between Being and beings. This ontological difference is given a respiratory interpretation as the difference of inspiration and expiration of Being and beings. To clarify the respiratory dimensions of ontological difference, Berndtson includes an examination of Zen Buddhism. In Zen, emphasis is on the breathing practice of *zazen*, as well as on the notion of *kū* (emptiness, sky, space, and air). These ideas from Zen will be understood ontologically within the context of ontological difference. In addition to Merleau-Ponty, Heidegger, and Zen, Gaston Bachelard's aerial poetics, as well as Luce Irigaray's aerial and respiratory thinking, are used to elaborate what this new respiratory ontology could be and how it would define basic ontological questions concerning, for example, what is a thing and what is not a thing. The basic insight of this respiratory ontology will be that it is not object- or thing-related, but atmosphere-related.

Lenart Škof argues in his chapter that breath perhaps was (and still is) the most neglected way of self-affection in the history of Western thought. By first introducing aerial elements in the thoughts of Feuerbach and Nietzsche, he continues by analyzing the most recent work of Luce Irigaray, in which a new ontology of sexual difference and breath is offered. Irigaray has proposed in her writings that humanity must search for a new way of intersubjective and communal dwelling known as the "Age of the Breath" (or, in terms of Christianity, the "Age of the Spirit"). In his chapter, Škof radicalizes Irigaray's thought by introducing Schelling's ontology of co-breathing from his famous *Human Freedom* essay and by thinking of a breath in a deeper ontological sense. According to Škof, breath could thus be a sign of our own path toward future divinization of our selves, of becoming more linked to the spiritual breath, and thus fully autonomous. The wounds of the world, as ontological fractures in the very core of our Being, are to be cured through our sensitivization of the breath. Finally, Škof argues that this is to be achieved by the means of a new pneumatic covenant, based on a new temporality of an ethical encounter as mutual ethical co-breathing, and, finally, of human as well as divine exchange of our spiritual breath(s).

In his chapter, Rolf Elberfeld discusses breath as a central aesthetic category within Chinese and Japanese traditions. First, he offers a semantic clarification of the meaning of various words for breathing and continues by elaborating on *qi/ki* as an aesthetic phenomenon in China and Japan. The main part of his chapter is dedicated to the aesthetical elements in Nō theater: here Elberfeld focuses on Zeami's (1363–1443) famous treatise on aesthetics and its implications for the mutual resonance between actor and audience via the mutual exchange of breath. For Elberfeld, aesthetic and artistic practices—such as Taiji, Qigong, music, Butoh dance, ink painting, drawing—as well as treatises in aesthetics are of vital importance for our time. Through an understanding of Asian cultures of breathing, according to Elberfeld, we are able to direct more attention to neglected elements within extant Western aesthetical theories and thus become more sensitized to the role of breath.

Silvia Benso puts thinking of breath in relation to Pre-Socratic tradition and its echoes in Levinas. We know that the Pre-Socratics held the elements fire, earth, water, and air of key importance. Benso's elaboration of Levinas's thought in this respect is highly important for the evolving tradition of the new respiratory philosophy we are proposing in this volume. We know that, for Levinas, inspiration represents a key concept, and that he regards the lungs as an ethical organ. Breathing, for Levinas, is *in-spiration*, a continuous process of ethical circulation of air, of our reaching of the other in an ethical way. Benso first discusses in detail the proto-respiratory philosophy of the pre-Socratics (particularly Anaximenes) and continues by elaborating the psychism and air in Levinas's main works (*Totality and Infinity* and *Otherwise than Being*). By drawing on rich deposits of respiratory phenomena in Levinas (psyche, air, inspiration/ expiration, spirit, lung), Benso aims to point to ethical subjectivity as enabling us to interpret the *pneuma* of psychism as a gift and donation for the other—an inspiration for-the-other, as it were, and toward the other in an ethical exchange yet to come.

Tamara Ditrich discusses in her chapter one of the key conceptual tools in Buddhist meditational practices, namely, mindfulness of breathing. This is one of the key methods in traditional as well as modern Buddhist contemplative practices. It also has a wide spectrum of uses in contemporary humanities and social sciences, and—in one or another version of this doctrine—especially in contemporary methods of psychology, psychiatry, and health science. Ditrich first explores breath in ancient Indian religion (Vedas, early ascetic movements) and then proceeds toward situating mindfulness in its original Buddhist contexts (early Buddhism). It is known that Buddha first attained his awakening through mindfulness of breathing. Ditrich analyzes textual evidence for mindfulness of breathing in a detailed manner in the rest of her chapter. In the conclusion of the chapter, she reflects on broader ethical usages of mindfulness (Buddhism itself did not develop a special philosophical discipline of ethics) and also views it as a constituent part of the meditation of loving kindness.

James Morley offers in his chapter an interpretation of the yoga practice of *prāṇāyāma* (breath control) influenced by the thought of Maurice Merleau-Ponty. This approach to yoga is less concerned with comparison between Merleau-Ponty's thought and the texts of classical yoga than with the elucidation of the actual experience of breath control through the constructs provided by Merleau-Ponty's extension of Husserl's philosophy of the lived-body. The discussion of yoga can answer certain pedagogical goals, but it can never finally be severed from *doing* yoga. Academic discourse centered entirely on the theoretical concepts of yoga philosophies must to some extent remain incomplete. Patañjali's *Yoga Sūtra* is itself a manual of practice. It is for this reason that Morley chooses to take as the basis of his study the commentary of the scholar-practitioner T.K.V. Desikachar, rather than a more exclusively theoretical commentary. In so doing, he approaches yogic breath work as an experience or phenomenon and not only in the context of a series of academic debates.

Jana Rošker's chapter deals with the concept of *qi* in Chinese philosophy—especially in the light of its role as a vital force of cosmic and human breath. According to Rošker, this concept is one of the most difficult and complex notions in Chinese ideational history. Rošker first analyzes various translations of *qi* in order to show how the concept has been misused and has diverged from its original meaning. Later in her chapter, she interprets *qi* in various philosophical, physiological, psychological, and ethical dimensions. Rošker shows that on a semantical level, *qi* is related to air, and especially to breath as the origin of the living world. One of her conclusions is that in a Chinese holistic worldview, *qi* can simultaneously be both immanent and transcendent and, along with being the source of life, its vital rhythm and nourishing could also be understood as "creativity" or a potential that enables us to function in a creative (and autonomous) way.

Tadashi Ogawa's contribution tackles wind, air, and breath from the holistic philosophico-medical point of view. Ogawa discusses the medical philosophy of Japanese thinker Kaibara Ekiken (1630–1713), a contemporary of Pascal and Leibniz, writing in his books on cosmic, philosophical, and medical aspects of our being-in-the-world through the cultivation of breath and breathing. For Ekiken (being both natural philosopher and Shintoist), human being is born in the atmospherical and ontological space between heaven and earth, and, clearly, this means that her existential basis is closely related to *ki* (Japanese for *qi*) as their basic principle and also—more concretely and naturally—the wind spirit. Ogawa analyzes Ekiken's books and searches for relations between the meanings of *ki* and related words that mean "breath." Ogawa explores the relation of *ki* and "breathing" in the context of Ekiken's writings in great detail, comparing them to Plato (the inner fire of the body movement versus the inhalation and exhalation of air) and Christianity (the divine workings of the Holy Spirit). Finally, Ogawa reflects on the practice of health (medical prescriptions and daily regimen as related to everyday activities) and its cosmic and philosophical implications.

Kevin Hart breathes into his chapter the poetic world of the late American poet Mark Strand. Hart walks through Strand's poems, paying special attention to "Breath," a poem that is Strand's most extensive treatment of our selfhood in its various physiological and spiritual layers. By reading Strand's poetry, according to Hart, we might at first think that breath is a mirror, but in a more fundamental poetic sense, breath *is* the medium of our language, its words, breaths, and thoughts.

Breath is somehow (poetically, but also naturally) related to the moves of our body, to our personal autonomy, which flows from our internal space(s) toward the other, in an ongoing dialectical encounter between the two, in a process of proximity and love, resembling Celan's designation of our poetic dwelling with the beautiful expression *Atemwende*, or "turning of our breath," enabling a new being in the world for us. Hart also tackles in his chapter the more hidden presence of breath in Mark Strand's poetry. In some of his more sublime poems, and in dialogue with Whitman, Rilke, and Stevens, Strand evokes in magical poetic moments the dependence of poetry, longing, and poetic salvation on breath and breathing.

Jones Irwin's chapter is a dialogue between Derrida and Artaud on the topic of breath. Derrida's encounter with Artaud is first analyzed, followed by a reading of Artaud with particular focus on the body, breath, and expression. For Artaud, flesh emphasizes the return to reality and, as he shows in his *Theatre of Cruelty*, breath as flesh's lifeforce has been too often suffocated by metaphysics. We need to think of breath beyond the metaphysical, both in Derrida and Artaud. Thus, the body will be reborn. Irwin shows in his chapter how a re-inspiration of breath is to be achieved in Artaud's philosophical project and, at the same time, how fragile this new embodied breathing can be.

In his chapter, John Durham Peters writes on the media of breathing. His approach is not limited by a narrow understanding of media but brings an innovative, expanded conception that includes technologies or techniques of our selves (such as cultures of breath), animal bodies and their breathful selves, and nature as revealed through technology. Durham Peters distinguishes between many arts of breathing. Especially illuminating are his original thoughts on a unique respiratory signature of each person, or even natural being. His analysis of cetaceans (whales, dolphins) and their breathing apparatus is without doubt among the most original accounts on animal and interspecies philosophy ever written. His comparative animal phenomenology, based on breath techniques, brings new insights into many fields in the humanities, particularly philosophy. In an idiosyncratic manner, Durham Peters also introduces and analyzes the term "cloud" as a new atmospheric media of breathing and concludes his chapter with the art of writing and vowels as the breathed part of language.

Marijn Nieuwenhuis takes us one step further in our rethinking of the breath. As a political scientist, he focuses in his work on the "politics of the air" and deals with questions of technology, pollution, security, territory, and governance. He provides a genealogical historiography of how knowledge of breathing has emerged and continues to evolve as an interest of governance. Nieuwenhuis is situated in the "Western" experience of breathing from Aristotle and ancient Greece, through Christianity all the way to the modern era. He elaborates on a more recent biopolitics of pneumatic therapy and the thanatopolitics of "gassing." He thus argues in his conclusions that breathing and knowledge of breathing have always been in interest to the governing of bodies.

Drew Leder addresses in his chapter breath as a theater for the play of health and illness. For him, in medical contexts, breath should be regarded not only as a respiratory fact in our organs but should play a much more sophisticated role. He thus introduces in his chapter the concept of a "hinge," as an interface, a living nexus between voluntary and involuntary, visible and invisible, interior and exterior. He elaborates on various techniques and medical traditions (including Daoist, Ayurvedic, Buddhist, Yogic breath) and argues in his conclusions for a more mindful approach toward our bodies-selves in medical as well as other life contexts.

Havi Carel's chapter presents a philosophical framework for the understanding of breath and breathlessness in terms of respiratory medicine. She first deals with the symptom of breathlessness within the clinic and outside it. Breathlessness, according to Carel, is a pathological derivative of many and varied physical, cultural, and religious forms, usages, and technologies of breathing. Breathlessness as an "invisible" but extremely dangerous symptom appears in a number of dangerous diseases. But for Carel, this symptom also needs a complex phenomenological elaboration. Phenomenological approach enables us to see deeper—that is, into the very logic (physiological, psychological, existential, cultural, spiritual) of this symptom. It also gives a new meaning to the personal and always unique experience of a bodily breakdown, or, as proposed by Carel, "bodily doubt" of an individual. This enables Carel to ask how this knowledge could be transmitted into the inherent logic of the clinic. She thus wishes to articulate the symptom and give phenomenology of breathlessness a new ethical meaning. Phenomenological reflection of breathlessness can help sufferers (patients) and doctors, in Carel's opinion, to develop a reflective stance from which to think about the painful experiences of illness and breathlessness and, importantly, to develop new knowledge and new strategies for those directly involved in these processes—in order to be able to treat them with care and ethical resilience.

In her chapter, Magdalena Górska presents a feminist politics of breathing. For Górska, breathing is situated in a natural and existential shared space of human and inhuman life forms. In these contexts, it clearly is represented in different respiratory forms. Through Karen Barad's concept of an "ethico-onto-epistemological" constitution, Górska wishes to engage with breathing as a relational enactment in all its environmental, social, and cultural practices. One of these contexts is related to various corpomaterial situations, as proposed by Górska, that is, in the worldly metabolization of oxygen, such as coal mining and suffocation by smog and pollution, among others. From these unequal exposures to air and its mutual sharing, inequalities in health follow as direct consequences. But also, in a more philosophico-ethico-political sense, with Górska, it really matters in our lives "how one's life is breathable." Feminist studies enable us to think of these processes within a broader context of various oppressive social structures. Upon this basis, Górska understands breathing as a force that enables social and environmental transformation to engage with oppressive structures and enable individuals to achieve their *freedom to breathe*.

David Abram concludes the collection with his chapter, "The Commonwealth of Breath." In a meditative-reflective manner, he argues that we need to create spaces of proximity that are not void and meaningless but filled with an atmosphere of air and breath. Abram thinks of the breathing atmosphere we need to regain for ourselves, and for our human and nonhuman others. For this purpose, he deals with Inuit and Yupik cosmology, and their understanding of *Sila*, a mysterious breath-like power, or spiritual essence residing in nature and in ourselves as its part. Abram also presents us with another example from Amerindian Dineh (or Navajo) people and *Nilch'i* as atmosphere, the Holy Wind, or the whole body of the air, as a medium of all beings. Finally, he draws on pueblo cultures from New Mexico and their emphasis on *kachinas*, or spirit ancestors. Above all, Abram is aware that this sacred, and especially oral, tradition should be regarded with the greatest respect and greatest care. In the conclusion to his chapter, Abram returns to his own Jewish tradition, and to *ruaḥ* as unseen presence in the Hebrew alphabet, arguing again for respect for a language that is not written but spoken and breathed. Since today we live in the world of forgetting of the breath, including in our languages and its media, Abram's message is a precious gift to our written respiratory project in philosophy.

Notes

1. One of the first explicit uses of the notion of "respiratory philosophy" can be found in Petri Berndtson's "The Inspiration and the Expiration of Being: The Immense Lung and the Cosmic Breathing as the Sources of Dreams, Poetry and Philosophy," in *Thinking in Dialogue with Humanities: Paths into the Phenomenology of Merleau-Ponty*, ed. Karel Novotný et al. (Bucharest: Zeta Books, 2010), 281–293.

2. Lenart Škof and Emily A. Holmes, *Breathing with Luce Irigaray* (London: Bloomsbury, 2013), 1–2 and 11.

3. Luce Irigaray, *The Forgetting of Air in Martin Heidegger*, trans. Mary Beth Mader (Austin: University of Texas Press, 1999).

4. Škof and Holmes, *Breathing with Luce Irigaray*, 9.

5. This notion of "great breather" is taken from Gaston Bachelard. For Bachelard, Johann Wolfgang von Goethe is an example of "a great breather," as he "breathes as the earth breathes. Goethe breathes with all his lungs as the earth breathes with all its atmosphere. The man who reaches the glory of breathing breathes cosmically." Gaston Bachelard, *The Poetics of Reverie: Childhood, Language, and the Cosmos*, trans. Daniel Russell (Boston: Beacon Press, 1971), 180–181.

6. Elias Canetti, *The Human Province*, trans. Joachim Neugtoschel (New York: Seabury Press, 1978), 194.

7. Hazrat Inayat Khan, "Breath," in *The Art of Being*.

8. Hazrat Inayat Khan, "The Mystery of Breath," in *In an Eastern Rose Garden*.

9. Hazrat Inayat Khan, "Pasi Anfas: Breath," in *The Gathas*.

10. Luce Irigaray, *Between East and West: From Singularity to Community*, trans. Stephen Pluhácek (New York: Columbia University Press, 2002).

11. Shinichi Suzuki in Robert E. Carter, *The Japanese Arts and Self-Cultivation* (Albany: State University of New York Press, 2008), 32.

12. Ibid.

13. Maurice Merleau-Ponty, *Notes des cours au Collège de France 1958–1959 et 1960–1961* (Paris: Éditions Gallimard, 1996), 39.

14. René Descartes, *Meditations and Other Metaphysical Writings*, trans. Desmond M. Clarke (London: Penguin Books, 2003), 30.

15. For more on Descartes's forgetting of breathing see Lenart Škof, *Breath of Proximity: Intersubjectivity, Ethics and Peace* (Dordrecht: Springer, 2015), 129–131.

16. This sentence is very much inspired by Irigaray, who wrote: "The forgetting of breathing in our tradition is almost universal." Irigaray, *Between East and West*, 77.

17. Elias Canetti, *The Secret Heart of the Clock: Notes, Aphorisms, Fragments 1973–1985*, trans. Joel Agee (New York: Farrar, Straus, and Giroux, 1989), 10–11.

18. Elias Canetti, *The Memoirs of Elias Canetti*, trans. Joachim Neugtoschel and Ralph Manheim (New York: Farrar, Straus, and Giroux, 1999), 491. This translation is an alteration of Neugtoschel's and Manheim's translation based on the original text offered by Chunjie Zhang, "Social Disintegration and Chinese Culture: The Reception of China in *Die Blendung*," in *The Worlds of Elias Canetti: Centenary Essays*, ed. William Collins Donahue and Julian Preece (Newcastle: Cambridge Scholars Publishing, 2007), 146.

19. This translation combines two translations of Zhuangzi's text. These translations are Fung Yu-lan, *Chuang-Tzu: A New Selected Translation with an Exposition of the Philosophy of Kuo Hsiang* (Heidelberg: Springer, 2016), 41; and Burton Watson, *Zhuangzi: Basic Writings* (New York: Columbia University Press, 2003), 74.

20. Herbert A. Gilles, *Chuang Tzu: Taoist Philosopher and Chinese Mystic* (London and New York: Routledge, 2005), 72. See also Dennis Lewis, *The Tao of Natural Breathing: For Health, Well-Being, and Inner Growth* (Berkeley, CA: Rodmell Press, 2006), 99–100.

21. Khan, "Breath."

22. Martin Heidegger, *The Basic Problems of Phenomenology*, trans. Albert Hofstadter (Bloomington and Indianapolis: Indiana University Press, 1988), 11.

23. Khan, "Breath." My emphasis.

24. Ibid.

25. Hazrat Inayat Khan, "The Power of Silence," in *Art of Being*. See also Khan, "Breath," in which he states the following connected to this task of the mystic: "Every school of mystics has, as its most important and sacred teaching in the way of attainment, the control and understanding of the mystery of breath."

26. Gaston Bachelard, *The Poetics of Space*, trans. Maria Jolas (Boston: Beacon Press, 1994), 52.

27. Maurice Merleau-Ponty, *Phenomenology of Perception*, trans. Donald A. Landes (London and New York: Routledge, 2012), lxxxv.

28. Canetti, *Memoirs of Elias Canetti*, 601.

29. Luce Irigaray, "Ethical Gestures Toward the Other," *Poligrafi* 15, no. 57 (2010): 3f.

30. Ibid., 4.

31. Irigaray, *The Forgetting of Air in Martin Heidegger*.

32. Canetti, *Secret Heart of the Clock*, 51.

Bibliography

Bachelard, Gaston. *The Poetics of Reverie: Childhood, Language, and the Cosmos.* Translated by Daniel Russell. Boston: Beacon Press, 1971.

Bachelard, Gaston. *The Poetics of Space*. Translated by Maria Jolas. Boston: Beacon Press, 1994.

Berndtson, Petri. "The Inspiration and the Expiration of Being: The Immense Lung and the Cosmic Breathing as the Sources of Dreams, Poetry and Philosophy." In *Thinking in Dialogue with Humanities: Paths into the Phenomenology of Merleau-Ponty*, edited by Karel Novotný, Taylor S. Hammer, Anne Gléonec, and Petr Specián, 281–293. Bucharest: Zeta Books, 2010.

Canetti, Elias. *The Human Province*. Translated by Joachim Neugtoschel. New York: Seabury Press, 1978.

Canetti, Elias. *The Memoirs of Elias Canetti*. Translated by Joachim Neugtoschel and Ralph Manheim. New York: Farrar, Straus, and Giroux, 1999.

Canetti, Elias. *The Secret Heart of the Clock: Notes, Aphorisms, Fragments 1973–1985.* Translated by Joel Agee. New York: Farrar, Straus, and Giroux, 1989.

Carter, Robert E. *The Japanese Arts and Self-Cultivation*. Albany: State University of New York Press, 2008.

Descartes, René. *Meditations and Other Metaphysical Writings*. Translated by Desmond M. Clarke. London: Penguin Books, 2003.

Gilles, Herbert A. *Chuang Tzu: Taoist Philosopher and Chinese Mystic*. London and New York: Routledge, 2005.

Heidegger, Martin. *The Basic Problems of Phenomenology*. Translated by Albert Hofstadter. Bloomington & Indianapolis: Indiana University Press, 1988.

Irigaray, Luce. *Between East and West: From Singularity to Community*. Translated by Stephen Pluhácek. New York: Columbia University Press, 2002.

Irigaray, Luce. *The Forgetting of Air in Martin Heidegger*. Translated by Mary Beth Mader. Austin: University of Texas Press, 1999.

Irigaray, Luce. "Ethical Gestures Toward the Other." *Poligrafi* 15, no. 57 (2010): 3–23.

Khan, Hazrat Inayat. "The Power of Silence." In *Art of Being*. Accessed October 28, 2016. https://wahiduddin.net/mv2/VIII/VIII_1_18.htm.

Khan, Hazrat Inayat. "The Mystery of Breath." In *In an Eastern Rose Garden*. Accessed October 28, 2016. https://wahiduddin.net/mv2/VII/VII_13.htm.

Khan, Hazrat Inayat. "Breath." In *The Art of Being*. Accessed October 28, 2016. https://wahiduddin.net/mv2/VIII/VIII_1_17.htm.

Khan, Hazrat Inayat. "Pasi Anfas: Breath." In *The Gathas*. Accessed October 28, 2016. https://wahiduddin.net/mv2/XIII/XIII_10.htm.

Lewis, Dennis. *The Tao of Natural Breathing: For Health, Well-Being, and Inner Growth.* Berkeley, CA: Rodmell Press, 2006.

Merleau-Ponty, Maurice. *Notes des cours au Collège de France 1958–1959 et 1960–1961.* Paris: Éditions Gallimard, 1996.

Merleau-Ponty, Maurice. *Phenomenology of Perception.* Translated by Donald A. Landes. London and New York: Routledge, 2012.

Škof, Lenart, and Emily A. Holmes. *Breathing with Luce Irigaray.* London: Bloomsbury, 2013.

Škof, Lenart. *Breath of Proximity: Intersubjectivity, Ethics and Peace.* Dordrecht: Springer, 2015.

Watson, Burton, trans. *Zhuangzi: Basic Writings.* New York: Columbia University Press, 2003.

Yu-lan, Fung, trans. *Chuang-Tzu: A New Selected Translation with an Exposition of the Philosophy of Kuo Hsiang.* Heidelberg: Springer, 2016.

Zhang, Chunjie. "Social Disintegration and Chinese Culture; The Reception of China in *Die Blendung*." In *The Worlds of Elias Canetti: Centenary Essays*, edited by William Collins Donahue and Julian Preece, 127–150. Newcastle: Cambridge Scholars Publishing, 2007.

I

Philosophical Atmospheres of Breathing

1

Logos and *Psyche*

A Hermeneutics of Breathing

DAVID MICHAEL KLEINBERG-LEVIN

The soul has its own Logos [nature, law, truth, language], which develops according to its needs. (Heraclitus, Fragment 115)[1]

You could never in your search find the limits of the soul, though you travelled as far as you could: so deep is its Logos [nature, law, truth, speech]. (Heraclitus, Fragment 45)

The hidden harmony is stronger than the visible. (Heraclitus, Fragment 54)

We speak of "inspiration." This word should be taken literally. There really is an inspiration and expiration of being. (Merleau-Ponty, "Eye and Mind")[2]

Prologue

I

This chapter contains seven strands of thought, which I have attempted to weave together to form a text that—although abbreviated for this publication—remains rich in implications beyond what could be discussed here: (1) Merleau-Ponty's

This essay was originally written in 1982 and published, in 1984, in *Research in Phenomenology* 14 (1984): 121–147. It has been revised for publication in this anthology, primarily because of changes in my thinking.

phenomenology of the lived body of experience, and in particular, his discussion of the role of the respiratory body in the infant's constitution of space; (2) an interpretation of Kierkegaard's discussion, in *Fear and Trembling*, of the connection between prayer and breathing; (3) the psychoanalytic (Freudian) understanding of ego process, and the critical revision of this understanding in Lacan's attempt to break out of the conservativism in Freud's ego psychology; (4) the radical diagnosis of ego process in the teachings of Tibetan Buddhism, which not only articulates *in theory* the connection between ego process and the body of lived experience, but offers in addition an ancient traditional knowledge in regard to the *meditative* body of respiration and the method for working with patterns of breath to "deconstruct" ego process; (5) Heidegger's hermeneutical phenomenology of the human condition in the light of this question; (6) the obscure but deeply inspiring fragments of Heraclitus, who calls our attention to the mysterious "pact" which binds the *psyche* to a hidden *Logos*; and finally, (7) the Jungian analytical psychology, which articulates the "phenomenology of the Self" against a back-ground of images, symbols, myths, and texts in which the *Logos*, and of course *Psyche*, are figures of great importance.

II

What is the significance of the fact that "psyche" is a word that bears two different meanings? What are we to make of this doubleness of reference: *psyche*, under-stood as "breath," and *Psyche*, understood as "soul," "spirit," "Self." Our attempt here is to understand this vital relationship through a hermeneutical examination of texts concerned with the experience of breathing.

For me, this experience with breathing is joyous, and has the quality of "song." It seems that *Psyche* understands and experiences some measure of onto-logical fulfillment when, in the elemental form of *psyche*, she receives the gift of the primordial *Logos* and reciprocates that gift, giving her thanks in a deeply gathered breathing, a breathing that speaks, a breathing that sings.

III

Heidegger's thinking and Jung's research converge, and a striking focus of their convergence is the cosmology of the pre-Socratics. Both of them found themselves deeply attracted to the utterances of Heraclitus; both unquestionably found in those fragments a deep source of inspiration. It is they who led me to Heraclitus. So I would like, now, to continue the generation of texts, weaving their various stories around the figures of *Logos* and *Psyche*.

The extant fragments from Heraclitus (45, 115) call upon us to give thought to the *psyche* and the *Logos*. But what do these words mean? Let us begin with a consideration of *psyche*. Its first meaning, as what Heidegger would call an "elemental word," refers us to breath and breathing. Its *second*, or *derivative* meaning, though, refers us to the soul, to spirit, and to the Self. In what sense, or way, is *psyche*, understood elementally as breath, related to *Psyche*, understood as Self? In this chapter, I shall argue that breathing and the Self—*psyche* and *Psyche*—are indeed related, and that the Logos is deeply involved in this relationship. I shall further argue that in meditative work with breathing, the open repose into which we settle, and the clarity of awareness that it facilitates, can be a powerful source of transformative energy for the process of self-development and self-fulfillment—the process which, in his "phenomenology of the Self," Carl Jung called "individuation."

Now, for both Jung and Heidegger, the Self must not be reductively identified with the ego. As we shall understand it here, the term "ego" basically refers to a tightly organized spatiotemporal structure polarized into an ego-subject and its co-emergent object: a structure in the emergence and maintenance of which the experience of anxiety (or "paranoia," in Lacan's terminology) figures very prominently, and which, for the most part, and even in its more stable levels and configurations, assumes the function of a massively defensive system. (So far, we are staying very close to Freud's own account, e.g., in *Inhibitions, Symptoms, and Anxiety*. Relative to the ego, however, the *Self* constitutes a much more open, much more expansive system of integration and wholeness. Instead of a high level of anxiety and a massive organization of self-destructive defenses, the Self is strong enough, integrated enough, to be more trusting, more open, and centered in a calm, clearly felt field of energy. The Self stands for *an ever-deepening experience* of living and for a *wholeness* in relation to that experience that is not defensively closed off.

Breathing (in the primary sense of *psyche*) is not only essential for biological survival; it assumes a privileged function in the processes of developing self-awareness and deconstructing self-identifications: processes leading to, and constitutive of, an authentic "individuation," a never-ending dialectic, "going beyond" ego. The human Self (*Psyche*) begins with, and begins as, a breathing body (a *psyche*). Consequently, the *fulfillment* of the Self calls for a hermeneutical return to recollect, and retrieve, a vital sense of this *primordial* psyche, a primordial (i.e., undeveloped) Self. Many ancient traditions therefore teach that breathing is the path of the ego's adventure on its way to Selfhood.

Now let us consider the word *Logos*. This word seems to have three meanings: (1) According to Heidegger, *Logos* is a name for being, name for everything that in any way or sense may be said to be. *Logos* (capitalized) is the most primordial *articulation* of being. And this primordiality also makes of it, at the same time, the most deeply *ontological* articulation of being. (2) Less debatable is the more customary meaning: *logos* (not capitalized) refers to the word, and to speech. (The corresponding verb form, *legein*, refers to speaking, bringing words to speech.) (3) But, as Heidegger points out in his work on the "Logos" Fragment of Heraclitus, *Logos* and *Legein*, as primordial articulation of being, also bear a more "elemental" meaning, viz., "gathering" and "shaping," or "laying-down" (a meaning that, in relation to Psyche, is a "laying claim" to its mindfulness regarding the way that psyche, as breathing, is a gathering and shaping of the surrounding air, the "atmosphere"). How do these three senses relate to the two senses of *psyche*—breath (*psyche*) and Self (*Psyche*)?

In this chapter, I shall attempt to show that—and also how—*psyche* in its *elemental* sense, as a unity of the corporeal and the spiritual, that is, as breathing, is, in truth, a *legein*, a *logos*, in the correspondingly *elemental* sense of a gathering and shaping. Breathing (*psyche* in the elemental sense) is, first of all, a primordial gesture of gathering: it is our first, and most, primordial openness to the elemental being of the world; and it gathers around the living breathing being a sphere of air—an elemental atmosphere. Breathing is therefore our first and most primordial articulation (*logos*) of being, the gathering of an elemental Fourfold (earth and sky, mortals and gods, the embodied projection of our ideals) by inhaling and exhaling gestures, spontaneous instinctive gestures of giving out and receiving in. Breathing is also, however, a *legein* in the elemental sense of a *laying-down*, a *shaping*: in its gathering, and *as* a gathering, our breathing participates in the primordial laying-down, or say shaping, of a communicative space, a field of communication. Breathing is, in truth, our first (albeit un-self-aware) experience of the *possibility* of speech; it is our most primordial *articulation* of the conditions necessary for speech. Due to its rhythmic patterns, breathing lays down the law, the meter (*metron*), for the poetry of mortal speech. Inhibiting itself, restricting and then releasing itself, our breathing *gives way* to speech. And speech is *born*, accordingly, in the "sacrifice" of breath. *Logos* (in the sense of "human speech") presupposes *psyche*, the gift of breath, for the gift of speech is given first of all to the breath. Breathing gives the primordial *Logos* (law) to our speech (*logos*), because it is *through* the breath (*psyche*) that the *Logos* is first gathered up so that it may enter this speech.

Furthermore, having articulated the relation that binds *logos* (speech) and *psyche* (breath), I want to suggest that *logos* (still understood as "speech") also bears a special relation—but of course a very different one—to *Psyche*, Self; for it is *by grace of* the word, the breath brought to speech, that we are human beings, are able to rise to the stature of Selfhood, as befits the freedom of our nature. It is only in speech that the truly *human* is born; and it is only when we have entered into the depths of our language and made our flesh at home in its tones and inflections, resonances and reflections, that we can take the steps of becoming a Self. *Psyche* as breath, then, makes possible the self-understanding articulation (*logos*) by virtue of which it can *become* a true Self.

Finally, I want to observe that *both* "breath" *and* "Self" are deeply dependent upon, and deeply obedient (*zugehörig*) to, the *primordial Logos*—that which Heidegger understands as an ancient name for that which makes possible what *is*—the being, or law, of beings. According to him, the *Logos* named by Heraclitus is that which lay out the conditions that *unify* all beings within an open wholeness, *gathering* them into themselves and *letting them come forth* into an unconcealment, a truth (*aletheia*), where they may *rest* in themselves and *as* themselves. The primordial *Logos*, then, is that which first *lays down,* or *shapes* for our breathing a primordial clearing, a primordial space of openness, a hospitable atmosphere; and it is *by grace* of this primordial clearing that the body of breath (*psyche*) is *enabled* to gather all it needs for its elemental nurture, attunement, and wholesomeness. But the *Logos*, the law and condition of the possibility of being, is also that immeasurable depth, that openness and ingathered wholeness, *in relation to which,* and *thanks to which,* the life of the *Self* is gathered into *its own* unfathomable depth: there where the *hidden* body of "nature"—the "Law" of the *Self's* ever-unfolding self-understanding—is already laid down for its free appropriation.

The *Logos* is a primordial gathering of the *Psyche's* body of breath; and in its great gathering, it *lays claim* to that breath, bestowing rhythm and shape. This claim is like a promise that requires "redemption." It is in fact redeemed by a breathing which, becoming the thinker's "song," *retrieves* the *Logos* in a recollection that dis-closes it in its most primordial gathering *as that which has always already been presencing* in and through our mortal breathing—or rather, as that which, inseparable from the being of *psyche,* lays down the Law (*Logos*) for *Psyche* while *laying claim* to its breathing body. It may be said, and with justice, therefore, that the claim of *Logos* is ultimately to be redeemed in a thoughtful saying, a *speaking* that lets itself *open up* to the deepest resonances of being. But a thoughtful *breathing* may also, by itself, respond to the claim. For breathing constitutes the *emergence* of an articulatory process, a process obedient, of course, to the lawfulness constitutive of language; but it is in breathing that we come closest to the most primordial level of being, that level to which, and by which, the speech of the Self is most deeply attuned.

IV

The text that follows focuses on our experience of breathing. However, inasmuch as the infant's mastery of breathing is required for the acquisition and ongoing use of language, this focus belongs in an essential way to my reflections on the nature of language. My working assumption is that we need a phenomenological understanding of the place that breathing constitutes in the onto-psychogenesis, and unfolding, of our body of speech (logos).

I think it is also true that "fundamental ontology" requires a phenomeno-logical, hermeneutical, and existential interpretation of the nature of language. Sooner or later, this interpretation further specifies a radical reflection focused on the retrieval, the "recollection" of our primordial experience in entering the world of speech through the modulation of our breathing. But an interpretation focused on speaking cannot avoid the task of reflecting on the nature of our breathing. This task is all the more imperative, however, inasmuch as the *Logos*, that which the most ancient Greek thinkers heard and named, originally gave itself, originally articulated itself, in the primordial form of a "breathing." Breathing is our body's first openness to the world—to being. Fundamental ontology must eventually concern itself with the *Logos* that manifests, primordially, as a "lived body" of breath.

Our interpretative strategy (a "conjunction," primarily, of Heidegger and Merleau-Ponty) will be to take up Heidegger's so-called "question of being" *as* a question concerning the being of our breathing. This question translates, however, into a question concerning the appropriation of our natural capacity for breathing. More specifically, the "question of being" translates into a reflection which, in the most radical way, *calls into question* our characteristically "normal," adult, and everyday mode of breathing. For such reflection, this mode of breathing is needlessly pained: shallow, tight, and constricted by anxiety and defensiveness. As we begin to get more in touch with our experiencing of this way of breathing, we might begin to realize, to feel, its characteristic unsatisfactoriness. Thus we might find ourselves deeply motivated, deeply moved, to seek, to question, and to prepare for, a deeper, more expansive, more fulfilling experience. This is what the Buddhist practices of mindfulness are designed to encourage.[3]

Now, our reflections are to be understood as "ontological" in precisely this sense: that, in calling our normal and habitual breathing into question, they attempt to call attention to the possibility of a deeper, more primordial experience of breathing. Our reflections suggest the possibility, moreover, that we may enjoy ever deeper, and ever more primordial experience with breathing, as we find ourselves *able*, by virtue of a gently disciplined attentiveness, to open out—and then open out even more—to that most open openness, disclosing ever more wonders in regard to the world we have been taking for granted.

Questioning the human *Psyche* in depth, our attempt at radical reflection begins to articulate the *Logos* that lays claim to, and which therefore is always and already implicit in, its body of breath. In keeping with the two senses of *legein*—laying out and gathering—I would like to suggest that, in an atmosphere of "normal" breathing, a more hermeneutical experience—and one, therefore, more in touch with that which is primordial—would be that of a breathing rhythmically measured by our heartfelt awareness of the *Logos*, as that which always and already underlies the participation of our breath in speech and gathers its far-reaching motility into the ring of the Fourfold, the unity of earth and sky, mortals and embodied ideals. Experienced in its primordial depth, our breathing in and our breathing out poetize a communicative ring of truth and prepare for the Fourfold the atmosphere of its open expanse.

Understanding herself as *originally* a breath-body, *Psyche* fulfills herself and redeems her own true ontological nature *as Psyche* when she reflectively recollects *for speech* the deeply moving song of the primordial *Logos*, the *Logos* thanks to whose gathering and laying-out our mortal's poor articulation of being is *enabled* to become the singing of our heartfelt song. Only the song of thought, by virtue of its deep resonance, can fully correspond (*homologein*) to the depth of the human *Psyche*. Only the song of thought, open and responsive to the deepest resonance, is truly appropriate to the recollection of *Logos*, the terms of being. Only the song of thought is a true retrieval of the *Logos* that, in its appropriation of Psyche, gathers and lays claim to our breathing, giving it rhythm and shape. And only our song, by a gathering of *soundful* breath homologous to the gathering of the *Logos* itself, can fully redeem the gift of speech that is given, first of all, to our breathing, in the primordial harmony (*Stimmung*) of *psyche* and *Logos*.

A Hermeneutics of Breathing

An ontological understanding of the fact that we are *beings who breathe* ought to be regarded as truly fundamental. Breathing, after all, is the most basic condition of nature in which we find ourselves (it is our *Befindlichkeit*)—and, in truth, it is our most primordial level of attunement or adjustment (*Stimmung*). We will begin the main text of our reflections, as we must, with a phenomenological characterization of the process of breathing as it is normally experienced. But even the breathing taken to be "normal" is in fact neurotic, or pathological: a symptom of our finitude, our vulnerability. More specifically, the symptom is an anxiety that restricts and suffocates our breathing. In the normal situation, of course, the symptomatology may be very deeply, or very cleverly, concealed. It may not appear directly, but only, instead, in displacement: in a nervous cough, for example, or in a nervous habit of clearing the throat. Or, even more indirectly, the anxiety may not appear except in some psychopathology of speech: a compulsion to fill silence, for example, or in stuttering.

The interpretation we will be considering here attempts, hermeneutically, to return to a body of breath more primordial than the one we normally experience as adults. Can we "recollect" such a body? Can we "retrieve" it for thought? Can we elicit from our everyday ontic experience of ourselves what I would like to call its innate potential? Can we, going deeply into our breathing, retrieve an inspiring sense of openness and a gathering *ecstasis* that our breathing in its most primordial form (i.e., in the pre-ontological way of breathing characteristic of the healthy infant) already prefigures and anticipates? Recognizing our experience in the healthy infant, we shall want to say, I think, that the primordial body of breath (a bodily felt sense of which we always still hold within us as adults) is a body without real duality: no fixed or rigid tissues, no impermeable walls, no solid boundaries, no airtight defenses. In order to get some sense of this truth, we might ask ourselves: Where does the breath end and the wind begin? Is there any point in the atmosphere that is a matter of indifference to our breathing? Breathing is our most fundamental openness, our most fundamental experience of nonduality. When, through our understanding of this, our breathing begins to realize its pre-ontologically given potential, we are likely to find that it issues in a speaking that is correspondingly charged with the inspirational energy of being as a whole.

Before we are able to speak, that is, in our infancy, we are already breathing, participating in the world in a relationship of the most intimate taking and giving. With every exchange of air, every gesture of breathing in and breathing out, we find ourselves woven into the currents of an atmosphere, an encompassing presence, in fact, from which we are inseparable, and without which it would be impossible for us to survive. This atmosphere is an elemental region of being; it provides the air we need to breathe, and consequently need, in order to speak. It forms, indeed, an utterly open field of energy.

Breathing is our very first teaching—a silent teaching—in a life of interdependency, continuity, relationship, giving, and receiving. Our first teaching is one of perfect integration, harmony, nonduality. Breathing comes naturally; it is so rudimentary that it requires no action of volition, no attention or thought. But, for that very reason, the *wisdom* in breathing is the most difficult, and the very last to be learned. What is closest and most familiar is taken for granted; it is farthest from our thought. If we would learn *Gelassenheit*, learn a way of being that is not the will to power, we must first give thought to our breathing. Only when our breathing is free, released from this power, will it be giving to our speech a breath that is truly drawn from the whole of being, and that returns to that openness with every word.

In "The Child's Relations with Others," Merleau-Ponty points out that, at the very moment of the child's birth, "the body is already a respiratory body. Not only the mouth, but the whole respiratory apparatus gives the child a kind of experience of space."[4] This is an observation of great importance, but Merleau-Ponty leaves it to us to draw out the ontological implications. If breathing actually participates in the constitution of our "lived" space, if its rhythms, its expansiveness, its tightness or calmness, vigorously contribute to the structuring of our being-in-space, then we might reasonably expect that changes in breathing (e.g., changes induced by exercises that are calming and relaxing) would bring about corresponding changes in our experience of space, our being-in-space. Since this space, however, is also a social space, a space that reflects, and in fact partially constitutes, our social being, our "personality," our temperament and social attunement, we might expect to find that changes in patterns or habits of breathing would bring about correlative changes in our space of being-with-others. Furthermore, since the process of learning to speak and communicate with others requires the disciplined use (i.e., the restriction and mastery) of our "natural" pattern of breathing, both the child's acquisition of speech and the adult's accession to a deeper, more tranquil and restful level of breathing are moments in which we should be able to observe the emergence and constitution of correspondingly significant transformations in the character of our communicative space, our space of being-with-others.

Now inasmuch as all human beings are endowed with the same respiratory system, our experience of being-in-space will be basically the same for all. But two points need to be made here. The first is that there will always be individual differences as well, since what is in question is not simply a physical system, but rather the embodiment of being human. And we breathe not only in an atmosphere, but in an entire world of nature, and of other human beings. Breathing, then, and the space breathing significantly participates in co-constituting, will always be conditioned to some extent by cultural norms, social interactions, our moods, states of mind, and passing feelings, as well as, of course, by our acquisition of language. Moreover, as the pre-personal body-subject (i.e., the infant) gradually emerges from its primordial breathing space and progressively differentiates itself until apparently fully self-enclosed, it will begin to respond, from that ego-cen-tric place, to the character of the "objective" space it has already participated in organizing. Space tends then to be experienced in its otherness; it is "outside" the body. Our initial sense of the integration of breathing—our original experience of *ecstasis*—somehow dies into silence.

Thus, if anxiety (the Latin word, *angustia*, means "narrowness") seizes and restricts the respiratory process of an infant or child, the character of the space that would henceforth begin to take shape will inevitably correspond, in its reflective otherness, to the child's state of anxiety. Even though the child's anxiety actually contributed to the character of his space, so long as that space is experienced in its absolute difference and is not recognized for what it really is, it will itself be present as a source of terrible anxiety. Noting that the Greek word for what we call "breath" is *psyche*, Frederick Perls, founder of the Gestalt Therapy method, writes: "anxiety, the disturbance of breathing, accompanies any disturbance of the self-function; thus the first step in therapy is contacting the breathing."[5] Anxiety is always a question of boundaries: the closing off of openness, a break in continu-ity. The space of anxiety is a space whose character is experienced as oppressive, perhaps even suffocating. In an atmosphere of intense anxiety, breathing may become extremely difficult, labored, possibly threatening our very survival. And, since the rhythmic pattern of our breathing also generates a basic, inwardly felt sense of time, disturbances in breathing will manifest, sooner or later, as disturbances in some dimension of our being-in-time. By the same token, deep-seated anxieties in relation to time, or to our death in time, will likewise manifest in problems of a respiratory nature.

Breathing is the gift of our original integration into the wholeness and openness of worldly existence. But we lose contact with this gift and its meaning for our life. Anxiety is thus a potentially useful reminder. For, anxiety discloses the truth that breathing is the most fundamental bodily dimension of our ontological well-being, and is always somehow implicated in every one of our existential pathologies.

Now we come to our second point of importance. Merleau-Ponty's discussion suggests the thought that, as the growing child undergoes many metamorphoses in keeping with its potential, so its body of breathing undergoes a corresponding evolution, a corresponding succession of developments, in keeping with its ownmost potential (Heidegger speaks of *das eigenste Seinkönnen*). But what is that potential? Is it merely physical, or anatomical? Can we say that the innate potential of the primordial body of respiration is actualized and fulfilled when it is, as it were, "functioning normally?" Is the character of breathing in the stage of adulthood incapable of further evolution? Should we even content ourselves with the fulfillment our breathing finds in the expressiveness and communicativeness of everyday speech? The Greek meaning of the word *psyche* should make us uncomfortable with any simple or ready-made answer.

Heidegger devotes much thought, in *Being and Time*, to the ontological significance of our experience of anxiety. But his interpretation is seriously incomplete, for it leaves unthought the deep relationship between anxiety and breathing. And, *a fortiori*, it leaves unthought the ontological significance of breathing itself, as an experience of our primordial openness to the world—to being.

Kierkegaard may be of help to us here in our attempt to get some clearer sense of the potential inherent in our primordial body of respiration. In *The Sickness Unto Death* (*SD*), he states that, "without possibility, a man cannot, as it were, draw breath."[6] He then elaborates his analogy:

> Personality is a synthesis of possibility and necessity. The condition of its survival is therefore analogous to breathing (respiration), which is an in- and a-spiration. The self of the determinist cannot breathe, for it is impossible to breathe necessity alone, which taken pure and simple suffocates the human self. (*SD*, 174)

Is this merely a useful analogy, or is there not, perhaps, a deeper affinity than our standard sense would grasp? The "personality" Kierkegaard has in mind is a Self, a spiritual human being: in a word, *Psyche*, given a Christian reincarnation. Breathing beings will suffocate unless they have space to breathe: a space, as it were, of possibility. Breathing beings will also suffocate unless they have time to breathe: a time that is not so pressing that it becomes impossible to breathe. (When we feel pressured, rushed, tensed by the pressing demands of a "current" of time that is "flowing" too swiftly, we find ourselves short of breath, or breathing with difficulty.) But beings capable of spiritual development are beings capable of a more developed breath. The space and time that would correspond to a spiritually developed breathing would therefore be a space, and a time, of the greatest possibility.

The spirit, Psyche, needs an openness within which to breathe. (Breathing itself, of course, is always an opening, though its expansiveness is variable.) More specifically, however, we need the openness of *truth* if we are really to breathe freely. The truth is an opening that sets us free. It sets us free by granting our being a new degree, or new kind, of openness. Now, our appropriation for this openness is one that we always *experience*, regardless of our *theory* of truth, as constituting a "space" in which we may breathe more freely, more expansively. Thus, it is not at all accidental that the *Gestalt* shift is called the "Aha!" moment of experience. (The reader should say "Aha!" out loud, here, and listen for the movement of breath, which is released through the widely opened mouth.) Deeply felt personal insights, personal discoveries, are always accompanied by, and always issue in, an expansive breath of relief. The moment of insight is a moment of sudden opening; the truth that releases the spirit also releases, at the same time, the spirit's body of breath. In the openness (*ek-stasis*) of a new truth, and in the speaking thereof, mortals breathe more easily. The *truth* of mortal breathing is an experience of its restful gathering and ecstasy. What Kierkegaard says is: "only the man whose being has been so shaken that he became spirit by understanding that all things are possible, only he has had dealings with God" (*SD*, 174).

Kierkegaard himself makes the connection between spiritual existence and breathing, for he writes: "So, to pray is to breathe, and possibility is for the self what oxygen is for breathing" (*SD*, 173). The connection undoubtedly is mediated by the phenomenon of language, for he concludes the paragraph asseverating that, without the time-space of possibility, by which he understands the time-space first opened up and maintained by God, "man is essentially as speechless as the brutes" (*SD*, 174). Breathing and prayer—the breathing of prayer—are equally necessary. Furthermore, it is Kierkegaard's belief that, without the openness of the human relationship with God, our breathing cannot have the "inspiration" of authentic speech. Kierkegaard writes earlier in that same paragraph:

> But for the possibility alone or for the necessity alone to supply the conditions for the breathing of prayer is no more possible than it is for a man to breathe oxygen alone or nitrogen alone. For in order to pray, there must be a God. (*SD*, 173)

These passages are extremely suggestive. I would like to draw out of them three propositions that are worthy, and also in need, of further thought

1. Speech is a spiritual development of breathing.
2. Prayer is the spiritual fulfillment of speech.
3. In prayer, in "the breathing of prayer," our breathing is consecrated and brought to fulfillment.

But this constellation of propositions moves me to propose a fourth thought, namely:

    4. Breathing itself, and as such, is essentially a mode of prayer.

If we surrender our dualistic conceptions—of mind as separate from body, of spirit and flesh as irreconcilable opposites, of the body that breathes as nothing but a physical system of respiration, and of prayer as a special form, or content, of words—then we are free at last to give breathing the *gift* of our mindfulness, which in this instance means that we recognize in breathing itself its ownmost ontological potential: to be so infused with awareness that it becomes an inhalation and expiration, a prayer of love, belonging to the dimensions of the cosmos.

    Breathing *becomes* the prayer it essentially *is*, in the ultimate sense of nonduality, when the prayer is not "imposed" upon it from outside its own most natural way of being, but is, rather, a breathing that, simply by its constant mindfulness, gives praise and repeated thanks. The body that breathes prayerfully, the body whose breathing is a spontaneous prayer, is the ontological, hermeneutical *fulfillment* of the primordial body of breath.

    Now we need to make more explicit the psychogenesis of this ontological body of breath, this breathing that is an organ of being. What is the *process* of its metamorphosis? Is there a "middle" stage, or a mediating moment, such as, for example, the body-subject as an egological body of breath? Could we perhaps understand this ego-body as the characteristically *personal* dimension of the breathing body, and as that realm in which the decisive existential turn presents itself for the first time as a possibility? The possibility I mean here is that we could break out of the confinements, the restrictions, that will bind our breathing for as long as it continues to belong to the egological body. What we are considering, then, is the possibility of working with the breath on the basis of our self-understanding. Instead of our current way of breathing, which—if we are honest with ourselves—we must acknowledge to be basically rather shallow, tight, tense, and vulnerable to all kinds of pressures and anxieties, we could *give mindfulness* to the expansion and deepening of our breathing. For this expansion and deepening is a potential that is always already given; and it is innately implicit in the infant's primordial body of breath. But this potential cannot be realized on its own, that is, by nature alone. It requires cultivation; it requires the gift of attentiveness; it requires the practice of a certain mindfulness, opening its world; it requires a trust in the benevolence, the goodness, of our atmosphere; it requires a breathing that is, as such, a spontaneous prayer. And yet, only the ego can resolve to open, to deepen and expand, its body of breath. Only the ego can do this, even though it means the subsiding of the ego and its co-emergent body, or in other words, the sublimation of ego (and the ego's personal body, which comes into being together with it) into the more open, freer breathing of the *trans-personal* body, the breathing body in which the Self, the deeply fulfilled *psyche*, may be at one with the whole of being through every breath it gives and takes.

Although Kierkegaard introduces the *idea* of a connection between breathing and the attitude of prayer, he has nothing to say about how, as a matter of existence, we can experience this essential connection. We may presume, from what he has said, that it must be possible to deepen our awareness, and deepen our understanding, of the "prayerful" essence of breathing. But how are we to proceed? How is prayer to be embodied in breathing? How is breathing to be turned into prayer? For answers to these questions, it would seem that we must be prepared to break out of our cultural tradition. Perhaps, long ago, there was a time when our own tradition could have handed down the teachings, the practices, that seem to be called for. But surely not now. Now we must reach out, beyond our Western frontiers, to receive teachings that come from cultures far away that are very different from our own.

Let us begin to flesh out our phenomenological understanding of breath in relation to the ego and its body by attending to the account we find in *Gesture of Balance*. Its author is a Tibetan scholar, teacher, and physician whose qualifications as a representative of the ancient Buddhist wisdom among his people are beyond question. According to this teacher, the human body is not only a physical entity made up of skin, bones, muscles, and internal organs; it is an organic system of energy patterns, such that the space *outside* the body and the space that the body *occupies* are not really separate. Body and its space constitute a natural dynamic unity, like water flowing into water. The solidity of the body is an illusion—or, more accurately, a sociocultural construction.[7]

Giving attention to our breathing, we could begin practices that bring calmness and rest to the body of breath. This would in turn clarify bodily awareness and allow the ego to relax its vigilant reign. Gradually, the ego-body's defensive boundaries could then be surrendered, opening up the human being to greater dimensions of spatiotemporal participation. According to the teachings of this tradition, it is possible for our body of breath to extend its awareness to the outermost atmosphere, so that we are inspired by its vastness and give to it our attention, hence our thanks, with every breath we expire. These practices disclose the *ontological* body of breath, a body whose breathing is open to the energy fields of the cosmos, a breathing already implicit, as a potential, in the "objective" body that is subject to the emergence and rule of the ego.

Let us now proceed, drawing on the teachings of another Tibetan, to penetrate the nature of the *ego* in its relation to the body and its space. Chögyam Trungpa's *Meditation in Action* will be useful in taking our understanding another step. We are virtually compelled to go, once again, outside our own cultural tradition, when it is a question of examining ego process from the standpoint of a psychology not centered in, and not defined by reference to, the egological structure. Only very recently, for example in the work of Carl Jung, Jacques Lacan, and Heinz Kohut, have the ego processes articulated by Freud been subject to an extensive yet sympathetic critique from a standpoint outside ego psychology. Trungpa suggests that "It is not a question of going into some inward depth, but rather of widening and expanding outwards."[8] And he proceeds to diagnose and deconstruct the egological structure of our bodily existence:

> Here, too, the teaching of selflessness plays a very important part. This is not merely a question of denying the existence of Ego, for Ego is something relative. Where there is an external person, a higher being, or the concept of something which is separate from oneself, then we tend to think that because there is something outside there must be something here as well. The external phenomenon sometimes becomes such an overwhelming thing and seems to have all sorts of seductive or aggressive qualities, so we erect a kind of defence mechanism against it, failing to see that it is itself a continuity of the external thing. We try to segregate ourselves from the external, and this creates a kind of gigantic bubble in us which consists of nothing but air and water, or, in this case, fear and the reflection of the external thing. So this huge bubble prevents any fresh air from coming in, and that is "I"—the Ego. In that sense, the Ego certainly exists. But it is in fact fictitious. Having established that [Ego], one generally wants to create some external idol or refuge. Subconsciously one knows that this "I" is only a bubble and it could burst at any moment, so one tries to protect it as much as one can—either consciously or subconsciously. In fact, we have achieved such skill at protecting this Ego that [. . .] even if other things are broken this would be preserved. That is why the concept of Egolessness is not really a question of whether there is a Self or not, [. . .] rather, it is the taking away of that concept of the bubble. Having done so, one doesn't have to deliberately destroy the Ego or deliberately condemn God. And when that barrier is removed one can expand and swim through straightaway.[9]

In the mindfulness of "meditation," then, it is possible literally to *breathe away* the Ego; we can breathe it into an utterly open flow of energy, so that we are free to draw our inspiration from the whole of being, and free, also, to *expire* into its utterly open time and space. (Of course, the kind of experience to which I am referring is one that requires years of the most strenuous discipline as its preparation. And even then, its "higher" mode of stability and permanence will always be in question.)

What does Kierkegaard say to us in the *Concluding Unscientific Postscript*? He reminds us: "An existing individual is constantly in process of becoming."[10] The wisdom that our breathing, our breath-body, preserves and sustains, the wisdom that our breathing has in it to teach us, is none other than this truth: the boundaries and ends of the process of becoming are as vast as the very openness of being.

But becoming is generally accompanied by anxiety. So the breathing of mortals is always attended by a certain suffocating anxiety, insofar as egological restrictions are successful in bearing heavily on our breathing. In fact, so long as our breathing belongs to an egologically restricted embodiment (i.e., a "lived body" experienced exclusively through ego-defined and ego-controlled processes), it will be restricted by the anxiety that generates egological defensiveness. This, in turn, affects our bodily being in time and space. Lacan, for example, would refer us to the experience of "paranoia" that he considers to be coterminous with the rule of the ego-system,[11] with its "attributes of permanence, identity and substantiality."[12]

Let us now articulate in more phenomenological detail the profile of this egological structure. What is the phenomenology of its *formation*? What is the phenomenology of its *functioning*, once it establishes its rule as master of our bodily being-in-the-world? In his report on "Space Therapy and the Maitri Project," Marvin Casper describes the character of the space therapy project that Trungpa designed as a way to apply Tibetan Buddhist psychology and the practice of attention to the problem of mental disorder. This description will, I think, complete the picture we need to have in order to understand the ontology, and the onto-psychogenesis, of breathing. Casper writes:

> According to Buddhist psychology, the basis of neurosis is the tendency to solidify energy into a barrier that separates space into two entities, "I" and "Other," the space in here and the space out there. This process is technically termed "dualistic fixation." First, there is the initial creation of the barrier, the sensing of other, and then the inference of "inner" or "I." This is the birth of ego. We identify with what is in here and struggle to relate to what is out there. The barrier causes an imbalance between inside and outside. The struggle to redress the imbalance further solidifies the wall. The irony of the barrier-creating process is that we lose track of the fact that we have created the barrier and, instead, act as if it was always there.
>
> After the initial creation of "I" and "Other," "I" *feels* the territory outside itself, determining if it is threatening, attractive, or uninteresting. *Feeling* the environment is *followed* by: impulsive action—passion, aggression, or ignoring—pulling in what is seductive; pushing away what is threatening or repelling; ignoring what is uninteresting or irritating. But feeling and impulsive action are crude ways of defending and enhancing ego. [. . .] The different stages of ego development—the initial split of "I" and "Other," feeling, impulse, conceptualization, and the various fantasy worlds, are technically

referred to as the five *skandhas*. From moment to moment the five *skandhas* are recreated in such a manner that it seems like the ego drama is continuous. Clinging to the apparent continuity and solidity of ego, or ceaselessly trying to maintain I and Mine, is the root of neurosis. This effort clashes with the inevitability of change, with the everrecurring death and birth of ego and, therefore, causes suffering.

The degree of neurosis and suffering that a person experiences is related to the amount of inner space and clarity available to him.[13]

This analysis of ego process, summarizing ancient Buddhist *Abhidhamma* psychology, now begins to appear in the "radical" thinking of our own culture—in the work of Lacan, for example. Our surprise will perhaps diminish, however, as we begin to understand the steps of thought that led to his repudiation of "ego psychology," despite his commitment to the continuation of Freudian psychoanalysis. Although we will, in part, be traversing the same ground a second time, I think it might nevertheless prove to be worth our time to take a brief look at Lacan's position. Some new points, points of some importance, I believe, will also emerge; and the Buddhist analysis on which I have relied to develop some of the steps in my argument may happily lose at least some of its initial strangeness.

According to Lacan, what the "I" refers to (namely, the "subject") cannot be properly described as an "ego."[14] The drawing of this distinction, like Jung's insistence on the difference between ego and Self, and the Buddhist differentiation of ego and life-without-ego, is surely of the greatest importance for a psychology that aspires to bring to humanity a vision of liberation, and not merely a word of relief. With stunning boldness, Lacan concludes his analysis arguing that "the ego is structured exactly like a symptom. [. . .] It is the human symptom par excellence, it is the mental malady of man."[15] It is his belief that the ego is nothing but a "projection" constituted through an adaptive process of self-alienation, and that it is essentially a structure of paranoia. Hence its defenses are in effect merely, as he puts it, "imaginary inertias that it concentrates against the message of the unconscious."[16]

It is Lacan's contention, argued most rigorously in his early paper on "The Mirror Stage as Formative of the Function of the I as Revealed in Psychoanalytic Experience," that the formation of the ego, precipitated, or at least facilitated, by the child's encounter with himself through the reflection it sees in the mirror, represents the terminus of a process in which, for the first time, a total unity organizes, and in effect replaces, the child's prior experience of himself as a fragmented, discontinuous, dismembered being. Thanks to the mirror, the child acquires a sense of bodily self-identity. However, this experience is potentially as much a curse as it is a blessing. First of all, the "achievement" is so powerful, and so immediately central for the child, that it tends to become idealized: projected and cathected as a model for all further stages where integration is necessary and new processes of identification need to take place. Second, it must be noted that the installation of the ego is an identity that takes place through a "form" that is "other," that is, "exterior": the child's first identity is therefore a structure formed in the most extreme "alienation." Thus, although this encounter with the mirror meets a crucial need, it also at the same time casts a spell, so captivating the child that further self-transformations may not be welcomed to take place. The child tends to *cling* to the identity achieved, cling, however precariously, to its first *real* triumph over impermanence, instability, and the felt turbulence of bodily movements without any egological agency to unify them into an existential whole. For Lacan, then, this process of ego-formation, necessary though it is for the young child, often entails "the assumption of the armour ["inertia"] of an alienating identity, which will mark with its rigid structure the subject's entire mental development."[17]

To the extent that one clings to this egological structure (and perhaps Lacan believes that we all tend to cling to it in some degree), so that new situations in life, and most especially, new stages in life development, are repeatedly greeted by paranoia and a massive system of impenetrable defenses, the ego and the body it inhabits may indeed be characterized as a "symptom" of pathology. According to Lacan, therefore, a healthy human life cannot be accurately conceptualized in the framework of terms formulated by "ego psychology." Psychology in general, and psychoanalysis in particular, must begin to articulate the process of personal growth, the process Jung calls "individuation," through which the stage of ego-logical rule (strictly defined, here, in terms of a massive system of painful and unnecessary defenses against fresh experiencing) can be authentically surpassed, or transcended (*aufgehoben*).

The psychologies of the Self that have emerged from within our own cultural tradition (Jung, Harry Stack Sullivan, Lacan, Kohut, Rogers), and which I want to connect with the wonderful psychology implicit in the notion of "psyche" handed down to us in the Heraclitus's *Fragments* (45, 115), are very promising and encouraging developments. But the fragments from Heraclitus, reminding us of the immeasurable depth of the *Psyche* and relating this depth to the *Logos*, make it clear that we still are very much in need, needing to give thought to the dimensions of the Self's mode of being. Since the earliest, most elemental sense of *Psyche* (Self) we know unmistakably calls attention to the body of breath, it certainly seems appropriate that we should attend to this body of breath as a way of "sublating," and passing beyond, the egological structure and its body. The calming and relaxing of our breathing, and thereby its expansion, its releasement, its openness, would seem to be one crucial phase in this process.

Now, in his "Letter on Humanism" (LH), Heidegger takes pains to spell out very clearly his ontological interpretation of human being (*Dasein*). *Dasein* "occurs essentially as 'thrown,'" he writes: thrown as into the openness or clearing of being.[18] The human being, "in his essence, is eksistent as into the openness of being" (LH, 229). "The ecstatic essence of man consists in ek-sistence . . ." (LH, 205). To be fully human, in the sense of measuring up to the human potential, is to live "an ecstatic inherence in the truth of being" (LH, 205).

But we must be very careful, here, to avoid an egological "inflation," that is, a narcissistic capturing of this expansive existential dimension. Openness is only *half* the story. In "What is Metaphysics?" (WIM), Heidegger reminds us that "*Da-sein* means: being held out into the nothing."[19] Relentlessly pressing his point, he tells us that, "without the original revelation of the nothing, no selfhood, no freedom" (WIM, 106). An encounter with nothingness is, he holds, of the most decisive importance for the unfolding of human being; it is that existential moment of trial through which each human being must pass, and pass alone, if the ecstatic openness of being is ever to be given and found. "In the clear night of the nothing of anxiety, the original openness of beings as such arises: that they *are* beings—and *not* nothing" (WIM, 105).

"Originary," or "primal," anxiety—anxiety experienced with an understanding of its ontological dimensionality, its essential sense—is an experience of the most total, most unqualified nothingness. And it can only be interpreted as the Ego's response to an openness that it perceives, or feels, to be a deadly threat to its identity, the space of its authority, a well-defended and well-controlled world. Originary anxiety is the Ego's defense when it experiences the openness and finitude of its existence as a nothingness that threatens its very survival. For some of us, this openness is not attractive; on the contrary, it may be extremely threatening, should it appear to require the "death" of the Ego. What is in fact called for, however, is *not* the death of the Ego, but only, rather, our willingness to give up our exclusive identification with the Ego's defensively restricted sphere of subjectivity. Ontologically understood, anxiety in breathing is symptomatic of Psyche's excessive attachment to an egologically restricted breath-body, and manifests its dread before the possibility of an openness-to-being that psyche's Ego can only comprehend as a total annihilation of being.

Our breath-taking adventure, then, consists in a willingness to place our trust, our "ecstatic inherence," in a truth that transcends the authority of Ego. For the truth is that openness and nothingness are "the same," not two, and it is the Ego's defensive work of projection that first introduces this life-threatening duality into an atmosphere of being otherwise congenial to mortal dwelling.

When our speaking arises from within a breath-body whose breathing is inspired by the whole of time and space and reciprocates that gift of breath, that gift of living energy that permeates its entire body, with speech that stays in touch with the breath it expires, we are able to communicate farther and wider than we might have imagined. And our words can become words of creative power and deep compassion, words whose communicativeness comes from, and returns to, the energy continuum, the *Logos*, in silent breath. Speaking that arises from the silence contacted by this free breathing reaches into the four corners of the

Fourfold that breathing itself continuously gathers: it reaches, therefore, into the realm of the gods, and the realm of mortals; and it receives the offerings of the earth and the sky. Speaking that issues from such breathing is a speaking that is as expansive, as spacious, as powerful, as the very atmosphere we breathe.

The path of thinking is for us an adventure with breathing. And there is no telling, in advance, what will transpire. Mortals who are determined to walk that path, regardless of the possible difficulties, must be, as Rilke reminds us, "more daring by a breath."[20] The text of "What Is Metaphysics?" does not mention this line of verse. But it is probable that Heidegger had it in mind when he wrote, there, about a daring that defies, or overcomes existential anxiety (WIM, 108). The "daring ones," the poets and thinkers who are more daring than others by nothing, perhaps, but a breath, may also experience anxiety. But their understanding of breathing and its rhythm somehow sustains them. For their breathing is experienced as drawn from, and expires into, the ecstatic breathing of being as a whole.

Rilke brings this experience to words with a clarity that can help us understand it. In one of his *Sonnets to Orpheus*, in lines Heidegger does not discuss, Rilke proclaims the poet's recognition of a breathing that poetizes, a breathing in which there is no longer an I who breathes, but only the transpersonal continuum of a breathing in which I rhythmically happen: a breathing, therefore, that holds me open in the *wholeness* of cosmic events:

> Breathing, you invisible poem! / World-space constantly in pure / interchange with our own being. Counterpoise, / wherein I rhythmically happen / [. . .] How many of these places in space have already been / within me! Many a wind / is like a son to me.[21]

When our breathing breathes away ego's boundaries, counterpoise prevails and the will is neutralized. This is *Gelassenheit*, an equilibrium in our mooded being for which only this adventure with breathing can prepare us.

In "What Are Poets For?" (WD), Heidegger writes a long meditation on Rilke's words, "daring by a breath." In this essay we will read that,

> being, which holds all beings in the balance, thus always draws particular beings towards itself—towards itself as the center. Being, as the venture, holds all beings, as being ventured, in this draft. But this center of the attracting drawing withdraws at the same time from all beings. In this fashion, the center gives over all beings to the venture as which they are ventured. (WD, 104)

We have been attempting to understand this process, which Heidegger calls a "gathering release," by giving thought to our experience of breathing and finding our truest centeredness in the elemental atmosphere whose inspiring openness can draw out our breath into the openness. We might hope that, in this openness, it would become possible for our breathing to gather the Fourfold—the earth and the sky, mortals and loftiest ideals—into an embrace of great peace: "Silent friend of many distances, feel how your breath is still increasing space."[22]

Notes

1. See Kathleen Freeman, *Ancilla to the Pre-Socratic Philosophers* (Cambridge, MA: Harvard University Press, 1978), 32, 27, and 28. Freeman has translated Diels's German-language translation from the original Greek fragments, *Die Fragmente der Vorsokratiker*. For Heidegger's discussion of Fragments 45 and 115, see his "Logik: Heraklits Lehre vom Logos," in *Heraklit, Gesamtausgabe*, vol. 55, ed. Manfred Frings (Frankfurt am Main: Vittorio Klostermann, 1979), 279–318, 353–359. As a drawing-in (*Einholen*) and an expanding (*Ausholen*), human beings breathe in the manner of a gathering (*legein*). When such breathing is understood and experienced with awareness, it becomes appropriate (*homologein*) in relation to the primordial *Logos*: it becomes a repetition that discloses the primordial *Logos* as a primordially articulate gathering. I am grateful to Manfred Frings for calling my attention to this Heidegger text, and, more importantly, for encouraging me to persevere in questioning Heidegger's texts in regard to the way that the *Logos* lays claim to the psyche's body of breath.

2. Maurice Merleau-Ponty, *The Primacy of Perception*, ed. James M. Eddie (Evanston, IL: Northwestern University Press, 1964), 167.

3. See Chögyam Trungpa, *The Foundations of Mindfulness* (Berkeley, CA: Shambhala), 8–14. I have slightly altered the form, but not the wording of the text.

4. Merleau-Ponty, *Primacy of Perception*, 122. Breathing, speaking, and hearing are, no less than our motility, involved in our corporeal spatialization, and in our sense of space as such. Breathing is also fundamental, because of its constant rhythm, as a measure of time: it participates in the constitution of our "inner sense" of temporality.

5. Frederick Perls et al., *Gestalt Therapy; Excitement and Growth in the Human Personality* (New York: Dell, 1951), 401.

6. Søren Kierkegaard, *The Sickness Unto Death*, trans. Walter Lowrie (Princeton: Princeton University Press, 1968), 172–173. Future references to this text will appear as *SD* followed by the page number.

7. Tarthang Tulku, *Gesture of Balance* (Berkeley, CA: Dharma Publishing, 1977), 54–56.

8. Chögyam Trungpa, *Meditation in Action* (Berkeley, CA: Shambhala, 1969), 54.

9. Ibid., 55–56.

10. Søren Kierkegaard, *Concluding Unscientific Postscript to the Philosophical Fragments*, trans. David F. Swenson (Princeton, NJ: Princeton University Press, 1941), 79. For a good discussion of the nature and stages of this process, see Carl Rogers, "A Process Conception of Psychotherapy," in *On Becoming a Person* (Boston: Houghton Mifflin Co., 1961), 125–159 and 351.

11. See the chapter "On Paranoia and its Relationship to Aggressivity" in Jacques Lacan, *Ecrits: A Selection*, trans. Alan Sheridan (New York: W.W. Norton,

1977). See also Jacques Lacan, "Some Reflections on the Ego," *International Journal of Psycho-Analysis* 34 (1953): 11–17.

12. See the chapter "The Mirror Stage as Formative of the Function of the I as Revealed in Psychoanalytic Experience," in Lacan, *Ecrits*, 17.

13. Marvin Caspar, "Space Therapy and the Maitri Project," *The Journal of Transpersonal Psychology* 6, no. 1 (1974): 57–59.

14. See Lacan, "Some Reflections on the Ego," 16; Lacan, *Ecrits*, 90; and see also Jean Laplanche and Jean-Bertrand Pontalis, *The Language of Psychoanalysis*, trans. D. Nicholson-Smith (New York: W.W. Norton, 1973).

15. Jacques Lacan, *Le Seminaire: Livre I. Les Ecrits techniques de Freud*, ed. J.-A. Miller (Paris: Editions du Seuil, 1975), 22.

16. See the chapter "The Agency of the Letter in the Unconscious, or Reason Since Freud" in Lacan, *Ecrits*, 168f.

17. Lacan, *Ecrits*, 4.

18. "Letter on Humanism," in Martin Heidegger, *Basic Writings*, ed. David Farrell Krell (New York: Harper & Row, 1977), 207. Future references to this text will be indicated by LH, followed by page numbers.

19. "What Is Metaphysics?," in Heidegger, *Basic Writings*, 105. Future references will be indicated by WIM, followed by page numbers.

20. See Martin Heidegger, "What Are Poets For?," in *Poetry, Language, Thought*, Martin Heidegger, trans. Albert Hofstadter (New York: Harper & Row, 1977), 91–142. Text cited hereafter as WD. Note Rilke's reference to our need for "unshieldedness."

21. Rainer Maria Rilke, *Sonnets to Orpheus*, trans. M.D. Herter Norton (New York: W.W. Norton, 1962), Second Part, First Sonnet, 71.

22. Rilke, *Sonnets to Orpheus*, Part 2, Sonnet 29, 127.

Bibliography

Caspar, Marvin. "Space Therapy and the Maitri Project." *The Journal of Transpersonal Psychology* 6, no. 1 (1974): 57–67.

Freeman, Kathleen. *Ancilla to the Pre-Socratic Philosophers*. Cambridge, MA: Harvard University Press, 1978.

Heidegger, Martin. *Basic Writings*. Edited by David Farrell Krell. New York: Harper & Row, 1977.

Heidegger, Martin. *Heraklit. Gesamtausgabe*, vol. 55. Edited by Manfred Frings. Frankfurt am Main: Vittorio Klostermann, 1979.

Heidegger, Martin. "What Are Poets For?" In *Poetry, Language, Thought*, translated by Albert Hofstadter, 91–142. New York: Harper & Row, 1977.

Kierkegaard, Søren. *Concluding Unscientific Postscript to the Philosophical Fragments*. Translated by David F. Swenson. Princeton, NJ: Princeton University Press, 1941.

Kierkegaard, Søren. *The Sickness Unto Death*. Translated by Walter Lowrie. Princeton, NJ: Princeton University Press, 1968.

Lacan, Jacques. *Ecrits: A Selection*. Translated by Alan Sheridan. New York: W.W. Norton, 1977.

Lacan, Jacques. *Le Seminaire: Livre I. Les Ecrits techniques de Freud.* Edited by J.-A. Miller. Paris: Editions du Seuil, 1975.

Lacan, Jacques. "Some Reflections on the Ego." *International Journal of Psycho-Analysis* 34 (1953): 11–17.

Laplanche, Jean, and Jean-Bertrand Pontalis. *The Language of Psychoanalysis.* Translated by D. Nicholson-Smith. New York: W.W. Norton, 1973.

Merleau-Ponty, Maurice. *The Primacy of Perception.* Edited by James M. Eddie. Evanston, IL: Northwestern University Press, 1964.

Perls, Frederick, Ralph Hefferline, and Paul Goodman. *Gestalt Therapy; Excitement and Growth in the Human Personality.* New York: Dell, 1951.

Rilke, Rainer Maria. *Sonnets to Orpheus.* Translated by M.D. Herter Norton. New York: W.W. Norton, 1962.

Rogers, Carl. *On Becoming a Person: A Therapist's View on Psychotherapy.* Boston: Houghton Mifflin, 1961.

Trungpa, Chögyam. *The Foundations of Mindfulness.* Berkeley, CA: Shambhala, 1976.

Trungpa, Chögyam. *Meditation in Action.* Berkeley, CA: Shambhala, 1969.

Tulku, Tarthang. Gesture of Balance. Berkeley, CA: Dharma Publishing, 1977.

2

The Possibility of a
New Respiratory Ontology

PETRI BERNDTSON

Ontology Is Everywhere

In this chapter I will investigate the relation between respiration and ontology. The motivating question for me in this investigation is this: Can breathing, or respiration, teach us an ontology? This may seem rather a strange question for many, as in our Western philosophical tradition, to quote Luce Irigaray, "[t]he forgetting of breathing [. . .] is almost universal."[1] This forgetting of breathing is even deeper in ontology than in other spheres of philosophy.

My quest to investigate the relation between ontology and breathing is inspired, in the first place, by Maurice Merleau-Ponty. In an interview with Madeleine Chapsal in 1958, he says the following: "The ontological problem posed by Heidegger and Sartre is now more than ever the order of the day."[2] This means, according to Merleau-Ponty as well as Martin Heidegger and Jean-Paul Sartre, that "philosophy must redefine Being."[3] Traditionally, ontology has been understood as a part of metaphysics that studies, investigates, or interrogates Being, existence, and reality, and metaphysics has been understood as one of the fundamental branches of philosophy, along with epistemology, ethics, logic, and aesthetics. What happens with Heidegger and Sartre is that ontology is no longer one of the essential parts of philosophy, but becomes synonymous with philosophy itself. In *Being and Time*, Heidegger writes: "Philosophy is universal phenomenological ontology," which means that "the fundamental theme of philosophy [is] Being."[4] In *The Basic Problems of Phenomenology*, Heidegger states this even more strongly, saying: "Being is the proper and sole theme of philosophy."[5] The later Merleau-Ponty agrees with Heidegger that philosophy is synonymous with ontology and that the task of philosophy as ontology is to perpetually "redefine Being." In this same interview, Merleau-Ponty specifies this ontological task as follows: "In particular, [philosophy as ontology] must redefine the connections between what is a thing and what is not a thing, between being and nothingness, and between the positive and the negative. It must reformulate what the traditional correlation between the object and the subject [. . .] does not adequately express."[6] From Merleau-Ponty's point of view, we must add the relation between the visible and the invisible to the list of issues of what philosophy, or ontology, must redefine. Basically, these particular ontological issues that must be especially redefined refer to what Heidegger and Merleau-Ponty call the ontological difference between beings and Being. Beings (in singular "a being") refer to things and objects that are positive. So, what about Being? Being is not a being, that is, it is *not* a positive thing or object, and thus it refers to nothingness and negativity. In one of the working notes of *The Visible and the Invisible*, Merleau-Ponty defines Being as follows: "Being = the perceived world [. . .] [T]his perceptual world is at bottom Being in Heidegger's sense."[7] The world is "universal Being."[8] *The Visible and the Invisible* also states that "Being [is] universal dimensionality"[9] and that "[e]ach field is a dimensionality, and Being is dimensionality itself."[10] This universal dimensionality as dimensionality itself is "the field of all fields."[11] Being, or the perceptual world, is the field of all fields. Positive beings (things and objects) appear against the background of negative Being[12] or within the universal field of Being (the world as the field of all fields or dimensionality). This means that the field of all fields, the universal dimensionality, or the world, is not a being. Being as the universal dimensionality, or the world, in Heidegger's words, is that which "makes beings as beings possible in *what* and *how* they are."[13] As it is Being that makes beings possible, it means that Being is always "prior to all beings."[14] One way of stating this is to say that Being as the meaningful context, horizon, or field has always a priority to the things or objects that appear within this context.

What is truly interesting in Merleau-Ponty's view of ontology is that he strongly emphasizes the idea that "[o]ntology is everywhere—in the painter's articulation of the world, in the scientist's flashes of insight drawn from things, in the passions, in the modes of labor and sociality. There is an ontological history, a deployment of our relation with Being, or a modulation of the relation of being to nothingness."[15] This means that each and every one of these spheres of life, as well as all the other spheres, as they all are always already within Being and thus relating with Being, have defined at least implicitly in their own way their "relation with Being." Each sphere of life has its own deployment of relation with Being and its own modulation of the relation of being to nothingness. Thus, all of the spheres of life have their own definition, however hidden it might be, of Being, which means that they all have at least a latent understanding of what is a thing and what is not a thing, what is visible and what is invisible. Merleau-Ponty himself is extremely interested in interrogating the painter's ontological articulation of the world. In the last published work of his life, "Eye and Mind," as well as in the lecture courses of his final years, Merleau-Ponty emphasizes this question concerning the ontology of the painting. It is his understanding that philosophy "will be reborn"[16] with the help of painters. This means that philosophy will find a "new ontology"[17] by interrogating the painter's articulation of the world, or the painter's relation with Being, as an absolutely new way of thinking. In "Eye and Mind," Merleau-Ponty says of this absolutely new way of thinking the following: "This philosophy, which is still to be made, is what animates the painter—not when he expresses opinions about the world but in that instant when his vision becomes gesture, when, in Cézanne's words, he 'thinks in painting.' "[18] Painters are the masters of vision, and this new ontology is and will be purely visual ontology that philosophy can learn from. In other words, it is a new chiasmic ontology of the *visible* world inspired by painters. In this "new philosophy,"[19] or "new ontology," we need, according to Merleau-Ponty, to "consult our senses"[20] as the painters do, and thus it becomes possible that "perception [especially vision[21]], teaches us an ontology that it alone can reveal to us."[22] This "new philosophy" of vision, as was already emphasized, is very much inspired by painters, whose "gaze interrogate the [visible] things"[23] and for whom the "world is [. . .] nothing but visible"[24]. Merleau-Ponty suggests that in this "closer relationship with" painters, philosophy "will be reborn" as a "new perceptual ontology"[25] of the visible.

Ontology of Inspiration and Expiration of Being

Now if "ontology is [truly] everywhere" would this not mean that there is also an ontology to be found in breathing? In a highly cryptic manner, Merleau-Ponty himself briefly points toward this possible respiratory ontology when he writes in "Eye and Mind": "What is called 'inspiration' should be taken literally: there is really and truly inspiration and expiration of Being, respiration within Being."[26] But Merleau-Ponty does not say anything else about this ontology of "inspiration and expiration of Being." Just previously in connection to painters, I quoted Merleau-Ponty's words: "perception teaches us an ontology that it alone can reveal to us." All of this raises the following important questions. Could this mean in reference to our respiratory relation with Being as "respiration within Being" that respiration can also teach us an ontology that it alone can reveal to us? If so, what kind of ontology could this respiratory ontology be? And how could breathing teach us, and how could we learn from it this possible respiratory ontology? If Merleau-Ponty's new perceptual ontology of the visible is inspired by painters, then from whom could we possibly get help in our effort to give an expression to this new respiratory ontology? Who could inspire us to redefine Being in respiratory terms? In order to make a choice from whom we could perhaps receive help in our effort to redefine our respiratory relation with Being we must first understand how, according to Merleau-Ponty, the philosopher could learn a new ontology. He writes in *The Visible and the Invisible*: "The philosopher speaks, but this is a weakness in him, and an inexplicable weakness: he should keep silent, coincide in silence, and rejoin in Being a philosophy that is there already made."[27] In this way he is able to "hearken" the silence of Being that speaks "within himself."[28] So according to Merleau-Ponty, within Being there is already made a philosophy, or an ontology, and for this reason our relation to Being can teach us this philosophy or ontology. Of this philosophy, he also writes: "Philosophy, precisely as 'Being speaking within us,' expression of the mute experience by itself."[29] What would this mean if these ontological formulations would be understood as formulations concerning "inspiration and expiration of Being, respiration within Being"? It would mean that the philosopher should keep silent and hearken inspiration and expiration of Being, speaking within himself in order to learn a philosophy, that is, a respiratory philosophy. Earlier we asked if respiration, or breathing, could teach us an ontology. So we could say that if we would learn to hearken "the mute experience" of "inspiration and expiration of Being, respiration within Being," that is, this experiential respiratory silence as it speaks within us, it could perhaps teach us a new respiratory ontology or philosophy as an absolutely new way of thinking.

In order to understand better what "there is really and truly inspiration and expiration of Being, respiration within Being" could mean, we must remember the ontological difference between beings and Being to which we referred at the beginning of this chapter. In respiratory terms, this ontological difference would mean that there is a difference between beings and inspiration and expiration of Being. It was said earlier that in Merleau-Ponty's view Being is the world as the field of all fields and the universal dimensionality. Thus, we could interpret "inspiration and expiration of Being" to mean inspiration and expiration of the world, or of the perceptual world, and inhalation and exhalation of universal dimensionality as the field of all fields. And what comes to "respiration within Being" we could similarly understand as respiration within the perceptual world and as respiration within the universal dimensionality. According to Merleau-Ponty "we are within Being,"[30] which I would interpret to mean that we are "respiration within Being" and thus our being-in-the-world is in respiratory terms breathing-in-the-world.

The Zen Masters and the Breathing Practice of *Zazen* as the Possible Guides toward a Respiratory Ontology

I choose as our mentors in breathing the Japanese Zen masters for whom a certain kind of "practice of breathing,"[31] which they call *zazen*, is the most essential part of Zen. So let us investigate how they could perhaps inspire us to articulate a new ontology, or new philosophy, of inspiration and expiration of Being. Could *zazen* as practice of breathing, that is, as respiration within Being, teach us an ontology? And how could respiration teach us to redefine Being, that is, for example, to redefine, to use Merleau-Ponty's words, "the connections between what is a thing and what is not a thing, between being and nothingness, and between the positive and the negative"?

According to Japanese Aikido Master Shinichi Suzuki, "nothing is more important than breathing, breathing, breathing."[32] By practicing regularly one's breath through breathing practices he says that there comes a moment when you "have entered a world of nothing but breathing. You will feel as if it is the universal, not yourself, who is doing the breathing."[33] Eventually, as you continue to practice breathing, Suzuki says, "you will come to comprehend yourself as a part of the universal."[34] To become part of the universal is the goal of Zen Buddhism, that is, to experience a participation in universal breathing.

The most important practice of Zen Buddhism is called *zazen*. There is no Zen without the practice of *zazen*, as one of the most famous Zen Masters Dōgen says: "Practicing Zen is *zazen*."[35] The Japanese word *zazen* means "seated-meditation"[36] or "sitting meditation."[37] The Japanese word *za* means "to sit"[38] and *zen* means "meditation."[39] *Zazen* is essentially a meditative breathing practice, or a form of mindfulness of breathing, in which a practitioner silently sits commonly in a full-lotus or half-lotus posture and follows the breathing process as mindfully as possible. In order to be mindful of breathing one needs to learn to keep silent, and thus *zazen* is also a practice of "cultivation of a profound silence."[40] Before we go deeper into the practice of *zazen* let us try to understand very briefly what Dōgen actually says with his phrase "Practicing Zen is *zazen*." If we interpret this phrase literally it means "Practicing Zen, that is, meditation is *zazen*, that is, seated-meditation." Thus for Dōgen, practicing meditation is seated meditation. Meditation is a way of looking at the world with the deepest and fullest sense of awareness or mindfulness in a manner in which the practitioner perpetually tries to deepen and enlarge his or her way of looking at reality. So what is Zen? So what is meditation? One possible answer to this question is the following given by D.T. Suzuki: "Zen wants us to acquire an entirely new point of view whereby to look into the mysteries of life and the secrets of nature."[41] This "entirely new point of view" is born out of the experience of *zazen* and actually the experience of *zazen* itself is this entirely new point of view.

In his modern classic of Zen literature, *Zen Mind, Beginner's Mind*, Zen master Shunryu Suzuki, who followed deeply the ideas of Dōgen, describes this *zazen*-meditation practice as an "entirely new point of view":

> When we practice *zazen* our mind always follows our breathing. When we inhale, the air comes into the inner world. When we exhale, the

air goes out to the outer world. The inner world is limitless, and the outer world is also limitless. We say "inner world" or "outer world," but actually there is just one whole world. In this limitless world, our throat is like a swinging door. The air comes in and goes out like someone passing through a swinging door. If you think, "I breathe," the "I" is extra. There is no you to say "I." What we call "I" is just a swinging door which moves when we inhale and when we exhale. When your mind is pure and calm enough to follow this movement, there is nothing: no "I," no world, no mind nor body; just a swinging door. So when we practice zazen, all that exists is the movement of the breathing, but we are aware of this movement.[42]

From the above quotations from Japanese Zen Buddhists it seems that the purpose of Zen through the practice of *zazen* is to enter into the "world of nothing but breathing." It is important to note that Shinichi Suzuki does not call this world simply a world of breathing, but "a world of *nothing* but breathing." And Shunryu Suzuki connects breathing and nothing, as he says that "[w]hen your mind is pure and calm enough to follow this movement [of breathing], *there is nothing*: no 'I,' no world, no mind nor body; just a swinging door. So when we practice *zazen*, all that exists is the movement of the breathing." Also in his book *The Method of Zen*, Eugen Herrigel[43] writes about the experiential interrelation between breathing and nothing in a regular practice of *zazen* as conscious breathing: "Finally *you are nothing but breathing—you are breathed.*"[44] So when one dives into the depths of *zazen* meditation-practice as mindfulness of breathing, one has a possibility to experience, or realize, that there is nothing, that is, no "I," no world, no mind nor body, as Shunryu Suzuki says. There is nothing but an experience of breathing, that is, the experiential movement of breathing. There is "a world of nothing but breathing." There is nothing but a "limitless world" of aerial exchange. And as there is no "I" in this experience of nothing but breathing then it is not an experience of "I breathe," but an experience that the universal "is doing the breathing," as Shinichi Suzuki says. Shunryu Suzuki also connects this breathing with "the universal": "So when you practice *zazen*, your mind should be concentrated on your breathing. This kind of activity is *the fundamental activity of the universal being*."[45] Or "[a]ctually what you are doing [as you practice *zazen*], however, is just sitting and being aware of the *universal activity* [. . .] [of] the swinging door."[46] "To be aware of the movement [of breathing] does not mean to be aware of your small self, rather your *universal nature*, or Buddha nature [. . .] it is actually the true experience of life through Zen practice."[47] The small self refers to the "I." This "true experience of life" as the universal being, or universal activity, is called in Zen by many different names. For example, in his book *Hara: The Vital Center of Man*, Karlfried Graf Dürckheim[48] calls this universal force "it," "Great Power," and "Great Respiration" as he describes this "true experience of life" as the experience of nothing but breathing:

It generally takes a long time before a beginner, turning his conscious attention to his breathing, grasps the truth that not he but 'it' breathes, and that he may confidently surrender even his breathing to the Great Power which keeps him alive without his assistance. This feeling that 'it breathes' not that 'I breathe,' [. . .] is one of the greatest, most impressive, and most blissful experiences at the beginning of the [Zen] Way. [. . .] [It is the experience of] the Great Respiration [which] means yielding oneself without reservation to the cosmic movement of ebb and flow.[49]

Kū, the Breath and the World of Aerial Emptiness

In the above descriptions of the experience of breathing, the notion of "nothing" plays an important role. Shinichi Suzuki used this notion as he spoke of "a world of *nothing* but breathing." Shunryu Suzuki said that "when we practice *zazen,* all that exists is the movement of the breathing," "there is *nothing*: no 'I,' no world, no mind nor body." And Herrigel's words "you are *nothing* but breathing." What is the meaning of this nothing? It can be said that in Zen terminology the "nothing" and *zazen* as mindfulness of breathing are connected in an essential way. In order to understand this connection it is important to know that in many instances the Zen notion of nothing, or nothingness, is synonymous with the notion of "emptiness." We can equate the "world of nothing" with "the world of emptiness."[50] In order to "grasp emptiness," that is, the world of emptiness, one needs to transcend the reality of things and objects, that is, the reality of beings. According to Heinrich Dumoulin's book *Zen Enlightenment,* "One who clings to no particular being gains the unobstructed view of vast emptiness."[51] The Japanese word for emptiness is "kū," which does not mean only emptiness, but also "the sky," "space," and "the air."[52] In Zen literature, commentators do not tend to emphasize these different meanings of the word *kū,* as the word is generally translated only as "emptiness." But if the Zen notion of nothing as emptiness is also, at the same time, "the sky," "space," and "the air," then this would open the whole interrogation into new dimensionalities. This would mean, for example, the word *kū* as the air would connect with *zazen* as a breathing practice in an interesting way. Also it is important to know that this Japanese word is a translation of the Sanskrit word for emptiness "śūnyatā." In his essay "The Deconstruction of Buddhism," David Loy writes of *śūnyatā*:

> The important term *śūnya* and its substantive *śūnyatā* are [. . .] very difficult to translate. They derive from the Sanskrit root *śū,* which means "to be swollen," both like a hollow balloon and like a pregnant woman; there the usual English translation "empty" and "emptiness" must be supplemented with the notion of "pregnant with possibilities."

(Sprung's translation uses the cumbersome "absence of being in things.") Rather than *śūnyatā* being solely a negative concept, however, Nāgārjuna emphasizes that it is only because everything is *śūnya* [empty] that any change, including spiritual transformation, is possible.[53]

This Sanskrit etymology of the word *śūnyatā* is highly interesting if considered from the perspective of *zazen* as a breathing practice. How so? Because in the process of breathing, during inhalation the body swells as it fills with air. But in *zazen* the body swells most in the area of the belly because *zazen* is abdominal breathing.[54] So in reference to the etymological meaning of *śūnyatā*, we could very well say that in *zazen* the belly of the practitioner swells like a hollow balloon or becomes swollen like a pregnant woman's belly. With each breath, the world of emptiness as the world of air makes the practitioner of *zazen* swollen. In Zen, the practice of *zazen* is deeply connected to spiritual transformation. In general, we can say that all breathing practices of different wisdom traditions of the East focus on attaining some form of spiritual transformation.[55]

Heidegger on *Kū*, Emptiness, and Nothing as well as the Forgetting of Air in Heidegger

Now what is very interesting is that Heidegger examines the theme of *kū* as emptiness in relation to Being in "A Dialogue on Language between a Japanese and an Inquirer." It is important to remember that in the beginning of my chapter we quoted Merleau-Ponty, who said: "The ontological problem posed by Heidegger and Sartre is now more than ever the order of the day." In this same interview, Merleau-Ponty also says: "Both Heidegger and Sartre have long maintained, and quite rightly, that philosophy must redefine Being."[56] In this dialogue Heidegger is truly redefining Being as he considers its connection to the Japanese notion of *kū*. Heidegger translates *kū* as "emptiness, the open, the sky,"[57] and thus the Japanese in the dialogue says: "*Kū* does indeed name emptiness and the open, and yet it means essentially more than that which is merely suprasensuous."[58] Later in this dialogue, the Japanese says that "*Kū*, the open, the sky's emptiness, means more than the supra-sensible,"[59] which is boundless. And as *kū* is suprasensible it cannot be "perceived by the senses."[60] This means that one cannot see, hear, or touch *kū* as emptiness, open space, or the sky. It is important to understand that this reference to perceiving by the senses means that since *kū* is not a thing or an object it cannot be "perceived by the senses."[61] What is extremely important in this dialogue is that in it Heidegger connects the Japanese emptiness (*kū*) and his notion of Being as the Japanese says: "To us [Japanese], emptiness [*kū*] is the loftiest name for what you mean to say with the word 'Being.'"[62] One of the most famous descriptions concerning the phenomenon of emptiness by Heidegger can be found in his essay titled "The Thing" in which he speaks about a jug as follows:

> When we fill the jug, the pouring that fills it flows into the empty jug. The emptiness, the void, is what does the vessel's holding. The empty space, this nothing of the jug, is what the jug is as the holding vessel [. . .] But if the holding is done by the jug's void, then the potter who forms sides and bottom on his wheel does not, strictly speaking, make the jug. He only shapes the clay. No—he shapes the void. For it, in it, and out of it, he forms the clay into the form. From start to finish the potter takes hold of the impalpable void and brings it forth as the container in the shape of a containing vessel. The jug's void determines all the handling in the process of making the vessel. The vessel's thingness does not lie at all in the material of which it consists, but in the void that holds.[63]

In this description Heidegger does not refer explicitly to the Japanese *kū* as emptiness, but what he says here is not in any manner in disagreement with the statement: "To us [Japanese], emptiness [*kū*] is the loftiest name for what you mean to say with the word 'Being.'" As said earlier in reference to *kū*, that "emptiness is [the] same as nothingness,"[64] we also see in this quotation on the jug that emptiness and nothing are the same; that is, the emptiness as "the empty space" of the jug and the "nothing of the jug" are the same. As said in reference to *kū*, that it is suprasensible and cannot be perceived by the senses, also here in connection to the emptiness, or nothing, of the jug this emptiness or void is impalpable, as Heidegger speaks of "the impalpable void" that the "potter takes hold of." What Heidegger says after his description of the emptiness of the jug is extremely important to our discussion here. Heidegger asks: "is the jug really empty?" The answer to this question depends, according to Heidegger, on the perspective one takes while investigating the jug, as the following words reveal:

> Physical science assures us that the jug is filled with air and with everything that goes to make up the air's mixture. We allowed ourselves to be misled by a semipoetic way of looking at things when we pointed to the void of the jug in order to define its acting as a container. But as soon as we agree to study the actual jug scientifically, in regard to its reality, the facts turn out differently. When we pour wine into the jug, the air that already fills the jug is simply displaced by a liquid. Considered scientifically, to fill a jug means to exchange one filling for another. These statements of physics are correct. By means of them, science represents something real, by which it is objectively controlled. But—is this reality the jug? No. Science

always encounters only what *its* kind of representation has admitted beforehand as an object possible for science.[65]

Here we can see that, according to Heidegger, what he calls "a semipoetic way of looking at things," which is actually a phenomenological way of looking at the world, reveals the jug's holding as emptiness or void, but from the perspective of physical science there is no emptiness or nothing because that which we understand phenomenologically, or semipoetically, as emptiness (empty space), nothing, or void is actually air. But here I would argue that Heidegger is wrong. His wrongness is deeply connected to his understanding of *kū*. He defined *kū* as emptiness, open space, and the sky. But the word *kū* also means "the air," as already mentioned, and this Japanese word is not in any manner part of the perspective of the physical sciences. So it seems that, according to Heidegger, emptiness, or nothing, cannot be phenomenologically, or semipoetically, at the same time also air. If we would listen in our Western philosophical tradition not to Heidegger but to the aerial poetic thinking of Gaston Bachelard, we could learn to understand that the phenomenon of air and the nothing belong together. So instead of making the Heideggerian choice between the semipoetic way of looking at the world and the physical scientific way of looking at the world, I suggest that we choose the Bachelardian aerial poetic way. Bachelard writes in his book *Air and Dreams*: "air brings *nothing*. It gives *nothing*. It is the immense glory of a Nothing."[66] It can be said that air appears to us as nothing or that the experience of air gives us the primordial experience of nothing. When we think within the atmosphere of aerial poetics the empty jug and the nothing of the jug, we could say that the air gives the jug its emptiness and that aerially the jug is full of nothing. It is fully empty of air. Its nothingness is the nothingness of air. Or when we enter a room that does not have a single thing in it, we say that the room is empty or that there is nothing there, but in fact the room is full of air, which makes it possible for us to be there as breathing beings; but at the same time, it is this air that gives us the experience of nothing. We call the experiential air "nothing" because it is not a thing. It is a "no thing." It cannot be seen, because it is invisible, and in its invisibility and emptiness it gives us a chance to see visible things that appear within this invisible atmosphere of air. This air in the empty room cannot be heard, because it is silent, and in its silence it provides the condition of possibility for hearing sounds. Air cannot be grasped into one's fist because it is impalpable void, and for this reason, for example, it does not phenomenologically have surface or form like things have. In these ways, the phenomenon of air is suprasensuous; that is, it cannot be perceived by the senses as an object or a thing. So if the Japanese *kū* is the loftiest name for what Heidegger means to express with the word "Being," then we can add that *kū* does not mean only emptiness, the open, space, and the sky, but also the air. Then we can speak of the atmosphere of air as the open and empty space. This would mean that we could say that the emptiness of air, the nothing of air (Bachelard), or the open air is the loftiest name for Heidegger's Being.

Respiration, the Clearing of Air, and the Essence of Human Existence

Without referring to the Japanese *kū* or to Bachelard's aerial poetics of nothing, Luce Irigaray says: "air appears as the element that goes hand in hand with [Heidegger's] Being."[67] In her book *The Forgetting of Air in Martin Heidegger*, Irigaray also speaks of the "open air" and "clearing of air."[68] The two other names in addition to "emptiness" for what Heidegger means to say with the word "Being" are "the open" and "the clearing."[69] Irigaray writes about the clearing of air as follows: "The clearing of air is a clearing for appearing and disappearing, for presence and absence."[70] In connection to Irigaray's radicalization of Heidegger's clearing (*Lichtung*), Peter Sloterdijk writes in his book *Terror from the Air*: "Luce Irigaray has even suggested that Heidegger's concept of *Lichtung* be bracketed and replaced by a meditation on air—the 'airing' instead of 'clearing.' [*Luftung statt Lichtung.*]"[71] Irigaray's aerial reformulation of Heidegger's clearing as "the clearing of air" refers very clearly to his text "The End of Philosophy and the Task of Thinking," in which he writes: "The clearing is the open region for everything that becomes present and absent."[72] The next sentence of this text by Heidegger says: "It is necessary for thinking to become explicitly aware of the matter here called clearing." If there is any essence of human being, according to Heidegger, it is our perpetual relatedness to this clearing of Being. This relatedness is openness. This essence of human existence is "what we ourselves always already are,"[73] and that is openness to the clearing of Being. This essential openness of human being is also understood as standing-in, and thus Heidegger can write: "In order that beings can come to presence [. . .] what is needed is the standing-in [*Innestehen*] of the human being [. . .] in the clearing."[74] In the aerial atmosphere of our investigation, this means that it is necessary for thinking to become explicitly aware of the clearing of air and the aerial emptiness. This would mean, according to Irigaray, that as the clearing of Being and the clearing of air go hand in hand we could suggest that the essence of human being should be rethought from the aerial perspective, which would mean essentially that the essence of human being as that which we ourselves always already are would be perpetual openness to the clearing of air and standing-in the atmosphere of open air as the nothing of air.

In the beginning of this chapter it was stated that we are respiration within Being, and thus our being-in-the-world in respiratory terms is breathing-in-the-world. As Being is the world as the field of all fields and the universal dimensionality, we also state that we are respiration within the world and within the universal dimensionality. Later in the chapter, it was stated that the Japanese *kū* as "emptiness is the loftiest name for [. . .] the word 'Being.'" It was also revealed that this word *kū* can also be translated as "the sky, space and the air" and that emptiness is synonymous with nothing. If we now combine these ideas of Merleau-Ponty, Heidegger, and Zen together we could say that we are respiration within the world of emptiness, within the world of nothing, within space and within the air. It was also stated, with the help of Bachelard, that air and nothing belong essentially together because air "gives *nothing*" and is thus "the immense glory of a Nothing." We also learned that, according to Irigaray, Being as the clearing goes hand in hand with air as "the clearing of air." Thus we could say that we are respiration within Being as the clearing of air. It was also stated, according to Heidegger, the essence of human existence as "what we ourselves always already are" is our relation with Being as openness to, or "standing-within,"[75] the clearing of Being. If we interpret this essence of human existence in the atmosphere of everything that we have previously stated we could perhaps say: the essence of human existence is that we are respiration within Being as respiratory openness to the aerial world of emptiness and the clearing of air.

The Ontological Priority of Merleau-Ponty's Respiratory Body and the Respiratory Essence of Human Existence

To make this respiratory interpretation of "what we ourselves always already are" more explicit, it is useful to quote Merleau-Ponty's text "The Child's Relations with Others" in which he very briefly states: "at the beginning of the child's life [. . .] the body is already a respiratory body. The whole respiratory apparatus gives the child a kind of experience of space. After that, other regions of the body intervene and come into prominence."[76] In Merleau-Ponty's view, I do not *have* a body as I *am* a body or I am my own body. This means that there is no "I," that is, neither subjectivity nor selfhood, without, or separated from, the body. "[O]ur body [. . .] is a *natural self.*"[77] For Merleau-Ponty, the lived body is the foundation of human existence, subjectivity and selfhood, and at the same time it is also essentially our perpetual relation with the world. In ontological terms, this means that the lived body is essentially always already openness to Being. Body's being-in-the-world as the foundation of human existence and subjectivity has many different dimensions. These dimensions are, for example, perception (perceptual being-in-the-world), movement (kinesthetic being-in-the-world), sociality, practicality, and speech. Merleau-Ponty is most famous for his investigations of the body's perceptual openness to the world, which includes, for example, the visual, auditory, and tactile relations with the world. What Merleau-Ponty clearly says in this brief citation on the "respiratory body" is that the lived body's all the other ways of being-in-the-world come *after* our embodied respiratory openness. This would mean that the respiratory body as respiratory openness is the foundation upon which all the "other regions of the body" are grounded. These other regions of the body are, for example, "the life of my eyes, hands, [feet, genitals,] and ears, which are so many natural selves"[78] as various ways of being-in-the-world. Based on this idea of Merleau-Ponty that the body is a natural self, David Michael Kleinberg-Levin interprets this citation concerning the child's "respiratory body" as follows: "The human Self [. . .] begins with, and begins as, a breathing body."[79] In his analysis of the ontological fundamentality and priority of this Merleau-Ponty's "respiratory body" Kleinberg-Levin has also expressed the following three important statements: (1) "Breathing [. . .] is our first and most primordial openness to [. . .] a sphere of air";[80] (2) "Breathing is our most fundamental openness"[81]; and (3) "Breathing is our body's first openness to Being."[82] With these three statements, Kleinberg-Levin has made a huge service to the beginnings of the ontology of breathing. In these ontological statements, he connects this "respiratory body" with Merleau-Ponty's other respiratory notion of "inspiration and expiration of Being," which he interprets through the conjoining of Merleau-Ponty's concept of the lived body and Heidegger's ontological analysis of the essence of human existence as openness to Being. Before I brought into discussion Merleau-Ponty's notion of the "respiratory body" and Kleinberg-Levin's ontological interrogation of it, I suggested that perhaps the essence of human existence is that we are respiration within Being as respiratory openness to the aerial world of emptiness and the clearing of air. Now, after introducing both Merleau-Ponty's "respiratory body," which always already has the priority in relation to other regions of the body, and Kleinberg-Levin's three ontological statements, which can be understood as "ontological implications"[83] of Merleau-Ponty's respiratory body, we can with more confidence suggest that truly the essence of human existence—that is, "what we ourselves always already are" as openness to the clearing of Being—should be rethought in respiratory terms, as we are respiration within Being. One of the ways of rephrasing this essence of human existence, in which we combine Heidegger's "what we ourselves always already are" and the Merleau-Pontian we are respiration within Being, would be the following statement: *we ourselves always already are respiration within Being.*

The Respiratory Encounter of *Zazen* and the Merleau-Pontian Ontological Hearkening

Let us return to the question of *zazen* as a meditative breathing practice in connection to learning a new ontology of breathing. Earlier in this chapter we chose the Zen masters as our initial mentors who could perhaps guide us in our way toward this new respiratory ontology. From Dōgen, we learned that "practicing Zen is *zazen.*" *Zazen* was understood as just sitting silently and being aware of the movement of breathing. Shunryu Suzuki said, "When mind is pure and calm enough to follow this movement [of breathing], there is nothing." But only when one becomes as silent as possible can the mind be pure and calm enough. Thus, *zazen* was also understood as a "cultivation of a profound silence." Now if we ponder with more awareness the things we said before we first introduced Zen and *zazen* in this chapter, we can note that the Zen masters where chosen very carefully as our mentors to help us to learn and create a new respiratory ontology. How is this so? We quoted Merleau-Ponty's words: "The philosopher speaks, but this a weakness in him, and an inexplicable weakness: he should keep silent, coincide in silence, and rejoin in Being a philosophy that is there already-made." It is this silence of Being that the philosopher "hearkens to within himself." We also quoted the following working note: "Philosophy, precisely as 'Being speaking within us,' expression of the mute experience by itself, is creation." We interpreted these words as the words of "inspiration and expiration of Being, respiration within Being" and through this interpretation the philosopher became the one who listens deeply in silence inspiration and expiration of Being speaking within himself. Now we can note that this task of the philosopher is to hearken the essence of human existence, as we ourselves always already are respiration within Being speaking within us. This Being speaks within us with each and every breath, as it is inspiration and expiration of Being. And we can note that this sounds almost exactly like what the practitioner of *zazen*-meditation also does as he sits silently following as carefully as possible the movement of breathing. So, both the respiratory philosopher and the practitioner of *zazen* should keep silent in order to cultivate silence, coincide in silence, and listen to the breath. If earlier we said with the mouth of Dōgen that "practicing Zen is *zazen*," now I suggest that we could also say: practicing respiratory philosophy, or respiratory ontology, is *zazen*. What I mean by this is that the ontological method of respiratory philosophy is to silently hearken breathing as mindfully as possible.

In the very beginning of this chapter, we said in reference to Merleau-Ponty's idea of giving rebirth to philosophy through painting the following: For Merleau-Ponty, painters are the masters of vision, and this new ontology is and will be purely visual ontology that philosophy can learn from them. In other words, it is a new chiasmic ontology of the *visible* world inspired by the painters. In this "new philosophy," or "new ontology," we need to "consult our senses" as the painters do, and thus it becomes possible that "perception [, especially vision,] teaches us an ontology that it alone can reveal to us." This "new philosophy" of vision is very much inspired by the painters whose "gaze interrogate the [visible] things" and for whom the "world is [. . .] nothing but visible." So in a "closer relationship with" the painters' philosophy "will be reborn" as a "new perceptual ontology" of the visible. Now we could translate and mutate all of this into the task of respiratory ontology. For us who are seeking to create this new respiratory ontology, the Zen masters are the masters of breathing, and this new ontology is and will be purely a breathing ontology, and philosophy can learn from these masters of the breath. In other words, it is a new chiasmic ontology of the *invisible breathing* world inspired by the Zen masters. In this "new philosophy" or "new ontology," we need to consult our breathing as the Zen masters do, and thus it becomes possible that respiration teaches us an ontology that it alone can reveal to us. This "new philosophy" of respiration is very much inspired by the Zen masters, whose breaths interrogate the invisible *kū* as the aerial emptiness and for whom the world is "a world of nothing but breathing." So, we might conclude that a "closer relationship with" the Zen masters philosophy "will be reborn" as a new respiratory ontology of the aerial invisibility and nothingness.

So, what does the respiratory philosopher do as he sits silently in *zazen* in order to learn a new ontology of inspiration and expiration of Being? First of all, in *zazen*, in the words of D.T. Suzuki, he "acquires an entirely new point of view whereby to look into the mysteries of life and the secrets of nature." This entirely new point of view is to look into the mysteries of life according to breath and in collaboration with breathing, and thus he takes very seriously in a principal manner Shinichi Suzuki's words that "nothing is more important than breathing, breathing, breathing." Nothing is more important than breathing because everything is explored from this respiratory perspective. Without the experience of the breath, this entirely new point of view does not exist. In *zazen* one chooses to place all one's efforts to listening and becoming familiar with this entirely new way of experiencing in which life is encountered and viewed within the silence of inspiration and expiration of Being. As Being equals the world as the field of all fields and as the universal dimensionality, this means, in other words, that the respiratory philosopher listens and experiences mindfully the silence of inhalation and exhalation of the world as the field of all fields and as the universal dimensionality. I suggest that this world is the world that we have heard Shinichi Suzuki call the "world of nothing but breathing." In *zazen*, the respiratory philosopher's being-in-the-world is being-in-the-world-of-nothing-but-breathing. This would mean that the world of nothing but breathing is the field of all fields and the universal dimensionality of his whole existence. Everything is then essentially intertwined with this respiratory world. If, according to Merleau-Ponty, philosophy is precisely Being speaking within us, then for respiratory philosophers, philosophy, or ontology, is the world of nothing but breathing speaking within us. In *zazen*, we place and attune ourselves in such a way that we are ready to listen and learn what this respiratory world can teach us. So, we are ready to learn ontology that only respiration can teach us. We listen to how respiration as an entirely new point of view redefines Being and how it thus redefines the connections between what is a thing and what is not a thing, between being and nothingness, between the positive and the negative, and between the visible and the invisible.

The Object- and Thing-Related Ontologies and the Atmospheric Ontology of the World of Nothing but Breathing

The most fundamental difference to other approaches, for example of seeing and of touching, is that respiration is not at all in the first place a relation to beings, that is, to things and objects. Our eyes gaze at, look at, and stare at things. Our hands grasp, caress, manipulate, fondle, push, pull, and destroy things. Our everyday life is built out of ceaseless dealings with things and objects in practical, social, emotional, theoretical, and perceptual ways. All of these different ways are dependent on their relation to things and objects. Our whole life is surrounded by things and objects. This means that there are theoretical objects of thought, practical objects of manipulation, emotional objects of affection, and social objects of communication. All the fields of life, for example, from religion to science, from cooking to sports, and from agriculture to politics, are founded upon their own collections of things and objects. When Merleau-Ponty says that "ontology is everywhere," he means that every field, level, and sphere of life defines the connections between what is a thing and what is not a thing in their own various ways, which means they all have their own kind of ontology (for example, what can be called regional ontologies) that differ from each other. But as all of their focus is in some collection of beings, they are all, in the first place, thing- or object-oriented ontologies. This includes also the various philosophical ontologies of the West as they are based, in the first place, on the life of the eyes, which always connect us primordially with things. As these thing-related ontologies always in some way define the relation between what is a thing and what is not a thing, it is important to ask how "no things" are defined. What is *not* a thing for these ontologies is still essentially intertwined with what is a thing. For example, the *various ways of how to approach* things and *what kind of meanings and relations* these various things have within a certain field or sphere of life are not things, but they are intimately interconnected with the things of the given field, and their meaning is constituted in a relation with the things of that field of life. Also, for example, the phenomenon of consciousness, which is often understood as something that is not a thing, is still understood in its relation to things as consciousness of things and sometimes even also as a thing (the Cartesian "thinking thing").

The thing-orientation is true even in the case of well-refined philosophical ontologies, for example, of Heidegger or Merleau-Ponty. Both of their ontologies are highly aware of the ontological difference between Being and beings, but still for both of them the starting point of philosophizing is thing-oriented. In their ontologies, things are investigated within that which is not a thing (horizon or clearing[84]) and which makes these things appear as things. Both of these well-refined phenomenological ontologies have fragmentary hints toward an ontology, as we have witnessed in this chapter, which would not be, in the first place, thing-oriented, but neither of them really gives true awakening toward this kind of new ontology. It *might be* that only an ontology that takes its starting point from respiration as a relation to the atmosphere of open and free air can become really and truly an atmosphere-oriented ontology in which all relations to things are primordially constituted by the respiratory atmospheric experience that has always already a priority over thing-relations. The life of the breath anticipates the life of the eye and the hand. All of this is truly the reason why the Zen masters and their primary practice of *zazen* are so crucially important for this new respiratory ontology, as *zazen* does not take its point of departure *either* from the thing-related approach, which completely forgets Being, *or* even from a much more ontologically refined thing-clearing/horizon-related Gestalt approach, which is perpetually aware of the ontological difference of Being and beings, while it studies things, but from the atmospheric approach, in which the practice of *zazen* does not, in the first place, relate us with things. *Zazen* as mindfulness of breathing opens us directly without any mediation of things to the atmospheric world of no-thing, that is, to *kū* as emptiness, nothingness, and the invisible air. In Merleau-Ponty's words we could call this atmospheric world of no-thing "natural negativity" that is "always already there" before any appearance of positive things and as their condition of possibility. The world of emptiness, the world of nothing, the "limitless world"[85] (Shunryu Suzuki), "inspiration and expiration of Being"[86] (Merleau-Ponty), the "Great Respiration"[87] (Dürckheim), and the aerial world of "the immense glory of a Nothing"[88] (Bachelard) as the "clearing of air"[89] (Irigaray) are the world that Shinichi Suzuki calls the "world of nothing but breathing."[90] Within this new atmospheric approach of *zazen*, we must let the silently sitting breathing body as respiratory openness to the world of nothing but breathing, which is the essence of human existence (we ourselves are always already respiration within Being), teach us again and again what the connections are between Being and a being, between what is a thing and what is not a thing, between positive and negative, and between visible and invisible. The Zen Masters can teach to the respiratory philosopher how to sit in our essential existence of respiratory openness for hours without any reference to the world of things while revealing in that pure act of sitting who we really always already are as respiration within Being. When Dumoulin writes in his book *Zen Enlightenment*, "[o]ne who clings to no particular being gains the unobstructed view of vast emptiness," it is important to understand that this is exactly what occurs in *zazen*, as breathing never clings to any particular being. It actually does not cling to beings at all, as breathing is not in the first place a relation with beings, but with *kū* as atmospheric aerial emptiness. It is important to remember that even Heidegger called *kū* "the loftiest name for what [we] mean to say with the word 'Being.'" When the respiratory philosopher learns to just sit in his essence of respiratory openness to *kū*, he could perhaps reach the state in which he just follows or listens to the "universal activity of the swinging door," which moves with every exhalation and inhalation when "you will feel as if it is the universal, not yourself, who is doing the breathing." At that moment, according to the Zen Masters, "the true experience of life through" *zazen* reveals to us our "universal nature," which is also called our "Buddha nature"—that is, the experience of enlightenment. So, according to the Zen Masters, the deep awareness of what I have called the respiratory essence of human existence and what they call the "universal nature," the "universal being," or the "Buddha nature" is the enlightenment experience of *kū* or *śūnyatā*. The deepest truth of our existence lies in the depths of our essential and most fundamental openness as respiratory openness. For this reason, Dōgen says very simply: "The breath of Buddha [the Awakened One] is the entire universe; that is all we need [to] learn."[91] But to learn "the breath of Buddha," that is, the breath of the Awakened One as the breath that perpetually sojourns in the entire world of aerial emptiness without clinging and limiting itself to things is extremely difficult, despite breath being the primordial essence of human existence. When ontological investigation learns to take its perpetual point of departure in its task to redefine "the loftiest name for" Being within "the breath of Buddha" as the constant deepening of our essential respiratory openness to the "world of nothing but breathing," the ontological revolution of new atmospheric respiratory ontology will have truly begun.

Notes

1. Luce Irigaray, *Between East and West: From Singularity to Community*, trans. Stephen Pluhácek (New York: Columbia University Press, 2002), 77.

2. Maurice Merleau-Ponty, "Merleau-Ponty in Person: An Interview with Madeleine Chapsal, February 17, 1958," in *The Merleau-Ponty Reader*, ed. Ted Toadvine and Leonard Lawlor (Evanston, IL: Northwestern University Press, 2007), 387.

3. Merleau-Ponty, "Merleau-Ponty in Person," 386.

4. Martin Heidegger, *Being and Time: A Translation of Sein und Zeit*, trans. Joan Stambaugh (Albany: State University of New York Press, 1996), 33–34.

5. Martin Heidegger, *The Basic Problems of Phenomenology*, trans. Albert Hofstadter (Bloomington and Indianapolis: Indiana University Press, 1982), 11.

6. Merleau-Ponty, "Merleau-Ponty in Person," 386–387.

7. Maurice Merleau-Ponty, *The Visible and the Invisible: Followed by Working Notes*, ed. Claude Lefort, trans. Alphonso Lingis (Evanston, IL: Northwestern University Press, 1968), 170.

8. Ibid.

9. Ibid., 236.

10. Ibid., 227.

11. Maurice Merleau-Ponty, *Phenomenology of Perception*, trans. Donald A. Landes (London and New York: Routledge, 2012), 366.

12. Merleau-Ponty calls Being "natural negativity," as it is not a positive thing that is present in a way beings are. Within the level or logic of positive and visible things, Being appears as absence and invisibility. It is invisible and intangible absence as it cannot be seen by the eyes or grasped by the hands. So from the perspective of positive beings (things, objects), it is negativity. But it is important to understand that Being as natural negativity is always already there around and between positive (seen and touched) things as their invisible and intangible background, field, or atmosphere.

It is their hidden or latent condition of possibility. Merleau-Ponty writes of Being as negativity as follows: "it is a natural negativity, a first institution, always already there" (*The Visible and the Invisible*, 216). Being as natural negativity is always already there as the hidden or absent field of all fields, that makes it possible that positive beings can appear to us as beings.

13. Heidegger, *Basic Problems of Phenomenology*, 324.

14. Martin Heidegger, "Letter on Humanism," in *Basic Writings*, Martin Heidegger, ed. David Farrell Krell (San Francisco: Harper, 1993), 255.

15. Merleau-Ponty, "Merleau-Ponty in Person," 387. As ontology and philosophy are synonymous, Merleau-Ponty can also write that "[p]hilosophy is everywhere, even in the 'facts,' and it nowhere has a private realm which shelters it from life's contagion." Maurice Merleau-Ponty, *Signs*, trans. Richard C. McCleary (Evanston, IL: Northwestern University Press, 1964), 130.

16. Maurice Merleau-Ponty, *Notes des cours au Collège de France 1958–1959 et 1960–1961* (Paris: Éditions Gallimard, 1996), 39.

17. Merleau-Ponty, *The Visible and the Invisible*, 169.

18. Maurice Merleau-Ponty, "Eye and Mind," in *The Merleau-Ponty Reader*, ed. Ted Toadvine and Leonard Lawlor (Evanston, IL: Northwestern University Press, 2007), 367–368.

19. Maurice Merleau-Ponty, "Phenomenology and Psychoanalysis: Preface to Hesnard's *L'Oeuvre de Freud*," in *The Essential Writings of Merleau-Ponty*, ed. Alden L. Fischer (New York: Harcourt, Brace & World, 1961), 81.

20. Maurice Merleau-Ponty, *The World of Perception*, trans. Oliver Davis (London and New York: Routledge, 2004), 40.

21. Merleau-Ponty, "Eye and Mind," 375.

22. Maurice Merleau-Ponty, *Nature: Course Notes from the Collège de France*, trans. Robert Vallier (Evanston, IL: Northwestern University Press, 2003), 40.

23. Merleau-Ponty, *The Visible and the Invisible*, 103. The translation has been slightly modified.

24. Merleau-Ponty, "Eye and Mind," 357.

25. Lawrence Hass, *Merleau-Ponty's Philosophy* (Bloomington and Indianapolis: Indiana University Press, 2008), 27.

26. Merleau-Ponty, "Eye and Mind," 358. The translation has been modified. See the original text: Maurice Merleau-Ponty, *L'Œil et l'Esprit* (Paris: Gallimard, 1964), 31–32.

27. Merleau-Ponty, *The Visible and the Invisible*, 125.

28. Ibid.

29. Ibid., 197.

30. Ibid., 128.

31. Karlfried Graf von Dürckheim, *Hara: The Vital Centre of Man*, trans. Sylvia-Monica von Kospoth (London: George Allen & Unwin, 1977), 152–164. See also Irigaray, *Between East and West*, 7.

32. Shinichi Suzuki quoted by Robert E. Carter, *The Japanese Arts and Self-Cultivation* (Albany: State University of New York Press, 2008), 32.

33. Ibid.

34. Ibid.

35. Zen Master Dōgen, *Beyond Thinking: A Guide to Zen Meditation*, ed. Kazuaki Tanahashi, (Boston and London: Shambhala, 2004), 7.

36. Helen J. Baroni, *The Illustrated Encyclopedia of Zen Buddhism* (New York: The Rosen Publishing Group, 2002), 385.

37. Norman Fischer, introduction to *Beyond Thinking: A Guide to Zen Meditation*, by Zen Master Dōgen (Boston and London: Shambhala, 2004), xxvi.

38. Daisetz Teitaro Suzuki, *An Introduction to Zen Buddhism* (New York: Grove Press, 1964), 34n2.

39. Baroni, *Illustrated Encyclopedia of Zen Buddhism*, vi.

40. Philip Kapleau, *The Three Pillars of Zen: Teaching, Practice, Enlightenment* (Boston: Beacon Press, 1967), 9.

41. Suzuki, *Introduction to Zen Buddhism*, 59.

42. Shunryu Suzuki, *Zen Mind, Beginner's Mind* (New York and Tokyo: Weather-hill, 1995), 29.

43. Eugen Herrigel (1884–1955) was a German philosopher who studied Zen in Japan in the 1920s.

44. Eugen Herrigel, *The Method of Zen* (New York: Vintage Books, 1974), 38. My emphasis.

45. Suzuki, *Zen Mind*, 31. My emphasis.

46. Ibid., 30. My emphasis.

47. Ibid., 29. My emphasis.

48. Karlfried Graf Dürckheim (1896–1988) was a German diplomat, psycho-therapist, and Zen Master who studied Zen in Japan between 1938 and 1947.

49. Dürckheim, *Hara*, 157–158 and 161. See also Alan Watts, *The Way of Zen* (New York: Vintage Books, 1989), 120. It is important to notice that this formula-tion of "It breathes me" can also be found outside of Zen context, for example, from Gaston Bachelard's book *The Poetics of Reverie*, as follows: " 'It breathes me.' In other words, the world comes to breathe within me; I participate in the good breathing of the world; I am plunged into a breathing world. Everything breathes in the world. The good breathing which is going to cure me of my asthma, of my anguish, is a cosmic breathing." Gaston Bachelard, *The Poetics of Reverie: Childhood, Language, and the Cosmos*, trans. Daniel Russell (Boston: Beacon Press, 1971), 179. In these quota-tions from Dürckheim and Bachelard we can also notice that both connect the "It breathes" to the notion of cosmic, that is, to "the cosmic movement of ebb and flow" and to "a cosmic breathing." The experience that instead of "I breathe" it is "It" that "breathes me" is also very similar to Merleau-Ponty's account of perceptual experience in general as he writes: "if I wanted to express perceptual experience with precision, I would have to say that *one* perceives in me, and not that I perceive" (*Phenomenol-ogy of Perception*, 223). Also the expression of the "Great Respiration" reminds me of Merleau-Ponty's expression of "some immense external lung" that takes over my own breathing in the process of falling asleep. See ibid., 219. See my following articles on Merleau-Ponty's notion of "some immense external lung": Petri Berndtson, "The Inspiration and the Expiration of Being: The Immense Lung and the Cosmic Breath-

ing as the Sources of Dreams, Poetry and Philosophy," in *Thinking in Dialogue with Humanities: Paths into the Phenomenology of Merleau-Ponty*, ed. Karel Novotný et al. (Bucharest: Zeta Books, 2010), 281–293; Petri Berndtson, "The Respiratory Constitution of Space and its Connection to the Origin of Space," *Scientific Papers University of Latvia* 765 (2011): 80–86; Petri Berndtson, "The Primordial Respiratory Peace and the Possibility of Cultivation of Breathing as a Method of Peacemaking," in *The Poesis of Peace*, ed. Klaus-Gerd Giesen et al. (London: Routledge, 2017).

50. Heinrich Dumoulin, *Zen Enlightenment: Origins and Meaning*, trans. John C. Maraldo (Boston and London: Weatherhill, 2007), 117; and Yuasa Yasuo, *Overcoming Modernity: Synchronicity and Image-Thinking*, trans. Shigenori Nagatomo and John W.M. Krummel (Albany: State University of New York Press, 2008), 84.

51. Dumoulin, *Zen Enlightenment*, 119.

52. Hee-Jin Kim, *Dōgen on Meditation and Thinking: A Reflection on His View of Zen* (Albany: State University of New York Press, 2007), 43.

53. David Loy, "The Deconstruction of Buddhism," in *Derrida and Negative Theology*, ed. Harold Coward and Toby Foshay (Albany: State University of New York Press, 1992), 233. See also Carl Olson, *The A to Z of Buddhism* (Lanham, MD: Scarecrow Press, 2009), 217–218.

54. See more about the relation between *zazen* and abdominal breathing in Kenneth Kushner, *One Arrow, One Life: Zen, Archery, Enlightenment* (North Clarendon, VT: Tuttle Publishing, 2000), 28–31. See also what in comparison to *zazen*, for example, Gay Hendricks says about diaphragmatic breathing: "In healthy diaphragmatic breathing, the belly muscles are relaxed, allowing *the abdomen to swell with the in-breath*." Gay Hendricks, *Conscious Breathing: Breathwork for Health, Stress Release, and Personal Mastery* (New York: Bantam Books, 1995), 59. My emphasis.

55. Irigaray, *Between East and West*, 7.

56. Merleau-Ponty, "Merleau-Ponty in Person," 386.

57. Martin Heidegger, *On the Way to Language*, trans. Peter D. Hertz (New York: Harper & Row, 1971), 14.

58. Ibid., 15.

59. Ibid., 46. See also ibid., 41.

60. Ibid., 46.

61. This phrasing that *kū* cannot be "perceived by the senses" raises the question can this be true or this is an oversimplification? As *kū* is not an object or a thing, but "emptiness, the open, and the sky," we still experience *kū*. We just do not experience it as an experience of an object or a thing, but as an experience of the open, emptiness, or sky. Can the senses perceive the open or the empty? At least I see the sky, but it is important to understand that the sky is not a thing, but a background against which objects appear. These objects, for example, are clouds. As *kū* is also "air" we experience it constantly in an implicit manner and have an intimate and sensitive contact with it as it ceaselessly touches us or as we touch it without purposely doing so. This sensitivity is not a perception of a thing or an object, but an atmospheric perception that surrounds us constantly. A good example of this perpetual aerial sensitivity is how we experience the warmth and coldness of the air without intentionally grasping

46 Petri Berndtson

something as an object, and this perpetual experience constitutes in a very deep manner the whole of our existence.

62. Heidegger, *On the Way to Language*, 19.

63. Martin Heidegger, *Poetry, Language, Thought*, trans. Albert Hofstadter (New York: Harper Perennial, 2001), 167.

64. Heidegger, *On the Way to Language*, 19.

65. Heidegger, *Poetry, Language, Thought*, 167–168.

66. Gaston Bachelard, *Air and Dreams: An Essay on the Imagination of Movement*, trans. Edith R. Farrell and C. Frederick Farrell (Dallas: The Dallas Institute Publications, 1988), 136.

67. Luce Irigaray, "From *The Forgetting of Air* to *To Be Two*," in *Feminist Interpretations of Martin Heidegger*, ed. Nancy J. Holland and Patricia Huntington (University Park: The Pennsylvania University Press, 2001), 309.

68. Luce Irigaray, *The Forgetting of Air in Martin Heidegger*, trans. Mary Beth Mader (Austin: University of Texas Press, 1999), 9, 19, 41–42 and 73.

69. Heidegger writes: "The open [. . .] is Being itself." Heidegger, *Parmenides*, trans. André Schuwer and Richard Rojcewic (Bloomington and Indianapolis: Indiana University Press, 1992), 150. According to Heidegger "Being [. . .] is the clearing itself." Heidegger, "Letter on Humanism," 240.

70. Irigaray, *Forgetting of Air*, 9.

71. Peter Sloterdijk, *Terror from the Air*, trans. Amy Patton and Steve Corcoran (Los Angeles: Semiotext(e), 2009), 93.

72. Heidegger, "The End of Philosophy and the Task of Thinking," in *Basic Writings*, Martin Heidegger, ed. David Farrell Krell (San Francisco: Harper, 1993), 442.

73. Martin Heidegger, *Zollikon Seminars: Protocols—Conversations—Letters*, ed. Medard Boss, trans. Franz Mayr and Richard Askay (Evanston, IL: Northwestern University Press, 2001), 217.

74. Ibid., 176.

75. Ibid., 185

76. Maurice Merleau-Ponty, "The Child's Relations with Others," in *The Primacy of Perception*, Maurice Merleau-Ponty, ed. James M. Edie (Evanston, IL: Northwestern University Press, 1964), 122.

77. Merleau-Ponty, *Phenomenology of Perception*, 174.

78. Ibid., 224.

79. David Michael Levin, "Logos and Psyche: Hermeneutics of Breathing," *Research in Phenomenology* 14 (1984): 124. This quotation is from the original version of David Kleinberg-Levin's article. An improved and updated version of this same article appears in this volume.

80. Ibid.

81. Ibid., 129. This same formulation can also be found in Kleinberg-Levin's book *Before the Voice of Reason: Echoes of Responsibility in Merleau-Ponty's Ecology and Levinas's Ethics* (Albany: State University of New York Press, 2008), 79.

82. Levin, "Logos and Psyche," 126.

83. Ibid., 129.

84. This horizon, or clearing, of Being can be in Heidegger's case, for example, the "Fourfold" in its complex network (the "gathering" of earth, sky, mortals, and divinities) which constitutes the thing; see Andrew J. Mitchell, "The Fourfold," in *Martin Heidegger: Key Concepts*, ed. Bret W. Davis (Durham, UK: Acumen, 2010), 208. In Merleau-Ponty's case, this horizon of Being in which the thing is constituted is the "Flesh" as the intertwining of chiasmic relations between the seer who is as vision "an operative nothingness" (invisibility, negativity) and the seen as a visible and positive thing; see Merleau-Ponty, *The Visible and the Invisible*, 76. In both of these cases, the thing is placed completely in a new dimension that is not a thing itself, but still these meaningful contexts in their nuanced networks show how the thing appears as a thing and how there would not be meaningful things without these contexts that constitute them. In Heidegger's words: "Da-sein [human being in its essential openness] *must always be seen* as being-in-the-world, *as concern for things*." Heidegger, *Zollikon Seminars*, 159 (my emphasis). In Merleau-Ponty's words, the foundational philosophical approach is based on the wisdom of the eye, which teaches the philosopher to see the things in an authentic questioning manner, as he writes: "Philosophy is the perceptual faith questioning itself about itself [. . .] It is not only philosophy, it is *first the gaze* that questions the things." Merleau-Ponty, *The Visible and the Invisible*, 103. (The translation has been slightly modified. My emphasis.) *Zazen*, in contrast to these approaches, offers the philosopher a way out of the whole game of things as its primary approach to Being. The practice of *zazen* could truly radicalize Heidegger's and Merleau-Ponty's thought. *Zazen* is the way literally, that is, really and truly "to think Being without beings." Martin Heidegger, *On Time and Being*, trans. Joan Stambaugh (New York: Harper & Row, 1972), 24. So, the basic difference is that Heidegger and Merleau-Ponty consider our relation to things within the horizons of Being (within what is not a thing) and Zen as practice of *zazen* considers our direct relation to *kū* without the mediation of things. If Heidegger gives us the clue "to think Being without beings" and Merleau-Ponty gives us the clue of "respiration within Being" without ever saying anything about it, then *zazen* teaches us what these clues can truly mean as an openness to Being and thus to ontology.

85. Suzuki, *Zen Mind*, 29.

86. Merleau-Ponty, "Eye and Mind," 358.

87. Dürckheim, *Hara*, 161.

88. Bachelard, *Air and Dreams*, 136.

89. Irigaray, *Forgetting of Air*, 9.

90. Shinichi Suzuki quoted by Carter, *Japanese Arts*, 32.

91. Zenji Dōgen, *Shobogenzo (The Eye and Treasury of the True Law)*, trans. Kosen Nishiyama (Tokyo: Nakayama Shobo, 1988), 182. "The breath of Buddha," that is, the breath of the Awakened One, is deeply connected to the experience of enlightenment as the experience of *kū* (emptiness, air). Yuasa writes of *kū* as follows: "*kū* [Chin., *kōng*: 空; Skrt., *śūnya*] is a word that carries such meanings as 'empty' and 'having no content,' and is an expression indicating the dimension that goes beyond actuality [of things], that is, the transcendental dimension known through the lived experience of *nirvāna*." Yuasa, *Overcoming Modernity*, 84. The experience of *kū*, of enlightenment, and of *nirvāna* are the same fundamental experience. This enlightened experience of aerial

emptiness is revealed to us through the practice of *zazen*, as this pure sitting with the breath little by little cultivates itself into the "breath of Buddha" that is wide awake to the perpetual respiratory experience of the "world of nothing but breathing" as "the transcendental dimension" pregnant with possibilities "beyond actuality" of all things.

Bibliography

Bachelard, Gaston. *Air and Dreams: An Essay on the Imagination of Movement*. Translated by Edith R. Farrell and C. Frederick Farrell. Dallas: The Dallas Institute Publications, 2002.

Bachelard, Gaston. *The Poetics of Reverie: Childhood, Language, and the Cosmos*. Translated by Daniel Russell. Boston: Beacon Press, 1971.

Baroni, Helen J. *The Illustrated Encyclopedia of Zen Buddhism*. New York: The Rosen Publishing Group, 2002.

Berndtson, Petri. "The Inspiration and the Expiration of Being: The Immense Lung and the Cosmic Breathing as the Sources of Dreams, Poetry and Philosophy." In *Thinking in Dialogue with Humanities: Paths into the Phenomenology of Merleau-Ponty*, edited by Karel Novotný, Taylor S. Hammer, Anne Gléonec, and Petr Specián, 281–293. Bucharest: Zeta Books, 2010.

Berndtson, Petri. "The Primordial Respiratory Peace and the Possibility of Cultivation of Breathing as a Method of Peacemaking." In *The Poesis of Peace: Narratives, Cultures and Philosophies*, edited by Klaus-Gerd Giesen, Carool Kersten, and Lenart Škof. London: Routledge, 2017.

Berndtson, Petri. "The Respiratory Constitution of Space and its Connection to the Origin of Space." *Scientific Papers University of Latvia* 765 (2011): 80–86.

Carter, Robert E. *The Japanese Arts and Self-Cultivation*. Albany: State University of New York Press, 2008.

Dōgen, Zenji. *Shobogenzo (The Eye and Treasury of the True Law)*. Translated by Kosen Nishiyama. Tokyo: Nakayama Shobo, 1988.

Dōgen, Zen Master. *Beyond Thinking: A Guide to Zen Meditation*. Edited by Kazuaki Tanahashi. Boston and London: Shambhala, 2004.

Dumoulin, Heinrich. *Zen Enlightenment: Origins and Meaning*. Translated by John C. Maraldo. Boston and London: Weatherhill, 2007.

Dürckheim, Karlfried Graf von. *Hara: The Vital Centre of Man*. Translated by Sylvia-Monica von Kospoth. London: George Allen & Unwin, 1977.

Fischer, Norman. Introduction to *Beyond Thinking: A Guide to Zen Meditation*, by Zen Master Dōgen, xxiii–xxxiv. Boston and London: Shambhala, 2004.

Hass, Lawrence. *Merleau-Ponty's Philosophy*. Bloomington and Indianapolis: Indiana University Press, 2008.

Heidegger, Martin. *The Basic Problems of Phenomenology*. Translated by Albert Hofstadter. Bloomington & Indianapolis: Indiana University Press, 1982.

Heidegger, Martin. *Being and Time: A Translation of Sein und Zeit*. Translated by Joan Stambaugh. Albany: State University of New York Press, 1996.

Heidegger, Martin. "The End of Philosophy and the Task of Thinking." In *Basic Writings*, Martin Heidegger, edited by David Farrell Krell, 427–449. San Francisco: Harper, 1993.

Heidegger, Martin. "Letter on Humanism." In *Basic Writings*, Martin Heidegger, edited by David Farrell Krell, 213–267. San Francisco: Harper, 1993.

Heidegger, Martin. *On Time and Being*. Translated by Joan Stambaugh. New York: Harper & Row, 1972.

Heidegger, Martin. *On the Way to Language*. Translated by Peter D. Hertz. New York: Harper & Row, 1971.

Heidegger, Martin. *Parmenides*. Translated by André Schuwer and Richard Rojcewic. Bloomington and Indianapolis: Indiana University Press, 1992.

Heidegger, Martin. *Poetry, Language, Thought*. Translated by Albert Hofstadter. New York: Harper Perennial, 2001.

Heidegger, Martin. *Zollikon Seminars: Protocols—Conversations—Letters*. Edited by Medard Boss and translated by Franz Mayr and Richard Askay. Evanston, IL: Northwestern University Press, 2001.

Hendricks, Gay. *Conscious Breathing: Breathwork for Health, Stress Release, and Personal Mastery*. New York: Bantam Books, 1995.

Herrigel, Eugen. *The Method of Zen*. New York: Vintage Books, 1974.

Irigaray, Luce. *Between East and West: From Singularity to Community*. Translated by Stephen Pluháček. New York: Columbia University Press, 2002.

Irigaray, Luce. *The Forgetting of Air in Martin Heidegger*. Translated by Mary Beth Mader. Austin: University of Texas Press, 1999.

Irigaray, Luce. "From *The Forgetting of Air* to *To Be Two*." In *Feminist Interpretations of Martin Heidegger*, edited by Nancy J. Holland and Patricia Huntington, 309–315. University Park: The Pennsylvania University Press, 2001.

Kapleau, Philip. *The Three Pillars of Zen: Teaching, Practice, Enlightenment*. Boston: Beacon Press, 1967.

Kim, Hee-Jin. *Dōgen on Meditation and Thinking: A Reflection on His View of Zen*. Albany: State University of New York Press, 2007.

Kleinberg-Levin, David Michael. *Before the Voice of Reason: Echoes of Responsibility in Merleau-Ponty's Ecology and Levinas's Ethics*. Albany: State University of New York Press, 2008.

Kushner, Kenneth. *One Arrow, One Life: Zen, Archery, Enlightenment*. North Clarendon, VT: Tuttle Publishing, 2000.

Levin, David Michael. "Logos and Psyche: Hermeneutics of Breathing." *Research in Phenomenology* 14 (1984): 121–147.

Loy, David. "The Deconstruction of Buddhism." In *Derrida and Negative Theology*, edited by Harold Coward and Toby Foshay, 227–253. Albany: State University of New York Press, 1992.

Merleau-Ponty, Maurice. "The Child's Relations with Others." In *The Primacy of Perception*, Maurice Merleau-Ponty, edited by James M. Edie, 96–155. Evanston, IL: Northwestern University Press, 1964.

Merleau-Ponty, Maurice. "Eye and Mind." In *The Merleau-Ponty Reader*, edited by Ted Toadvine and Leonard Lawlor, 351–378. Evanston, IL: Northwestern University Press, 2007.

Merleau-Ponty, Maurice. *L'Œil et l'Esprit*. Paris: Gallimard, 1964.

Merleau-Ponty, Maurice. "Merleau-Ponty in Person: An Interview with Madeleine Chapsal, February 17, 1958." In *The Merleau-Ponty Reader*, edited by Ted Toadvine and Leonard Lawlor, 379–391. Evanston, IL: Northwestern University Press, 2007.

Merleau-Ponty, Maurice. *Nature: Course Notes from the Collège de France*. Translated by Robert Vallier. Evanston, IL: Northwestern University Press, 2003.

Merleau-Ponty, Maurice. *Notes des cours au Collège de France 1958–1959 et 1960–1961*. Paris: Éditions Gallimard, 1996.

Merleau-Ponty, Maurice. "Phenomenology and Psychoanalysis: Preface to Hesnard's *L'Oeuvre de Freud*." In *The Essential Writings of Merleau-Ponty*, edited by Alden L. Fischer. New York: Harcourt, Brace & World, 1961.

Merleau-Ponty, Maurice. *Phenomenology of Perception*. Translated by Donald A. Landes. London and New York: Routledge, 2012.

Merleau-Ponty, Maurice. *Signs*. Translated by Richard C. McCleary. Evanston, IL: Northwestern University Press, 1964.

Merleau-Ponty, Maurice. *The Visible and the Invisible: Followed by Working Notes*. Edited by Claude Lefort and translated by Alphonso Lingis. Evanston, IL: Northwestern University Press, 1968.

Merleau-Ponty, Maurice. *The World of Perception*. Translated by Oliver Davis. London and New York: Routledge, 2004.

Mitchell, Andrew J. "The Fourfold." In *Martin Heidegger: Key Concepts*, edited by Bret W. Davis, 208–218. Durham, UK: Acumen, 2010.

Olson, Carl. *The A to Z of Buddhism*. Lanham, MD: The Scarecrow Press, 2009.

Sloterdijk, Peter. *Terror from the Air*. Translated by Amy Patton and Steve Corcoran. Los Angeles: Semiotext(e), 2009.

Suzuki, Daisetz Teitaro. *An Introduction to Zen Buddhism*. New York: Grove Press, 1964.

Suzuki, Shunryu. *Zen Mind, Beginner's Mind*. New York and Tokyo: Weatherhill, 1995.

Watts, Alan. *The Way of Zen*. New York: Vintage Books, 1989.

Yuasa, Yasuo. *Overcoming Modernity: Synchronicity and Image-Thinking*. Translated by Shigenori Nagatomo and John W.M. Krummel. Albany: State University of New York Press, 2008.

3

Breath as a Way of Self-Affection

On New Topologies of Transcendence and Self-Transcendence

LENART ŠKOF

For not even spirit itself is supreme; it is but spirit,
or the breath of love. (Schelling)[1]

Language is nothing but the realization of the species, the mediation of the I and Thou [. . .] The word's element is air, the most spiritual and universal medium of life. (Feuerbach)[2]

Anyone who knows how to breathe the air of my writings knows that it is an air of the heights, a bracing air. You must be made for it, or else you are in no little danger of catching cold in it. The ice is near, the solitude is immense—but how peacefully everything lies in the light! how freely you breathe! how much you feel to be beneath you! (Nietzsche)[3]

Something has happened—an event, or an advent—an encounter between humans. A breath or soul has been born, brought forth by two others. There are now living beings for whom we lack the ways of approaching, the gestures and words for drawing nearer to one another, for exchanging. (Irigaray)[4]

Before Breath Is Born: In Search for a New Self-Affection

The question of epistemological foundations of our religious and theological thinking is perhaps one of the most difficult questions in philosophy: it deals with both theoretical as well as practical layers of our being-in-the-world; moreover, it is also related to the most intimate layers of our personal and social life (questions of life and death, family and kin, our values in social and political environments, our ethical attitudes) that we possess and inhabit. Moreover, for philosophy of religion, today the question would be how to relate our self-transcendence to the transcendence of the irreducible otherness of the other—in other words, how to relate in a new way our most intimate (also sexed) ontological layers with the other, and ultimately God/dess still to come. But it seems that we do not yet have the dialectics to enable this encounter. We pray for this *event* (Caputo),[5] which resides in a yet unknown place and time, as our longing, but also as our forgetting.

Traditionally, Western metaphysics has armed (male) philosophers with the knowledge needed for the encounter with the unknown or dangerous, and at the same moment given them permission to safeguard the place, occupied only for themselves, and which they firmly held only for sustaining and perpetuating this powerful self-affection. With Feuerbach's *philosophy of sensibility*[6] and with Nietzsche's *revaluation of all values*,[7] for the first time in the history of Western thought the existing topologies of this kind of selfhood (soul, spirit, subjectivity) have been radically undermined—both from the theoretical as well as from the practical sense (self-affection as both natural affection in Feuerbach as well as an artistic practice in Nietzsche). With Feuerbach and Nietzsche the philosopher, and man, is now put into an entirely new relational space that he never before occupied: he is now close to the primordial (macrocosmical) constellation of the elements of nature (water, air, earth, and fire) and to the *pulsation* of his body (the microcosm)—as radically exposed by Nietzsche; he is also reminded of his sex (Feuerbach being the first philosopher to address this new dialectics of inter-subjectivity)[8] and thus exposed in an entirely new way to sexual difference; finally, with both Feuerbach and Nietzsche, the philosopher for the first time was faced with the death of a God he had known and worshipped for centuries. In this, both thinkers (and, as we'll see, also Irigaray) are close to pre-Socratic thought. Additionally, Nietzsche reminds us in his *Antichrist*[9] that we need to search for truth also in the traditions of the East (i.e., within ancient Indo-Iranian civilizational circle)—such as in his invocation of the Zarathustra and his high praise of Buddha (in this, Nietzsche remained Schopenhauer's best successor; we may also add the Upanishadic thought).[10] Sadly, Feuerbach's philosophy soon went into oblivion, allegedly superseded by Marxist thought and only resuscitated after more than a century by Irigaray's philosophical project.

Maybe phenomenology was first to learn this lesson in its entirety: Husserl and Heidegger have each in his own way decided to brush aside all of the old philosophical sediments from our spiritual legacies.[11] Husserl's phenomenological reduction in his *Ideen* and Heidegger's *Being and Time* are without doubt two of the key events in the history of Western thinking. Since then, phenomenology has enabled philosophers to dwell closer to the body, closer to our senses (of ethical/bodily proximity, hearing, caress and touch—as in Merleau-Ponty and Levinas, but also in Nancy, Henry, Marion, and especially Chrétien; but, with one exception[12]—not yet breath—as our "ontological" sense), and, later also in an intercultural sense, to interpret our various lifeworlds only as parts of a pluriform world culture, which is hermeneutically open, eventual, and never enclosed into the one interpretative framework, or the one Truth. But according to Irigaray, cultivating oneself requires a different kind of self-affection that still "seems to be lacking for us Westerners."[13] The self-affection, which already was a part of classical philosophical training from Parmenides to Hegel, but which also extended to Husserl and Heidegger, did not cultivate the relationality as a way of our individual becoming; that is, self-affection toward the other was not defined in a proper dialectical way—in a way that would safeguard *both* my subjectivity and the other's transcendence in his or her difference and full autonomy. Of course, philosophy always was relational in a sense of some temporality of me and the other, the Real, or, ultimately, a God, but not in a sense of an "ecstasy of an encounter"[14]—in an ethically radicalized mode of between-two, based on the ontology of self-affection, sexual difference, and our mutual mesocosmical *breathing*.[15] This very encounter inaugurates and at the same moment safeguards the new radicalized ontology (at first as *a*theology) of the two, which in its essence is both religious (cf. Irigaray's sensible transcendental) and ethical. What is the ontology of self-affection, then?

In her more recent works, Luce Irigaray works on what I would call "the sexuate ontology of radical subjectivity."[16] Her thinking is based on the notion of *auto-* or *self-affection*. In order to be able to get to the ontological layer of her teachings on sensible transcendental and breath, it is first necessary to understand this notion, as proposed in her later writings. We find it for the first time in *The Way of Love* from 2002, in the Introduction:

> An encounter between two different subjects implies that each one attends to remaining itself. And that cannot amount to a simple voluntarist gesture but depends on our ability for "*auto-affection*"—another word that I did not find in the dictionary. Without this, we cannot respect the other as other, and he, or she, cannot respect us. It is not a question, to be sure, of extrapolating into some essence—mine or that of the other—but of a critical gesture for a return to oneself which does not stay in suspension in immutable truths or essences but which provides a faithfulness to oneself in becoming.[17]

Later known as self-affection, this is in my opinion a key to understanding her philosophical teaching on sexual difference and our ethical becoming. Irigaray's greatest contribution to philosophy is without doubt the introduction of an idiosyncratic dialectical *dyad* into the very core of our ontology and epistemology.

This dyad is always formed by two, who are different (sexual difference is here understood as an ontological paradigm, and clearly not as a call to heteronorma- tivity), and "not united by genealogy or hierarchy."[18] Self-affection thus teaches us to become two, without appropriating or annihilating the other as other, or without being alienated from our own becoming in subjectivity. The becom- ing of subjectivity also refers to an idiosyncratic logic of a difference between masculine and feminine world(s), since men and women have different accesses to maternal genealogies, to the rhythms of nature, and to sexual becoming and belonging through mutual desire and love. We breathe the same air, but we breathe it differently. We all want to achieve our humanity, but we can achieve it only dialectically—by respecting our differences in an intersubjective and intercultural sense. Irigaray concludes *In the Beginning, She Was* with the following thoughts:

> Self-affection is neither secondary nor unnecessary. Self-affection— which once more does not amount to a mere auto-eroticism—is a much necessary for being human as bread is. Self-affection is the basis and the first condition of human dignity. There is no culture, no democracy, without the preservation of self-affection for each one.
>
> Self-affection today needs a return to our own body, our own breath, a care about our life in order not to become subjected to technologies, to money, to power, to neutralization in a universal "someone," to assimilation into an anonymous world, to the solitude of individualism.
>
> Self-affection needs faithfulness to oneself, respect for the other in their singularity, reciprocity in desire and love—more generally, in humanity. We have to rediscover and cultivate self-affection start- ing, at each time and in every situation, from two, two who respect their difference, in order to preserve the survival and the becoming of humanity, for each one and for all of us.[19]

But still, what does self-affection offer that is not available to us in Western philosophical history? Here we need to return to Feuerbach and Nietzsche (and their appeal to the body and its practices of self-affection), and also introduce Eastern teachings (from yoga and Buddhism: silence as a mode of self-affection, and the related practice of meditation), which are strong influences on Irigaray[20] and form the fertile ground for her thinking. With Feuerbach, we are witnessing the first philosophical elaboration of intersubjectivity in the entire Western his- tory of philosophy: according to the German thinker, a man and a woman are two beings, fully dependent on Nature (via food, water, air, etc.), but thus also fully dependent on each other. They are sharing each other's finite lifeworlds with the interchange of breathing, touching, and various gestures (such as language), which form a dialectical encounter between any pair of two sensible subjectivities.

But in this relational process, my and your finitude also confront the limit—an infinite transcendence of the other, which is ontologically unsurmountable. For Feuerbach, this is the true and first meaning of any religion and love. Nietzsche clearly radicalized this constellation with his appeal to the body and its immanent life and thus with his absolute rejection of any kind of subjectivity having soul or spirit as its immaterial cause, even hypostacized as a God. It seems that Irigaray translates and develops both concepts—Feuerbach's sensitivity and Nietzsche's will—to her idiosyncratic notion of *self-affection*. There is no logical procedure nor moralistic rule (or religious authority) that could guide us in this dynamics and dialectics of self-affection: and this is where Eastern training (yoga, meditation, Buddha's teachings) enters into the very core of Irigaray's thought. In yoga and Buddhism, the predominance of vital and spiritual breath is clearly represented in their meditational and practical methods, where emptying our ordinary modes of selfhood is a key to our attentiveness (or mindfulness). Now, in order to secure a future world for us, we need to reorient toward dwelling first in our interiority, with self-affection guiding us—in order to inaugurate and enable silence and listening. But to which ontological layer, or reality, will this silence refer? To whom are we first destined to listen? This still is a mystery. We first need to create a sanctuary in ourselves—a place for the advent of *pure breath*, which will be the first sign of compassion and love. As stated in *Una nuova cultura dell'energia*, "thanks to a practice of self-affection"[21] we have become settled in ourselves, protecting life as such—in order to be able to share it with the others. Silence and listening (first to ourselves: meditation, yoga, other spiritual practices) are therefore signs of our self-affection—first toward ourselves, and then toward others (from nature and animals, to human beings and gods, or vice versa). Silence and listening are two modes of our attentiveness, which first is an ontological, and later, as developed in an intersubjective way, also a moral disposition of ourselves, a genuine and ontological dyadic mode of relationality. As argued in one of my previous essays on Irigaray's notion of attentiveness,

> [b]eing attentive to the needs of others is not a simple act or a moral disposition but something more: it is the ideal—but as a certain passivity, an emptying of ourselves, a labelling with "nothingness" of our everyday aims and goals. In a theological language, all of this would be very close to a state of grace. Irigaray devoted much of her later work to the new culture of proximity and intersubjectivity, based on the elements that may, in our opinion, enable us to construct new ethical spaces in ourselves for the welcome of the other. But attentiveness is first of all related to our self-affection. [. . .] Attentiveness is a relational virtue, but of a pre-reflective character: it shows us that we, as individuals, have sociality (and God) already in ourselves. Attentiveness thus opens an ethical space of transcendence of the

other—of his or her irreducible difference to me, or my subjectivity. Only on this ground an ethical gesture, fully respectful of the other and of the needs of others, can emerge. The intersubjective space has thus been revealed and opened to us in a new way.[22]

In this sense, we first need to respect ourselves, being attentive to our inner breath, which always already pulsates in us (although we may not always sense its weak pulsation and it may be obstructed by various obstacles) and enables us to share it with the others, in a respectful, nondiscriminating, and nonpossessing way.

Wound of the World: Freedom and the Love of Breath

To stand in the shadow
of the scar up in the air.

To stand-for-no-one-and-nothing.
Unrecognized,
for you
alone.

With all there is room for in that,
even without
language.[23]

Now it is time to proceed to the ontology of breath. In *Una nuova cultura dell'energia* we read:

If we are conscious of a fact that our life exists only because of our breathing, it is necessary to become autonomous beings. This is why we cannot remain alive on the elementary level of life of a newborn at the beginning of his existence. We need to accept the responsibility for our life and transform it to human existence. This is why we need to safeguard and develop our breathing but also to teach to create the reserve of disposable breath [*una riserva di soffio disponibile*]: a soul, which allows us, that our breath is not dependent only to some necessities we are facing. This, in fact, is the first meaning of the word soul.[24]

According to Irigaray, breath must be a path of our spiritual becoming. When we are born, we breathe autonomously for the first time, but our breath still depends on others who give us food, shelter, and love. In the beginning of our spiritual life,

When we do have breath at our disposal, we become more or
less at the mercy of the reactions of the breathing.
L. Irigaray

Breath as a Way of Self-Affection   57

breath is never uninterrupted, never pure, and we do not yet possess the energy
by ourselves to bring our breath into an equilibrium and peace. We are born with
a body and with a soul (our senses, language), but spiritually we first depend on
others and thus do not yet breathe in an autonomous way. We do not yet have
the reserve of breath at our disposal. In almost all religions of the world we find
a cosmological myth or narrative related to breath energy or breathing, giving us
spiritual guidance and, as it were, the reserve of breath we first need for keeping
and maintaining ourselves in our self-affection, and then for having its share for
others in our compassion. In the form of "wind," "air," "cosmic breath" or "spirit"
(*lil, ruaḥ, aer, pneuma, spiritus, anima, prāṇa, qi, ki, mana* . . .), this substance
is the essential link between microcosmic and macrocosmic realities, between
immanence (our body) and transcendence (other), enabling finite human beings
to access other spiritual beings, the cosmos, and its gods, ultimately, to become
spiritual and express in themselves the infinite. This is the path of divinization, and
this is what I understand as freedom in a truly ontological sense. But Schelling (in
his *Philosophical Inquiries into the Nature of Human Freedom*) went even deeper
with his elaborations on the primordial breath: for him, breath of love (*der Hauch
der Liebe*) is the very foundation of God/Ground—which existed even before
there was a foundation. He argued that in the beginning (ontologically) there is
an original gesture of "co-breathing" (*Konspiration*)[25] which, once inflamed with
inner fever, becomes fractured and inflamed with evil, and the core of our being
is wounded. Human being is born from the wound of the world and is essentially
and ontologically vulnerable (in Christianity this is expressed in the doctrine of
original sin; in Eastern doctrines it is *karma*). To breathe autonomously, to express
freedom in every move of our muscles, to possess the reserve of breath (freedom)
for every gesture of our soul, is our highest goal. But how can we achieve this
spiritual transformation of our being?

This is a very deep level of ontology (and theology) indeed, and it is in my
opinion perhaps the most original account or question posited on the cosmological
and theological foundation of human being in the entire history of philosophy.
Life is born out of the primordial longing of God within itself, which is love,
or, more precisely, the breath of love. Within this primordial breath there is a
movement, an exhalation and inhalation,[26] as it were, of this ground, which is
the archetype of all pulsation and all life (but also of our ontological wound of
death). Within Christianity this movement is clearly expressed in the Trinitarian
teaching, where God himself must become incarnated and wounded in order
to be able to bring the hope of salvation to the world; and it is precisely in the
Holy Spirit that Father sends his Son to the world.[27] The mysterious logic of the
trinitarian co-relationality and co-breathing (*conspiratio*) of three divine persons is
visible precisely in this primordial and anarchic exhalation and inhalation of the
Ground itself, the pulsation of its archetypal life, for Schelling. It is in *pneuma*,
as represented by the Holy Spirit, that every living being receives the share of his

or her vital breath, as its reserve, which is soul. For Roberto M. Unger, whose experimental pragmatist thinking is in many respects very close to Irigaray's philosophy, Jesus Christ "was a concentrated embodiment of divine energy [. . .] the activity of spirit that we find in our experience of transcendence and that we rediscover at work in evolving nature."[28] We may say that this movement is a *paradigm* of our own becoming—as a progression of difference from the ground of our being, as already being wounded, and finite, to the possibility of our own infinite longing through the awakening and mysterious grace of this primordial breath. But also of our death. This is how we transcend ourselves and become spiritual, and how our finite self is becoming awakened and infinite. But one more step needs to be taken: it is the question of the role of breath and sexual difference as related to the sensible transcendental and feminine divine. For Irigaray, it is of no coincidence that Jesus, as our savior, has been incarnated in a young virgin since women have a privileged access to the breath. For Irigaray, Mary is already autonomous in relation to her mother, and her breath has not yet been mingled with the breath of another human being. She is called by an angel to awaken not only her vital breath, but also the spiritual breath inside her.[29]

According to Irigaray, the incarnation of Christ in a young woman marks the advent of a new epoch (new age) of our spiritual becoming, now with a mother (a woman) and her male child (a man) being both chosen for this revelatory and redemptive task. We might here remember another young woman and a virgin—namely, Antigone from the Greek tradition, and Creon, who has chosen to follow the diabolic[30] path by literally taking breath and freedom (and possibility for her to share her life and spiritual breath with others in the future) from her—as a woman. Antigone dies, but her death (by herself she has *withdrawn her breath* from this world)[31] is of divine and redemptory character. We know that Hegel and Irigaray both think that her mission might have been even higher than that of Christ. Through her radically apolitical and thus ethical act of safeguarding her brother (a corpse) a symbolic burial, she regains for all of us the lost cosmic order. As Mary has now shared her breath with Jesus, and thus enabled with this sharing a new life—now of a savior, her gesture will open a new possibility for a future epoch (*the Age of the Spirit*), in which, according to Irigaray, we all will become autonomous in our breath, and when we, men and women, will become linked to divine breath.[32] In this way, the essence of religion is now affirmed by Irigaray through acknowledging the special role of women—as being in a closer relation than men to the breath of life.

But to become enlightened by the power of self-affection is not possible without grace. For Caputo, Jesus dispersed grace all around the world, and if we could touch his garment, Caputo writes, we could *feel* this grace among us, close to us, as an energy, circulating in his body, as filled with *pneuma*, or the divine breath.[33] The pneumatic grace of his body is related to the first breath he receives from the Holy Spirit, and from his Mother, being spiritually linked by, as it were, a pneumatic covenant. But the first grace we all receive is through the gesture of sharing the breath in the womb of our mothers, as already beautifully explained by Irigaray. We could now also say that, similarly to Jesus and his birth, Buddha's enlightenment and his redemptory role for the world, on the other side, has been explained in an analogous narrative in *Gaṇḍavyūha*, a Mahāyāna sūtra from the fourth century CE. We know that in Indian mythology we have a strong acknowledgment of sexual difference from the very beginning—as in divine couples throughout the Hindu (also Vedic) cosmology and universe, and later in yoga and especially Hindu and Buddhist Tantra. Now, in this sacred Buddhist text, Māyā, the mother of Śākyamuni Buddha, welcomes in her body the *bodhisattva*, ascending from the *Tuṣita* Heaven into her womb and being born as Buddha into this world. But Māyā's womb is able to welcome many other bodhisattvas, and her body "came to embrace the entire world" and "became as expansive as ether."[34] This gesture of the mother of all Buddhas, past, present, and future, is another crucial mark of the *pneumatic bond* between a young woman and a young man, securing, as Irigaray would say, first, respect for life and cosmic order, then for generational order, and, finally, for sexual differentiation.[35] They all represent and embrace all that we need to preserve in order to safeguard *a life* and its breath in their immanence—within the cosmos, within ourselves, and within community.

Transcending Our Finiteness: Toward Sharing of the Divine Breath in Humans

Now it is my wish to wind up this chapter with a meditation on an ethics of breath. First, a return to Nietzsche is needed: Gaston Bachelard, in his beautiful and seminal series of books on the four elements elaborates on Nietzsche in his book on air and depicts him there as an *aerial philosopher*. For Bachelard, air is intrinsically linked to our imagination and freedom, to the "philosophy of absolute becoming," to the "*awareness of the free moment*,"[36] to what opens to us in the future. For him, air indeed is a substance of our freedom. In the process of re-evaluating all values, air and breathing represent the most crucial parts. For Bachelard—and this now is really important—Nietzsche's doctrine involves the *whole being* and represents the transformation of its *vital energy*.[37] We have seen, that for our dwelling in the ontological realm of pure breath, a new self-affection was needed, one being able to acknowledge and, as it were, follow the movements of the Holy Breath in Jesus, or another type of Cosmic/Vital Breath (*prāṇa*) in Buddha,[38] one being able to abide in silence and listening and closest proximity to the pure breath. We need to nurture, I have argued, a space in our interiority (microcosm, the body, *psyche*—as breathing), to be able to empty, or forget in ourselves all projections that were hindering the ethical encounter with the other, in his or her singularity and difference.

But to move to the ethical world now: here silence is the principal value of the threshold. It enables us to listen first to the movements of our inner breath, to the pulsation (inspiration and expiration) of life in ourselves (this now is not a path of ontology anymore but of ethics),[39] and at the same moment, in an ethical temporality and an exchange of respiratory energies I wish to explain in this last part, also be attuned to the pulsation of breath and life in the other being. This is how the first memory of our ethical obligation is born. This movement and transformation of our self-affection, and our entire being really, inaugurates a new philosophical discipline—the ethical pneumatology—*qua* respiration in our being in relation to the other. To enter the plane of ethics let us first reintroduce these words of Irigaray:

> Something has happened—an event, or an advent—an encounter between humans. A breath or soul has been born, brought forth by two others. There are now living beings for whom we lack the ways of approaching, the gestures and words for drawing nearer to one another, for exchanging.[40]

The temporality of ethical encounter is without doubt one of the most difficult questions of ethics. I have already mentioned the Irigarayan concept of the ecstasy of encounter, as a radicalized intersubjective mode of between-two, based on our self-affection, sexual difference, and mutual mesocosmical breathing. In my self-affection (based in silence and listening) I am first infused with my basic ontological attentiveness—toward breath as an exhalation and inhalation of Being, as a paradigm of a progression of first difference (pulsation, life, sexual difference); but in this I am always already wounded with my finiteness and my ontological link to the pure breath is broken. This wound is our longing to become *more* that we are in this present moment, and to become awakened in our *spirituality* (*spiritus* = breath and respiration), but this is only possible with the help of the other, as she is transcending my finite world. Ontological attentiveness and my self-affection thus transform into an ethical attentiveness, for which the *reserve of breath* is needed, one that I will now be able to share with the other. Our task here is to become an embodied soul in which there would be an imagination of the future event, of the *advent* of the other—for which a revolution of our culture of sentiments indeed is needed.[41] This marks the beginning of any religious gesture, if religion is understood as a horizontal rather than vertical link between two subjects, and as a horizontal order within communities. This shift from verticality does not mean that we cannot use the name "God" in this encounter anymore. "God" now is the name for the reserve of breath, or an excess of breath, which as a vital breath-energy is available to us as a gift, a grace of the moment of our encounter with the other.

We have seen that in Trinity we have an exhalation and inhalation as a mysterious logic of the trinitarian co-relationality and co-breathing (*conspiratio*) of the three divine persons. In Schelling, this is visible in the primordial and anarchic exhalation and inhalation of the Ground itself, the pulsation of its archetypal life. Now I would like to discuss this trinitarian pneumatics in a radicalized ethico-spiritual sense. In Mark 15:37 we read about the death of Jesus Christ: "Then Jesus gave a loud cry and breathed his last [*eksepneusen*]." I will argue here that, from this moment of His last breath until the moment of resurrection and giving his breath to the disciples, the co-breathing in Trinity is in crisis. There are two moments we need to acknowledge here: first, from the very moment of His last breath breathed into the world, when Jesus dies for us, humanity also partakes in this trinitarian crisis; it is without the reserve of breath and witnesses the cosmic crisis, or coming of a cosmic night (Mark 15:33: "When it was noon, darkness came over the whole land until three in the afternoon."). Second, it is in faith of a woman—Mary Magdalene—that resurrected Jesus will first reappear, and only later *breathe* the reserve of breath back onto His disciples (John 20:22—"When he had said this, he breathed on them and said to them, Receive the Holy Spirit"). We know that for Irigaray, as Mary is "spiritual ancestor and spiritual mother of Jesus,"[42] analogously now the resurrected Jesus is bringing the Holy Spirit and thus spiritual autonomy to Mary Magdalene, as *mater familias*, or the first apostle (Schüssler-Fiorenza),[43] and then all of humanity. In the gospel of John we are witnessing the peak moment of the trinitarian crisis, when in famous *noli me tangere* passage (*me mou haptou*) Jesus says to Mary Magdalene not to hold on him, because he "has not yet ascended to Father" (John 20:17). According to my interpretation of this passage, the prohibition of touching his body (Jesus is represented by the *neaniskos* in the gospel of Mark) does not relate to the logic of haptology[44] but rather to an original and idiosyncratic pneumatic meaning: it is the touching within an *ethico-pneumatic interval* between/of two autonomous bodies and breaths that we are witnessing here, an encounter of a divine character, inaugurating a new spiritual bond—the coming of love to this world, when men and women will become spiritual brothers and sisters in love by compassionately sharing their spiritual breaths in the community-to-come. But this *touching without touch* means that we have two subjectivities, two self-affections (also marked by sexual difference) indeed—one already divine, the other becoming divine, which now for the first time are dwelling within the transcendence of each other; pure love and compassion (*agape, caritas*) can emerge only from this *interval of breath* between them.

It is precisely this event that marks the advent of the third age of human-ity—*the age of the Spirit*, when the task of humanity will be to "become itself divine breath."[45] The coming of this epoch of breath is thus based on both self-affectivity and love as visible in this idiosyncratic encounter between Jesus Christ and Mary Magdalene. The reserve of breath has now been regained—one that only can heal the wound of the world as the fraction in the very core of our being. It is our task to get this reserve for ourselves (faith, grace, our soul), to become spiritual in a way to in-breathe or let into ourselves the breath of love, and share it with others, in an encounter of spiritual energies—which now is divine by itself—as an exchange of pure breath in its primordial rhythm of exhalation and inhalation. This now is the *co-breathing* of two autonomous persons in an atmosphere of freedom and grace.[46]

Notes

1. F.W.J. Schelling, *Philosophical Inquiries into the Nature of Human Freedom*, trans. J. Gutman (La Salle, IL.: Open Court, 1989), 86.
2. Cited from Marx W. Wartofsky, *Feuerbach* (Cambridge: Cambridge University Press, 1977), 182.
3. Friedrich Nietzsche, *Ecce Homo* (Oxford: Oxford University Press, 2007), 4.
4. Luce Irigaray, *Sharing the World* (London: Continuum, 2008), 31.
5. John D. Caputo, *The Insistence of God* (Bloomington and Indianapolis: Indiana University Press, 2013).
6. On Feuerbach see my *Breath of Proximity* (Lenart Škof, *Breath of Proximity: Intersubjectivity, Ethics and Peace* [Dordrecht: Springer, 2015], chap. 5).
7. Nietzsche, *Ecce homo*, 88.
8. Cf. Ludwig Feuerbach, *The Essence of Christianity*, trans. George Eliot (Amherst, NY: Prometheus Books, 1989), 91–92: "Flesh and blood is life, and life alone is corporeal reality. But flesh and blood is nothing without the oxygen of sexual distinction."
9. See Friedrich Nietzsche, *The Anti-Christ: Curse of Christianity*, chap. 20–23, in *The Nietzsche Reader*, ed. K.A. Pearson and D. Large (Oxford: Blackwell, 2006), 486–499. Cf. also his praise of Islamic Spain in chap. 60 of the same book.
10. Schopenhauer was without doubt the first Western philosopher to deconstruct Hegelian Eurocentrist thought on the progression of world cultures on a vertical East-West civilizational axis. But Schopenhauer's methodological problem lies in his inability to escape his metaphysical presuppositions that fully captured his otherwise beautiful and informed knowledge (and respect) of Hinduism, Buddhism, and other Eastern and Southeastern religious traditions. Cf. on this my paper on Schopenhauer and world religions: Lenart Škof, "Metaphysical Ethics Reconsidered: Schopenhauer, Compassion and World Religions," *Schopenhauer Jahrbuch* 87 (2006): 101–117. On Upanishads see chap. 2 of Škof, *Breath of Proximity*.
11. In this chapter I will not discuss analogous developments in classical American pragmatism (Peirce, James, Dewey, Mead). More on this in my book *Pragmatist Variations on Ethical and Intercultural Life* (Lanham, MD: Lexington Books, 2012).
12. I think of breath in Merleau-Ponty's philosophy. See on this important relation Petri Berndtson's chapter 2 of this book.
13. Luce Irigaray, *In the Beginning, She Was* (London: Bloomsbury, 2013), 159.
14. Irigaray, *Sharing the World*, 78ff.
15. In this chapter, the term "mesocosm" is used in a sense as propounded and defended throughout my *Breath of Proximity*. Mesocosm was there interpreted

as "a sign of our awakening of an ethical and spiritual breath, which is the task and ontological property of each individual" (Škof, *Breath of Proximity*, 36). As a term, the "mesocosm" originates from a book on Newar religion authored by Robert I. Levy and Kedar Raj Rajopadhyaya, titled *Mesocosm: Hinduism and the Organization of a Traditional Newar City of Nepal* (Berkeley: University of California Press, 1990). In his beautiful exposition of a Vedic ritual, Michael Witzel argues for the reconstruction of this term within the Vedic magical interpretation of the world; cf. the Introduction in Michael Witzel, *Kaṭha Āraṇyaka* (Cambridge, MA: Harvard University Press, 2004), xln129. Cf. also Michael Witzel, "Macrocosm, Mesocosm, and Microcosm: The Persistent Nature of 'Hindu' Beliefs and Symbolic Forms," *International Journal of Hindu Studies* 1, no. 3 (1997), 501–539. See on this Škof, *Breath of Proximity*, 4n3.

16. In this chapter, I will mostly refer to Luce Irigaray's most recent books, that is, those forming the so-called "third stage" of her thought, among them especially: *The Way of Love* (2002), *Between East and West* (2002), *Sharing the world* (2008), *In the Beginning, She Was* (2013), and *Una nuova cultura dell'energia. Al di là di Oriente e Occidente* (2013).

17. Luce Irigaray, *The Way of Love* (London: Continuum, 2002), xiv.

18. Irigaray, *In the Beginning, She Was*, 160.

19. Ibid., 161f.

20. Apart from Schelling and Heidegger (and Levinas)—but more on this relation in the second part of my chapter.

21. Irigaray, *Una nuova cultura dell'energia: Al di là di Oriente e Occidente* (Torino: Bollati Boringhieri, 2013), 31 (my translation).

22. Lenart Škof, "Breath of Hospitality: Silence, Listening, Care," *Nursing Ethics* 23, no. 8 (Dec 2016): 902–909. doi:10.1177/0969733015587779.

23. Paul Celan, *Poems of Paul Celan*, trans. M. Hamburger (New York: Persea Books, 2002), 209 (from *Atemwende*, 1967).

24. Irigaray, *Una nuova cultura dell'energia,* 29 (my translation).

25. Schelling, *Philosophical Inquiries into the Nature of Human Freedom*, 70. Schelling uses here the rare Latinate-German word *Konspiration*, which he takes from Lat. *conspiro* ("to breathe together"); this word is of course related to *spiritus*). See on this my interpretation in Škof, *Breath of Proximity*, chap. 3, and especially Jason Wirth, *The conspiracy of life: Meditations on Schelling and his time* (Albany: State University of New York Press, 2003), 2.

26. Cf. ibid., 2f. In one of the most ancient speculative Vedic hymns "Creation" (*Ṛgveda* X.129, from around the tenth century BC), we find the most precise explanation of this cosmic *breathing* of the Ground/Foundation of Being (That One, or *tad ekam*) itself: "That One breathed without wind by its independent will. There existed nothing else beyond that"; *The Rigveda*, trans. S.W. Jamison and J.P. Brereton (Oxford: Oxford University Press, 2014), 1608. I have analyzed this Vedic hymn and compared it with Schelling's ontology in detail on many different occasions, cf. especially Škof, *Breath of Proximity*, chap. 3. The poet-philosopher of this hymn argues that even before there were any signs of the existent or nonexistent, of death or life proper, there breathed this first One—by its own mysterious and "independent will"; ibid.

27. Cf. Mt 1:18, Lk 1:35. Also for Schelling "God must become Man in order that man may be brought back to God."; Schelling, *Philosophical Inquiries into the Nature of Human Freedom,* 57. But he also knows, that man "is formed in his mother's womb."; ibid., 35.

28. Roberto Mangabeira Unger, *The Religion of the Future* (Cambridge, MA: Harvard University Press, 2007), 261. Cf. also his previous book *The Self Awakened: Pragmatism unbound* (Cambridge, MA, and London: Harvard University Press, 2007). On cosmic Jesus see Caputo's *The Insistence of God*: "I treat Jesus as a Judeo-pagan prophet and healer, in tune with the animals and the elements, in whose body the elements dance their cosmic dance, supplying as it does a conduit through which the elements flow, and I treat the elements as a cosmic grace which is channeled by the body of Jesus."; Caputo, *Insistence of God*, 251f. This indeed is a simply beautiful depiction of Jesus in his cosmico-theological role. Of course, among the four elements, *pneuma* holds the most exquisite position, since his entire body is filled with this cosmic wind, or spiritual energy ("Yeshua was the sort of man whose *pneuma* filled any room that he entered"; ibid., 254).

29. Luce Irigaray, *Il mistero di Maria* (Roma: Paoline, 2010), 13f.

30. Creon is a paradigm for the progression of evil (the politics of power, tyranny, authority) into the world of free and living breath: "Miming the living, the diabolic does not breathe, or does not breathe any longer. It takes away the air from the others, from the world. It suffocates with its sterile repetitions, its presumptuous imitations, with its wishes deprived of respect for life." Luce Irigaray, *Key Writings* (London: Continuum, 2004), 166.

31. Antigone's justice and her life are of a cosmic origin. With his deed, Creon has inflicted this world with the diabolic, an evil that cosmic order. Cf. Job 34:14–15: "If he should take back his spirit to himself, / and gather to himself his breath, / all flesh would perish together, and all mortals return to dust." *The Holy Bible*, NRSV, Nashville, TN: Thomas Nelson Publishers 1990. Verse 15 reads better in French translation: "toute chair expirerait à la fois . . ."; *La Bible, TOB* (Paris: Editions de Cerf, 1988). This precisely is God's spiritual breath *as reserve* for the humanity, as we will see later.

32. Irigaray, *Key Writings*, 168. Also, Irigaray states: "God is us, we are divine if we are woman and man in a perfect way." Ibid., 169.

33. Ibid., 252.

34. *Buddhist Scriptures*, ed. Donald S. Lopez, Jr. (London: Penguin, 2004), 132.

35. Irigaray, *In the Beginning, She Was*, 119–135. "The maternal genealogy favours the values of life, of generation, of growth." Ibid., 127.

36. Gaston Bachelard, *Air and Dreams: An Essay on the Imagination of Movement*, trans. E.R. Farrell and C.F. Farrell (Dallas, TX: The Dallas Institute of Humanities and Culture, 2011), chap. 5, "Nietzsche and the Ascensional Psyche," 136–137.

37. Ibid., 127.

38. See about Buddha's and Jesus' role for the future of humanity in Irigaray, *Una nuova cultura dell'energia*, 120. They represent, for her, a paradigm of a new global community, based on heart, breath, listening, language, and thinking.

39. On *respiratory ontology* in Bachelard and especially in Merleau-Ponty's thought see Petri Berndtson, "The Inspiration and expiration of Being: The Immense Lung and the Cosmic Breathing as the Sources of Dreams, Poetry and Philosophy," in *Thinking in Dialogue: Paths into the Phenomenology of Merleau-Ponty*, ed. K. Novotný, T.S. Hammer, A. Gléonec, and P. Špecián (Bucharest: Zeta Books 2010), 281–293. See on Merleau-Ponty's phenomenology of breathing Berndtson's chapter in this book. Merleau-Ponty writes in his *Eye and Mind*: "We speak of 'inspiration,' and the word should be taken literally. There really is inspiration and expiration of Being, respiration in Being, action and passion so slightly discernable that it becomes impossible to distinguish between who sees and who is seen, who paints and what is painted." Cit. after ibid., 282.

40. Irigaray, *Sharing the World*, 31.

41. Cf. here my essay "Breath of hospitality: Silence, listening, care": "[W]e are lacking a genuine culture of attentiveness and care; our 'globalised' culture is not sensitive enough to the personal, sociopolitical and environmental needs of others. Perhaps a personal revolution of a kind is needed, to be able to secure in a most intimate sense—taking place first within ourselves—a new place for the welcome of the other. This new culture of hospitality for which we are hoping is not related to resolving some form of a political conflict; neither is it achievable by a simple exchange of words within a discourse or communication that we already know and use. This culture demands from us to reorient our senses towards others: for this, a new culture of intersubjectivity is needed. But, before we are able to welcome the other in her or his subjectivity, we will first require a new culture of sensitivity, based on our self-affection." Škof, "Breath of hospitality," 2f.).

42. Chap. "The Redemption of Women" in Irigaray, *Key writings*, 152. See also her insightful thoughts on the *Assumption of Mary* on page 163: "[. . .] whose virginity allows her to rise into heaven without any death or resurrection similar to those of her son." I elaborate on this in my essay "God, Incarnation in the Feminine, and Imaginary of the Third Presence" (private copy—ahead of print, to be published in the journal *Bogoslovni vestnik*).

43. Cf. Elizabeth Schussler-Fiorenza, *In memory of Her: Feminist Theological Reconstruction of Christian Origins* (Minneapolis, MN: Fortress, 1983), 333.

44. Cf. on haptology as related to the dead body of Christ in tomb Gregg Lambert, "Untouchable," in *Derrida and Religion*, ed. Yvonne Sherwood and Kevin Hart (New York and London: Routledge, 2005), 363–374.

45. Irigaray, *Key writings*, 168 ("The Age of the Breath").

46. In chap. 70 of his main work, Schopenhauer argues that this faith does not originate in ourselves, but "like something coming to us from outside"; Arthur Schopenhauer, *The World as Will and Representation*, vol. 1, trans. E.F.J. Payne (New York: Dover, 1969), 406. This new birth is grace, which, for Schopenhauer, constitutes our freedom (freedom of the will), based on faith (which is knowledge, for Schopenhauer). With this effect, our motives, previously based on the "kingdom of nature," are thus a part of the "kingdom of grace"; ibid., 408. This is precisely what Irigaray

wanted to say with her statement, namely, that "our breath is not dependent only to some necessities we are facing." Irigaray, *Una nuova cultura dell'energia*, 29.

Bibliography

Bachelard, Gaston. *Air and Dreams: An Essay on the Imagination of Movement.* Translated by E.R. Farrell and C.F. Farrell. Dallas, TX: The Dallas Institute of Humanities and Culture, 2011.

Berndtson, Petri. "The Inspiration and Expiration of Being: The Immense Lung and the Cosmic Breathing as the Sources of Dreams, Poetry and Philosophy." In *Thinking in Dialogue: Paths into the Phenomenology of Merleau-Ponty*, edited by Karel Novotný, Taylor S. Hammer, Anne Gléonec, and Petr Špecián, 281–293. Bucharest: Zeta Books 2010.

Buddhist Scriptures. Edited by Donald S. Lopez, Jr. London: Penguin, 2004.

Caputo, John D. *The Insistence of God.* Bloomington and Indianapolis: Indiana University Press, 2013.

Celan, Paul. *Poems of Paul Celan.* Translated by Michael Hamburger. New York: Persea Books, 2002.

Feuerbach, Ludwig. *The Essence of Christianity.* Translated by George Eliot. Amherst, NY: Prometheus Books, 1989.

The Holy Bible. New Revised Standard Version. Nashville, TN: Thomas Nelson Publishers, 1990.

Irigaray, Luce. *Between East and West: From Singularity to Community.* Translated by Stephen Pluháček. Delhi: New Age Books, 2005.

Irigaray, Luce. *Il mistero di Maria.* Roma: Paoline, 2010.

Irigaray, Luce. *In the Beginning, She Was.* London: Bloomsbury, 2013.

Irigaray, Luce. *Key Writings.* London: Continuum, 2004.

Irigaray, Luce. *Sharing the World.* London: Continuum, 2008.

Irigaray, Luce. *Una nuova cultura dell'energia: Al di là di Oriente e Occidente.* Torino: Bollati Boringhieri, 2013.

Irigaray, Luce. *The Way of Love.* London: Continuum, 2002.

La Bible, TOB. Paris: Editions de Cerf, 1988.

Lambert, Greg. "Untouchable." In *Derrida and Religion*, edited by Yvonne Sherwood and Kevin Hart, 363–374. New York and London: Routledge, 2005.

Levy, Robert I., and Kedar Raj Rajopadhyaya. *Mesocosm: Hinduism and the Organization of a Traditional Newar City of Nepal.* Berkeley: University of California Press, 1990.

Nietzsche, Friedrich. *The Anti-Christ: Curse of Christianity.* In *The Nietzsche Reader*, edited by K.A. Pearson and D. Large, 486–499. Oxford: Blackwell, 2006.

Nietzsche, Friedrich. *Ecce Homo.* Translated by D. Large. Oxford: Oxford University Press, 2007.

The Rigveda. Translated by S.W. Jamison and J.P. Brereton. Oxford: Oxford University Press, 2014.

Schelling, Friedrich Wilhelm Joseph. *Philosophical Inquiries into the Nature of Human Freedom.* Translated by J. Gutman. La Salle, IL: Open Court, 1989.

Schopenhauer, Arthur. *The World as Will and Representation.* Vol. 1. Translated by E.F.J. Payne. New York: Dover, 1969.

Schussler-Fiorenza, Elizabeth. *In Memory of Her: Feminist Theological Reconstruction of Christian Origins.* Minneapolis, MN: Fortress, 1983.

Škof, Lenart. "Breath of Hospitality: Silence, Listening, Care." *Nursing Ethics* 23, no. 8 (Dec 2016): 902–909. doi:10.1177/0969733015587779.

Škof, Lenart. *Breath of Proximity: Intersubjectivity, Ethics and Peace.* Dordrecht: Springer, 2015.

Škof, Lenart. "Metaphysical Ethics Reconsidered: Schopenhauer, Compassion and World Religions." *Schopenhauer Jahrbuch* 87 (2006): 101–117.

Škof, Lenart. *Pragmatist Variations on Ethical and Intercultural Life.* Lanham, MD: Lexington Books, 2012.

Unger, Roberto Mangabeira. *The Religion of the Future.* Cambridge, MA: Harvard University Press, 2007.

Unger, Roberto Mangabeira. *The Self Awakened: Pragmatism Unbound.* Cambridge, MA, and London: Harvard University Press, 2007.

Wartofsky, Marx W. *Feuerbach.* Cambridge: Cambridge University Press, 1977.

Wirth, Jason. *The Conspiracy of Life: Meditations on Schelling and His Time.* Albany: State University of New York Press, 2003.

Witzel, Michael. *Kaṭha Āraṇyaka.* Cambridge, MA: Harvard University Press, 2004.

Witzel, Michael. "Macrocosm, Mesocosm, and Microcosm: The Persistent Nature of 'Hindu' Beliefs and Symbolic Forms." *International Journal of Hindu Studies* 1, no. 3 (1997): 501–539.

4

Aesthetics of Breathing

Some Reflections

ROLF ELBERFELD

Introduction

On the one hand, breathing is an involuntary and mostly unconscious action necessary for our physical survival. On the other hand, breathing can also be consciously controlled and cultivated in an extremely diverse range of manners. Breathing is therefore a performance that resides between nature and culture. Two of the most important forms of cultivating breathing for humans are speaking and singing. Neither activity would be possible without breathing. Although this is the case, breathing has hardly been taken into account at all to date in philosophical aesthetics in Europe. The situation is different in the case of the old approaches to aesthetics in East Asia, where breathing is seen as a central aesthetic category in writing and ink painting, theater, and music, and often the first to unlock the meaning in the respective art. The aesthetics of breathing thus must be designed in a manner that enables it to describe anew the aesthetic practices in the artistic traditions of Europe.

Breathing means that we are all *always* in a relationship with our environment. We breathe in that which surrounds us. We do not inhale only air. We also inhale dust, liquids, bacteria, and lots more. That which we breathe out is mixed with what is found in our bodies. In rooms with large numbers of people we are particularly engaged in an intimate exchange through breathing. In such situations, it can sometimes be hard to get air, and we must get out into the open. In every situation, we react through the way we breathe. Breathing is a reflection of the situation in which we find ourselves.

Breathing reflects not only our relationship with that which surrounds us but also reflects our sensory perception, our physical processes, our feelings, and our thoughts. If we hear music that really touches us, our breathing changes. If we have a problem with our circulation, our breathing changes. If we feel deep sadness or extreme joy, our breathing changes. If we think intensively, our breathing also changes. Looked at more closely, our breathing undermines the distinction between physiology and psychology, between body and soul. When breathing, meaning turns into physical performance, and physical performance becomes meaning. This has been confirmed by medical trials: "Breathing proved to be a highly sensitive physiological parameter linked to both objective requirements (motor function) and subjective assessments of sensitivity."[1]

But breathing is not only in constant resonance with all of the processes mentioned, it can also cause intensive change to or significantly influence these processes. If I prepare for an evening concert through an extended period of breathing meditation, I will hear the music differently. If I have practiced and calmed my breath over a long period of time, my circulation will be different. If I have learned to control my breathing in a conscious manner, intensive feelings can be experienced differently. Even my thoughts will change as a result of cultivating my breathing. My breathing is therefore in constant interaction with all situations in which I find myself. Whether I can control these situations through my practiced breathing or not is a question of cultivating my breathing. If I have linked my life to a *culture of breathing*, it is possible to include breathing actively in all actions. If this is not the case, I am more or less at the mercy of the reactions of my breathing. This becomes clear, for example, if I am unable to control my breathing or my nervousness in any way during oral examinations or interviews. If you practice breathing over an extended period of time, in many cases it will be less common for you to become flustered. This is linked to the fact that calm, controlled breathing achieves a different type of attention. Calm, controlled breathing focuses the body so, for example, the creation and effect of feelings can be experienced in a more attentive manner. This effect of breathing can on the one hand be important for ethical questions,[2] and on the other it can play a key role in aesthetics.

As is generally known, *cultures of breathing* have developed in various traditions in Asia, and *Yoga*, *Taijiquan*, and *Judō* are now particularly widespread in the West too. The meaning of these *cultures of breathing* for religions, human cohabitation, and the development of arts in Asia has not been sufficiently investigated for many years. In the following I will limit myself to looking at aspects of the aesthetics of breathing in China and Japan.

The Semantic Field 氣 (*Qi/Ki*) in Chinese and Japanese

In the old Chinese language, a word or character developed that originally meant the word "breathing." Within the Western languages, many people are familiar with expressions such as the Chinese *Qigong* or the Japanese *Aikidō*. In the Chinese expression of *Qigong* 氣功, the first character is "qi," which would be "ki" (Aikidō 合気道) in Japanese. This character is one of the most evocative and richest in meaning in both the Chinese and Japanese languages. The history of its use stretches back over three millennia.

> In addition to *dao, yin* and *yang*, the concept of *qi* [. . .] is without doubt one of the most fundamental terms in Chinese thought. The many potential translations range from breath, touch, steam over the *pneuma*, ether, fluid, influences, power and constellation energy to world substance, substance and matter energy.[3]

One of the fundamental meanings of the character is breathing. All further meanings are closely linked to this fundamental meaning. Over millennia, the term has developed not only in the linguistic usage within Chinese medicine but also with regard to the weather, atmosphere, and other subtle phenomena. In addition, it is used extensively in Chinese philosophy and aesthetics:

> The Chinese character *qi* 氣 shows a diverse link between phenomena within the Chinese experience and interpretation of the world. We should therefore understand *qi* as a central paradigm in the philosophical determination of the world and humanity. Using the various manners of speaking which formed as a result of observations in various areas, it is possible to show from this perspective that in Chinese intellectual history with *qi* circumscribed phenomenal existence poured into patterns of thinking which were used to ensure the intellectual penetration of *movement, relationships* and *references*. The concept of *Qi* stands for a fundamental effort, which is contrary to the Parmenidean-Platonic-Aristotelian processing of ontology for the western world in a diametrical manner.[4]

Qi, understood as breathing, is a fundamental movement in life through which relationships of many types are created and designed. When breathing, life can be experienced as a dependent arising (Sanskrit: *pratītyasamutpāda*) in movements and relationships. To this day, this manifests itself primarily in the Japanese language, in which there are many expressions formed in combination with the character *ki*. In Japanese, it is said that "thin breathing" means that someone is nervous, while "long breathing" means the person is patient. "Large breathing" means that someone is generous, and "small breathing" that someone is nervous. It also means that if the breath of two people meets, these people work together well as a team and when the breath turns in a circle then the person is particularly attentive to even the smallest fluctuations.[5]

These experiences became a central starting point for the development of various arts in East Asia.

Qi/Ki (氣/気) as an Aesthetic Phenomenon in China and Japan

The Chinese character *qi* has been extensively used in the classics of Chinese philosophy since the fifth century BC. Its use in the field of aesthetics in the narrow sense, however, started with the relevant treatises on mountain water painting (*shan shui hua* 山水畫). Around the year 500, in China, Xie He 謝赫 wrote a preface to a text on old painting in which he makes a distinction between "six methods of painting" (*hua liu fa* 畫六法). The first point on this list contains a maxim that has continued to be highly significant in Chinese ink painting to this day: 氣韻生動 (*qi yun sheng dong*). Mathias Obert translates this to " 'Attunement in breathing,' which means 'living self-movement.' "[6] Another translation of this expression is "breathing resonating [in] living movement." Obert indicates the expression with reference to the first part of the meaning:

> The word *yun* 韻 originally meant the acoustic phenomenon of rever-
> beration, and therefore also the unison of individual tones and the
> rhyming of words. Primarily, it is the correspondence phenomenon
> of individual sounds which correspond to one another that was
> described in greater detail and reflected on above that is meant. In
> musical and poetic sounds, however, the existence of phenomena of
> this type can be perceived overall as an "attunement." At the same, the
> fact that certain circumstances promote a reverberation or unison of
> this type can be perceived as the peculiar "attunement" of a situation
> or as the directly atmospheric nature of poetic design. Transferred to
> the individual circumstances that pervade human existence, includ-
> ing in the field of anthropology, *yun* 韻 is ultimately understood as
> a "prevailing mood" of physical and spiritual significance which can
> also be viewed from a sensory perspective as an "attunement" of the
> individual appearance and demeanour and as personal style. If the
> basic alignment of a human life is determined aesthetically as the
> oscillating correspondence of all his moments, this clearly shows
> that in order to perceive this a "reverberation" or a "resonance" is

required which evokes the person in question in their counterpart.[7]

The sensory mood and fluctuation events that come to our attention here are fundamentally to be understood and realized via the medium of breathing (*qi*). However, this designation can be understood only against the background of the long history of the word and of the meanings that this Chinese character has had in Chinese and Japanese. In the description, Obert refers to sensual, mood-related, and emotive levels, as well as individual and interpersonal levels. The phenomenon of breathing must be situated in a mesh of this kind. It comprises, breaks through, and penetrates levels that are adjacent to one another like substantially separate entities in the worst-case scenario in conventional descriptions. The penetration of the various levels into one another through the descriptive word *qi* has extensive consequences, for example, for what it means to look at a Chinese mountain water painting (Shanshuihua 山水畫). Obert shows how, for example, criteria for the living interaction with mountain water paintings develop, culminating in the breathing attunement of picture and viewer in a common movement designed to change the viewer himself into *the picture* at leisure. The descriptive levels of the *qi* therefore break through the distinction between aesthetics relating only to the works of art or only to the reception of the works of art, as the work of art is simply not finished before an interaction of me and the work of art took place, which in every case transforms me and the work of art. *Qi* makes reference to a dense entanglement of sensory levels, feelings, physical sensations, and moods demonstrated in various manners in the practice of the arts in East Asia that transcend the distinction between subject and object.

How few of these connections are known in Europe can also be shown using an example from the field of the Japanese Nō theater. In the following I want to include two quotations from an old Japanese text on Nō aesthetics. The text is a very famous treatise on aesthetics by Zeami 世阿弥 (1363–1443) on Nō theater. This form of theater, which is still performed on large Nō theater stages to this day, developed a form of expression, primarily thanks to Zeami, which is closely linked to breathing. In the following quote, Zeami describes the situation right at the start of the text in which the actor uses his voice for the first time, which has to be brought precisely in line with the sound of the musicians through his breathing:

> It is the breathing (*ki*) that sustains the pitch. If you focus on the pitch of the flute first and use this occasion to match the breathing (*ki*) with it, then close your eyes, draw in a breath, and only after that produce the voice, your voice will come forth from within the pitch from the start. When you focus exclusively on the pitch and let your voice loose without having first matched it to the breathing

(*ki*), it is difficult at first for the voice to come forth from within the pitch. Since we best produce our voice only after having established the pitch within the *ki*, we say, as a rule, "First pitch, second breathing (*ki*), third voice."[8]

調子をば機が持つなり。吹物の調子を音取りて、機に合はせすまして、目をふさぎて、息を内へ引きて、さて声を出だせば、声先調子の中より出づるなり。調子ばかりを音取りて、機にも合はせずして声を出だせば、声先調子に合ふ事、左右なく無し。調子をば機に籠めて声を出だすがゆゑに、一調・二機・三声とは定むるなり。

In this passage, the focus is primarily on the actor's breathing in combination with the music. Breathing plays a key role in mutual resonance among actors and musicians. The following passage discusses further interactions shown within breathing:

When you appear in a *sarugaku* performance, you will have an opportunity to begin singing the *sashigoto* and *issei*. It isn't good to begin too soon. Nor should you be too late. You should, I'd say, emerge from the green room, take a few steps onto the *hashigakari*, direct your attention all about, and begin to sing at that very moment when the audience waits in anticipation, all as one, with the thought, "Look, he's just about to begin singing." This way of responding to the feeling of the audience and singing right then is how you fit the moment to the excitement. Once this moment has passed by, even by a little bit, the feeling of the audience slackens, and if you begin then, belatedly, it will not match their excitement. This moment lies in the breathing of the spectators. What I mean in saying that the moment lies in the breathing of the people is that this is an opportunity the actor should use his excitement to watch for. [. . .] It is the most opportune moment in the entire day.[9]

まづ、楽屋より出でて、橋がかりに歩み止まりて、諸万をうかがひて、「すは声を出だすよ」と、諸人一同に待ち受けて声をなはちに、声を出だすべし。これ、諸人の心を受けて声を出だす、時節感当なり。この時節少しも過ぐれば、また諸人の心緩くなりて、後に物を言ひ出だせば、万人の感に当たらず。この時節は、ただ見物の人の機にあり。人の機にある時節といつば、為手の感より見する際なり。これ、万人の見心を為手ひとりの眼精へ引き入るる際なり。

The situation being described here is fundamentally characterized by the fact that actors and audience members form a dense field of unity in breathing, as Obert has described for looking at a Chinese mountain water painting. Both actors and audience members are equally responsible for whether the temporal unity and the temporal oscillation are achieved from the start or not. The two central expressions—excitement and breathing—are characterized by the fact that they comprise both the individual and the common. If the actor takes on the hearts of everyone, he is able to find the right moment to start the song from his "excitement." This excitement is demonstrated in an individual manner in his entire body as the mood of everyone. On the other hand, the start also depends on the breath of the audience. This fine overlapping of moods and oscillations is what Nō theater is about. This means that all expression movements are carried out relatively slowly in order to provide an opportunity for the fine resonance to correspond to the entire range of feelings. The performance is not about pursuing the dramatic development of a new piece, but about experiencing a piece that has been known for a long time in the individual, never recurring, unique situation of the current performance in its sensory, emotive, and lived meaning as an existential exercise, the final horizon of which is life and death.[10]

In the background to both examples there are breathing practices that have been carried out in India, China, Japan, and other places in Asia for centuries. There has still yet to be a comprehensive review of these breathing practices, and this is a large desideratum of research. In both examples, it becomes clear that both the aesthetic experience of the artists and the audience is linked to breathing. This observation provides an opportunity to ask questions about the possibilities of an aesthetic of breathing for present art.

Breathing as an Aesthetic Practice

Both in mountain water painting in China and in Japanese Nō theater, breathing plays a key role as an aesthetic category. This is demonstrated via the respective art both in practice and in theoretical treatises. The following questions arise here: To what extent can these aesthetic approaches and aesthetic descriptions from ancient China or Japan be enlightening for modern aesthetic practices? Would it be conceivable to place breathing itself at the center of aesthetic descriptions by primarily talking about the dynamic conditions in the forms of art? What qualities of breathing can be distinguished by artists and audience members? Is it possible, for example, to say that a play has a dynamic effect on the audience member only if this is shown in the audience member's breathing? Is it possible to assume that it is the transfer of the breath by means of which an artistic event becomes effective and physical? What happens exactly when a dancer spends so much time on the stage that she is no longer able to stay in line with the audience members' breathing? How does audience members' breathing change if a person cuts open his skin in front of them? Perhaps you could say at this stage in the twentieth century increasing numbers of artistic designs have been developed in

Europe and North America that want to transport linguistic meaning to a decreasing extent and rather attempt to penetrate the breathing and people's breath to form this from the inside and transform it.

If we listen to a song with lyrics, it is not only the singer who is breathing. If we go and see a play, it is not only the actors who are breathing. From the training of singers and actors, we know that they spend a large amount of time practicing their breathing, while the listeners and audience members go to concerts or to the theater without doing any breathing exercises. If breathing is taken seriously as a basic aesthetic category, we can ask ourselves whether during a particularly intensive evening at the theater both the actor *and* the audience members are guided into dense breathing. It is also possible to ask the question of how an audience prepared for breathing changes the intensity of the play.

The questions open up the field of theoretical attention, which has to date not yet been played through in Western aesthetics. Only once you are aware of your attention and your breathing in aesthetic processes does the scope of the issue become clear. Sensitized by the Asian *cultures of breathing*, a new field of research therefore opens up to reflect on aesthetic practices. Equipped with this attention, it is then possible to observe that the old *cultures of breathing* are still alive in contemporary productions in East Asia. To conclude my chapter, I want to describe two examples, one from Taiwan and the other from Japan, in which breathing plays a key role in aesthetic practice.

The Cloud Gate Dance Theatre (雲門舞集 *Yunmen wuji*), founded by Lin Hwai-min (林懷民) in 1973, is the first independent dance company in Taiwan. In order to enable initial access to their world of movement, it is particularly important to look at which daily exercises are borne out in the dance. In the case of the dancers at the *Yunmen wuji*, there are a mixture focusing on East Asian movement arts. The dancers predominantly practice *Taiji* and certain forms of *Qigong,* in addition to forms of movement from the Chinese opera, *modern dance,* and ballet. They also practice sitting meditation in order to develop special forms of consciousness and attention. At the level of exercise practice, a developmental form of physical movement is created that is fundamentally different from European practice but which, however, is only visible and can only be experienced in the dance after a process of practice lasting many years. The practiced movements are not simply techniques; they are ways of exercising, the aim of which is to combine people not only with themselves but ultimately also with the entire cosmos. Breathing plays a key role in particular in the East Asian movement arts and meditation practices on which the exercises are based. Both in *Taiji* and in *Qigong,* individual movements are always carried out in direct coordination with breathing. A sliding form of movement carried out with attention from the entire body is created. The movements of the dances of the *Yunmen Wuji* that have been created since 1998 (Moon Water, Cursive I, Cursive II, Smoke, White)[11] appear not to have a start or an end. Everything is always moving. A means of dealing

with the constant change is present. Particularly, this is also motivated by philosophical and aesthetic development in ancient China. It is not an "I" that starts
the movement, but rather movements of the *Qi* flow through everything, in other
words synchronized by the movements of breathing. *Qi*, or breathing, does not
adhere to an inside or an outside. You could call this the medium in which form
is first identified. The dancers are in a state of constant flux, so a transformation
process becomes visible by means of the movements of the individual becoming
the breathing resonance of the common movement. Without particular attention
being paid to breathing and many years spent practicing breathing, the quality of
movement that can be observed in the dancers would not be possible.

An entirely different form of movement linked to breathing can be observed
in the Butoh dancer Tanaka Min (田中泯). Like Lin, Tanaka started to seek his
own path in the world of dance in the early 1970s. He started to look for places
in nature or in public spaces where he could dance, mostly naked except for his
penis, which was wrapped in a bandage. In the coming years, he developed his
dance and his forms of practice further. He placed particular focus on natural
movements, so he lay in a river for a number of hours to use the resonances
achieved by the flowing movements of the river to practice dancing. Over time,
he developed his own training method, which he called "body weather." The
movements created in the dancing body using this method cannot be said to be
beautiful in either a harmonic or a classical sense. There are many breaks in the
movements and much twitching, reminiscent of the physical blockade everyone
has in them. In 2006, Tanaka Min ended his career as a stage dancer with a piece
entitled "Transparent Body Falling Off" (*tōtai datsuraku* 透体脱落).[12] Particularly,
a longer scene in this piece is determined by the breathing movement of the
dancer. In this scene, Tanaka slowly takes his clothes off and then stands nearly
naked, with just a bandage on his penis. While the dancer stands there and his
body twitches with numerous micromovements, the breathing movements become
increasingly obvious and clear. He then slowly moves his head backward, and the
hands follow from above the stomach upward. Once the hands have settled on
the shoulders, he extends them out to one side. The head is placed into the nape
of the neck. The further the hands and arms are extended, the more strongly the
breathing movement of the entire chest can be perceived. It becomes apparent how
the breathing movements direct and penetrate the movements of the entire body.
The entire dancing body becomes the breathing movement. After this sequence,
Tanaka brings his arms back in front of his body. He slowly falls to the floor
and creeps backward on the sandy floor into the darkness as if in slow motion.

Both Lin Hwai-min and Tanaka Min use breathing and the movements of
breathing to design their dance in an explicit manner. This is certainly not possible
in the same way in all aesthetic practices. However, if the attention is drawn to
the breathing, it becomes clear that breathing always plays a role in every aesthetic
practice, be it explicit or implicit. The painting of pictures can very explicitly be

accompanied by breathing. The writing and reading of texts can be combined with breathing, as can be observed for example in Samuel Beckett. In this sense, an aesthetic of breathing could develop the attention to the breathing processes in aesthetic processes. Here, the focus was on describing the respective function of breathing in the respective aesthetic practice. Since breathing accompanies all activities carried out by humans, breathing often remains inconspicuous. When looked at closer, however, it is clear that breathing also was and is of key importance in the European tradition of arts and aesthetic practices. Further research in this area could contribute to a much richer understanding of the cultures of breathing in Europe as well.

Notes

1. Brigitta Danusa-Nideröst, "Motivierte Aufmerksamkeit und Atmung" [Motivated Attention and Breathing], Postdoc thesis (Zurich: Swiss Federal Institute of Technology Zurich, 2001), 9.

2. See Lenart Škof, "Ethics of Breath: Towards New Ethical Spaces of Intersubjectivity," in "Bodily Proximity," ed. Sigrid Hackenberg Y Almansa and Lenart Škof, *Poligrafi* 17, 65–66 (2012): 199–210.

3. Gudula Linck, "Qi. Zur Geschichte eines Begriffs—von numinoser Atmosphäre zu Materie / Energie" [Qi. On the History of a Term—From Numinous Atmosphere to Matter/Energy], *Studia Religiosa Helvetica* 6/7 (2000/2001): 200.

4. Mathias Obert, "Das Phänomen qi 氣 und die Grundlegung der Ästhetik im vormodernen China" [The Phenomenon of *qi* 氣 and the Foundation of Aesthetics in Pre-Modern China], *Zeitschrift der Deutschen Morgenländischen Gesellschaft* 157, no. 1 (2007): 167.

5. For more information see Rolf Elberfeld, *Sprache und Sprachen. Eine philosophische Grundorientierung* [*Language and Languages. A Basic Philosophical Orientation*] (Freiburg im Breisgau: Karl Alber, 2012), 303–311, 396–402.

6. Mathias Obert, *Welt als Bild. Die theoretische Grundlegung der chinesischen Berg-Wasser-Malerei zwischen dem 5. und dem 12. Jahrhundert* [*The World as an Image. The Theoretical Basis of Chinese Mountain Water Painting Between the 5th and the 12th Centuries*] (Freiburg im Breisgau: Karl Alber, 2007), 182.

7. Ibid., 183ff.

8. Zeami, *Performance Notes*, trans. Tom Hare (New York: Columbia University Press, 2008), 97. Translation slightly amended.

9. Ibid., 103f.

10. For an interpretation of this expansion of aesthetic practice in East Asia, see Rolf Elberfeld, "Einteilung der Künste in interkultureller Perspektive" [Division of the Arts in Intercultural Perspectives,] *Polylog: Zeitschrift für interkulturelles Philosophieren* 9 (2003): 57–64.

11. Sections from the pieces are easily accessible on *YouTube*. The pieces *Cursive II* and *Wild Cursive* are recommended in particular.

12. This piece can be found on *YouTube*. The part on which I will primarily focus below can be found by searching music (live electronics): Noguchi/dance: in Tanaka '06 Tokyo (6/6), accessed June 5, 2016.

Bibliography

Danusa-Nideröst, Brigitta. "Motivierte Aufmerksamkeit und Atmung." [Motivated Attention and Breathing.] Postdoc thesis, Swiss Federal Institute of Technology Zurich, 2001.

Elberfeld, Rolf. "Einteilung der Künste in interkultureller Perspektive." [Division of the Arts in Intercultural Perspectives.] *Polylog: Zeitschrift für interkulturelles Philosophieren* 9 (2003): 57–64.

Elberfeld, Rolf. *Sprache und Sprachen. Eine philosophische Grundorientierung.* [Language and Languages. A Basic Philosophical Orientation.] Freiburg im Breisgau: Karl Alber, 2012.

Linck, Gudula. "Qi. Zur Geschichte eines Begriffs—von numinoser Atmosphäre zu Materie/Energie." [Qi. On the History of a Term—From Numinous Atmosphere to Matter/Energy.] *Studia Religiosa Helvetica* 6/7 (2000/2001): 195–210.

Obert, Mathias. "Das Phänomen qi 氣 und die Grundlegung der Ästhetik im vormodernen China." [The Phenomenon of qi 氣 and the Foundation of Aesthetics in Pre-Modern China.] *Zeitschrift der Deutschen Morgenländischen Gesellschaft* 157, no. 1 (2007): 160–192.

Obert, Mathias. *Welt als Bild. Die theoretische Grundlegung der chinesischen Berg-Wasser-Malerei zwischen dem 5. und dem 12. Jahrhundert.* [The World as an Image. The Theoretical Basis of Chinese Mountain Water Painting Between the 5th and the 12th Centuries.] Freiburg im Breisgau: Karl Alber, 2007.

Škof, Lenart. "Ethics of Breath: Towards New Ethical Spaces of Intersubjectivity." In "Bodily Proximity," edited by Sigrid Hackenberg Y Almansa and Lenart Škof. *Poligrafi* 17, 65–66 (2012): 199–210.

Zeami. *Performance Notes.* Translated by Tom Hare. New York: Columbia University Press, 2008.

II

Philosophical Traditions of Breathing

5

The Breathing of the Air

Pre-Socratic Echoes in Levinas

SILVIA BENSO

Are not we Westerners, from California to the Urals, nourished by the Bible
as much as by the Presocratics?

—Levinas, "No Identity," *CPP* 148

Pre-Socratic Presences

Relinquishing the rhetorical interrogation in the above epigram, let us restate it
positively: "We Westerners [. . .]" Others have already explored some of the ways
in which Levinas's philosophy is sustained by the Biblical inspiration. And Levinas
himself is willing to recognize, at various points in his essays, the presence of the
Socratic, Platonic, and even Aristotelian legacy (to stay with some major Greek,
post-Socratic thinkers) within his own thought. Is Levinas also nourished by the
pre-Socratics, as his statement suggests? And what would a Levinasian reading
of the pre-Socratics reveal? Would different possibilities of philosophical thinking open up, within the very origins of Greek philosophy, if one were to let the
Levinasian inspiration breathe through such an originary thinking? These are the
questions I would like to take up in this chapter. After a necessary brief, certainly
unsystematic excursus on some pre-Socratic themes that might be said to echo
in Levinas's philosophy, I will focus more specifically on the presence in Levinas
of a rather minor, but thus even more significant pre-Socratic thinker, namely,
Anaximenes and his "theory" that air is the *arche* of all things. Some ways in

which pre-Socratic thinkers and themes resonate in Levinas's thought are more
evident than others, insofar as such echoes are identified by Levinas himself.
Indeed, there are moments when Levinas is highly critical of themes inaugurated
by the pre-Socratic tradition. Thus, an equal criticism associates the two giants of
pre-Socratic philosophy (which some, such as Nietzsche,[1] see as representatives of
two very different, distinct tendencies within Western philosophy): Parmenides,
the philosopher of being and unity, and Heraclitus, the philosopher of becoming and *polemos*. Levinas's contention with Parmenides as being at the origin of
a recurrent attempt, within the Western tradition, at reading being in terms of
unity and, more specifically, in terms of a unity of being and thought—that is,
in terms of a reassembling of differences within the circularity of thought—is
well known, since it implicitly inspires much of the pages and themes unfolded
in *Totality and Infinity* (*TI*, cf. 33–52). In *Time and the Other* (*TO*), Levinas
declares his programmatic intention to distance himself philosophically from
Parmenides when writing that "it is toward a pluralism that does not merge
into unity that I should like to make my way, and, if this can be dared, break
with Parmenides" (*TO*, 42). What is here rejected is Parmenides's *hen kai pan*,
the monism of the logic of the One in which all possibilities for proximity with
the Other are denied in favor of a mysticism of representation prescribing either
unity in the object, as in religious mysticism (which Levinas constantly rejects),
or unity in the subject, as in all theories of the conformation of the object to
the subject whether configured in a Cartesian, Kantian, Hegelian, or even Husserlian and Heideggerian mode. Analogously evident is Levinas's condemnation,
which once again inspires much of the opening pages of *Totality and Infinity*,
of the Heraclitean motif of being as *polemos*, which ends up in an ontology of
war in which the other is seen as the enemy to be conquered, subsumed, and
annihilated. "We do not need obscure fragments of Heraclitus to prove that being
reveals itself as war to philosophical thought, that war does not only affect it as
the most patent fact, but as the very patency, or the truth, of the real" (*TI*, 21),
Levinas states. Far from seeing Parmenides and Heraclitus as separate, like and
yet unlike Heidegger, Levinas unites them as being the necessary counterparts in
a project that aims at denying what he calls "the eschatology of messianic peace"
inspired by the idea of the Infinite, "a relation with *a surplus always exterior to
the totality*" (*TI*, 22). Thus, he writes, "the visage of being that shows itself in war
is fixed in the concept of totality, which dominates Western philosophy" (*TI*, 21).
Heraclitean ontology of war (and annihilation) and Parmenidean logic of totality and unity are two explications, one practical and one theoretical as it were,
of a same attitude toward alterity and transcendence. True becoming, then, the
true passage from the same to the other is not that indicated by the Heraclitean
movement of flux. Rather, in agreement with the appearance, in Plato's *Theaetetus*
(152a–e), of Protagoras, for whom "man [appears] as measure of all things, that
is, [is] measured by nothing, comparing all things but incomparable," for Levinas,

who rehabilitates the great sophist, "a multiplicity of sentients would be the very *mode* in which a becoming is possible" (*TI*, 59–60).

Beside the ones just indicated, there are other places where a remainder of pre-Socratic inspirations is acknowledged as playing more positive roles in Levinas's thinking. Although the concept of *il y a* is not the final point in Levinas's project, nevertheless it cannot be denied that such a notion plays an essential part in enabling the constitution of a subjectivity capable of responding to the appeal of the Other, that is, capable of making itself ethical. Without the *il y a*, in fact, without this resurgence of being that never allows for escapes or exits into nothingness (and here the subscription to Parmenides's prohibition of the path of nonbeing should be evident), the I could easily find a way of contenting and thus quieting itself in a quasi-Buddhist notion of emptiness or nothingness, or in the death brought about by suicide. But the inability to rest upon itself, the impossibility to sleep, even in death, the wakefulness to which the *il y a* forces the I is also what prepares the I, in its exposure and vigilance, to the possibility of later being disrupted by the Other. And it is what provides the I with the elements that will enable the I to remedy the thirst, hunger, and nakedness of the Other, to welcome the Other not with empty hands.

The Heraclitean moment in the notion of the *il y a* is recalled by Levinas himself when, in a page of *Time and the Other*, he writes that "if it were necessary to compare the notion of the *there is* with a great theme of classical philosophy, I would think of Heraclitus. Not to the myth of the river in which one cannot bathe twice, but to Cratylus's version of the river in which one cannot bathe even once; where the very fixity of unity, the form of every existent, cannot be constituted" (*TO*, 49). Still in the same context, Levinas dismisses possible Anaximandrean reminiscences of the *apeiron*, an indefinite infinite to which one might be tempted to assimilate the *il y a*. "The indeterminate ground spoken of in philosophy textbooks," Levinas writes without citing any names, "is already a being—an entity—a something. It already falls under the category of the substantive. It already has that elementary personality characteristic of every existent" (*TO*, 47–48), whereas what Levinas has in mind when speaking of the *il y a* is the "very work of being" (*TO*, 48), verbal and not substantive or subjective, and therefore anonymous and impersonal—as in *Existence and Existents* (*EE*, 57–64).

In *Time and the Other* as well as in *Existence and Existents* such anonymity and impersonality is exemplified through expressions such as "it is raining" (*TO*, 47; *EE*, 58), "it is hot" (*TO*, 47), "it is warm (*EE*, 58), "it is night" (*EE*, 48), "a heavy atmosphere" (*EE*, 58), thus possibly suggesting an affinity with the general realm of what the pre-Socratic, naturalist philosophers, namely Thales and Anaximenes but also Empedocles (who, however, similarly to Anaximander, identified such a general realm with specific, particularized beings), might have called *physis*—nature in its preobjective, prescientific meaning. Could pre-Socratic *physis* resonate, then, in the *il y a*? To ask this question means to ask about the place of nature in Levinas's thought both with respect to being and in relation to the beyond being; that is, it means to ask, among other things, whether ethical subjectivity requires a breaking open and a relinquishing of the self's natural attitude or whether ethical subjectivity is to an extent rooted in nature, although certainly it is not grounded there since its reason of being comes from the transcendence of the alterity of the Other.

Pre-Socratic *physis*, or the natural elements to which many of the pre-Socratics refer, falls, properly, under what Levinas calls "the elemental" (*TI*, 131). What is the relation between the elemental and the *il y a*, that is, between the pre-Socratic conception of elemental *physis* and the *il y a* on which the I as hypostasis, as substance raises (*EE*), but which it leaves behind in its move toward ethical subjectivity, toward subjectivity without autonomous substance or substantivity? Indeed, the elemental shares many features with the *il y a*. Like the *il y a*, the elemental is indeterminate, boundless, timeless, without origin: it is "a common fund or terrain, essentially non-possessable, 'nobody's,'" Levinas writes (*TI*, 131), and continues: "the depth of the element prolongs it till it is lost in the earth and in the heavens. 'Nothing ends, nothing begins'" (*TI*, 131). Content without form (*TI*, 131), the elemental is pure "qualit[y] without support [. . .] adjectiv[e] without substantive," quality "determining nothing" (*TI*, 132), and thus anonymous like the *il y a*: it "presents us as it were the reverse of reality, without origin in being. [. . .] Hence we can say that the element comes to us from nowhere; the side it presents to us does not determine an object, remains entirely anonymous. *C'est du vent, de la terre, de la mere, du ciel, de l'air*" (*TI*, 132). Self-sufficient, incapable of raising any questions regarding "what is the 'other side'" of it, the elemental calls for a "bathing," for an "immersion [. . .] not convertible into exteriority" (*TI*, 132)—what Levinas names "enjoyment—an ultimate relation with the substantial plenitude of being, with its materiality" (*TI*, 133).

Yet, in Levinas the elemental is not *simply physis* (although *physis* is elemental), and the elemental is not the *il y a*, which means also that *physis* is not the *il y a*. First of all, the elemental is not simply *physis* in the sense of the natural elements as understood by the pre-Socratics insofar as Levinas certainly includes in it earth, sea, sky, air (*TI*, 132), light (*TI*, 130), but also, and in a sense surprisingly, city (*TI*, 131). That is, the elemental escapes the distinction and separation between natural and artificial, between *physis* and *techne*, perhaps allowing for an understanding of both as forms of *poiesis*, perhaps enabling a reading of technology as an inevitable component of nature, or perhaps opening up some other possibility of discourse that cannot be explored in the context of this chapter. Second, for Levinas, the elemental is not the *il y a*. Whereas in the *il y a* Levinas stresses the verbal aspect without a substantive to support such verbality, what is stressed in the elemental is the qualitative aspect without substantiality. Thus, the two forms of anonymity differ. The *il y a* refers to an impersonal anonymity, to the sheer event of being without form or content because prior and indifferent to both. The elemental instead refers to an anonymity that is already identified and identifiable, personalized or hypostasized, as it were, through a certain way (a certain quality) of its being, which thus becomes its content; it is an anonymity where what remains undetermined is not the content but the form, the face, the absence of which compels Levinas to talk about the gods of nature as pagan, mythical, faceless deities with whom no personal relation can be entertained.

This lack of complete coincidence between the elemental and the *il y a* also means that being and nature do not coincide in Levinas. Nature is already a way of being, an existent, a content, a mode of carving oneself a niche in the anonymity of the *il y a*. As we know from other places in Levinas's philosophy, there are other ways of being: the egology or egoism of the ontological subject (which thus is not necessarily natural), the being-for-the-other of ethical subjectivity, the beyond-being of transcendence (whether God or the Other) to name a few. This lack of coincidence between nature and the *il y a* allows for the possibility, I argue, that, unlike the *il y a*, nature for Levinas may already be spiritual, that is, open to the ethical, or perhaps, which amounts to the same, that spirit may already be natural because in fact nature is beyond the separation between materiality and spirituality, mind and body, matter and soul. It is at this point that Anaximenes's "theory" of air being the *arche* of all things becomes interesting.[2]

Aer, Psyche, Pneuma in Anaximenes

We know very little, almost nothing certain about Anaximenes's life and activities. Certainly in the eyes of the contemporary reader, often trained in the shadow of Nietzsche and Heidegger, among the three Milesians Anaximander appears more prominent than his "associate" Anaximenes.[3] According to Diogenes Laertius, however, Theophrastus (Aristotle's pupil) wrote an entire monograph on Anaximenes,[4] which signals the recognition Anaximenes enjoyed in the ancient world, and thus the possibly widespread influence of his thinking.[5] Although the theory of *pneuma*—pneumatology—occupies an important place in the theories of the medical schools as they developed in the fifth century BCE, and received its most complete and significant form in the doctrines of the Stoics, it is in Anaximenes that its first philosophical mention occurs according to a longstanding tradition in the West.[6] Therefore, it is to him that I turn regardless of the only alleged authenticity of the fragment in which such a theory appears (some alterations and rewording might in fact have occurred, but this would not radically change the general sense of the quotation).

As handed down to the tradition by Aetius, the words commonly accepted as a direct quotation from Anaximenes are as such: "As our soul [*psyche*], he says, being air [*aer*] holds us together and controls us, so does wind [or breath; *pneuma*] and air [*aer*] enclose the whole world. (Air [*aer*] and wind [*pneuma*] are synonymous here)."[7] The *psyche* is *aer*, *aer* and *pneuma* are synonyms, therefore the *psyche* is also *pneuma*.

First of all, a brief semantic observation. It is questionable what Anaximenes exactly meant by *aer*, whether atmospheric air (invisible) or, as in Homer, mist and vapor (visible). There is no doubt, however, that for Anaximenes air is something substantial, and indeed the basic form of substance. Whether such substantiality retains material or spiritual features or neither is part of what I would like to address here. In the fragment reproduced above, even more radical than the association between air and breath (breath is, after all, in a merely physiological sense, warm air) is the suggestion that our soul—the *psyche*—is not only air but also, and at the same time, *pneuma*. In other words, the soul is indeed assimilated to a natural, physical principle (*aer*) that is seen at work in the entire universe (thus also suggesting, but it is not our interest here, an analogy if not a structural coincidence between microcosm and macrocosm). By itself, this move would amount to understanding the soul in terms of its physical makeup, of what has later been named "matter," and would subject it to obedience to the deterministic, mechanistic laws that are seen at work in the universe of physicality. What would derive would be a philosophical vision in which the psychic dimension otherwise known as spirituality would be reduced to its natural, physical, material component. However, there is something else going on in Anaximenes's fragment.

Moreover and more notably, through Aetius's clarification that air and breath are synonymous, the soul is also associated with another term, *pneuma*, a word indicating a component that, besides physically making it up, enlivens the soul, makes it mobile, pulsating, active, verbal, and not substantive, and in this sense subtracts it from immediate association with the pure materiality of air and renders it certainly forceful, vital, organic, and, with a terminology that will appear only later, almost spiritual, although perhaps of a peculiar spirit. In fact, there is no *pneuma*, no breath (substantive) except that in breathing (verbal), and breathing is a pulmonary activity (and not a status) of taking in and letting out, of inspiration and expiration. It is breathing, not simple air that individualizes the human being, that gives him or her subjectivity, and that ultimately constitutes his or her soul. Such an activity of breathing provides physiological as well as psychological, physical as well as spiritual life, and in this sense, more than a material element (as air is) *pneuma* is a force, a lifeforce. If it is a lifeforce, it is certainly natural, but is it still truly material? Even, is it truly physical, or is it already also something else?[8]

Yet *pneuma*, we are told in Aetius's remark, is nothing else than air, a material, physical, natural element that, present at the cosmic level—that is to say, outside—is internalized and externalized by the soul so as to nourish, sustain, even make possible the life of the *psyche*, which itself then *is* air. This is why the soul is in fact air: because the soul is the air-breathing that by bringing the air from outside inside and back gives the soul its subsistence. The soul is itself this movement of the air, this inhaling and exhaling, this folding itself in and turning itself out, this pulsating lung in which the inside (properly, the soul) is always already the outside (the air) and vice versa. Without air there is no breathing, without breathing there is no soul, without air there is no soul. To exhale the last breath is to stop breathing, to die. But the lack of air certainly brings about the last breath, and all dying is, in a way, a gasping for air, for more air, a suffocating. Is air itself, then, the lifeforce expressed by the term *pneuma*? Is the natural, physical element already pervaded by a spiritual dimension, so as to justify the classical description of the first philosophers as hylozoists, that is, as those who see matter (*hyle*) as in itself provided by a principle of animation (*zoon*)? And is this animation the spiritual?

What is ultimately going on in Anaximenes's association of *psyche, aer*, and *pneuma*? Is Anaximenes simply reducing the psychological, what the tradition has later understood as the spiritual aspect of human beings to its natural, physical, material makeup? This is indeed the sense in which the Stoics understood *pneuma*. But the Stoics also wrote after Plato's theorization of the division between the soul and the body; thus, in a way, they were forced to operate a choice between the materiality and immateriality of *pneuma* (and they opted for the former). Or is Anaximenes spiritualizing nature, physicality, and materiality? The spiritual dimension shadowed in the term *pneuma* was not lost to the Septuagints, who generally translated the Hebrew form *ruah* (wind, breath, but also the spirit of God) with *pneuma*, and also used *pneuma* in a context where pagan Greek would have used *thymos* or *psyche*.[9] What are the nature and status of the *psyche*, this peculiar entity that seems to be at once material (*aer*) and nonmaterial (*pneuma*) except that the apparently nonmaterial aspect, the *pneuma*, is then allegedly solved back into its material dimension as *aer*?

Some suggestions as how to cast some light on these questions surprisingly come from Hegel. In his *Lectures on the Philosophy of History*, commenting on Anaximenes's fragment, Hegel translates Anximenes's *pneuma* with *Geist*, spirit,[10] and writes that "Anaximenes shows very clearly the nature of his essence in the soul, and he thus points out what may be called the transition of natural philosophy into the philosophy of consciousness."[11] Certainly Hegel's understanding of the history of philosophy is oriented by his attempt at reading all moments of such a history as transitional to the full manifestation of spirit accomplished in nineteenth-century German philosophy. With respect to Anaximenes, however, even if one does not subscribe to Hegel's general historiography, one thing becomes clear through his remark: by marking the transition from nature to consciousness Anaximenes in fact situates himself at the turning point of that transition, as the one who perhaps renders the transition possible but possibly without himself being completely part of it. That is, in Anaximenes the split between nature and consciousness, body and mind, matter and spirit, as well as that between microcosm and macrocosm, which will become evident in Platonic philosophy (although there too it is only by taking care of bodily needs in a certain way that the life of the mind or spirit can develop), is not yet fully at work. *Psyche*, *aer*, and *pneuma* remain in the ambiguity that enables the transition to occur: they interact and feed on one another in such a manner that each nourishes the other, so that nature, or what will later appear as corporeality, physicality, or materiality, is in fact the source, origin, and aliment of spirituality. In other words, nature is itself spiritual while remaining nature, and vice versa. And all this emerges through the somewhat ambiguous notion of *pneuma* in its correlation with *aer* and *psyche*. As Irigaray states in a different context (and remarking on the concept of breathing in terms that however speak the language of the tradition of the split), in breathing "nature becomes spirit while remaining nature."[12]

This very attitude of thought, which situates itself before or beyond the split defining and characterizing so much of Western philosophy between materiality and spirituality with all the conceptual corollaries attached, is present also in Levinas, who explicitly discusses the notion of psychism both in *Totality and Infinity* and in *Otherwise than Being*. In a sense that I will try to elucidate, the two descriptions resemble Anaximenes's double association of the *psyche* with *aer* and *pneuma*, respectively, while at the same time they contribute to let emerge and disclose the meaning of the ambiguity contained in Anaximenes's own account.

Psychism and Air in *Totality and Infinity*

In *Totality and Infinity* Levinas generally does not speak of the psyche or soul but of psychism or psychic life, and understands it as "an event in being" (TI, 54), "a dimension in being, a dimension of non-essence, beyond the possible and impossible" (*TI*, 56). As such, psychism belongs to the movement of separation through which the I constitutes itself on the background of the il y a, but also on the background of all forms of totalization aimed at encompassing the self. Psychism is what constitutes the I in its individuality; "it is the feat of radical separation" (*TI*, 54). In this sense, psychism is not a purely theoretical moment, but rather an existential one: "it is already a way of being, resistance to the totality" (*TI*, 54), and thus act of freedom with respect both to one's own origin and to the universality of history. The tradition has tried to express the irreducibility of the psychism of the I to the common, totalizing time of history through the notion of "the eternity of the soul" (*TI*, 57). But the concept of eternity as "perenniality" does not mark a separation that is radical with respect to common history. Rather, the separation is radical only if "each being has its own time, that is, its interiority" that interrupts historical time—that is, only if each being is born and dies. Thus, birth and death are inherent components of psychism, which makes both possible. Psychism means not existence as eternity, but discontinuity in historical time, for Levinas. The life of the soul is made of birth and death, physical appearance and disappearance. It is human life.

The way in which psychism defines itself is through enjoyment which, according to the description in the section of *Totality and Infinity* devoted to "Interiority and Economy," is grounded on corporeity, sensibility, affectivity, bodily needs that want to be satisfied, happiness. Enjoyment neither relates to the things of the world through an instrumental, "utilitarian schematism" (*TI*, 110) that makes the I see them as tools, implements, fuels, or, in general, means, nor do they appear as goals. Rather, enjoyment provides us with an immersion in the fullness of life which, in itself, is "*love of life*" (*TI*, 112)—not life in abstract but life in its very contents, which are thus lived, and "the act of living these contents is *ipso facto* a content of life" (*TI*, 111). In enjoyment, the reliance, the dependency on the contents of life, the "living from [. . .]" such contents turns the I into an autonomous, independent subject, into an egoism, or, precisely, into a psychism.

As already noticed, it is such a psychism, specified as sensibility, "and not matter that provides a principle of individuation" (*TI*, 59), Levinas remarks. That is to say, in Levinas what we would otherwise call spiritual life, what he terms "psychism" is not separated from bodily life, sensibility, and corporeality. The body for Levinas is not "an object among other objects, but [rather . . .] the very regime in which separation holds sway [. . .] the 'how' of this separation and so to speak [. . .] an adverb rather than [. . .] a substantive" (*TI*, 163). Life is a body, and the body is "the presence of [an] equivocation" (*TI*, 164) between "on the one hand *to stand* [*se tenir*], to be master of oneself, and, on the other hand, to stand on the earth, to be in the *other*, and thus to be encumbered by one's body" (*TI*, 164). The two aspects are not distinct and in succession; rather, "their simultaneity constitutes the body" (*TI*, 165), which also means that there is "no *duality*—lived body and physical body—which would have to be reconciled" (*TI*, 165). The psychism situates itself before or beyond the distinction into body and soul, body and mind, and thus, unlike much philosophical thinking of Platonic (or Platonist, I will not address the difference here) descent, beyond the need for their reconciliation. With a clear reference to Plato's myths of the soul as recounted at various places in his philosophy, Levinas states that "consciousness does not fall into a body—is not incarnated; it is a disincarnation—or, more precisely, a postponing of the corporeity of the body" (*TI*, 165–166). That is, consciousness, which Levinas characterizes as a being "related to the element in which one is settled as to what is not yet there" (*TI*, 166), is intertwined with the body, has its origin in the body, arises out of the body as a taking time, a taking distance "with respect to the element to which the I is given over" (*TI*, 166).

Moreover, sensibility, or rather, this "incarnate thought" (*TI*, 164), this psychism, is not made to coincide either with matter or with nature. As sensibility, the body, "a sector of an elemental reality" (*TI*, 165), immerses itself in the elementality of matter, elementality which, as we have seen, can be natural as well as artificial or technological. But sensibility is already separation, already psychism, whereas matter, or the elemental, is pure quality in which no separation is possible, since "as qualities, the differences still relate to the community of a genus" (*TI*, 59), that is to say, to a totality. On the other hand, the body is not immediately nature because the body exists as already animated by its psychism, the body is its psychism, or better, psychism is "sensible self-reference" (*TI*, 59), whereas for Levinas nature is not animated, is not separate, does not possess an interiority of its own. Nevertheless, matter as well as the elemental (both natural and technological) for Levinas can only and always be approached from the perspective of the psychism of the I, through the "sensible self-reference" that in enjoyment bathes itself in such dimensions, and that through dwelling, possession, labor, and consciousness gains a stable hold on such dimensions. In other words, it is not only the body but also matter and the elemental that are already spiritual, inscribed in the economy through which the I attains its own individuality and separation—or matter, the elemental, the body are already cultural because in fact they are before and beyond the distinction between nature and culture as a specific dimension of humankind. As Levinas writes against a whole tradition that has rather mainly equated bodily pleasures with animality, "to enjoy without utility, in pure loss, gratuitously, without referring to anything else, in pure expenditure—this is the human" (*TI*, 133). As in Anaximenes, psychism is air, being steeped in the elemental as the source of one's independence and happiness, sensible enjoyment, nourishment.

The love of life that Levinas displays in these pages of *Totality and Infinity* is the feeling of innocent, sinless, guilt-free *eudaimonia* with which the pre-Socratic philosophers were generally capable of approaching the universe; of being completely present to it while representing its *genesis*, its *arche* to themselves; of being in harmony with it. The injustice of which Anaximander speaks has precisely to do, according to Levinas's reading of Heidegger's interpretation in "The Anaximander Fragment," with a "put[ting] into question [of] the ego's natural position as subject, its perseverance—the perseverance of its good conscience—in its being. It puts into question its *conatus essendi*, the stubbornness of its being" ("Diachrony and Representation"; *TO*, 108). If it puts such "an indiscreet—or 'unjust'—presence" into question, however, this does not mean the uprooting or elimination of such a "positive moment" of separation (*TI*, 53), since "the plurality required for conversation [and, one could add, for the ethical relation] results from the interiority with which each term is 'endowed,' the psychism, its egoist and sensible self-reference" (*TI*, 59).

In *Totality and Infinity*, the psychism is characterized as an egoism that actually enables the I to separate itself from the anonymity of the *il y a*, of pure being. As such, it represents an ontological moment in the activity of self-constitution of the I—it is a moment through which the I establishes *its own being*, its having its own beginning and end, its own birth and death, in short, its own time. What animates such a moment, however? As Anaximenes indicates, the *psyche* is *aer*, substantive presence, substantiality, that is, in Levinas's language, persistence in one's own being; but it is also *pneuma*, verbality, vital force, breathing. What gives the psychism its life, its animation, its *pneuma*, according to Levinas? What is "the very pneuma of the psyche" (*Otherwise than Being*; OB, 69, 141)?

The Pneuma of Psychism in *Otherwise than Being*

In *Otherwise than Being*, the psychism of the I (which Lingis's translation renders as *psyche*) is discussed once again in relation to concepts, already associated to it in *Totality and Infinity*, such as sensibility, enjoyment, the body. But here psychism undergoes a "coring out [*dénucléation*]" for which "the nucleus of the ego is cored out" (*OB*, 64). Thus, psychism is no longer described as egoism, as separatedness of the I, but rather as "the form of a peculiar dephasing, a loosening up or unclamping of identity: the same prevented from coinciding with itself" (*OB*, 68). This emptying-out, which does not entail "an abdication of the same" but rather "an abnegation of oneself fully responsible for the other" (*OB*, 68–69) is brought about, through the notions of responsibility, substitution, the one-for-the-other, by the presence of the Other, who then constitutes the very *pneuma* of psychism, its animation. As Levinas defines it, psychism now signifies "the other in me, a malady of identity, both accused and *self*, the same for the other, the same by the other. Qui pro quo, it is a substitution" (*OB*, 69). From substantive identity, like the air-like psychism of *Totality and Infinity*, the I now turns into verbality, movement, breathing through which the other penetrates the I and, through a "traumatic hold" (*OB*, 141), a claim and a command placed on the same, destabilizes the substantive identity of the I and renders it verbal, responsive, responsible, for-the-other rather than for-itself, active of an activity that is, in fact, a passivity, a receptivity, a welcoming, and, ultimately, a donation—the donation of hospitality. "An openness of the self to the other [. . .] breathing is transcendence in the form of opening up," Levinas writes in the concluding pages of *Otherwise than Being* (*OB*, 181). Psychism is then a deep inspiration (*OB*, 141)—an inspiring, breathing the other in as well as a being inspired, animated by the other who thus constitutes the I in its very substantial identity as a destabilized self. Yet, "this pneumatism is not nonbeing; it is disinterestedness, excluded middle of essence, besides being and nonbeing" (*OB*, 181). As for Anaximenes, *aer* and *pneuma* are synonyms, and the *psyche* is both. It is the breathing, the verbality, the animation by the other that ultimately gives the soul its identity, its nonsubstantive substance, its being—its *aer*.

Such an animation does not occur at the level of cognition, theory, or intentionality, claims Levinas. Rather, it is only possible at the level of the body, through an incarnation. "The animation, the very pneuma of the psyche, alterity in identity, is the identity of a body exposed to the other, becoming 'for the other,' the possibility of giving" (*OB*, 69). The other lays claim on the I, inspires the I as an other who is hungry, thirsty, naked, in need of protection, of a home. Thus, the counterpart of such an inspiration, the movement of expiration through which the breath makes itself breathing, what Levinas will call elsewhere in *Otherwise than Being* testimony or "witness," can only unfold itself through the donation of bodily, corporeal, material goods. Once again, as in *Totality and Infinity*, psychism, which the tradition has understood as nonmaterial, spiritual being, is described and defined through the body, corporeal donation, giving one's body, one's breath as nourishment, as source of life—"psychism in the form of a hand that gives even the bread taken from its mouth" (*OB*, 67). The body thus is retrieved from its confinement in that Cartesian (but, even before, Platonic) order of materiality for which the body and the soul "have no common space where they can touch" (*OB*, 70). Rather, the body is already an "animated body or an incarnate identity" (*OB*, 71), and psychism is defined as "the way in which a relationship between uneven terms, without any common time, arrives at relationship" (*OB*, 70). That is to say, psychism is neither spiritual nor material, is "an accord, a chord, which is possible only as an arpeggio" (*OB*, 70). As for Anaximenes, the *psyche* is *aer* and *pneuma*, or the proximity of both, and psychism results into a subject "of flesh and blood," an individual "that is hungry and eats, entrails in a skin, and thus capable of giving the bread out of his [or her] mouth, or giving his [or her] skin" (*OB*, 77). Ultimately, Levinas identifies psychism with "the maternal body" (*OB*, 67), the only one for which even the activity of breathing for itself, the in-taking of the air that gives the I its substantiality, becomes a breathing for the other, "a further deep breathing even in the breath cut short by the wind of alterity" (*OB*, 180). In turn, the subject is defined as "a lung at the bottom of his substance" (*OB*, 180).

To say that psychism is an animated body, a lung, does not imply, however, a return to or a lapsing into animality. Animality (or the organic body) and the animated body are not the same thing. An animal is driven by its *conatus essendi*, entirely caught in the sphere of ontological self-assertion; the animal lives in being, and the signification of sensibility as signifyingness for-the-other completely escapes it. Conversely, the incarnate body may certainly give in to its own *conatus essendi*, since "there is an insurmountable ambiguity there: the incarnate body [. . .] can lose its signification" (*OB*, 79), and the human subject ends up engaging in an animalistic life style, which is what ontology ultimately is. But the incarnate body, psychism can also live what we may call the "spirituality" of the elemental, that is, sensibility as ethical signification. Rather than a deficiency, the ambiguity is then "the condition of vulnerability itself, that is, of sensibility as signification" (*OB*, 80). As Levinas phrases it, "perhaps animality is only the soul's still being too short of breath" (*OB*, 181), that is, the soul's inability to engage in the movement of inspiration by the other "that is already expiration" (*OB*, 182). This movement "is the longest breath there is, spirit," Levinas remarks, asking: "Is man not the living being capable of the longest breath in inspiration, without a stopping point, and in expiration, without return?" (*OB*, 182).

This also means that it is not the body in itself that belongs to animality, or to ontology, since the body is already possibility of being for-the-other. Ethical subjectivity is distinct from animals' life but not thereby from nature, since nature is alien to the distinction between body and mind, matter and spirit or soul. By engaging in an ethical life, by inspiring the air of the Other as the *pneuma* of one's own breathing, psychism does not relinquish its natural status, does not distance itself from its own nature; if anything, it separates itself from animals and *their* way of being within nature. Ethics is not unnatural for the psychism; in this sense, for Levinas as well as for Anaximenes, *pneuma* is *aer*; the vital principle is proximity with and not distance from the natural element, since the natural element is alien to—it is before or beyond—all dichotomies.

The *pneuma* of psychism, its inspiration and animation, is the appeal by the other so that the elemental that the I enjoys becomes a gift and a donation for the other. Without the elemental, which is not pure being (*il y a*) but already a way of being, ethical subjectivity, the breathing subject, a subject inspired by and responsive to the other would not be possible. Matter, the elemental (whether natural or technological) and its transformation through labor and work, in which the ontological I bathes so as to constitute itself in its substantiality, are already potentially spiritual in the sense that they are already open to the dimension that properly constitutes the psychism in its breathing aspect—or rather, they are beyond such a distinction between materiality and spirituality. As Levinas very clearly puts it, "matter is the very locus of the for-the-other" (*OB*, 77), that is to say, matter and the elemental are the place of the ethical not only because they are instrumental to the ethical, but also because they are already open to it, they are what makes the ethical responsiveness concrete and actual. As Levinas has it, in order to be ethical, in order to be able to give the very bread one eats, "one has first to enjoy one's bread, not to have the merit of giving it, but in order to give it with one's heart, to give oneself in giving it" (*OB*, 72). Nature belongs not to pure being, toward which the ontological movement of the hypostasis is necessary for the constitution of an identity, but rather to a pre-ontological way of being that, precisely because it is pre-ontological, allows for a beyond being, for hospitality. Thus, *aer* is *pneuma* also in the sense that physical, natural elements contain within themselves, rather, are the possibility for the welcoming of the other.

In Place of a Conclusion

Once again, let us ask the question Levinas asks: "Are not we Westerners, from California to the Urals, nourished by the Bible as much as by the Pre-Socratics?" Is Levinas influenced by Anaximenes as much as he is by the Bible in his understanding of psychism as egoism of the self, enjoyment, sensibility, incarnate body, subject of flesh and blood, maternal body? Very likely the answer to the question is "No," and an analysis of the Biblical concept of *ruaḥ* would probably show the Jewish ground of Levinas's understanding of such a notion. My point in this chapter, however, is not that of retracing the roots of Levinas's thought as much as showing the proximity between the Jewish inspiration and the Greek tradition of the origins on the notion of psychism. Such a proximity becomes possible precisely through Levinas's own understanding of psychism. Within that psychism, which Western philosophy has understood mainly as a spiritual and immaterial principle, Levinas retrieves the naturalistic, material element, and thus situates himself, with Anaximenes, before or rather beyond the split between materiality and immateriality, body and soul, nature and spirit that Anaximenes itself has contributed to originate while remaining at its threshold, at least according to Hegel's interpretation quoted earlier in the chapter. There is no doubt that such a Greek understanding of psychism is obliterated throughout much of the rest of the history of Western philosophy, covered up and bent in a more immaterial, spiritualistic direction by a certain interpretation of Plato known as Platonism, and further elided by Christian metaphysics. But what would it mean, for Western philosophy, to reread its own origin, its own history, its own conceptualizations in light of such a different, and yet not foreign understanding of psychism, the breath of which can be perceived through the inspiration of Levinas? What would it mean, for philosophy, to read itself against the grain of its own interpretative tradition, inspired by the presence of the other that the Jewish, religious tradition represents? If led by such an inspiration, could it find within itself those very themes to which the inspiration has opened it up? Could the breath become its air, so that the inspiration would not suffocate philosophy by changing its nature—from philosophy to religion, or theology, or religious thinking? So that, rather, it would only redirect, deflect, or inflect the movement and direction of its breathing: not toward itself, but for-the-other, "wisdom of love" rather than love of wisdom, as Levinas has had occasion to say (*OB*, 162)? Would this not be the only possible sense of proximity, of a "contact across a distance" (*TI*, 172) between the two traditions, a contact in which the other manifests itself in "a mastery that does not conquer but teaches" (*TI*, 171)? "In Greek philosophy one can [. . .] discern traces of the ethical breaking through the ontological," Levinas remarks.[13] Not only can one, but rather one does indeed, I would argue.

Abbreviations of Works by Emmanuel Levinas

CPP   *Collected Philosophical Papers.* Translated by Alphonso Lingis. The Hague: Martinus Nijhoff, 1987.

EE   *Existence and Existents.* Translated by Alphonso Lingis. Pittsburgh, PA: Duquesne University Press, 2001 (originally published with Dordrecht: Kluwer, 1978 and reprinted with minor corrections 1988).

OB   *Otherwise than Being or Beyond Essence.* Translated by Alphonso Lingis. The Hague: Martinus Nijhoff, 1981.

TI   *Totality and Infinity.* Translated by Alphonso Lingis. Pittsburgh, PA: Duquesne University Press, 1969.

TO   *Time and the Other.* Translated by Richard A. Cohen. Pittsburgh, PA: Duquesne University Press, 1987.

Notes

1. See Friedrich Nietzsche, *Philosophy in the Tragic Age of the Greeks*, trans. Marianne Cowan (Washington, DC: Regnery, 1996).

2. It should be noted that the term *arche* is not used by the pre-Socratics; it is rather Aristotelian in the sense that Aristotle uses it when classifying his predecessors according to how many "first causes" they postulated (cf. *Physics* A, 2 184b15ff.; cf. *The Complete Works of Aristotle*, Vol. 1).

3. Cf. on this Fragment 2 of Theophrastus's work *Physicorum Opiniones*.

4. Diogenes Laertius, *Lives of the Eminent Philosophers*, Vol. 1 (London: William Heinemann, 1925), 5: 42.

5. John Burnet, *Early Greek Philosophy* (New York: Meridian, 1957), 78ff.

6. This is not to say that such a theory did not have a previous origin in the popular tradition, or that it was not formulated in previous authors, such as, for example, Homer.

7. Aetius I, 3, 4. (cit. from *The Presocratic Philosophers*, p. 158f.).

8. In conformity with their physical theories, the Stoic doctrine reads *pneuma* in entirely materialistic terms, and because of this it will be rejected by the later Christian thought, which, through a peculiar, Neoplatonist interpretation of the Platonic legacy, will consign such a rejection to medieval and modern philosophy. In this chapter I wonder, however, about the reduction of *pneuma* to a purely material dimension.

9. The cultural history of the term *pneuma*, as well as that of "spirit," is complex indeed. For such a history, see Gerard Verbeke, *L'évolution de la doctrine du pneuma du stoicism à S. Augustine* (New York: Garland, 1987), and Marie Isaacs, *The Concept of Spirit* (London: Heythrop, 1976).

10. See Georg Wilhelm Friedrich Hegel, *Lectures on the History of Philosophy*, Vol. 1, trans. Elisabeth S. Haldane and Frances H. Simson (New York: Humanities Press, 1974), 190.

11. Ibid.

12. Luce Irigaray, "A Breath That Touches in Words," in *I love to you*, trans. Alison Martin (New York: Routledge, 1996), 123.

13. See Emmanuel Levinas and Richard Kearney, "Dialogue with Emmanuel Levinas," in *Face to Face with Levinas*, ed. Richard A. Cohen (Albany: State University of New York Press, 1986), 25.

Bibliography

Burnet, John. *Early Greek Philosophy*. New York: Meridian, 1957.

The Complete Works of Aristotle (2 vols.). Edited by Jonathan Barnes. Princeton, NJ: Princeton University Press 1984.

Diogenes Laertius. *Lives of the Eminent Philosophers* (Vol. 1). Translated by R.D. Hicks. London: William Heinemann, 1925.

Hegel, Georg Wilhelm Friedrich. *Lectures on the History of Philosophy* (Vol. 1). Translated by Elisabeth S. Haldane and Frances H. Simson. New York: Humanities Press, 1974.

Irigaray, Luce. "A Breath That Touches in Words." In *I love to you*, translated by Alison Martin, 121–128. New York: Routledge, 1996.

Isaacs, Marie. *The Concept of Spirit*. London: Heythrop, 1976.

Levinas, Emmanuel, and Richard Kearney. "Dialogue with Emmanuel Levinas." In *Face to Face with Levinas*, edited by Richard A. Cohen, 13–34. Albany: State University of New York Press, 1986.

Nietzsche, Friedrich. *Philosophy in the Tragic Age of the Greeks*. Translated by Marianne Cowan. Washington, DC: Regnery, 1996.

The Presocratic Philosophers. Edited by G.S. Kirk, J.E. Raven, and M. Schofield. Cambridge: Cambridge University Press, 1999.

Verbeke, Gerard. *L'évolution de la doctrine du pneuma du stoicism à S. Augustine*. New York: Garland, 1987.

6

Mindfulness of Breathing in Early Buddhism

TAMARA DITRICH

Just as when, bhikkhus, in the last month of the hot season, a great
rain cloud, out of season, instantaneously dissolves and extinguishes
the stirred up dust and dirt, in the same way, bhikkhus, concentration through mindfulness of breathing, when cultivated and practiced
repeatedly, is peaceful and exalted, a sublime and pleasant abiding,
and it instantaneously dissolves and extinguishes harmful, unwholesome states whenever they arise. (S V, 54)[1]

Mindfulness of breathing is one of the key methods of meditation in most traditional and modern Buddhist contemplative practices. This chapter first situates the
significance of breath in the context of ancient Indian religious and philosophical
milieux, pointing out that earlier Indian conceptions of breath provide a context
for and influence early Buddhist teachings. It then focuses on the presentation
of mindfulness of breathing in early Buddhism, drawing from the Pāli Buddhist
canon of the Theravāda school; it investigates mindfulness as an implicitly ethical praxis within Buddhist teachings, and reflects on the intrinsic interrelation
between ethics and breath.

Breath in Ancient Indian Discourse

The Sanskrit term *prāṇa*, referring to breath,[2] occurs already in the earliest recorded
Indian text, the *Ṛgveda* (*RV*), a collection of hymns, probably from the middle of
the second millennium BCE.[3] For example, one of its most famous and rather

opaque hymns, the *Nāsadīyasūkta* (*RV*, 10.129), situates breathing at the stage before the creation took place, in an inexpressible, undifferentiated state, when "there was neither being not non-being."[4] In that pre-creative state, an enigmatic That One (*tad ekam*) "was breathing without breath / wind, by its own will,"[5] or in other words, That One was breathing breathlessly; it was only later on, as the hymn narrates, that cosmic creation would start with the appearance of heat, thought, and desire.[6] Later Vedic and other ancient Indian texts (e.g., the *Upaniṣads*, texts on yoga and tantra) would frequently revisit this theme by positioning meditation on breath as one of the vehicles for reaching (or returning to) that state without movement and differentiation, the pre-creative state beyond this world. Another very influential hymn, the *Puruṣasūkta* (*RV*, 10.90), narrates creation through a cosmic ritual, a sacrifice, in which the parts of the cosmic man (*puruṣa*) are interlinked with the parts of the cosmos; here, breath (*prāṇa*) is positioned as the origin of wind (or the god of wind, Vāyu).[7]

The cosmogonic role of breath is expanded in the commentaries on the Vedas, where the multiple correspondences, interactions, and correlations between the body and the world are evolved further, and linked to ritual, contemplative practices and their soteriological aims. For example, the *Aitareya Āraṇyaka* (*AitĀ*), which expounds on the interdependence between micro- and macrocosms, posits breath (*prāṇa*) as the agent that animates the body, equates it to the Vedic hymns (*AitĀ*, 2.1.4), and links it through speech to the entire cosmos (*AitĀ*, 2.1.6): "speech is united with breath, breath with the wind, the wind with all the gods, all the gods with the heavenly abode, and the heavenly abode with *brahman*" (*AitĀ*, 3.1.6).[8] Already in this early text, the dynamic structural model of the cosmos in its multiple interrelations to the human body indicate a perception of embodied individual that is not viewed as an independent entity but rather as a relational, interlinked, dynamic structure or process (*AitĀ*, 2.1–2.4). This model is repeatedly reflected, with abundant variations, in other Indian religious and philosophical traditions[9] including Buddhism, especially in its formula of dependent origination (Pāli *paṭiccasamuppāda*), which reinterprets and redefines this model in the light of its doctrine of nonself and nonsatisfactoriness of existence.[10]

The interconnection between the human being, ritual, and macrocosm is also one of the foundational premises of the *Upaniṣads*, a later body of texts included in the Vedic tradition, with the earliest ones dated in the pre-Buddhist period, in the seventh or sixth century BCE.[11] These texts portray the world as a totality of correlations, with a particular focus on the human body, its vital powers, cognition, spiritual core (*ātman*), and the Absolute (*brahman*). Already in the earliest *Upaniṣad*, the *Bṛhadāraṇyaka* (*BU*), breath is perceived as the essence of the bodily parts (*BU*, 1.3.19); together with speech and mind, it constitutes the self (*BU*, 1.3.20); and is related to various cosmic "realities," such as the wind (*BU*, 1.3.13), the waters, and the moon (*BU*, 1.5.13). The whole world is viewed to be "held up by breath" (*BU*, 1.3.23),[12] equated to the Absolute (*brahman*) (*BU*, 2.5.4, 3.9.9, 4.1.3),[13] and breath therefore is regarded as a vehicle for soteriological transformation (in direct parallel with Buddhist teachings, as will be shown below).

Breath is also centrally positioned in other Indian philosophical or religious systems and soteriological practices, as evidenced by the textual records of various ascetic movements (*śramaṇas*), focusing on bodily austerities and meditation, such as the Jainas and Ājīvikas.[14] Although historical information on these early ascetic traditions is scarce and the textual sources that we know today are dated mostly in the CE era, they probably stem from pre-Buddhist times.[15] Thus the earliest textual record of the yoga tradition, the *Yogasūtra*, viewed today as its *ur*-text, dedicates a section (2.49–2.53) to the practice of breath restraint (*prāṇāyāma*) as one of the "eight limbs of yoga" (*aṣṭāṅga yoga*) on the path to liberation.[16] Meditation on breathing greatly expanded in later Yogic schools, as well as in emerging Tantric traditions in the late first and the second millennium CE, which integrated a wide range of religious beliefs, cults, and practices of the time. Complex structures and models of physiology and psychology, linked to breath and subtle energies, evolved, and numerous new methods, rituals, and techniques developed, often of an esoteric nature.[17] To summarize, meditation on breath as a soteriological path has arguably been highly significant for most Indian traditions, their philosophies, cosmologies, and soteriological praxes, from the earliest records up to the present day. Hence, earlier Indian teachings on breath provide a context for and influence Buddhist teachings; this link seems to be have been largely overlooked by contemporary interpretations of mindfulness of breathing.

Situating Mindfulness of Breathing in the Pāli Buddhist Canon

Buddhism, likely emerging in the middle of the first millennium BCE[18] in northern India, reflected the religious and philosophical *milieux* of the time, to which it responded by integrating, reinterpreting, and challenging the existing traditions, both ascetic doctrines and practices of *śramaṇas,* as a well as the Vedic worldview and its ritual implementations. Although meditation centering on breath had probably developed already in pre-Buddhist religious traditions of ancient India, it was in Buddhism, according to the textual evidence we have today, that mindfulness of breathing was systematically and thoroughly explored, articulated, and firmly embedded within its discourse for the first time.

It seems that from the very beginning, mindfulness of breathing (*ānāpanasati*)[19] has been a key meditation practice: as narrated in the Pāli canon, the Buddha attained awakening (*bodhi*) through mindfulness of breathing (*S* V, 317) and continued to practice it thenceforth (*S* V, 326). Mindfulness of breathing was arguably perceived as a soteriological method on its own, which, "when cultivated and repeatedly practised, leads completely to disenchantment, detachment, cessation, peace, direct insight, awakening, *nibbāna*" (*A* I, 30).[20]

The word "mindfulness" is the contemporary English rendering of the Pāli term *sati*[21] (Sanskrit *smṛti*); it is primarily a meditational term, referring to contemplative awareness (or remembering) of mental and physical phenomena arising in the present moment.[22] It is frequently described as an ethical watchfulness, awareness as to whether the objects of mindfulness are ethically wholesome/ skillful (*kusala*)[23] or not; for example, *sati* is compared to a gatekeeper guarding a city's six gates (representing the six senses) from strangers (i.e., unwholesome mental states) (*S* IV, 194; *Vism*, 464).

The concept and practice of mindfulness is embedded within all the main models of Buddhist teachings, presented in the Pāli canon.[24] It is integrated in the fundamental model of Buddhist doctrine, that is, the four truths, which put forward (1) the nonsatisfactoriness of existence (*dukkha*); (2) craving (*taṅhā*) as its cause; (3) the possibility of liberation from suffering (*nibbāna*); and (4) the eightfold path that leads to deep transformation and awakening (*S* V, 420–424). The eightfold path proposes a holistic training, encompassing mind, speech, and body—the way one thinks, comprehends, communicates with other beings and acts—aiming toward liberation from suffering, that is, awakening from ignorance. The first two components of the eightfold path are about cultivation of wisdom (*paññā*), which comprises appropriate or right understanding (*sammā diṭṭhi*[25]) of the nature of physical and mental phenomena (*M* III, 71–72), and right intention (*sammā saṅkappa*) to cultivate wholesome or skillful (*kusala*) mental states (*S* V, 8–9; *M* I, 46–55; *M* III, 73). The next three components are concerned with morality/ethics (*sīla*), namely, the cultivation of right speech (*sammā-vācā*), right action (*sammā kammanta*), and right livelihood (*sammā ājīva*), aiming not to cause suffering for oneself and other living beings (*S* V, 9; *M* III, 73–75). The last three components are about meditation; they comprise right effort (*sammā vāyāma*) to cultivate and sustain ethical (*kusala*) mental states and prevent or avert nonethical ones (*akusala*); right meditative concentration (*sammā samādhi*) on a chosen object of contemplation; and right mindfulness (*sammā sati*) (*S* V, 9–10), which integrates ardency, clear comprehension, mindfulness, and relinquishment of desires and discontent in regards to the world. Thus, mindfulness is not viewed as a method on its own, but is a constituent, albeit an essential one, of the entire early Buddhist soteriological project, encompassing ethical training, meditation, and development of wisdom.

When mindfulness of breathing is discussed in early Buddhist sources, it is directly or indirectly indicated that right mindfulness is meant to be practiced in the context of the eightfold path, aiming for the development of wisdom, that is, insight into the three characteristics[26] of all phenomena and processes, leading to the final goal, *nibbāna* (*M* III, 245; *S* II, 32*).* Thus, mindfulness of breathing may be viewed as a soteriological method on its own, as evidenced in several texts dedicated solely to the mindfulness of breathing, particularly the collection of *suttas* in the *Ānāpānasaṃyutta* (*S* V, 311–341). These *suttas* describe the cultivation of mindful breathing (*S* V, 311–312, 317–320, 323–325), the development of the seven factors of awakening (*S* V, 312–313, 329), and the great fruition, that is, *nibbāna* (*S* V, 314, 326–328).

One of the most comprehensive texts on the cultivation of mindfulness of breathing is the *Ānāpānasatisutta* (*M* III, 78–88).[27] This *sutta* initially outlines, in sixteen steps, four areas of contemplation through mindfulness of breathing, starting with the body (*kāya*) (*M* III, 82). It instructs on mindful breathing in and out, knowing whether the breath is short or long, and training to experience the whole (breath) body and calming the "bodily formations." Having achieved calmness of the body, contemplation continues in the area of feelings (*vedanā*), experiencing rapture, happiness, mental formations, and their tranquility, which may indicate achievement of high concentration or meditative absorption (*jhāna*) (*M* III, 82–83). The third section of the *sutta* discusses contemplation of cognition (*citta*): through mindfulness of breathing the meditator experiences, gladdens, concentrates, and liberates cognition (*M* III, 83). The last section outlines contemplation of mental objects (*dhammas*) by contemplating their impermanence, fading away, cessation, and relinquishment (*M* III, 83).

Then the *sutta* delineates the four foundations of mindfulness, accomplished through mindfulness of breathing, and after each section reiterates that the meditator has to be "ardent (*ātāpī*), clearly comprehending (*sampajāno*) and mindful (*satimā*), having abandoned desires and discontent (*vineyya abhijjhādomanassaṃ*) in regards to the world (*loke*)."[28] The attribute "ardent" (*ātāpī*) relates to the endeavor to relinquish defilements (*kilesa*) (*Ps* I, 244), and clear comprehension (*sampajañña*) is explicated as wisdom (*paññā*) (*Dhs*, 16), or an understanding required for cultivation of wholesome qualities (*kusala*) and abandonment of the unwholesome ones (*A* I, 13). In addition, the meditator has also (temporarily) relinquished (*vineyya*) desires and ill will (*abhijjhādomanassaṃ*) concerning the world (*loke*).[29] Then, in the last section, the *sutta* outlines the development and cultivation of the seven factors of awakening (*bojjhaṅga*), that is, mindfulness (*sati*), investigation of *dhamma* (*dhammavicaya*), energy (*viriya*), joy (*pīti*), tranquility (*passaddhi*), concentration (*samādhi*) and equanimity (*upekkhā*). When these are fully accomplished, true knowledge and deliverance (*vijjāvimutti*), that is, *nibbāna*, is achieved (*M* III, 88).[30] Mindfulness of breathing can thus be viewed as a method, aiming to accomplish the goal of the eightfold path, and is intrinsically linked to all the other seven components of the path, that is, to moral/ethical virtues through freedom from desire and aversion, to wisdom through clear comprehension, and to meditation through sustained effort, concentration and mindfulness.

In other words, when articulated through the structural cognitive model of the Pāli *Abhidhamma*,[31] the cognition of the breath, when accompanied by mindfulness, is wholesome or ethical. How can this linking be upheld and explained? In Theravāda *Abhidhamma* texts (particularly in the first book, the *Dhammasaṅgaṇi*), the fundamental components or conditions (*dhammas*), which are involved in the mental and physical phenomena experienced, are determined, specified, and classified into four categories: cognition (*citta*), mental concomitants (*cetasika*), materiality (*rūpa*), and *nibbāna*.[32] Cognition (*citta*), which is defined as "that which knows its object, which cognizes"(*As*, 63),[33] arises, from moment to moment, in conjunction with several mental concomitants (*cetasika*), which determine, mark and affect, *how* the object of cognition is experienced. Over fifty such mental concomitants (*cetasika*) are identified and classified from an ethical perspective, that is, in relation to wholesomeness (*kusala*), whether they lead toward or away from suffering, toward or away from *nibbāna*.[34] The mental concomitants (*cetasika*) and cognition (*citta*) are momentary phenomena, instantaneously arising and passing away.[35] In a given moment of cognition, the mental concomitants (*cetasika*) arise together with cognition (*citta*) in various groupings, depending on their compatibility. The concomitants are classified as ethically variable, unwholesome, or wholesome: the variable concomitants occur every moment, always within either the wholesome or unwholesome groupings (which are in turn mutually exclusive): if the wholesome grouping arises the unwholesome cannot arise in the same moment and vice versa. Mindfulness is listed as a wholesome concomitant (*cetasika*)[36] and is therefore compatible with other wholesome ones, such as trust, wisdom, and compassion, but not with unwholesome ones, such as anger, greed, and conceit; when mindfulness is present, unwholesome mental concomitants cannot simultaneously be present. Thus, the entire analysis of human cognitive processes in the *Abhidhamma* is underpinned by the primary aim of Buddhist teachings, that is, liberation from suffering, to be achieved through the cultivation of wisdom, which is firmly founded on ethics (i.e., the wholesome).

In the *Abhidhammattha Saṅgaha*, mindfulness (*sati*) is classified as one of the nineteen wholesome mental concomitants (*cetasika*), which arise together at every moment of wholesome cognition (*citta*).[37] When mindfulness of breathing occurs, the air is the object that cognition (*citta*) cognizes through the sense of touch, in a wholesome way: in this case, cognition of breath arises in conjunction with mindfulness (*sati*), which remembers to pay attention to the touch of the breath as well as guards the mind from unwholesome states. At the moment of breathing mindfully, the wholesome cognition arises in conjunction with other "universal" mental concomitants, such as peace (*passaddhi*), lightness (*lahutā*), gentleness (*mudutā*), trust (*saddhā*), mental balance (*tatramajjhattatā*), absence of greed (*alobha*), and absence of aversion (*adosa*) (*Dhs*, 9).[38] The presence of mindfulness is thus indicated by other wholesome mental concomitants (*cetasikas*) that arise together in a group. Importantly, when the "universal" wholesome concomitants arise together, they can facilitate and allow other wholesome mental components to join them, such as compassion (*karuṇā*), sympathetic joy (*muditā*), and wisdom (*paññā*) (*Dhs*, 54–55).

In other words, as stated in the *Ānāpānasatisutta*, when each breath is cognized in a wholesome way, mindfully, peacefully and steadily, with clear understanding, having abandoned ill will and craving, the seven factors of awakening can be accomplished and liberation attained. Hence mindfulness of breathing is equated to "purity of virtue in the sense of restraint, purity of cognition in the sense of calm balance, and purity of view in the sense of insight" (*Patis* I, 184).[39] To summarize, in Buddhist discourse, mindfulness of breathing is intrinsically interrelated to ethical conduct, wholesome and peaceful mental states, and wisdom, that is, an insight that all *dhammas* are impermanent and empty of self (*M* 1, 230; *S* III, 133), which prompts conditions for liberation, *nibbāna*.

Mindfulness of Breathing and Ethics

In this chapter, the word "ethics" has been used to render the Pāli term *sīla*, meaning "character, habit, behavior, moral practice, good character, Buddhist ethics, code of morality" (*PED*, s.v.). In the Buddhist teachings, there are no exactly equivalent terms for ethics as Western discourse understands it (i.e., an independent branch of philosophy), nor, as mentioned earlier, is there a particular word or concept in the Pāli language for religion or philosophy. However, as pointed out by Keown, Buddhism provides a "systematic exposition of the normative ethical principles in terms of how the noble life should be led. The urgency now is for implementation rather than further speculation."[40] Thus "ethics" is used in this chapter with the sense of the Buddhist definition of wholesome and unwholesome cognition, which conditions wholesome or unwholesome behavior, respectively, leading toward or away from *nibbāna*.

Although Buddhism did not develop ethics as a separate theoretical discourse in a way that matches Western categorization, it may be argued that ethics underpins and is implied in all its main theoretical models, such as the four truths, the formula of dependent origination, the *Abhidhamma* analysis of cognition, all of them being grounded on the three postulated characteristics of all phenomena, that is, impermanence, nonsatisfactoriness, and nonself. This chapter seeks to clarify the idea that Buddhist ethical teachings are directly related to the notion of nonself (in conjunction with an insight into impermanence and nonsatisfactoriness), which establishes the fundamental premise for situating and actuating *sīla*, that is, wholesome, skillful, ethical speech, action, and livelihood. Buddhist teachings postulate that when insight into the absence of a permanent, separate intrinsic self is realized or, in other words, when wisdom (*paññā*) arises, the interconnectedness and interdependence of all the phenomena (within oneself and the entire cosmos) are understood. At this point, greed (*lobha*), aversion (*dosa*), delusion (*moha*), and other unwholesome mental concomitants cannot arise, since (by definition) they are not compatible with wisdom. Consequently thoughts, speech, and actions are then ethical, since they are founded on the absence of the notion "I am," or a separate entity. In other words, ethical conduct is at once the foundation of, as well as the result of, wisdom, which is viewed as the portal to *nibbāna*. Ethical problems are thus dissolved at the end of the Theravādin Buddhist soteriological path, since after awakening or reaching *arahatship*, nonethical states simply cannot occur any longer.

In this context, mindful breathing is ethical; it arises with wholesome qualities, or, if articulated in the language of the *Abhidhamma*, with wholesome mental concomitants (*cetasika*) among which three are concerned with the ethical aspect (*sīla*) of the eightfold path: right speech (*sammā-vācā*), right action (*sammā kammanta*), and right livelihood (*sammā ājīva*). Breath is thus perceived as an agency for mindfulness to create conditions for ethical development, which, in turn, is a foundation for soteriological knowledge or an understanding that the human body and mind and the entire cosmos are interdependent. This echoes the earliest Brahmānical vision of interlinked and interrelated micro- and macrocosms, connected through breathing, perceived as a soteriological vehicle.

Mindfulness of breathing is thus positioned as a precondition for an understanding of the interconnectedness of all mental and physical phenomena within and without. This may be indicated also in the recurring refrain of the *Satipaṭṭhānasutta*, which instructs that mindfulness is practiced in three modes: internally (*ajjhattaṃ*), or externally (*bahiddhā*), or internally and externally (*ajjhattabahiddhā*) (M I, 56–58; D II, 292–298). As I have discussed elsewhere,[41] these three modes may be interpreted in several ways. According to Buddhaghosa, an important Theravādin commentator presumably from the fifth century CE, mindfulness of breathing internally (*ajjhattaṃ*) would refer to one's own breathing (*attano*), externally (*bahiddhā*) to breathing of another (*parassa*), and internally and externally (*ajjhattabahiddhā*) alternatively to oneself and another (*kālena attano, kālena parassa*) (Ps I, 252, 270–273, 279–280, 286–287). A different interpretation, found only in one text in the Pāli canon, the *Satipaṭṭhānavibhaṅga* (Vibh, 194), interprets that mindful breathing internally and externally would mean experiencing "there is breathing," without reference to oneself or to any other, which may indicate that contemplation of breath takes place in conjunction with insight into nonself (*anattā*). The commentary on this passage, the *Sammohavinodanī* (Vibh-a, 261), further elaborates that contemplation takes place in reference neither to one's own body (*na attano kāyo*) nor another's (*na parass'eva kāyo*). This would mean that breathing is taking place mindfully with full cognizance or understanding of interdependence, within and without, and as discussed earlier, in conjunction with other wholesome (ethical) qualities, such as lightness, peace, trust, kindness, friendliness, love, compassion, and wisdom.

Among these qualities, love (*mettā*) has a special place in Buddhist tradition, and some comments are needed to situate it in this context. Meditation on love or loving kindness (*mettā*) has been one of the most popular meditation practices across the Buddhist world. The Pāli term *mettā* refers to "love, amity, sympathy, friendliness" (*PED*, s.v.); it is most commonly translated into English as "loving kindness."[42] In the Pāli canon, *mettā* is defined as the quality in beings which is "love, loving, friendliness, state of loving kindness, mental freedom" (*Vibh*, 86, 272; *Dhs*, 1056),[43] and equated with absence of anger (*adosa*) (*Dhs*, 188–189). This means, in the *Abhidhamma* analysis, that *mettā*, if interpreted as nonhatred (*adosa*), is a mental concomitant that occurs in all wholesome mental states, together with mindfulness. Hence, meditation on loving kindness is implicitly linked to mindfulness, wisdom, and the development of the seven factors of awakening (*S* V, 119–121). When there is absence of anger, it is presumed that one's thoughts, speech, and actions can be motivated by loving kindness. Likewise, the absence of greed implies generosity, the absence of delusion, and wisdom; once negative qualities are removed, one's thoughts, speech, and action can be wholesome, ethical.

Meditation on loving kindness is one of the four interrelated meditation practices, the so-called "divine abidings" (*brahmavihārās*).[44] The practice of *mettā* cultivates benevolence, kindness, and love, comparing it, in the *Mettāsutta* (*Sn*, 25–26), to the love of a mother for her only child, directed equally to all beings, boundlessly, without barriers, in all directions (*Vism*, 307). It is frequently stated in the Pāli canon, that loving kindness meditation abolishes anger (*A* I, 4) and resentment (*A* III, 189), motivates wholesome, kind, ethical thoughts, speech and action, and is a foundation for development of wisdom and ultimate liberation (*M* I, 351; *Sn*, 26), thus it is presented, similarly to mindfulness of breathing, as a soteriological method in its own right.

Loving kindness is proposed as a foundation for relating to all beings in a harmonious and wholesome way (*M* I, 207), from an ethical stance. Buddhist texts also propose such a relationship in the form of a noble friend, *kalyāṇamitta* (*SN*, 45.2), usually translated as a "good companion, virtuous friend, honest friend, a spiritual friend or adviser" (*PED*, s.v.).[45] The Pāli adjective *kalyāṇa* refers to "beautiful, auspicious, helpful, morally good," and *mitta* (Sanskrit *mitra*) to "friend" (*PED*, s.v.), the latter is a very important notion, already present in the earliest Indian and other Indo-European sources.[46] The word for friend (*mitta*) is defined in the *Sammohavinodanī* as one "who is lovingly friendly" (*Vibh-a*, 108),[47] thus linking it to loving kindness, *mettā*, which itself is an abstract noun derived from the word *mitta*. Having good friends (*kalyāṇamittatā*) is explained as associating with people "who have trust, virtue, are learned, generous and wise" (*Dhs*, 228).[48] The qualities of a good friend listed in the texts include generosity, forgiveness, forbearance, guarding others' secrets, and not deserting friends in trouble (*A* IV, 31).

In the Pāli canon, *kalyāṇamitta*, in the sense of spiritual friend, is a pivotal component of the Buddhist soteriological path. In words ascribed to the Buddha, a good friend, a virtuous companion, a spiritual guide represents the entire soteriological path (*S* V, 2),[49] and is essential for cultivation of the eightfold path

(*S* V, 3) and the seven factors of awakening (*S* V, 78). The term good friend (*kalyāṇamitta*) frequently refers to a meditation teacher, the Buddha himself being an example *par excellence*, who can guide, teach, inspire, and encourage meditators in their practice; hence, it is positioned in the center of Buddhist soteriological path.

To conclude, in this chapter, interrelated links were proposed—supported by textual evidence from the Pāli canon—among some of the key components of the Buddhist soteriological structure, namely, mindfulness of breathing, ethics, wisdom, liberation from suffering, love, kindness, and loving friendship. These interconnections are relevant for the ethical dilemmas of today and may inform, inspire, as well as, undoubtedly, require further exploration of the proposition that breathing mindfully is an ethical gesture, opening space for love, friendliness, and wisdom.

Abbreviations

Abbreviations and the quotation system of Pāli sources follow the *Critical Pāli Dictionary* (Epilegomena to vol. 1, 1948, pp. 5–36, and vol. 3, 1992, pp. II–VI). The numbers in the quotations of Pāli sources refer to the volume and page of the PTS edition (e.g., *M* I 21 refers to the *Majjhimanikāya*, vol. I, p. 21).

A   *Aṅguttaranikāya*. 5 vols. Edited by Richard Morris and Edmund Hardy. London: Pali Text Society, 1885–1900. Reprint. London: Pali Text Society, 1999–2013.

As   *Atthasālinī*. 1897. Edited by Edward Müller, revised by Lance Selwyn Cousins. London: Pali Text Society, 2011.

AitĀ   *The Aitareya Āraṇyaka*. Edited and translated by Arthur Berriedale Keith. Oxford: Clarendon Press, 1909.

BU   *Bṛhadāraṇyaka Upaniṣad*. In Patrick Olivelle, *The Early Upaniṣads: Annotated Text and Translation*, 29–165. New York and Oxford: Oxford University Press, 1998.

D   *Dīghanikāya*. 3 vols. Edited by Thomas William Rhys Davids and Joseph Edwards Carpenter. London: Pali Text Society, 1890–1911. Reprint. London: Pali Text Society, 1995–2007.

Dhs   *Dhammasaṅgaṇi*. Edited by Edward Müller. London: Pali Text Society, 1885. Reprint. London: Pali Text Society, 2001.

M   *Majjhimanikāya*. 3 vols. Edited by Vilhelm Trenckner and Robert Chalmers. London: Pali Text Society, 1888–1902. Reprint. London: Pali Text Society, 2013.

MW   Monier-Williams, Monier. *A Sanskrit-English Dictionary*. Oxford: Oxford University Press, 1899. Reprint. Delhi: Motilal Banarsidass, 1988.

Patis   *Paṭisambhidāmagga*. 2 vols. Edited by Arnold Charles Taylor. London: Pali Text Society, 1905, 1907. Reprint. London: Pali Text Society, 1979.

PED   *Pāli-English Dictionary.* Thomas William Rhys Davids and William Stede. London: Pali Text Society, 1921–1925.

Ps   *Papañcasūdanī, Majjhimanikāyāṭṭhakathā* of Buddhaghosa. 5 vols. Edited by J. H. Woods, D. Kośambi, and I. B. Horner. London: Pali Text Society, 1922–1938. Reprint. London: Pali Text Society, 1976–1979.

RV   *Die Hymnen des Ṛgveda.* 2 vols. Edited by Theodor Aufrecht. Bonn: A. Marcus, 1877. Reprint. Darmstadt: Wissenschaftliche Buchgesellschaft, 1955.

S   *Saṃyuttanikāya.* 5 vols. 1884–1898. Edited by Léon Feer. London: Pali Text Society, 1975–2006.

Sn   *Suttanipāta.* Edited by Dines Andersen and Helmer Smith. London: Pali Text Society, 1913. Reprint. London: Pali Text Society, 1990.

Vibh   *Vibhaṅga.* Edited by Caroline Augusta Foley Rhys Davids. London: Pali Text Society, 1904. Reprint. London: Pali Text Society, 2003.

Vibh-a *Sammohavinodanī.* 1923. Edited by A.P. Buddhadatta. PTS. 1980.

Vism   *Visuddhimagga.* Edited by Caroline Augusta Foley Rhys Davids. London: Pali Text Society, 1920–1921. Reprint. London: Pali Text Society, 1975.

W RV   Grassmann, Hermann. *Wörterbuch zum Rig-Veda.* Leipzig: F.A. Brockhaus, 1873. Reprint. Delhi: Motilal Banarsidass, 1999.

Notes

1. All translations from Pāli and Sanskrit are by the author.

2. In the *Ṛgveda,* the word *prāṇa* mainly signifies "breath, life breath" (*W RV,* s.v.), but in later Sanskrit texts, its semantic spectrum broadens, referring to "respiration, vital air, vitality, life energy, spirit, power" (MW, s.v.).

3. Michael Witzel, "The Development of the Vedic Canon and its Schools: The Social and Political Milieu," in *Inside the Texts, Beyond the Texts,* ed. Michael Witzel (Cambridge, MA: Department of Sanskrit and Indian Studies, Harvard University, 1997), 263.

4. *RV* 10.129.1a: *nāsad āsīn nó sád āsīt.*

5. *RV* 10.129.2c: *ānīd avātáṃ svadháyā tád ékam.*

6. For a detailed analysis of this hymn, see Joanna Jurewicz, *Fire and Cognition in the Ṛgveda* (Warszawa: Elipsa, 2010), 44–59.

7. *RV* 10.90.13d: *prāṇād vāyúr ajāyata.*

8. AitĀ 3.1.6: *vāk prāṇena saṃhitā. prāṇaḥ pavamānena pavamāno viśvair-devairviśve devāḥ svargeṇa lokena svargo loko brahmaṇā saiṣāvaraparā saṃhitā.*

9. In studies of ancient Indian discourse we generally use terms such as "religion" and "philosophy," however, there are no exact equivalents for these concepts in ancient Indian languages such as Pāli and Sanskrit. Consequently, the problems around the translation of ancient Indian sources (linguistic and cultural), and especially their key philosophical concepts, into modern Western languages, remain seriously problematic in modern scholarship.

10. Cf. Joanna Jurewicz, "Playing with Fire: The *pratītyasamutpāda* from the Perspective of Vedic Thought," *The Journal of the Pali Text Society* 26 (2000): 77–105.

11. Patrick Olivelle, *The Early Upaniṣads: Annotated Text and Translation* (New York and Oxford: Oxford University Press, 1998), 12–13.

12. *BU* 1.3.23: *prāṇena hīdaṃ sarvamuttabdham.*

13. *BU* 3.9.9: *prāṇa iti. sa brahma tyadityācakṣate.*

14. Johannes Bronkhorst, *The Two Traditions of Meditation in Ancient India* (Delhi: Motilal Banarsidass, 1993).

15. Johannes Bronkhorst, *The Two sources of Indian Asceticism* (Delhi: Motilal Banarsidass, 1998); Padmanabh S. Jaini, "Śramaṇas: Their Conflict with Brāhmaṇical Society," in *Collected Papers on Buddhist Studies*, ed. Padmanabh S. Jaini (Delhi: Motilal Banarsidass, 2001), 47–96.

16. Gerald James Larson, "An Old Problem Revisited: The Relation between Samkhya, Yoga and Buddhism," *Studien zur Indologie und Iranistik 15* (1989), 129–46; Ian Whicher, *The Integrity of the Yoga Darsana: A Reconsideration of Classical Yoga* (Albany: State University of New York Press, 1998).

17. For a comprehensive history of yoga and tantra, see Geoffrey Samuel, *The Origins of Yoga and Tantra: Indic Religions to the Thirteenth Century* (Cambridge: Cambridge University Press, 2008).

18. The textual history of early Indian traditions, especially for the BCE era, is very problematic and uncertain. For dating of the historical Buddha, see Heinz Bechert, *The Dating of the Historical Buddha. Die Datierung des historischen Buddha*, 3 vols. (Göttingen: Vandenhoeck and Ruprecht, 1991–1997).

19. Since from here onward the discussions are related to the Pāli canon, all the technical terms will be given in Pāli (mostly in parentheses).

20. *A* I 30: *Ekadhammo bhikkhave bhāvito bahulīkato ekantanibbidāya virāgāya nirodhāya upasamāya abhiññāya sambodhāya nibbānāya saṃvattati.*

21. *PED* (s.v.) "memory, recognition, wakefulness, mindfulness, alertness, lucidity."

22. For the meanings of *sati*, see Rupert Gethin, "On some definitions of mindfulness," *Contemporary Buddhism* 12, no. 1 (2011): 263–279; "Buddhist Conceptualizations of Mindfulness," in *Handbook of Mindfulness Theory, Research, and Practice*, ed. Kirk Warren Brown et al. (New York and London: Guilford Press, 2015), 9–41.

23. The adjective *kusala* refers to "virtuous, skillful, good, right" (*PED*, s.v.), commonly used to mark things that are wholesome, i.e., appropriate for or conducive to attainment of liberation from suffering (*dukkha*).

24. For a detailed discussion on presentations of mindfulness (*sati*) within the fundamental models of Buddhist discourse in the Pāli canon, see Tamara Ditrich, "Situating the Concept of Mindfulness in the Theravāda Tradition," *Asian Studies* 4, no. 2 (2016), 13–33.

25. The term *sammā* is rendered into English as "thoroughly, properly, in the right way, perfectly" (*PED*, s.v.), indicating appropriateness for achieving awakening.

26. The three characteristics are impermanence (*anicca*), nonsatisfactoriness (*dukkha*), and nonself (*anattā*).

27. For the English translation and traditional commentaries, see Ñāṇamoli, *Mindfulness of Breathing (Ānāpānasati)* (Kandy: Buddhist Publication Society, 1998).

28. *M* III, 83: *ātāpī sampajāno satimā, vineyya loke abhijjhādomanassaṃ*. Cf. *M* I, 56; *D* II, 290.

29. The world (*loka*) refers to the body, the feelings, the mind, and phenomena (*Ps* I 244) or, in other words, to the five aggregates of clinging (*Vibh* 195).

30. Similarly, the *Satipaṭṭhānasutta* (*M* I, 55–63; *D* II, 290–315) starts with mindfulness of breathing and ends with the seven factors of awakening, which lead to liberation.

31. The *Abhidhamma* (Pāli) is a collection of texts, usually dated in the third century BCE, which encompass, in terms of Western categories, philosophy, ethics, and psychology. The term *Abhidharma* (Sanskrit) is used to refer to the parallel teachings of non-Theravāda schools.

32. Bodhi, trans., *Abhidhammattha Saṅgaha: A Comprehensive Manual of Abhidhamma: Pali Text, Translation and Explanatory Guide* (Kandy: Buddhist Publication Society, 1993), 25.

33. As, 63: *Cittanti ārammaṇaṃ cintetīti cittaṃ vijānātīti attho.*

34. Thus the first book, the *Dhammasaṅgaṇi*, introduces in its very first sentence the overall topic and aim of the *Abhidhamma* through the question: "Which *dhammas* are wholesome or ethically skillful (*kusala*)?" (*Dhs*, 9: *katame dhammā kusalā?*)

35. Cf. Alexander von Rospatt, *The Buddhist Doctrine of Momentariness: A Survey of the Origins and Early Phase of this Doctrine up to Vasubandhu*. Stuttgart: F. Steiner Verlag, 1995.

36. Other schools, such as the Sarvāstivāda, position mindfulness both with skillful or unskillful cognition. However, right mindfulness is always viewed as wholesome.

37. Bodhi, *Abhidhammattha Saṅgaha*, 79.

38. Ibid.

39. *Paṭis* I 184: *saṃvaraṭṭhena sīlavisuddhi, avikkhepaṭṭhena cittavisuddhi, dassanaṭṭhena diṭṭhivisuddhi.*

40. Damien Keown, *The Nature of Buddhist Ethics* (New York: Palgrave, 1992), 2–3.

41. Tamara Ditrich, "Interpretations of the Terms *ajjhattaṃ* and *bahiddhā*: From the Pāli *Nikāyas* to the *Abhidhamma*," in *Text, History and Philosophy: Abhidharma across Buddhist Scholastic Traditions*, ed. Bart Dessein and Weijen Teng (Leiden and Boston: Brill, 2016), 108–145.

42. For a comprehensive study of *mettā*, see Harvey B. Aronson, *Love and Sympathy in Theravāda Buddhism* (Delhi: Motilal Banarsidass, 2008); Mudagamuwe Maithrimurthi, *Wohlwollen, Mitleid, Freude und Gleichmut* (Stuttgart: F. Steiner Verlag, 1999), 47–113.

43. *Vibh* 86: *metti mettāyanā mettāyitattaṃ mettā cetovimutti.*

44. The four divine abidings (*brahmavihārās*), which are probably of pre-Buddhist origin (*D* II, 250; *M* II, 76; *S* V, 115–121), encompass loving kindness (*mettā*); compassion (*karuṇā*), aiming to remove suffering of others; sympathetic joy (*muditā*), rejoicing at another's happiness; and equanimity (*upekkhā*) as a balanced even-mindedness.

45. For a detailed discussion of this term, see Steven Collins, "Kalyāṇamitta and Kalyāṇamittatā," *Journal of the Pali Text Society* 11 (1987): 51–72.

46. For the Vedic notion of *mitra*, see Jan Gonda, *The Vedic God Mitra* (Leiden: E.J. Brill, 1972); and for etymological links to Tocharian words for friendship, see Georges-Jean Pinault, "Tocharian Friendship," in *Evidence and Counter-Evidence. Essays in honour of Frederik Kortlandt*, ed. Alexander Lubotsky et al. (Amsterdam and New York: Rodopi, 2008), 431–451.

47. *Vibh-a*, 108: *mettāyantīti mittā*.

48. *Dhs*, 228: *ye te puggalā saddhā sīlavanto bahussutā cāgavanto paññāvanto*.

49. *S V*, 2: *sakalam eva hidam Ānanda brahmacariyaṃ yad idaṃ kalyāṇamittatā kalyāṇasahāyatā kalyāṇasampavaṅkatā*.

Bibliography

Aronson, Harvey B. *Love and Sympathy in Theravāda Buddhism*. Delhi: Motilal Banarsidass, 1980. Reprint. Delhi: Motilal Banarsidass, 2008.

Bechert, Heinz. *The Dating of the Historical Buddha. Die Datierung des historischen Buddha*. 3 vols. Göttingen: Vandenhoeck and Ruprecht, 1991–1997.

Bodhi, trans. *Abhidhammattha Saṅgaha: A Comprehensive Manual of Abhidhamma: Pali Text, Translation and Explanatory Guide*. Kandy: Buddhist Publication Society, 1993.

Bronkhorst, Johannes. *The Two Sources of Indian Asceticism*. 2nd edition. Delhi: Motilal Banarsidass, 1998.

Bronkhorst, Johannes. *The Two Traditions of Meditation in Ancient India*. Delhi: Motilal Banarsidass, 1993.

Collins, Steven. "Kalyāṇamitta and Kalyāṇamittatā." *Journal of the Pali Text Society* 11 (1987): 51–72.

Ditrich, Tamara. "Intepretations of the Terms *ajjhattaṃ* and *bahiddhā*: from the Pāli *Nikāyas* to the *Abhidhamma*." In *Text, History and Philosophy: Abhidharma across Buddhist Scholastic Traditions*, edited by Bart Dessein and Weijen Teng, 108–145. Leiden and Boston: Brill, 2016.

Ditrich, Tamara. "Situating the Concept of Mindfulness in the Theravāda Tradition." *Asian Studies* 4, no. 2 (2016): 13–33.

Gethin, Rupert. "Buddhist Conceptualizations of Mindfulness." In *Handbook of Mindfulness Theory, Research, and Practice*, edited by Kirk Warren Brown, J. David Creswell, and Richard M. Ryan, 9–41. New York and London: Guilford Press, 2015.

Gethin, Rupert. "On Some Definitions of Mindfulness." *Contemporary Buddhism* 12, no. 1 (2011): 263–279.

Gonda, Jan. *The Vedic God Mitra*. Orientalia Rheno-Traiectina, Vol. 30. Leiden: E.J. Brill, 1972.

Jaini, Padmanabh S. "Śramaṇas: Their Conflict with Brāhmaṇical Society." In *Collected Papers on Buddhist Studies*, edited by Padmanabh S. Jaini, 47–96. Delhi: Motilal Banarsidass, 2001.

Jurewicz, Joanna. *Fire and Cognition in the Ṛgveda*. Warszawa: Elipsa, 2010.

Jurewicz, Joanna. "Playing with Fire: The *pratītyasamutpāda* from the Perspective of Vedic Thought." *The Journal of the Pali text Society* 26 (2000): 77–105.

Keown, Damien. *The Nature of Buddhist Ethics*. New York: Palgrave, 1992.

Larson, Gerald James. "An Old Problem Revisited: The Relation between Samkhya, Yoga and Buddhism." *Studien zur Indologie und Iranistik* 15 (1989): 129–146.

Maithrimurthi, Mudagamuwe. *Wohlwollen, Mitleid, Freude und Gleichmut: eine ideengeschichtliche Untersuchung der vier apramāṇas in der buddhistischen Ethik und Spiritualität von den Anfängen bis hin zum frühen Yogācāra*. Stuttgart: F. Steiner Verlag, 1999.

Ñāṇamoli, trans. *Mindfulness of Breathing (Ānāpānasati): Buddhist Texts from the Pāli Canon and Extracts from the Pāli Commentaries*. 6th ed. Kandy: Buddhist Publication Society, 1998.

Olivelle, Patrick. *The Early Upaniṣads: Annotated Text and Translation*. New York and Oxford: Oxford University Press, 1998.

Pinault, Georges-Jean. "Tocharian Friendship." In *Evidence and Counter-Evidence. Essays in honour of Frederik Kortlandt*, edited by Alexander Lubotsky, Jos Schaeken, and Jeroen Wiedenhof, 431–451. Studies in Slavic and General Linguistics, Vol. 32. Amsterdam and New York: Rodopi, 2008.

Rospatt, Alexander von. *The Buddhist Doctrine of Momentariness: A Survey of the Origins and Early Phase of this Doctrine up to Vasubandhu*. Stuttgart: F. Steiner Verlag, 1995.

Samuel, Geoffrey. *The Origins of Yoga and Tantra: Indic Religions to the Thirteenth Century*. Cambridge: Cambridge University Press, 2008.

Whicher, Ian. *The Integrity of the Yoga Darsana: A Reconsideration of Classical Yoga*. SUNY Series in Religious Studies. Albany: State University of New York Press, 1988.

Witzel, Michael. "The Development of the Vedic Canon and its Schools: The Social and Political Milieu." In *Inside the Texts, Beyond the Texts*, edited by Michael Witzel, 257–345. Cambridge, MA: Department of Sanskrit and Indian Studies, Harvard University, 1997.

7

Inspiration and Expiration

Yoga Practice through Merleau-Ponty's Phenomenology of the Body

JAMES MORLEY

Introduction

This essay offers an interpretation of yoga practice of *prāṇāyāma* (breath control) that is influenced by the existential phenomenology of Merleau-Ponty.[1] My approach to yoga will be less concerned with comparison between Merleau-Ponty's thought and the texts of classical yoga than with the elucidation of the actual experience of breath control through the constructs provided by Merleau-Ponty's philosophy of the lived-body. The academic discussion of yoga can answer certain pedagogical goals, but it can never finally be severed from *doing* yoga. Academic discourse centered entirely on the theoretical concepts of yoga philosophies must to some extent remain incomplete. Patanajali's *Yoga Sūtra* is itself a manual of practice. It is for this reason that I have chosen to take as the basis of my study the commentary of the scholar-practitioner T.K.V. Desikachar, rather than a more exclusively theoretical commentary. In so doing, I have approached yoga as an experience or phenomenon and not only in the context of a series of academic debates.

While comparisons between yoga and phenomenology have been made, these studies have taken a different direction from the present study. Earlier comparative studies have been concerned with the thought of Merleau-Ponty's philosophical predecessor, Edmund Husserl, and the consonance between the transcendental aspects of his earlier thought and that of the more idealist schools of classical yoga.[2] While I will not contest the validity of these comparisons, I wish to offer another perspective on the yoga-phenomenology comparison that is less idealistic and more existential or concretely psychological in orientation. Thus, I shall proceed to show how this other version of phenomenology can make a fruitful contribution toward providing a framework from within the Western philosophical tradition for understanding the practice of breath-oriented yoga, just as transcendental phenomenology has already provided a means for establishing common conceptual grounds.

Summary of Conceptual Concurrences between Classical Yoga Concepts and Transcendental Phenomenology

Phenomenology in general seeks to comprehend the perceived or lived world prior to metaphysical categorizations. This is made possible by a method of radical reflection that is widely known as the "phenomenological reduction" or *epoché*, perhaps best explained as an absolute suspension of belief, doubt, or any kind of presupposition about the existence of the world and its objects. Earlier comparative studies of yoga and phenomenology have rightly stressed this particular aspect of phenomenology, first set out in Husserl's early published writings, as convergent with yogic meditative practices. Certain aspects of the yoga literature show a consonance with the *epoché* of transcendental phenomenology; this is especially evident in Patañjali's *Yoga Sūtra* where the Sanskrit term *nirodaha* can be shown to closely approach Husserl's *epoché*. Patañjali's classic summary of yoga as *citta vṛtti nirodha* roughly translates as "Yoga is the suspension (*nirodha*) of the fluctuations (*vṛtti*) of thought (*citta*)." Thus, *nirodha* is a rigorous meditation technique the goal of which is a purified perception (*puruṣa*) untainted by mental conditioning or habits such as present passions, future desires, or past impressions (*karma*). Nirodha is the route to attaining a pure consciousness (*samādhi*) that lies beyond the psychological mind (*citta*) and envelopes the division between perceiver and perceived.[3] As pure self-evident knowledge, *samādhi* can be occupied only by the practitioner but never described, for to do so would be to turn the experience into an object and hence distort its meaning. In a remarkably similar manner, Husserl distinguishes the "hidden 'I'" of transcendental subjectivity from the psychological ego still immersed within the subject-object bifurcation.[4] Like Patañjali, he advocates a transformation of the mental structures that inhibit clear perception in order to develop a reflexive "witness consciousness" toward our own process of perceiving the world. Built into both approaches is the ideal of a pure consciousness that remains as a residue of this methodological cleansing process: an *a priori* or pure subjectivity distinct from an external objective world.

Existential Phenomenology: The Critique of Pure Subjectivity

"Existential" phenomenology appeared through Heidegger's critique of the idea of a "pure subjectivity" cast in binary opposition to a "pure materiality."[5] Rejecting the convention in Western thought to think in terms of binary antonyms, Heidegger asserted that there can be no subjectivity apart from the world or, to put it another way: it is the *relation* between subject and world that is prior to their categorical division. Individual human beings are immersed within and arise out of existence generally. Heidegger's concept of *Dasein* (literally "there-being"), typically translated as "being-in-the-world," is that of a historically situated existence aware of itself as existing in a finite temporal horizon, that is, toward death. As a development of Husserl's earlier phenomenology of primarily transcendental subjectivity, Heidegger's *Dasein* is always already "in and of" the world. Hence, in existential phenomenology, human existence is adhered to the world, neither an internality nor an externality, subject nor object, but a spatiotemporal openness. Merleau-Ponty's contribution was to tighten the concept of *Dasein* through an existential-phenomenological rehabilitation of the human body.[6]

Merleau-Ponty's Conception of the Lived Body

Building on Husserl and Heidegger's revision of subjectivity as a self-world *relation* rather than a consciousness *apart* from the world, Merleau-Ponty focused on the "zero point" of this relation: the lived body *is* this relation, which he shows to be the precategorical ground sought by Husserl and Heidegger, that crosses subjectivity and objectivity. Merleau-Ponty highlights human sensory experience as emblematic of all metaphysical antonyms such as subject and object or interiority and exteriority. His term *sens* connotes both "sense experience" and "meaning." The lived body, in contrast to the medical or physical body, grounds personal life as well as the impersonal or objective dimension of nature of which it is a participant. "Now we must think of the human body [. . .] as that which perceives nature which it also inhabits."[7] The lived body is the embodied consciousness, a nexus between the twin roles of active agent of perception and the passive object of perception by others. The nexus may not be separated into subject and object or self and world, but is an irreducible foundation.

   Although we will remain with the term "lived body" for the purposes of this paper, it should be mentioned here that in his final work, *The Visible and the Invisible*, Merleau-Ponty adopts the term "flesh" to express the continuity between the surface and depth of the world and that of the body. The "lived body" of the earlier writings is recast as "flesh" in the later work, to capture its primordial or elemental character. Flesh contains the ambiguous interplay between subject and object, internal and external. Merleau-Ponty's new phrase "flesh-of-the-world" deliberately replaces Heidegger's "being-in-the-world," where the philosophical term "being" is not only laden with centuries of tradition but is itself an abstract and overly intellectualized term. "Flesh," on the other hand, better serves Merleau-Ponty's goal of bringing philosophy "down to earth;"[8] it captures the intimate, personal, embodied character of human life. To Merleau-Ponty, flesh is a way of describing not only the body, but the basic substance of the world. Rather than describing the body in terms of inanimate material elements, he turns convention around to view the external world in terms of the body's elemental corporeality.[9] Where "body" could suggest a complex system, "flesh" (*chair*) better expresses an elemental, raw dimension that is a crossing point between subject and object, body and world.

The Lived Body and Yoga

A concept of the lived body that refuses subject-object distinctions is especially relevant for the experience of yoga. Yoga not only affirms the existence of the external world, but employs the perceptual relation between the self and the world as the means of meditation practice. Control of the body is equated with the mastery of external nature, and this control is achieved through focusing the senses. The focus on sense experience grants primacy to the body. The body is understood as a microcosm of the external universe, or in Eliade's terms, the goal of yoga is to achieve a cosmic "homology" between the body and the world.[10] Breath control is the emblem or master metaphor of this goal.[11] The central place of the body in the theory and practice of yoga suggests a comparison with Merleau-Ponty's thesis of the primacy of the body and could serve as a point of mutual clarification.

Our habitual tendency, in our awareness of our bodies, is to separate the "outer" body in contact with the external world, from the "inner" body, that which we carry around inside ourselves. Such a separation tends to an alienation that we habitually experience in relation to our bodies. The objects of external sense become the focus of our experience, so that we tend to privilege that aspect of our body that is accessible to the external observer perspective. We think of ourselves in terms of our mirror images, that is, as images observable from an external point of view. Correspondingly, our perception is alienated from the sentient mass of our bodies, which is relegated to the margins of our ordinary experience. *Prāṇāyāma*, or breath control, integral to the practice of yoga, prevails against this alienation: it is the concrete experience of the body as a *relation* between inside and outside. To breathe is to pull external air into ourselves and to rhythmically release outward something of ourselves. This simple experience, so common to us all, is brought into focus by yoga practice.

Proprioception is inverted perception, the perception of the deep tissues of the body, of enclosed or encircled corporeal space. When we fall ill or experience extraordinary body sensations, perception becomes directed to the source of discomfort. Ill health makes us acutely aware of our potential for perceptual inversion: perception directed inward to the hollow of the body, rather than outward to the world. Unfortunately, in the case of illness, this is such an unpleasant experience that we tend to "depersonalize" our bodies, distance ourselves or "defend" ourselves from the trauma of pain. The yogic practice of *prāṇāyāma*, on the contrary, gives us proprioception outside the context of illness. Through the practice of postures (*āsana*) together with *prāṇāyāma*, we develop an inverted sense of our muscles, tendons, heart valves, and lung cavities. We come to live the opening and closing of these corporeal zones as we do with external visible limbs. We experience the expansion of the chest in inhalation, the quickened tempo of the heart, and the blood's flow through the course of the arteries. We incorporate the autonomic nervous system into the realm of the voluntary. We note how the lungs change tide between breaths, and the movement of interior contraction as expiration moves outward only to pause between breaths before beginning the cycle again. In the context of *āsana-prāṇāyāma* we focus only on breathing rhythms; we take up what is involuntary and appropriate it into what Husserl would call "the sphere of ownness."[12] In psychoanalytic language, we "cathect," occupy, or inhabit the corporeal space that is otherwise habitually relegated to the zone of external nature. I am made aware of the body, habitually experienced as an "outer body" in contact with the external world, as being also an "inner body," not just occupying physical space, but as inhabited, psychical space.

The experience of *prāṇāyāma* points us to a central aspect of Merleau-Ponty's philosophy of the lived body, that is, his explication of interiority and exteriority. Used conventionally, terms like "outside" and "inside" are inimical to Merleau-Ponty's project of collapsing the subject-object distinctions, that is, to the view that the body and the world are a continuum: "where are we to put the limit between the body and the world, since the world is flesh?"[13] "Outside" and "inside" seem to imply the exactly rigid demarcation between the thing and the surrounding world that Merleau-Ponty is arguing against. At the same time, the terms "inside" and "outside" become semantically necessary when we engage with the body's spatiality. Merleau-Ponty's descriptive language of spatiality, depth, or dimension surmounts this difficulty by framing interiority and exteriority in a way distinct from the Newtonian concept of abstract space that is purged of subjectivity.

In traditional philosophy, space is used in relation to inorganic matter and not, as Merleau-Ponty uses it, to understand the experientially *full* space of sentient flesh. Merleau-Ponty's focus on the human body as a mass of consciously *occupied* flesh recasts the meaning of space. Mass is the continuum of interior and exterior that defines human embodiment. The enclosed space of the body is, almost in yogic terms, a homology *with* and microcosm *of* the world. This is exemplified in the phenomenon of sight. The perceiving or sentient body brings objects into visibility as much as it is itself brought into visibility by the seeing power of other sentient beings. Thus, the active power of seeing is also interwoven with one's passive enclosure within the world of visible things. Yet, to see a visible world is to also maintain a distance. Seeing and being seen are not collapsed into one another.

> It is that the thickness of the flesh between the seer and the thing is constitutive for the thing of its visibility as for the seer of his corporeity. [. . .] It is for the same reason that I am at the heart of the visible and that I am far from it: because it has thickness and is thereby naturally destined to be seen as a body.[14]

Here, Merleau-Ponty uses the words "thickness" and "corporeity" as synonyms for body space. He continues: "The thickness of the body, far from rivalling that of the world, is on the contrary the sole means I have to go into the heart of the things, by making myself a world and making them flesh."[15] The concept of "flesh" expresses, crucially, the idea of *difference within identity*. As much as the surface of my body differentiates me from the objects around me, this differentiation is what also permits an empathy with the surface of the objects. So it is with depth: my body's spatial configuration as an occupied, or inhabited closure, is itself the means through which I apprehend the depth of the objects and entities around me as co-enclosures. Corporeity, then, is not matter in the Newtonian sense, but is closer to the traditional concept of "element" such as earth, air, fire, and water that combine quality with substance. The body, not seen as matter, but as an exemplar sensible, allows the "outside" to be drawn entirely within it: "In any case, once a body-world relationship is recognized, there is a ramification of my body and a ramification of my world and a correspondence between its inside and my outside, between my inside and its outside."[16]

Merleau-Ponty's explication of interiority and exteriority is immediately relevant to the practice of *prāṇāyāma*, through which we experience exactly this correspondence. Strikingly, his use of the metaphor of breathing to explain the self-world relation precisely applies to the experience of *prāṇāyāma*. In his last published paper, "Eye and Mind," he writes, "[w]e speak of 'inspiration' and the word should be taken literally. There really is an inspiration and an expiration of Being."[17]

Yoga and Reversibility

To grasp fully the nature of the corporeity as a relation of inside and outside, we must turn to Merleau-Ponty's appropriation of gestalt psychology's conception of the figure-ground dynamic. The gestalt psychologists posit that all perception is bound within certain perceptual laws, the most primary being that of field phenomena or figure-ground. We focus on an object at the cost of losing our focus on its background. This background, however, never disappears. In fact, it sustains the form of the object. The background is present through *holding* the object or offering the *field* through which it may come into focus. Visibility is possible through its invisible field. The important point here is that the structure of figure and ground is itself a totality. Moreover, this totality can invert: we can switch, or reverse, the figure and ground back and forth at will. Reversibility is at the heart of the figure-ground relation and is fundamental to Merleau-Ponty's philosophical project; in particular, it is intrinsic to his understanding of the self-world relation. There is a "correspondence between" my body's inside and the outside of the world and, reversibly, between the interiority of the world and my body's exterior. "If one wants metaphors, it would be better to say that the body sensed and the body sentient are as the obverse and reverse,"[18] thus there is a reversible relation between the body as it actively senses and the body as it is passively sensed by the life around it. Merleau-Ponty takes from Husserl the term "interwoven" (*verflockten*) and "within one another" (*ineinander*) to preserve the distinction between sensing and being sensed while also maintaining the mutually constitutive relation between these active and passive aspects of the human body.

The notion of reversibility, of the active and passive aspects of the human body as co-constitutive, may be seen to underlie Desikachar's description of yoga practice. In his manual of yoga practice, Desikachar asks the practitioner to recall that "yoga is the practice of observing oneself without judgement"[19] and goes on to define yoga informally as "something we experience inside, deep within our being. Yoga is not an external experience."[20] It is distinguished from other arts performed before an audience because "[w]e do it only for ourselves. *We are both observer and what is observed at the same time.* If we do not pay attention to ourselves in our practice, then we cannot call it yoga."[21] The state of yoga is described by Desikachar not only in terms of the observing "witness consciousness" but also as "what is observed." The identity of the practitioner is not extracted from the observable but is experienced as a totality that joins the observer and the observed.

In a working note to *The Visible and the Invisible*, Merleau-Ponty writes, "[t]he true philosophy" is to "apprehend what makes the leaving of oneself be a retiring into oneself, and vice versa. Grasp this chiasm, this reversal. That is the mind."[22] In much the same vein, Desikachar observes, commenting on *Yoga Sūtra* 1.12, "The state of yoga is achieved by simultaneously striving (*abhyāsa*) and letting go (*vairāgya*)."[23] The yogic technique of *pratyahara*, translated by Desikachar as "to withdraw oneself from that which nourishes the senses," lends itself to comparison to the figure-ground process central to Merleau-Ponty's thesis. While the term *pratyāhāra* is literally construed in terms of withdrawal, in practicing *pratyāhāra,* we concentrate on one sense object (of any sense) to exclude external distractions or push them into the background. Through *pratyāhāra* one develops an ability to perform, in gestalt terms, a figure-ground switch between general world and single object. In the figure-ground relation, deliberately adopted by the practitioner, any point of focus will do (such as an image or sound), but breath is the most paradigmatic point of focus. In breath extension, I focus on breath to put the rest of the perceived world into the background. But in yoga I paradoxically withdraw my senses to achieve control over my sensory processes: I diminish my senses to strengthen them. My perception becomes heightened once I learn to withdraw perception. The classical yoga tradition calls this *ekāgratā* or "one pointedness" to describe this yogic concentration. Once accomplished, concentration is held and sustained (*dhāraṇā*) by holding the point of focus, and a link or relation is developed between self and object; this is meditation proper (*dhyāna*). The subject engages with the point of focus until he or she is joined with and assumes the position of the point of focus (*samādhi*).

Conclusion

At the beginning of this essay, I offered a brief summary of how the goal of yoga practice, pure consciousness or *samādhi,* may be approached through Husserl's transcendental phenomenology. Specifically, I mentioned the convergence between the concept of *samādhi* and Husserl's concept of transcendental subjectivity. But when considering the concrete yoga practices required for the attainment of *samādhi,* the key practice, *prāṇāyāma* foregrounds the body in a manner not sufficiently acknowledged in earlier Husserl scholarship, which has hitherto been the sole basis for the comparison of yoga and phenomenology. In this context, without rejecting Husserl, we might productively turn to Merleau-Ponty's development of Husserl's later thought from the unpublished manuscripts. Merleau-Ponty's more existentially oriented phenomenology, which develops Husserl's key concept of the lived body, manifests a concurrence with yoga practice that takes greater account of the central role of the body in that practice. His explication of interiority and exteriority and his thesis of reversibility resonate with the phenomenological descriptions of yogic *prāṇāyāma,* as exemplified in the writings of the scholar-practitioner T.K.V. Desikachar. The significance or value of the comparison between Merleau-Ponty's thought and yoga is not that it attempts to impose a Western philosophical framework for an established non-Western tradition: such an attempt would do less than justice to the integrity of the yoga tradition. Rather, I hope to establish, even through this brief study, that yogic breathwork is an important resource for phenomenologists undertaking future research in the ongoing project prescribed by Merleau-Ponty: namely, to bring Western thought "down to earth" by focusing on the lived human body as philosophical and psychological ground.

Notes

1. This chapter was previously published in *Philosophy East and West* 51, no. 1 (2001). I wish to thank Roger T. Ames, Editor-in-Chief of *Philosophy East and West* and the University of Hawaii Press for their kind permission to reprint this material. I also wish to thank the Indian National Institute of Advanced Studies, Bangalore, India, for the 1998 research fellowship that enabled me to begin this research. Thanks are particularly due to Dr. Sundar Sarukkai whose friendship made this research possible.

2. See A. Paranjpe and K. Hanson, "On Dealing with the Stream of Consciousness: A Comparison of Husserl and Yoga," in *Asian Contributions to Psychology*, ed. A. Paranjpe, D. Ho, and R. Rieber (New York: Praeger Publishers, 1988), 215–231; R. Puligandla, "Phenomenological Reduction and Yogic Meditation," *Philosophy East and West* 20 (1970): 19–33; Ramakant Sinari, "The Method of Phenomenological Reduction and Yoga," *Philosophy East and West* 15 (1965): 217–228. All of the above focus exclusively on the earlier writings of Husserl as the point of comparison between phenomenology and Patañjali's *Yoga Sūtra*.

3. See Ian Whicher, "Nirodaha, Yoga Praxis and the Transformation of the Mind," *Journal of Indian Philosophy* 25 (1997): 1–67. Whicher provides a detailed etymological and philosophical analysis of the term *nirodha*. In brief, he claims the conventional translation of *nirodha* as "stopping the mind" does not do justice to the subtlety of the term and to yoga philosophy and practice in general.

4. Edmund Husserl, "Phenomenology," in *Encyclopedia Britannica* 17 (1951), 701.

5. In Martin Heidegger, *Being and Time*, trans. John Macquarrie and Edward Robinson (New York: Harper & Row, 1962).

6. In the, at that time, less known text of *Ideas II*, which was only published in German in 1951 and translated into English in 1989, we can see how Husserl himself was always already focused on the lived body. He states that every object, real or imagined, is in some kind of spatiotemporal orientation to the perceiver's body. Only through the body does the world become real. "[. . .] all that is thingly real in the surrounding world of the ego has its relation to the body"; Edmund Husserl, *Ideas pertaining to a Pure Phenomenology and to a Phenomenological Philosophy*, bk. 2, *Studies in the Phenomenology of Constitution*, trans. R. Rojcewicz and A. Schuwer (Boston: Kluwer Academic Publishers, 1989), 61. He even goes so far as to say: "Furthermore, obviously connected with this is the distinction the body acquires as the bearer of the zero point of orientation, the bearer of the here and now, out of which the pure ego intuits space and the whole world of the senses. Thus each thing that appears has *eo ipso* an orienting relation to the body, and this refers not only to what actually appears but to each thing that is supposed to be able to appear"; ibid. Thus, for the later Husserl, even a fantasy exists in relation to the corporeal "zero point" that is "the bearer of the here and now." From this we can see how Husserl, if not already moving in this direction, was actually the inspiration to Merleau-Ponty's emphasis on embodiment grounded on corporeal experience. It is thus likely that the transcendental ego, which is the basis of the comparative studies cited above, was misunderstood as ever being separated from the life-world.

7. Maurice Merleau-Ponty, *Themes from the Lectures at the College de France: 1952–1960*, trans. John O'Neill (Evanston, IL: Northwestern University Press, 1970; original work published 1968), 128. See also Maurice Merleau-Ponty, *Phenomenology of Perception*, trans. Colin Smith (London: Routledge and Kegan Paul, 1962; original work published 1945).

8. Maurice Merleau-Ponty, *The Primacy of Perception*, ed. and trans. James Edie (Evanston, IL: Northwestern University Press, 1964), 13.

9. Merleau-Ponty's reversal of convention here is akin to Kant's reversal of empiricist convention in his famous premise, "suppose that objects must conform to our knowledge." Immanuel Kant, *The Critique of Pure Reason*, trans. N. Kemp Smith (NY: Macmillan, 1929, original work published 1781), 22.

10. Mircea Eliade, *Yoga: Immortality and Freedom*, trans. W. Trask, (Princeton, NJ: Princeton University Press, 1969; originally published 1954), 97. Eliade's scholarly discussion of Haṭha yoga and tantrism is especially helpful; see ibid., 200–273.

11. *Yoga Sūtra*, II, 49–55. The standard academic translation by James Haughton Woods, *The Yoga System of Patanjali* (Varanasi: Motilal Banarsidass, 1966; originally published 1914 in Harvard Oriental Series, vol. 17). A more recent translation in a popular style is by Barbara Stoler Miller, *Yoga: Discipline of Freedom: The Yoga Sutras attributed to Patanjali* (Berkeley: University of California Press, 1996). The translation I have preferred, with a commentary directed toward practice and rooted in a living yoga tradition, is by T.K.V. Desikachar, *Patanjali's Yoga Sutras: An Introduction* (Madras: Affiliated East-West Press LTD, 1987).

12. Edmund Husserl, *Cartesian Meditations*, trans. Dorian Cairns (The Hague: Martinus Nijhoff, 1977), 92–99.

13. Maurice Merleau-Ponty, *The Visible and the Invisible*, ed. Claude Lefort and trans. Alphonso Lingis (Evanston, IL: Northwestern University Press, 1968), 138.

14. Merleau-Ponty, *The Visible and the Invisible*, 135.

15. Ibid., 135.

16. Merleau-Ponty, *The Visible and the Invisible*, 136n.

17. Merleau-Ponty, *Primacy of Perception*, 167.

18. Merleau-Ponty, *The Visible and the Invisible*, 138.

19. T.K.V. Desikachar, *The Heart of Yoga: Developing a Personal Practice* (Rochester, VT: Inner Traditions International, 1995), 23.

20. Ibid., 23.

21. Ibid., 23 (emphasis is mine).

22. Merleau-Ponty, *The Visible and the Invisible*, 199.

23. Desikachar, *Heart of Yoga*, 113n.

Bibliography

Desikachar, T.K.V. *The Heart of Yoga: Developing a Personal Practice*. Rochester, VT: Inner Traditions International, 1995.

Desikachar, T.K.V., trans. and comm. *Patañjali's Yoga Sutras: An Introduction*. Madras: Affiliated East-West Press LTD, 1987.

Eliade, Mircea. *Yoga: Immortality and Freedom*. Translated by W. Trask. Princeton, NJ: Princeton University Press, 1969.

Heidegger, Martin. *Being and Time*. Translated by John Macquarrie and Edward Robinson. New York: Harper & Row, 1962.

Husserl, Edmund. *Cartesian Meditations*. Translated by Dorian Cairns. The Hague: Martinus Nijhoff, 1977.

Husserl, Edmund. *Ideas Pertaining to a Pure Phenomenology and to a Phenomenological Philosophy*. Bk. 2, *Studies in the Phenomenology of Constitution*. Translated by R. Rojcewicz and A. Schuwer. Boston: Kluwer Academic Publishers, 1989.

Husserl, Edmund. "Phenomenology." In *Encyclopedia Britannica* 17 (1951).

Kant, Immanuel. *The Critique of Pure Reason*. Translated by N. Kemp Smith. New York: Macmillan, 1929.

Merleau-Ponty, Maurice. *Phenomenology of Perception*. Translated by Colin Smith. London: Routledge and Kegan Paul, 1962.

Merleau-Ponty, Maurice. *The Primacy of Perception*. Edited by James M. Edie. Evanston, IL: Northwestern University Press, 1964.

Merleau-Ponty, Maurice. *Themes from the Lectures at the College de France: 1952–1960*. Translated by John O'Neill. Evanston, IL: Northwestern University Press, 1970.

Merleau-Ponty, Maurice. *The Visible and the Invisible*. Edited by Claude Lefort and translated by Alphonso Lingis. Evanston, IL: Northwestern University Press, 1968.

Miller, Barbara Stoler, trans. *Yoga: Discipline of Freedom: The Yoga Sutras Attributed to Patañjali*. Berkeley: University of California Press, 1996.

Paranjpe, A., and K. Hanson, "On Dealing with the Stream of Consciousness: A Comparison of Husserl and Yoga." In *Asian Contributions to Psychology*, ed. A. Paranjpe, D. Ho, and R. Rieber, 215–231. New York: Praeger Publishers, 1988.

Puligandla, R. "Phenomenological Reduction and Yogic Meditation." *Philosophy East and West* 20 (1970): 19–33.

Sinari, Ramakant. "The Method of Phenomenological Reduction and Yoga." *Philosophy East and West* 15 (1965): 217–228.

Whicher, Ian. "Nirodaha, Yoga Praxis and the Transformation of the Mind." *Journal of Indian Philosophy* 25 (1997): 1–67.

8

The Concept of *Qi* in Chinese Philosophy

A Vital Force of Cosmic and Human Breath

JANA S. ROŠKER

Introduction

Since the very early Chinese philosophic discourses, the notion of *qi* belonged to the most basic categories for the understanding of reality. It is already mentioned in the *Guoyu* 國語 (*State Records*), a work that goes back to ca 500 BC. In this book, the notion *qi* apparently referred to an earthquake. According to this categorization, earthquakes were results of an imbalance of the *tu qi* 土氣 (the earthly *qi*). When the *yang qi* 陽氣 (the dynamic, active *qi*) was suppressed and could not get out, the situation resulted in the explosion of the *tuqi* (the *qi* of the earth).[1]

An earthquake, however, was only one of the many different ways of explaining natural events in terms of the dynamic of *qi*. The notion can already be found in the oracle inscriptions of the early Zhou Dynasty (1066–771 BC), symbolizing the cloudy vapors in the air.[2] It contained the idea of air and was therefore mostly connected with the process of breathing. Hence, it is probably not coincidental that already in the sources from the sixth century BC, the term *qi* is seen as the cause of natural events, and not only as a means to describe them.[3] In this context, one can already distinguish various versions of the theory of *qi*, including a theory of its close connection to the interactions of the five powers (*wu xing* 五行) that create life and the universe. In its recent form, it is mostly applied in the compound *kongqi* 空氣, which means air (in empty space). Hence, it is something that is physically real but at the same time invisible.

In most traditional sources, the notion implied an organic state, linked to breath. Since the exchange of gases and oxygen underlies any form of life as we know it, *qi* is of fundamental and vital significance for any organic existence. This organic state is internalized in the human body, but simultaneously it connects all existing beings in the universe that are endowed with life. Such a notion of *qi* can be found, for instance, in *Guanzi*,[4] in which we come across the notion of a quintessential *qi* (*jing qi* 精氣),[5] which is responsible for life: things live because they have *qi*[6]—as soon as they lose it, they die.[7]

Qi thus manifests itself as the vital force that underlays any form of life, as the principle of vital creativity, as the cause of any change and transformation, which in Chinese philosophy has been seen as the fundamental precondition of life. In the process of breathing, one can see the evidence of life. Breathing in air and breathing it out results in the circulation of blood in the body, and so *qi* implies the meaning of internal life force. This life force is by no means limited to the automatic bodily functions; on the contrary, it also produces consciousness and awareness, and thus comprises the very foundation for every form of knowledge and wisdom. Because it is the power of continuous change, it elevates and becomes a cosmic (and even cosmological)[8] power of creation.

> Eventually, the concept of qi acquires the meaning of both energy or force and vitality, and thus becomes "vital energy" or "vital force," but it has not lost its naturalistic or even materialistic reference of meaning. In fact, what we have observed about the visible natural qi can be extended to the invisible internal qi of an organism. It is even extended to the atmosphere—which is invisible but can be experienced.[9]

In the human body, however, *qi*'s activity does not remain limited to the function of breathing. It underlies every function of all organs, blood, and seminal fluids. It is also closely connected with the very bases of traditional Chinese medicine, for it underlies the invisible electric neural currents that represent the foundation for healing various diseases with acupuncture, acupressure, or with the help of psychosomatic exercises.

Although in ancient sources, the concept of *qi* has thus almost exclusively been associated with the meaning of some kind of vital power or vital energy, it appeared often as "matter" in the earliest French and English translations. This erroneous understanding is connected to some general problems of intercultural understandings. In order to understand the reasons for such misinterpretations of the notion *qi*, we must take a brief look into some important distinctions that mark the fundamental and paradigmatic differences between the European and the Chinese philosophies.

Some General Problems of
Intercultural Interpretations in Chinese Studies

Philosophic discourses from traditional China differ from those that have prevailed in the course of European ideational history in their basic paradigms. In this context, we must expose the principle of transcendence in immanence, which is essentially different from basic approaches applied in transcendental metaphysics. On the one hand, immanent, but simultaneously transcendent, notions are doubtless a necessary product of the classical Chinese holistic worldview. This is also the reason that the prevailing ideational discourses in traditional China did not create a notion of "pure transcendence" in the sense of exceeding one and transferring into another (usually "higher") sphere of metaphysical noumena. Such a holistic worldview is rooted in relations of antagonistic binary notions that are often named binary categories (*duili fanchou* 對立範疇). The mutual interactions between the two poles that form such a category are governed by the principle of correlative complementarity, which belongs to the fundamental paradigms of Chinese reasoning and which, *inter alia*, led to the formation of patterns of specific Chinese analogous reasoning.

Nevertheless, this holistic worldview was rigidly structured; it was by no means a homogenous unity in which everything was connected to everything else, without distinctions or demarcations. The classical Chinese worldview was thus logically ordered and its order was based on relatively strict binary oppositional patterns. Hence, the above-mentioned binary categories belong to the basic features of traditional Chinese philosophy. Such categories can be seen as dualities that seek to attain a state of actuality through relativity, which is expressed through the relation between two oppositional notions.[10]

> Distinctions are seen in binary terms, and primarily between pairs of opposites (with even figure and color reduced to square/round and white/black); having drawn them, and recognized some recurring or persisting pattern (for example large, round, hard, heavy, and white), we detach a stone from other things as we cut out a piece of cloth or chop off a piece of meat. Things are not seen as isolated, each with its own essential and accidental properties; on the contrary, distinguishing characteristics are seen as mostly relative.[11]

However, it is completely clear that as such, binary patterns are not only specific characteristics of Chinese philosophy; in their divisional effect, they create a basic condition for any form of human thought. Binary patterns have led to many various modes of reasoning.

One of them can be found in the model of Cartesian dualisms, which prevailed in premodern and modern Euro-American thought. The model that prevailed in Chinese ideational history differs in many aspects from these dualisms. A basic distinction between the two modes of binary reasoning is rooted in the aforementioned principle of complementarity, which governs the Chinese model. The dualistic model, as prevailed in Western philosophy, involves a dialectics posited on the relation between the mutually exclusive and polar opposites of thesis and antithesis, which are in mutual contradiction. This contradiction forms a tension, in which the mutual negation of thesis and antithesis creates a synthesis. The complementary model, on the other hand, is instead based on a noncontradictory opposition between the two anti-poles, which do not exclude, but rather complement each other, and which are also interdependent.[12] Such dual patterns cannot produce any separate synthesis in which the "positive" elements of the previous state could be preserved, while the "negative" ones would be eliminated. The Daoist philosopher Zhuangzi described such a binary relation as follows:

> This is why I am saying: why cannot we preserve truth and eliminate falseness? Why cannot we preserve order and eliminate chaos? Such thinking means that we do not understand the structure of nature, nor the state of being in which everything exists. This would mean preserving earth and eliminating heaven, preserving yin and eliminating yang. It is completely clear that this could not work.[13]

Such explanations of binary relations differ to a great extent from logocentric dualisms as were developed in the Hellenistic and Judeo-Christian traditions. The latter were namely based on mutual contradiction of the two anti-poles, tending to preserve one of the poles while abolishing the other. The most important specific features of complementary relations that distinguish them from the Cartesian type of dualisms are thus the noncontradictional opposition of the two anti-poles, their interdependence, their axiological equality, and their mutual supplementation.

What is important for our present study of the notion of *qi*, however, is the fact that such binary patterns also became visible in the basic paradigms, which defined the medieval and premodern Chinese cosmology. This cosmological (or ontological) paradigms were expressed through the mutually complementary interactions between the principles of *li* 理 and *qi*, whereby the former was understood as structure (or structural patterns) and the latter as (vital) creativeness. Hence, even though this cosmological system was binarily ordered, it is important to know that traditional Chinese thinkers never strictly distinguished between the spheres of matter and idea, or any other dualistic connotations resulting from this basic dichotomy.[14] In the system of classical Chinese cosmology, the world was not composed by matter and idea, or by material and ideational elements. It was created through correlative interactions between the dynamic, all-encompassing structural patterns *li* that were mutually compatible with and endowed with life through the vital potential or vital force(s) *qi*.[15]

While in ancient and early medieval China, the notion of *qi* has mostly been applied in the sense of an independent concept, things changed in later medieval and premodern China. In the scope of the Neo-Confucian philosophies of the Song (960–1279) and Ming (1368–1644) dynasties, it was seen as a part of the bipolar (or binary) category of structure (*li*) and creativeness (*qi*), which represented the basic cosmological pair that underlays every form of existence.[16]

The Binary Relation between *Qi* and *Li* and False Interpretations of the Notion *Qi*

When the first sinologists (who were mostly Christian missionaries) initially came to China in the seventeenth century, the prevailing ideology they encountered was based on the Neo-Confucian philosophy. Hence, for them, it was perfectly natural to interpret its bipolar conception of the world, consisting of something called *qi* and organized in accordance with something else called *li*, in terms of, respectively, matter and idea. However, in our view, the concept *li* cannot be understood as idea or principle in the "Western" sense, but rather as structure or a structural pattern, which can, of course, also pertain to the sphere of abstractions or ideas. Similarly, and based on a more profound understanding of Neo-Confucian philosophy, it is evident that the concept *qi* can hardly be understood as matter in the "Western" sense. In fact, the Neo-Confucian philosophers defined it as something not necessarily substantial, for air or even a vacuum (the great void *tai xu* 太虛) are composed of *qi*. Thus, it represents a concept that could be more appropriately defined as creativity, or a potential that functions in a creative way. Hence, Zhang Zai (1020–1077), a pioneer of the neo-Confucian thought, described it in the following way:

> In the great void, qi condenses and dissolves again. This can be compared to ice dissolving in water.[17]

According to most traditional Chinese interpretations, in its condensed form *qi* pertains to the sphere of matter, whereby it belongs to the sphere of abstract entities in its finest, most dispersed state.[18] However, the majority of traditional European and American sinologists have (as we have noted above) translated this concept as matter. To illustrate this point, we can cite the translation of the above-quoted passage by the renowned French sinologist from the beginning of the nineteenth century, Le Gall (1858–1916), in which the notion *qi* is clearly understood as atom(s):

Le condensation et les dispersions des atomes dans la T'ai-hiu peuvent
se comparer a la fonte de la glace dans l'eau.[19]

This translation of the concept *qi* is problematic, for it derives from a profoundly
intrinsic sense of the criteria, based on the model of Cartesian dualism. Although
Zhang Zai's comparison with water explicitly states that *qi* is a continuous state,
and not an aggregate of atoms, the analogy with matter was so deeply rooted in
Le Gall's perception that he automatically saw the notion *qi* as an entity, which
contains or is composed of atoms. Hence, for centuries, Le Gall and other sinologists who followed his reading have misled scholars regarding the question whether
traditional Chinese philosophy applied the concept of atomicity.[20]

The second term, or the concept *li*, indicates the notion of structure, a
structural pattern and the structural order of things. Taken as a whole, *li* represents a cosmic pattern, defining lines of movement or the dynamicity of men and
nature. These structural lines are seen as relations that define both the sphere of
ideas and that of phenomena. At the same time, they make possible the mutual
adjustment of binary oppositions with complementary functions, as well as their
orderly fusion within cosmic unity.

> The concept *li* is not obeyed or violated like a law; instead, one
> either goes with or against the grain of it, as in chopping wood. Le
> Gall translated it as *forme*, thus remolding the whole neo-Confucian
> cosmology after the analogy of Aristotelian form and matter (atoms).
> J. Percy Bruce instead translated this term as "law," thereby incor-
> porating into neo-Confucian terminology itself the wrong answer to
> the question "Are there laws of nature in China?"[21]

Instead, in these Neo-Confucian discourses, *li* and *qi* are complementary concepts,
which can be explained as a structure (or structural pattern) and a creative formative potential (creativity). Both are of immanent nature and can therefore be
realized in the spheres of both ideas and phenomena. Euro-American philosophy
offers no precise equivalents for these two terms. If we want to comprehend the
modes of their existence and their functions, we must first free ourselves from
reasoning in terms of Cartesian dualisms and try thinking based on the model
of analogy, which arose from and was prevalent in the immanent metaphysic of
traditional Chinese thought.

The Meaning of *Qi* on Different Levels

A.C. Graham points out that unlike the concept *li* that can mostly be expressed
only on a metaphorical level, *qi* is quite concrete,[22] since it really is—among other

things—the breath in our throats. However, as already mentioned, the notion of *qi* had mostly been applied as an independent concept long before the Neo-Confucian discourses. Already in Laozi's *Dao de jing* we come across passages that emphasize that concentrating on the natural flow of their breath enables human beings to remember their elementary nature and to become aware of their inseparable unity with the universe. "When people give undivided attention to the (vital) breath, and brings it to the utmost degree of pliancy, they can become as (tender) babes."[23] This connection between breath and mind was seen as important, because "the heart-mind can make the vital force (or breath of life) strong."[24]

> *Qi* is the source of life, dispersing into the air at death. Hence, *Qi* was not only seen as human breath, but also as the breath of the universe: "When the cosmic breath comes strongly, it is called wind."[25]

In addition to its fundamental meaning of human and simultaneously cosmic breath, the notion of *qi* has several different semantic connotations, which differ according to the referential framework in which it has been applied. These frameworks pertain to various fields, as for instance philosophy, physics, physiology, psychology, ethics, aesthetics, and so on.

The relationship between *qi* and human life in communities is evident in many East Asian sociopolitical, cultural, economic, and medical institutions. Based on this relation, a vernacular epistemology has been developed. Such an epistemology provides spiritual guidance for cultural, political, and economic conventions and everyday behavior.[26] "All that exists bears yin and embraces yang. Everything is infused with the breath of life to achieve harmony."[27] Hence, it is by no means coincidental that examples of disciplines and practices associated with *qi* include the martial arts, traditional Chinese medicine, architecture, agriculture, aesthetic production, and other pursuits.

On the philosophical level, *qi* can be compared to all sorts of gas, and especially to air, which is indispensable for breathing.[28] This basic connotation, tightly linked to the process of breathing in the sense of the most fundamental vital function of all life, will be explored in more detail in the next section. However, in order to gain an idea of the wide-ranged complexity of the term, let us first look to the meanings of *qi* in other significant fields of knowledge.

In physics, *qi* is similar to the idea of field. This idea has gained special importance in various practices of the bodily *qi*-cultivation, which was based on the so-called *qigong* 氣功 exercises. A *qi* field (*qi chang* 氣場) refers to the cultivation of an energy field that can allegedly be used for various healing or other benevolent purposes. In such practices, popular in contemporary China, a *qi* field is believed to be produced by breath control, visualization, and affirmation. All these techniques are psychological tools for observing the magnetic field that is a part of every organic entity.[29]

In traditional Chinese medicine, *qi* represents a form of wind[30] and the vital force, which makes any form of organic life possible. In traditional medical discourses, the concept of *qi* was often applied together with the term *xue* 血, which means blood. The term *xueqi* 血氣 was developed to express the essential function of the blood as it coursed through the arteries, bringing nutrients to the remotest parts of the body.[31] Hence, it often appears as the elementary source of vital energy, which preconditions every social activity: "They tasked their blood and breath to make out a code of laws."[32]

This relation between *qi* and blood was already clearly defined in the ancient medical book entitled *The Yellow Emperor's Classic of Internal Medicine* (黃帝內經). Their inseparable connection was seen as a necessary precondition for any form of life: "Blood and *qi* constitute human spirit. Therefore, they have to be cherished and cultivated."[33]

> It was perhaps the recognition of this intimate relationship between *qi* and blood that provided ancient theorists with the understanding necessary to construct a map of the pathways both these essential substances traversed throughout the entire human body. The deceptively simple phrase *xue qi* contains the gist of this interrelationship.[34]

But Confucius, on the other hand, often used the term *xueqi* in the sense of (male?) sexual potential:

> There are three things the superior man guards against: in youth, when the sexual powers are not yet settled, he guards against lust. When he is strong and his sexual powers are full of vitality, he guards against pugnacity. When he is old, and his sexual powers are decayed, he guards against lust.[35]

Shén qi 神氣 is another important compound applied in traditional Chinese medicine. The term *shen* connects *qi* with another of the essential entities indispensable to life itself. *Shen* means "spirit" and reflects the belief of ancient Chinese healers that human beings contain a spark of the eternal, indispensable for their existence. "Yet even this eternal flame could not burn without an invisible but essential substance, the breath of life: *qi*."[36] Hence, the phrase *shén qi* represented the medical concept of spirit, that is, of human innermost vitality. Zhuangzi, the most radical opponent of orthodox Confucianism, applies this term in the context of criticizing their shallow ambitions linked to their obsession with various techniques of body and mind cultivation. In his chapter *On Heaven and Earth*, a simple gardener warns Zi Gong 子貢, one of Confucius's most famous disciples, of excessively controlling the spirit and being excessively obsessed with the ancient "fitness" by saying: "You should forget the energy of your spirit, and neglect the care of your body."[37]

Qi is also an important notion within traditional Chinese aesthetics, including paintings, architecture, literature, music, and dance. All forms of Chinese art seem to be closely integrated and interrelated by *qi*. Calligraphy, for instance, is driven by "the pulse of *qi*."[38] In paintings, this pulse develops into "the charm of *qi*."[39] Similarly, literary expressions are also connected with the concept of *qi* and can be divided into two categories. Prose is usually motivated by "the momentum of *qi*,"[40] and poetry by its "romantic charm."[41] All these elements develop the aesthetic sense and function on many different levels of beauty appreciation.

Qi as the Breath and the Source of Life

In Chinese philosophy, the world was seen to be in constant motion, manifesting the changes of life. All these changes and movements were rooted in *qi*. Hence, this notion could be applied to explain all transformations and developments. Thus, it is by no means coincidental that it holds a premier position in classical Chinese thought. As we have seen, *qi* is the principal source of energy and matter, establishing simultaneously the elementary spirit of all human beings.[42] Therefore, *qi* was also seen as a connective medium through which living beings could harmonize their growth and development and become aware of their inherent connection with the forces of nature. The elementary meaning of *qi* is revealed through the holistic understanding of *breath*, which exposes the dynamic network connecting all existing beings in the universe, endowed with life.

This aspect is already visible in the earliest etymological explanation of the Chinese character, which expresses the notion. It was created as a semantic compound, consisting of the element 气, which originally depicted the shape of (rising) clouds,[43] and the radical 米, which means rice. According to some interpretations,[44] its earliest forms in the oracle inscriptions of the early Zhou Dynasty (1066–771 BC), symbolize the cloudy vapors in the air.[45] Zhuangzi applies the notion *qi* in this sense very often, for instance:

> On a whirlwind it mounts upwards as on the whorls of a goat's horn for 90,000 *li*, till, far removed from the cloudy vapours, it bears on its back the blue sky, and then it shapes its course for the South, and proceeds to the ocean there[46]. [. . .] (He) mounted on the clouds, drove along the flying dragons[47]. [. . .] Being such, he mounts on the clouds of the air, rides on the sun and moon, and rambles at ease beyond the four seas.[48]

The final ideogram 氣 suggests vapors rising from rice paddies. Such interpretations point out that the notion *qi* belongs to the typical terms of early agricultural China.[49] Other interpretations, based on definitions from the *Shuowen jieci* 說 文解字 (*Explaining Graphs and Analysing Characters*), an early second-century etymological dictionary, rather suggest that it depicts a man blowing on rice,[50] and that it means gas or breath. Such interpretations simultaneously point out the nourishing function of the concept *qi*. In later dictionaries, *qi* is often explicitly linked to the term "breathing."[51] This additional meaning came following the Yin (1600–1066 BC) and Zhou (1066–256 BC) periods. In this sense, *qi* is already defined in the ancient Confucian classics, the *Book of Rites* (*Li ji* 禮記).[52] In the course of later development, an alternate mode of writing the word *qi* developed and was used to express this meaning of breath. The character 炁 (with the same pronunciation) meant "the *qi* of breathing." This way of writing was primarily used by Daoists and practitioners of various arts related to the cultivation of *qi*.[53]

It is interesting that this feature of the concept of *qi* bears many resemblances to several similar notions developed in other ancient cultures:

> The ancient Hindus wrote of *prana*, the invisible "breath of life" that they cultivated through Yoga. Ancient Greeks described a concept which in several important aspects parallel the Chinese notion of *qi* with the word "*pneuma*." Like the Chinese *qi*, this Greek word is often translated into English as "breath"—with similarly misleading results. The Greek *pneuma*, like the Chinese concept of *qi*, was a complex idea that blended spiritual and material aspects of the vital essence of life into a comprehensive description of that without which life itself could not exist.[54]

Conclusion

One must rely on *qi* in order to live and to grow strong. Sickness decreases *qi* and death depletes it. If humans do not drink for days or eat for weeks, they still might not die, but they will surely die from not breathing *qi* for less than an hour.[55] Hence, *qi* was seen as something immensely precious, as the fundamental precondition of life.

In ancient Chinese philosophy, *qi* is thus a limitless source of all creation[56] forming an omnipresent cosmic creative flow. Since the ancient Chinese worldview was holistic, and based on an inseparable unification of heaven (or nature) and men (天人合一), this creative flow is visible in both cosmic and human breath. In this sense, *qi* is a basic vital rhythm connecting everything that exists in the great symphony of life.

Notes

1. 陽癉憤盈, 土氣震發 . . . 自今至于初吉, 陽氣俱蒸, 土膏其動. "Guoyu 國語 (State Records)," in *Chinese Text Project: Pre-Qin and Han*, accessed December 29, 2015, http://ctext.org/guo-yu.

2. Chung-Ying Cheng, "Qi (Ch'i): Vital Force," in *Encyclopedia of Chinese Philosophy*, ed. Antonio S. Cua (New York and London: Routledge, 2003), 615.

3. Ibid.

4. 管子; an important political text written in the Spring and Autumn period (770–476 BC).

5. "Guanzi 館子 (Master Guan)," in *Chinese Text Project: Pre-Qin and Han*, accessed December 29, 2015, http://ctext.org/guanzi.

6. 坦氣修通, 凡物開靜, 形生理. Ibid.

7. 有氣則生, 無氣則死. Ibid.

8. Jane Geaney, *Epistemology of the Senses in Early Chinese Thought* (Honolulu: University of Hawai'I Press, 2002), 9.

9. "Guanzi 館子 (Master Guan)."

10. Some generally best-known Chinese binary categories are *yinyang* 陰陽 (sunny and shady), *tiyong* 體用 (essence and function), *mingshi* 名實 (concept and actuality), *liqi* 理氣 (structure and phenomena), and *benmo* 本末 (roots and crown).

11. Agnus C. Graham, *Disputers of the Tao: Philosophical Argument in Ancient China* (Chicago: Open Court, 1989), 286.

12. Jana S. Rošker, "Structure and Creativeness: A Reinterpretation of the Neo-Confucian binary category Li and Qi," in *Origin(s) of Design in Nature: A Fresh, Interdisciplinary Look at How Design Emerges in Complex Systems, Especially Life*, ed. Liz Swan, Richard Gordon, and Jeseph Seckbach (New York: Springer, 2012), 280.

13. 故曰：蓋師是而無非, 師治而無亂乎？是未明天地之理, 萬物之情者也。是猶師天而無地, 師陰而無, 其不可行明矣. "Zhuangzi 莊子 (Master Zhuang)," in *Chinese Text Project: Pre-Qin and Han*, accessed December 29, 2015, http://ctext.org/zhuangzi.

14. As, for instance, distinctions between subject and object, substance and phenomena, creator and creation, etc.

15. See Rošker, "Structure and Creativeness," 280.

16. In the philosophy of Zhu Xi 朱熹 (1130–1200), who is the most well-known representative of the Neo-Confucian discourses, the binary patterns tended to transform into a semi-dualistic pattern (see Jana S. Rošker, *The Rebirth of the Moral Self: The Second Generation of Modern Confucians and their Modernization Discourses* [Hong Kong: Chinese University Press, 2016], xx) because they relied too heavily on a mechanistic rationality. Such approaches resulted in a deformation of the holistic tradition in philosophy, in which the binary poles of structure (*li*) and vital creativity (*qi*) were harmonized, thereby preserving the harmonic unity of facts, values, and the sphere of aesthetic experience. Hence, numerous scholars share the opinion that Neo-Confucian philosophers headed by Zhu Xi represented a turnaround in Chinese tradition. This was often expressed through the optics of its alleged "germs of dualism" (see for instance Alfred Forke, *Geschichte der mittelalterlichen Chinesischen Philosophie II* [Hamburg: R. Oldenbourg, 1934], 173). However, it was still a mixture between both models; and what matters most in the context of the present study is the fact that, even in their function of basic cosmological elements, *li* and *qi* were never seen as idea and matter respectively by any of the traditional Chinese philosophers—including Zhu Xi.

17. 氣之聚散於太虛由冰釋於水. Zhang Zai 張載, 正蒙 *Correction of Ignorance*, vol. 4 of *Xingli da quan: Kongzi wenhua da quan*, ed. Hu Guang (Jinan: Shandong youyi shushe, 1989), 389.

18. Huainanzi, a Han period (206 BC–AD 8) Daoist-oriented master of Chinese philosophy, said that before the birth of Heaven and Earth there was only a formless, fluid state called *taizhao*, like a clear transparent void. This void, which is the beginning of Dao, gave birth to the universe. The universe in turn produced *qi*. That part of *qi* that was light and limpid floated up to form Heaven, whereas the part of *qi* that was heavy and turbid coagulated to become earth. Therefore, *qi* can be understood as protomaterial, a vital creative force that gives "form" to everything in the universe. See Jian Xu, "Body, Discourse, and the Cultural Politics of Contemporary Chinese Qigong," *The Journal of Asian Studies* 58, no. 4 (1999): 967.

19. Stanislas P. Le Gall, *Le philosophe tchou hi, sa doctrine, son influence* (Ville de Saguenay: Chicoutimi, 2006), 49.

20. Graham, *Disputers of the Tao*, 61.

21. Ibid.

22. Ibid., 62.

23. 專氣致柔, 能嬰兒乎? "Laozi 老子: Daode jing 道德經 [The Book of Dao in and the Power of Virtue]," in *Chinese Text Project: Pre-Qin and Han*, accessed December 29, 2015, http://ctext.org/dao-de-jing.

24. 心使氣曰強. Ibid., 55.

25. 夫大塊噫氣, 其名為風. "Zhuangzi 莊子 (Master Zhuang)."

26. Sheng Kuan Chung, "Aesthetic Practice and Spirituality: 'Chi' in Traditional East Asian Brushwork," *Art Education* 59, no. 4 (2006): 34.

27. 萬物負陰而抱陽, 沖氣以為和. "Laozi 老子: Daode jing 道德經," 42.

28. See for instance the Confucian *Analects*: . . . 屏氣似不息者 。(. . . holding in his breath, as if he dared not breathe); "Lunyu 論語 (The Analects)," in *Chinese Text Project: Pre-Qin and Han*, accessed December 29, 2015, http://ctext.org/analects.

29. See Cunshan Li 李存山, "Qi, shiti yu changyou 氣, 實體與場有" [Qi, Substance and Field,] in *Chang yu you—Zhongwai zhexuede bijiao yu rongtong* [Field and Being: The Comparison and Fusion of Chinese and non-Chinese Philosophies,] ed. Luo Jiachang and Zheng Jiadong (Beijing: Dongfan chuban she, 1994), 132.

30. Just as traditional Chinese cosmogony holds that everything is produced through the movement and transformation of *qi*, so traditional Chinese medicine explains life as a concentration of this primal or vital potential. "The complications of the Chinese medical theory of *qi*, as articulated through the scheme of yin and yang, and the five powers (*wuxing* 五行), were basically derived from this fundamental understanding." The method of analyzing the factors of illness focuses almost exclusively on the war between *heteropathic* and *orthopathic qi*, the relations between climate or other environmental excesses (e.g. of heat, damp, wind) and physiological heat, damp, or sluggishness. See Elisabeth Hsu, "The Experience of Wind in Early and Medieval Chinese Medicine," in *Wind, Life, Health: Anthropological and Historical Perspectives. The Journal of the Royal Anthropological Institute* 13 (2007): 117.

31. Yu Huan Zhang and Rose Ken, *A Brief History of Qi* (Brookline: Paradigm Publications, 2001), 7.

32. 矜其血氣以規法度. "Zhuangzi 莊子 [Master Zhuang]."

33. 血氣者, 人之神, 不可不謹養. "Huangdi neijing 黃帝內經 [The Yellow Emperor's Classic of Internal Medicine]," in *Chinese Text Project: Pre-Qin and Han*, accessed September 21, 2015, http://ctext.org/huangdi-neijing.

34. Zhang and Ken, *Brief History*, 7.

35. 君子有三戒：少之時, 血氣未定, 戒之在色；及其壯也, 血氣方剛, 戒之在鬥；及其老也, 血氣既衰, 戒之在得. "Lunyu 論語 [The Analects]."

36. Ibid., 6.

37. 汝方將忘汝神氣, 墮汝形骸！ "Zhuangzi 莊子 [Master Zhuang]."

38. Zhang and Ken, *Brief History*, 61.

39. Ibid.

40. Ibid.

41. Ibid.

42. Zhang and Ken, *Brief History*, 61–62.

43. Originally, this element was written in the following way: 三. Later, it was gradually transformed into the present form, mainly to distinguish it from the character that depicts the numeral 3; see Zhang and Ken, *Brief History*, 3.

44. See for instance Cheng, "Qi (Ch'i)," 615.

45. Cheng, "Qi (Ch'i)," 615.

46. 翼若垂天之雲, 搏扶搖羊角而上者九萬里, 絕雲氣, 負青天, 然後圖南, 且適南冥也。"Zhuangzi 莊子 [Master Zhuang]."

47. 乘雲氣, 御飛龍 Ibid., 5.

48. 若然者, 乘雲氣, 騎日月, 而遊乎四海之外。Ibid.

49. Cheng, "Qi (Ch'i)," 615.

50. 饋客芻米也

51. See for instance the Guangyun 廣韻 dictionary from the tenth century: 氣: 氣息也.

52. Zhang and Ken, *A Brief History*, 4.

53. Ibid., 5.

54. Ibid., 15.

55. Ibid., viii.

56. Ibid., 19.

Bibliography

Cheng, Chung-Ying. "Qi (Ch'i): Vital Force." In *Encyclopedia of Chinese Philosophy*, edited by Antonio S. Cua, 615–617. New York and London: Routledge, 2003.

Chung, Sheng Kuan. "Aesthetic Practice and Spirituality: "Chi" in Traditional East Asian Brushwork." *Art Education* 59, no. 4 (2006): 33–38.

Forke, Alfred. *Geschichte der mittelalterlichen Chinesischen Philosophie II*. Hamburg: R. Oldenbourg, 1934.

Geaney, Jane. *Epistemology of the Senses in Early Chinese Thought*. Honolulu: University of Hawai'i Press, 2002.

Graham, Agnus C. *Disputers of the Tao: Philosophical Argument in Ancient China*. Chicago: Open Court, 1989.

"Guanzi 館子 (Master Guan)." In *Chinese Text Project: Pre-Qin and Han*. Accessed December 29, 2015. http://ctext.org/guanzi.

"Guoyu 國語 (State Records)." In *Chinese Text Project: Pre-Qin and Han*. Accessed December 29, 2015. http://ctext.org/guo-yu.

Hsu, Elisabeth. "The Experience of Wind in Early and Medieval Chinese Medicine." *Wind, Life, Health: Anthropological and Historical Perspectives, The Journal of the Royal Anthropological Institute* 13 (2007): S117–S134.

"Huangdi neijing 黃帝內經 (The Yellow Emperor's Classic of Internal Medicine)." In *Chinese Text Project: Pre-Qin and Han*. Accessed September 21, 2015. http://ctext.org/huangdi-neijing.

"Laozi 老子: Daode jing 道德經 (The Book of Dao in and the Power of Virtue)." In *Chinese Text Project: Pre-Qin and Han*. Accessed December 29, 2015. http://ctext.org/dao-de-jing.

Le Gall, Stanislas P. *Le philosophe tchou hi, sa doctrine, son influence*. Ville de Saguenay: Chicoutimi, 2006.

Li, Cunshan 李存山. "Qi, shiti yu changyou 氣, 實體與場有" [Qi, Substance and Field]. In *Chang yu you—Zhongwai zhexuede bijiao yu rongtong* [Field and Being: The Comparison and Fusion of Chinese and Non-Chinese Philosophies,] edited by Luo Jiachang and Zheng Jiadong, 123–135. Beijing: Dongfan chuban she, 1994.

"Lunyu 論語 [The Analects]." In *Chinese Text Project: Pre-Qin and Han*. Accessed December 29, 2015. http://ctext.org/analects.

Rošker, Jana S. *The Rebirth of the Moral Self: The Second Generation of Modern Confucians and Their Modernization Discourses*. Hong Kong: Chinese University Press, 2016.

Rošker, Jana S. "Structure and Creativeness: A Reinterpretation of the Neo-Confucian binary category Li and Qi." In *Origin(s) of Design in Nature: A Fresh, Interdisciplinary Look at How Design Emerges in Complex Systems, Especially Life*, edited by Liz Swan, Richard Gordon, and Jeseph Seckbach, 273–285. New York: Springer, 2012.

Xu, Jian. "Body, Discourse, and the Cultural Politics of Contemporary Chinese Qigong." *The Journal of Asian Studies* 58, no. 4 (1999): 961–991.

Zhang, Yu Huan, and Rose Ken. *A Brief History of Qi*. Brookline: Paradigm Publications, 2001.

Zhang Zai 張載. 正蒙 *Correction of Ignorance*. Vol. 4 of *Xingli da quan: Kongzi wenhua da quan*. Edited by Hu Guang. Jinan: Shandong youyi shushe, 1989.

"Zhuangzi 莊子 (Master Zhuang)." In *Chinese Text Project: Pre-Qin and Han*. Accessed December 29, 2015. http://ctext.org/zhuangzi.

9

Phenomenology of the Wind and the Possibility of Preventive Medicine

A Discussion of *Ki* (Wind) Following Kaibara Ekiken (1630–1713)

TADASHI OGAWA

In this chapter I would like to discuss the medical philosophy of Kaibara Ekiken, or Atsunobu Kaibara (1630–1713), especially with regard to his views on preventive medicine. Ekiken lived about the same time as Pascal and Leibniz, the scientist and philosopher of seventeenth-century Europe. Similarly, Ekiken was a scholar and physician trained in traditional medicine that originated in China and later developed in Japan. He was born into a scholarly family in Fukuoka. His father, however, died early, when Ekiken was a small child. He therefore continued his education through self-study in Fukuoka and Kyoto, the center of Japanese culture at that time. Ekiken eventually belonged to the anti-Neo-Confucianism movement, which flourished in Kyoto. The famous anti-movement representatives Jinsai Ito and Sorai Ogyū were to demand: "Back to the original writings of Confucius and Mencius!"—as they studied directly the texts of those two classical authors, both in the philological as well as literary sense. Ekiken, however, took a different approach, as he himself went back to the original works. Ekiken worked on *Hon-zogaku*, the study of *materia medica* (medical botany) and studied pharmacology and pharmacy. His book *Yamato Honzo*[1] is a famous, indeed a classic, book on plants in Japan. In fact, Ekiken was a working scientist and a "phenomenologist," not a philologist. Rooted in Japanese national and nature religion, rather than being a Buddhist, he was a Shintoist.[2]

Today, Ekiken has been aptly described as the first preventive medical doctor in Japan by Michio Matsuda, a famous physician and translator of Ekiken's writings. Ekiken's philosophy on medicine and its key moments is reflected in his well-known book on preventive medicine called *Yojokun*, published in 1713.[3] Along with his last work on the method, the Daigiroku,[4] meaning the document of great doubts, his publications were very important in educating people regarding health issues and preventive medicine. In addition, he wrote a significant book on the education of children, *Wazoku doushikun*.[5] His concept of "learning by following an example" can be said to lie at the core of Ekiken's pedagogy.

Ekiken's basic thesis for human existence is often repeated in his books. Man is born between heaven and earth. Heaven and earth for the human being are like father and mother. Man is the Spirit or the spirit of all things. Heaven and earth are the first cause of everything that exists in the world. Man is born as the correct *ki* and the right touch of the wind spirits of Heaven and Earth. Only a human being is the child of heaven and earth. The Japanese religion Shintoism is a religion of nature, and traditional Shintoism is closely related to Confucianism. For example, the author of *Shinto Denju*, Razan Hayashi, was a famous Confucian teacher and scholar. In any case, one could say that Ekiken was a Shintoist as well as a philosopher of nature.

Up to the age of sixty-nine, Ekiken was a teacher and an official of the feudal state in Fukuoka. He kept writing and publishing his ideas until his death at the age of eighty-four. At that time, the center for publications was in Kyoto. Almost all his books were written in his seventies. In his last major work, *Daigiroku*, published posthumously, Ekiken explained the title of the work in the preface as follows:

> After learning and studying there comes doubt, after doubt[,] thinking
> arises, and after thinking you will get new profit.[6]

Reading this, one might be reminded of the skeptical tenor in the Cartesian Meditations.

In *Daigiroku*, Ekiken asserted that *ri* was possible only as "*ri = ki*." *Ri* is the order and structure of the world, as in the order of the seasons being spring, summer, autumn, and winter. It could also be seen in the system of roads, relating, for instance, the hotel *Zur Sharfen Ecke* to the center of the city of Hildesheim in Germany. That is, there is a road that runs next to the university and there is the air of the wide, open, and flat field next to the road, which is nothing but the atmosphere of the city. Since the structure of those streets is considered to be a kind of *ri*, this *ri* is seen to be covered by an atmosphere, namely the *ki*. *Ri* and *ki* are thus not two separate principles; rather, *ri* is equated to *ki*. However, how can it be that these concepts are regarded as two separate things but at the same time still be considered as one?[7] Ekiken rejected this dualistic scheme of *ri* and *ki* in relation to the principles of the world. *Ri* and *ki* are what constitutes the real antithesis to *Shu-shi*, or the Neo-Confucianism. Ekiken thought that the structure of the world, *ri*, was fully merged with *ki*, so that *ri* becomes equal to *ki*. In this sense, you might wonder what *ki* is, or, more precisely, what the breathing or the wind is.

Where does Ekiken's thesis stand within the history of Confucianism? His thesis is opposite to the dualism of *ri* and *ki* in the *Shu-shi* philosophical theory. Ekiken described *ri* as the static structure and the system of paths that make up roads in the world. *Ki*, however, signifies the richness of contents, the air or the wind in the world. *Ki* is always associated with movement, including life movement, the movement of bodily life. The result of some strange-looking concept of *ki-ketsu* (*ki* means wind or *pneuma* and *ketsu* means blood, so *ki-ketsu* is translated literally as wind-blood).

Ekiken has thought hard about *ki* and endeavored to overcome the old dualism of *ki* and *ri* in the *Shu-shi* conceptualization. For him, the origin of the world and man is chaotic because of *ri* and *ki*, which are considered as *Taikyoku*. The term *Taikyoku* literally means border in the world, or rather the origin or groundlessness of the world. Ekiken believed *ri* and *ki* were melted together (*crasis*) with each other in the groundlessness of the world. In Greek philosophy, this distinction was made clear. *Mixis* means that different and independent elements or parts exist in an enclosing whole, such as pieces in a jigsaw puzzle. The parts are separate and independent. On the other hand, *crasis* has merged its parts in the enclosing whole. You can therefore equate, for example, the ratio of wine and water in a measuring container. Two different elements, wine and water, are thus fused together.

In the *Yojokun*, Ekiken reveals his thoughts on the concept of *ki* as follows: the process of inhaling and exhaling refers to the breath or air-wind from one's nose and mouth. Exhalation is the phenomenon in which impure wind comes from the interior of the body. Inhalation is the flow of *ki* from the outside into the body. Man dies when the cycle of inhalation and exhalation ceases. The *ki* in the human body is identical to the *ki* between heaven and earth. The *ki* in the outside of one's body and the one inside the body are mixed in the interior and exterior of the body. But *ki* inside the body is impure, because it coexists with the five internal organs. The *ki* between heaven and earth is clean and fresh.[8] Here, the nature of wind-philosophy further underlines the essence of what Ekiken has expressed in his work. The thesis contained therein could in fact be reformulated as a phenomenology of the wind. The practice of inhaling and exhaling was described by Ekiken as the method of measured breathing that regulates respiration. The regular practice of expelling the breath in small amounts makes breathing calm to the point that no breath is felt passing through the nose at all. The sense of small amounts of breath coming and going above the navel would be simply felt. This was one way that Ekiken suggested one could regulate one's energy.[9]

I have already argued on several occasions that a phenomenology of the wind would be possible for this thesis. My view on phenomenology is that the phenomena focusing on phenomenology are always intercultural. The phenomenon of wind is also an intercultural phenomenon. Human beings are born of the wind according to the Gospel of John (3:8) in the Bible. The wind here is spirit. People are born out of the wind in the world, and they live by the wind, in this instance understood as spirit. There is yet another parallel with the popular work of Ekiken, called *Yamato zokukun*. According to this work, human being is born of heaven and earth. Heaven and earth are thus a human being's father and mother. Human being is characterized by it (being) receiving *ki* (air, or *pneuma*) of heaven and earth. Therefore, one can say that human beings have *spiritus*.[10]

But what does *ki* mean? According to the Chinese letter for *ki* (氣), there is a relation between rice (米), cooking, and vapor. When cooking rice, water rises to steam. *Pneuma* or *spiritus* is connected to the movement of air, more precisely, to the inhaling and exhaling. Ekiken has, as already indicated, criticized the Confucian approach, known as *Shushi*, which presupposes a dualistic theory of *ri* and *ki*. In his major work, *Daigirokui*, the *taikyoku* is defined as follows: *tai* means the Great, and *kyoku* means the highest of the extremes.[11] In this sense, *taikyoku* refers to the origin of all beings. How do we understand and estimate that *taikyoku* is something positive? It is the ground of all being, in which *ki* and *ri* are associated with each other. Drawing on the expression of Hermann Schmitz, it means the chaotic multiplicity, in which *ki* and *ri* are fused.

Ki is also the breathing in and out, the movement of air from the exterior of the body into the body and vice versa, out of the interior of the body into the external world, that is, the lifeforce that is connected to bodily movement. What is meant here is the movement of life, which is allowed to flow. In short, *ki* is associated with the movement of life. Ekiken understood *ki* as vitality. *Ki* is the energy of life, and one has to wonder what influences the level of *ki* in the human body. In his medical philosophy, Ekiken used *ki-ketsu* as a term for wind-blood. His understanding of this technical term is connected to the blood and *ki*. Its English translation is *pneumatic-hemia*. Once you are comfortable, you get serenity, that is, a serene *pneumohemia*.

To stay healthy, the body must keep *pneumohemia* in motion. If *ki* is reduced in the body, a person becomes sick. If *ki* is increased, the person becomes healthy. In order to maintain good health, we need to consider what increases and decreases *ki* in the body. To this question of what would be important for health, Ekiken answers that eating, drinking, and sleeping are important, but only when done in moderation. He cautioned against sleeping or taking a nap after a meal, for example, since that could halt the constantly moving wind-blood and therefore be unhealthy. Many might be skeptical and wonder why too much sleep is unhealthy. The reason is quite simple. Too much sleep can pause the constantly moving *ki*, and sleep is seen to reduce *ki*. The end of this path is death. According to Ekiken, death means the complete cessation of or retreat from the living and healthy *ki*. Anything done in excess, be it eating, sleeping, or having sexual intercourse, is considered negative, since indulging in too much pleasure reduces *ki*. This theme, the reduction and propagation of *ki*, is the crux of a good and healthy life. Now, *ki* is the energy of life, and one might ask what influences the level of *ki* in the human body. Further, Ekiken categorized *ki* either as *yang* (light) or *yin* (darkness). If *ki* moves, the *ki* becomes *yang*, or bright. When *ki* solidifies, it becomes *yin*, or dark. In both cases, *ki* is associated with the movement of living power. In fact, as mentioned already, *ki* is the movement of life. Today people use the term *ki* in Japanese colloquial expressions as *yo-ki* (*yang-ki*) and *in-ki* (*yin–ki*). When a person is *yang-ki*, he is in good spirits. *Ki* is also the wind, which arises in human space.

The mood (*ki-bun*) or the atmosphere (*fun-i-ki*) are types of *ki*. The *ki* is wind and vitality, or life energy. The original Chinese word *ki* denotes a surrounding human natural sphere between heaven and earth, which often appears as a haze, vapor, or mist. The *ki* appears as air, wind, weather, climate, atmosphere, and so on. The *ki* is a kind of steam that surrounds any human existence, a special kind of mood, insofar as it is experienced in the vicinity of human existence. A Japanese term, *fuh-tei*, literally translated as wind-body, indicates the mood of or atmosphere in which a human being finds him- or herself. This word appears in Nō theater of *Zeami*. *Ki* is therefore a kind of wind, also to be understood as inhaling and exhaling. The breathing, the wind of the people, the wind of the human body, is indeed the consummation of life. *Ki* is the air and the wind.

Mencius understood the depth and scope of the appearance of *ki*. He said that *ki* would fill all body, provided the body is dominated by the will.[12] The willful Mencius was inspired by Daoism and brought the word *kozen-no-ki*, which expressed a strong, moving spiritual force of human existence. The meaning of *kozen-no-ki* is difficult to express. *Ki* is bigger, wider, and stronger than anything else. If *ki* is spread in the world, the scope of heaven and earth is filled entirely. There are two elements that feed *ki*. First is righteousness, as a result of fair and adequate acts. Second is the empty and formless way that unfolds between heaven and earth. The truth of the way is the opening of the world.

To sum up, *ki* has two explicit meanings. It refers to the moving, lively spiritual power, which is incorporated into the human body. On the other hand, *ki* is also the force or power in heaven and earth, the living and spiritual air. Mencius described the interconnection as the human assets of the will, in which both meanings of *ki* reach unity. A criticism could be that *ki* theory is typical of a particular tradition of East Asian thought, and that the typical East Asian phenomenon of *ki* remains strange to and different from European thought. Some may believe that any European attempts to understand the East Asian phenomenon of *ki* can only fail and that only East Asian thinking is suited to address *ki*. I oppose such perspectives and propose that *ki* is a universal cultural phenomenon.

Ki is the phenomenon of breath. Ekiken also had this important insight as regards this phenomenon. Breathing for him is to let unclean air flow out from the inside of the body, and fresh air from the outside to absorb it. The New Testament described a similar phenomenon and called it *pneuma*. Jesus told Nicodemus:

> The wind blows where it chooses, and you hear the sound of it, but you do not know where it comes from or where it goes. So it is with everyone who is born of the Spirit (John 3:8).

Wind and spirit are originally the same word in the Greek text: *pneuma*. The translation used for the same Greek word could arbitrarily vary depending on the context for other English expressions. *Anemos* was another Greek word for the wind as a pure natural phenomenon and used by Homer. Jesus actually used the same word in order to identify the wind with the spirit. The *pneuma* is the divine breath, the wind appearing as spirit. Human beings exist even as the wind. Men are children of the Divine Spirit. We humans have a spiritual existence that is as uncontrollable as the blowing wind. People come and breathe in the world between heaven and earth. It was the Greek, Platonic thought that anticipated this Christian thinking and so prepared the ground for the concept of wind as spirit.

In Plato's *Timaeus*, the human condition of breathing can be analogically described in relation to *ki*. The body acts both actively and passively when a man inhales and exhales, implying the movement of *ki* as air and spirit. What functions actively and passively in the incoming and outflowing breathing of the body moisturizes and cools the body with the air, which is received from the cold outer world. According to Plato, the inner fire of the body moves in accordance with the inhalation and exhalation of air. The body can assimilate according to the moving air as food. The movement of *ki* as breathing conveys the internal fire of the body. In the cold outside world, the human being maintains the fire of life. Thus Plato has shown how deep the body has rooted itself in the cold outer world. The inner fire of the body is mediated by the *ki* to which the cold outer world belongs. The *ki* brings physicality when breathing in and with the world in a single reference. This thought of Plato is expressed in the sentence *ergon kai pathos*,[13] the meaning of which has been explained in this way:

> [T]his, of course, is the phenomenon to which the name-giver (so we claim) assigned the names of *inhalation* and *exhalation*. This entire pattern of action and reaction, irrigating and cooling fire, supports their nutrition and life. For whenever the internal fire, united with the breath that passes in or out, follows it along, it surges up and down continually and makes its way through and into the belly, where it gets hold of the food and drink.[14]

What is the practice of health? An atmosphere of amenity is necessary for people to be able to play or talk together. In Europe as well as in Japan, there is a great fear among the elderly of becoming old and ill, such as with dementia. Japan is currently an aging society. Politically and economically this is very dangerous because the cost of medical treatment is increased. The number of young people is drastically decreasing, while dementia and Alzheimer's are increasing. In Ekiken's teaching, there were already many indications of a practice that can prevent dementia. Ekiken has proposed the importance of always moving physically or to being able to move, to sing, and to dance together. This was considered important because the means of dancing and singing could set *ki* in the body in motion.[15]

Today, Japanese physicians often say that three things are important for old people: first, chatting or talking together; second, walking together; and third, cooking. When you cook, you have to cut ingredients, such as meat and vegetables. You must cut those ingredients with your hands, using a knife or other device for the preparing of food. Not only that, but you also have to perform the overall design. This can be difficult for old people. Planning the entire process might prove extremely challenging for people with dementia. Ekiken thought that to do one thing for a long time reduced *ki* in the body. While a long walk is recommended, a long sleep is not. Sitting in the same place for a long period of time is also not recommended.

Almost all proposals of Ekiken are convincing and reasonable, even from today's perspective of medicine, with the exception of perhaps his thoughts on too much sleeping. According to Ekiken, taking a nap was not healthy. After dinner, one should go for a walk in the garden, at least for a hundred steps. If you absolutely need to take a nap, you should do that just by leaning against the wall while briefly closing your eyes. Long sleep during the day should be, however, avoided for health reasons. Thus, Ekiken recommended a short and deep sleep at night. But sleeping is actually good for life and health, as you can relax and thereby draw fresh life. But Ekiken thought that through sleeping the vitality of body would be lost. It would depend on *ki* or the *pneumohemia*. According to Ekiken, the vitality of the living flesh is nothing else than the *pneumohemia*. Because of the stillness of sleep, the wind-blood, the *pneumohemia* is no longer moving.

Why did Ekiken hold this view? Why should sleep, especially long sleep, be bad, even toxic, for health? I mentioned earlier the peculiar notion of *ki-ketsu*, *pneumohemia*. Ekiken has written that long sleep and a daily routine with a short nap in between prevents the movement of *pneumohemia*. The essential question for Ekiken was how to manage and keep the body moving. The humans must always keep the *ki-ketsu* in the living flesh in motion. The wind-blood is the essence of the lifeforce. No one until recently asked about the nature of *ki-ketsu*. Is it possible that the wind is fused with blood? Ekiken had insight about the importance of movement through the physical body. In the moving self, life is strong and vibrant. The movement of *ki-ketsu* makes life alive and active. The *ki* is the wind, the air, which is always moving. The wind or the air comes from the exterior of the living flesh so that we can stay alive. *Ki* is the movement and the motion of the wind. *Ketsu* is the blood that flows through all living flesh. The blood brings nourishment to the body. The synthesis of *ki* and *ketsu*, their "melting together," occurs through movement, in which motion and the mover are fused.

Pneumohaima is the moving and moved creature. Its tendency is the *pneumai*, the *ki* that is always moving. The *haima*, blood, is moved by its very nature. The *ki-ketsu*, the *pneumohaima*, is attracted by movement. Thus, our Japanese medical thinker of the seventeenth to eighteenth centuries, Ekiken, advised against frequent or long periods of sleep and to maintain movement. Too much sleep makes one's life unhealthy because *ki*, the lifeforce, is weakened through sleeping. Not only did Ekiken criticize oversleeping but also overeating. For best results, Ekiken recommended the following: one should daily consider and examine what increases health and what reduces *ki-ketsu*; it is thus very important to multiply the primordial *pneumai*, that is, *gen-ki*.

In summary, what is *ki*? Air and wind. Man lives by inhaling and exhaling the wind. Human existence is embedded in the lifeworld. We live in this world by establishing our mood or atmosphere.

Notes

1. You can find this book in the library of Kyoto University; see Kaibara, Ekiken, *Yamato Honzo* (Kyoto: Chobei Nagatam, 1761).

2. This chapter is based on a lecture I gave at a conference on breath in Hildesheim on July 2, 2015. The time of "modernity" in this context implies the era after the Meiji Restoration in 1868. I would like to draw your attention to the premodern period, such as the early Edo period. At that time in Edo, now known as Tokyo, the *Tokugawa shogunate* was all over Japan. In the early Edo period, the philosophical situation was one of transition within Confucianism. The classical Confucianism of Confucius and Mencius was overcome by Neo-Confucians of *Shushi* and *Oyomei*, such as *Shushi-gaku* (study of *Shushi*) and *Yomei-gaku* (study of *O-Yomei*). There was also a countermovement to Neo-Confucianism. Their motto was "Back to the real classical writing of Confucius and Mencius." Kaibara Ekiken belongs to the countermovement.

3. See Kaibara, *Yojokun*, trans. Michio Matsuda (Tokyo: Chuokoronsha, 1969); or Kaibara, Ekiken, *Yojokun*, ed. Nomonobu Ito (Tokyo: Kodansha Gakujutsu Bunko, 2013).

4. See Kaibara, *Daigiroku*, ed. Kengo Araki (Tokyo: Iwanami Shoten, 1970).

5. See Kaibara, *Yojyokun-Wazoku Dojikun* (Tokyo: Iwanami Universal Library, 1984).

6. Kaibara, *Daigiroku*, 10.

7. Ibid., 17.

8. Kaibara, *Yojokun-Life-Lessons from a Samurai*, trans. William Scott Wilson (Tokyo: Kodansha International, 2010).

9. Ibid.

10. See first paragraph of Kaibara Ekiken's *Yamato zokukun* (ed. Ishikawa Ken, Tokyo, 1977).

11. Kaibara, *Daigiroku*, 55.

12. Mencius, *Kosonchu (Chugokukoten-sen Chinese Classics Selection)*, ed. and trans. Osamu Kanaya (Tokyo: Asahi Bunko, 1955).

13. *The Holy Bible*, NSRV (Nashville, TN: Thomas Nelson, 1990), 94.

14. See Plato, *Timaeus*, 78e, in Plato, *Complete Works*, ed. John M. Cooper (Indianapolis and Cambridge: Hackett, 1997).

15. Kaibara, *Yojokun* (2013).

Bibliography

The Holy Bible (NSRV). Nashville, TN: Thomas Nelson, 1990.

Kaibara, Ekiken. *Daigiroku*. Edited by Kengo Araki. Tokyo: Iwanami Shoten, 1970.

Kaibara, Ekiken. *The Philosophy of Qi: The Record of Great Doubts*. Translated by Mary Evelyn Tucker. New York: Columbia University Press, 2007.

Kaibara, Ekiken. *Yamato Honzo*. Kyoto: Chobei Nagatam, 1761.

Kaibara, Ekiken. *Yamato zokukun*. Edited by Ishikawa Ken. Tokyo 1977.

Kaibara, Ekiken. *Yojokun-Life-Lessons from a Samurai*. Translated by William Scott Wilson. Tokyo: Kodansha International, 2010.

Kaibara, Ekiken. *Yojokun*. Edited by Nomonobu Ito. Tokyo: Kodansha Gakujutsu Bunko, 2013.

Kaibara, Ekiken. *Yojokun*. Translated by Michio Matsuda. Tokyo: Chuokoronsha, 1969.

Kaibara, Ekiken. *Yojokun-Wazoku Dojikun*. Tokyo: Iwanami Universal Library, 1984.

Mencius. *Kosonchu (Chugokukoten-sen Chinese Classics Selection)*. Edited and translated by Osamu Kanaya. Tokyo: Asahi Bunko, 1955.

Plato, *Complete Works*. Edited by John M. Cooper. Indianapolis and Cambridge: Hackett, 1997.

III

Voices and Media of Breathing

10

"Thoughts, that Breathe"

KEVIN HART

In memory of Mark Strand

In his Pindaric ode "The Progress of Poetry," Thomas Gray calls poetry "Thoughts, that breathe," and in doing so alerts us to two things at once.[1] First, we are invited to consider that poetry *thinks*, which is perhaps not what we expect to be told of lyric poetry. For there is a long tradition, going back at least to Plato, that denies that poets are serious thinkers and that, if their poems express thoughts, they cannot explain them satisfactorily.[2] Second, we are told that a poem is *alive*: it is not merely an aesthetic object, like a painting or a statue, but something that maintains an organic, temporal life, if not human then either above the human or beneath it. René Char beautifully captures the idea when he writes, "Le poème est l'amour réalisé du désir demeuré désir" (The poem is the realized love of desire remaining desire).[3] A poem is at once realized (a warm breath having cooled in the air) while still the longing that animated it (it continues to move and be warm while it is read). Thoughts that do not breathe, like the woman in Heraclides of Pontus's story (as recorded by Diogenes Laertius), subsist in a coma, become a yawn once fashion changes, or enter the world still born.[4] Breath, then, is a condition of possibility for poetry; and it is no surprise that this condition emerges as a theme of some poems. It occurs in thinking about what inspires a poem, in thinking of poetry as song, in the fleetingness of life as a common theme of lyric poetry, in figuring love as what allows that evanescence to gain sense, and in thinking of life as such.

Mark Strand breathed his last in Brooklyn on November 29, 2014. He was eighty years old, and his parting gift to us two months before his passing was a large *Collected Poems* (2014) on which one might meditate for decades.[5] For those

153

of us who had been reading him for almost forty years, his poems usually came
into focus by way of a contradiction. No one could fail to see how thoroughly he
had learned Rimbaud's lesson "Je est un autre."[6] The young French poet's lapidary
sentence taught Strand not so much that he could multiply voices within his work,
something he could have learned from Browning or Eliot. Rather, it confirmed a
terrifying realization that an alien self has always invaded what one might have
hoped to be the calm refuge of self. Sometimes that dark self can be a Muse.
"Somebody else has arrived. Somebody else is writing," he declares at the end of
"My Life by Somebody Else" (*Collected Poems; CP*, 124). At other times, the poetry
explores the eeriness of a doubled self. "The Mailman" tells the story of a letter
that contains "terrible personal news," which is delivered at midnight, and which
turns out to be written by the recipient (*CP*, 45). (Sometimes one can almost hear
Borges breathing behind the young Strand's back.[7]) The Kafkaesque "The Tunnel"
pictures a man who is at once threatened by someone standing outside his house
and is that man himself.[8] When Strand titles a poem " 'The Dreadful has Already
Happened,' " he does not mean to refer to Heidegger's grim summation of the
forgetfulness of being but to the intrusion of another self.[9] Perhaps only Maurice
Blanchot, especially in *Thomas l'obscur* (1941), has probed the phenomenon of an
otherness haunting the self as persistently and plangently as Strand has done.[10]

At the same time, Strand's poems are an endless exploration of selfhood
stripped of all accidents of personality, of an "I" whose statements often seem
uttered by oneself as one reads a poem because there is so very little information
given by which one could separate the "I" on the page from one's own. Strand's
is a world of night, of dreams and nightmares, of mirrors, of uncanny situations,
of mysterious rooms, of memories that wound, and of the disquieting approach
of death. Yet because the "I" is so disencumbered of superficial details, it is also
a world in which life is presented as nakedly as possible: birth, love (rebirth),
and death. Even when the earlier poetry is apparently personal, as in "Elegy for
My Father," very little indeed is told of Robert Strand or specific events shared
by father and son; it is the sharpness of loss that is felt, not the consolation of
anecdote that is offered. Yet as soon as one says "personal," a caveat is required,
for the poem's force is achieved in part by doubling Federico García Lorca's elegy
"Llanto por Ignacio Sánchez Mejías."[11]

These things, both somber and elated, constitute the content of Strand's
poetry, what comes to mind when we ask the simple question "What?" If we
also ask the question "Why?" and begin to look for Strand's explanations of his
declarations and images, often the pathos of the poetry—those stark registrations
of loss and loneliness—is overthrown by a self-mocking humor as sudden as it
is dark. "It is pointless to slash my wrists," he writes in "My Life by Somebody
Else." Why? "My hands / would fall off" (*CP*, 124). Yet it is also poetry about
poetry: not because it is overt criticism of other people's writing or because it
speaks without drawing on a fund of experience, but because it addresses the very

nature of inspiration. It tries to answer the question "How?"—the very question that binds together poetry and phenomenology. It does so by saying how poems themselves think, how they breathe, and how new breath must be found for American poetry in the late twentieth century. We can loosen the tight knot of these three questions by following the theme of breath in his poems and seeing the areas into which it reaches.

∾

"The Accident" is one of Strand's most powerful early narrative poems. It begins where another poem about a railway accident might well end—"A train runs over me"—and immediately offers an expected reaction: "I feel sorry / for the engineer" (*CP*, 42). The motif of breath enters the poem right away. The train driver "whispers" in the speaker's ear, and "blows" ashes from the sufferer's lips. He continues to murmur to the injured man, relating his own life story, until a flashlight frightens him away, leaving the casualty beside the train tracks. At home, the train driver imagines the speaker sprawled on the ground, "the faint blooms / of my breath / being swept away" (*CP*, 43). *Blooms:* although the man is mortally hurt, his breath still shows vitality, for we remember that a bloom contains the reproductive system of a plant. Even though the poem's last line reads, "The end of my life begins," we realize that the victim has been speaking the whole lyric, reproducing himself in the very poem that we are reading. Oddly, his dying breaths are more powerful than the huge brute forces of nature about him, "the heavy sheets / of the wind" that scatter the birds into the trees (*CP*, 43). It is an old boast: art is stronger than nature. Certainly the poem has outlasted any storm.

Reasons for Moving, in which "The Accident" appears, was published in 1968, toward the end of the age of "confessional" poetry. (Sylvia Plath had died in 1963, John Berryman would die in 1972, Anne Sexton in 1974, and Robert Lowell would pass away in 1977.) If Strand inherits anything from this school, it is chiefly in the mode of refusal, for at this stage of his writing, he tells us nothing about himself that we do not already know merely by being human. His desired genealogy, however, seems clear, since he testifies to it the year before his second book was published. *Another Republic*, an anthology of seventeen European and South American poets, which Strand co-edited with Charles Simic, was published in 1976.[12] Attempts had earlier been made to expand the canon of poetry read in America, chief among them being Robert Bly and William Duffy's *The Fifties: A Magazine of Poetry and General Opinion*, which continued as *The Sixties* and *The Seventies*. But *Another Republic* gathered together a range of poets other than those valued for the "deep image," some of whom Strand would doubtless like to count as inspirations: Julio Cortázar, Nicanor Parra, and above all Carlos Drummond de Andrade, whose work he had encountered in Elizabeth Bishop's fine translations and to the study of which he dedicated himself while on a Fulbright scholarship in Rio de Janeiro, Brazil, in 1965.[13]

Yet we should be careful not to take the authorial names in *Another Republic* as a family tree. For one thing, the anthology is co-edited: we should not presume that everything there speaks powerfully to Strand as a poet. Simic has his own interests and commitments. And for another thing, there are poets who inspire Strand but who are not in the anthology. There is Rafael Alberti, for one, among the Europeans, and American contemporaries such as Donald Justice, Louis Simpson, and of course Bishop also fall beyond the anthology's bounds.[14] Also, it must be said that sometimes poets learn most outside poetry, and when reading the early Strand we can sense prose writers—Borges, Buzzati, Kafka, Landolfi, and Schultz—giving him some of the air he needs to breathe. Also, the proximity of Wallace Stevens to Strand is evident from as early as "The Man in Black" up to the cantos of *Dark Harbor* (1993) and beyond. In poetry, though, as in the realm of faith, there is a strange "spiritual acoustics"; sometimes the voice that counts the most for one's own poetry seems to come from one writer but in fact comes from another.[15] On occasion it is not even a writer. Edward Hopper, Giorgio de Chirico, and René Magritte are significant for Strand, albeit in another way than Drummond de Andrade. They can evoke situations and moods, but do not indicate new ways of writing poems. The artist on whom one seizes at once covers a true forebear and gives one a membrane through which to hear what one needs to hear in order to write without undue anxiety.[16]

Not only did Strand read translations of Drummond de Andrade and others but also he translated poems from the Spanish and Portuguese himself, and, more importantly, undertook a complex translation of what inspired them when writing his own poems, especially those in his first four books.[17] Few things are as complex as "inspiration": the Muse who whispers in one's ear is no goddess but an amalgam of artists, esteemed and feared, alive and dead, whose prophecies and blandishments are commonly heard imperfectly. The most vital translations that Strand undertook are not quite translations; each of them is marked as "after" the poet named. To be sure, Lowell's *Imitations* (1961) is a model here, especially for poets who are not fluent in the language of the poem to be translated; but Strand's own word "after" bespeaks more than a modest knowledge of the foreign language as it is whispered in parentheses before or after a poem. For the word at once accepts a secondary rank for the translation with respect to the original poem—it is customarily beneath it in status as well as coming subsequent to it—while actively pursuing something in the original poem that is held to belong just as surely to the later poet as it has done to the earlier one. Drummond de Andrade's "Elegia 1938," for instance, becomes for Strand "Elegy 1969"; and we might judge better what it means for a poem to be "thoughts, that breathe" if we compare Strand's adaptation of the poem with a later translation of it. Consider the line "sentes calor e frio, falta de dinheiro, fome e desejo sexual" which is rendered faithfully enough as "you feel heat and cold, lack of money, hunger, and sexual desire." Under Strand's gaze, however, the line becomes, "you shiver in bed, you get hungry, you want a woman" (CF, 126).[18] Its concretion is palpable.

∿

"Breath" is Strand's most extensive treatment of the phenomenon, or rather (as we will see) phenomena named in the word, even though it takes root in the poem half way through. It begins with an undefined "you" who is to be meeting a similarly undefined "them" being told that the speaker remains where he has been. The second piece of information we—for each of us takes himself or herself to be addressed as "you"—are given to impart is that "I stand on one leg while the other one dreams" (CP, 91). If we think that the speaker is seeking to strengthen his ankles or, more darkly, to judge his risk of having a stroke, we will have gotten on the wrong track right away. We are hardly in a naturalist world when reading this poem, and we need to give full weight to the statement that the speaker's other leg is dreaming. He is saying that, rather than having two feet squarely on the ground, he is only partly balanced. Dreaming—poetry—keeps him unsteady, although, as he says, "this is the only way" for him to live.

The catalogue of peculiar statements is unrelenting. Next, we are instructed to say that "the lies I tell them are different / from the lies I tell myself" (CP, 91). The speaker recites poems, knowing, as Shakespeare's Touchstone says, "the truest poetry is the most feigning," and he presumably practices within the normal range of self-deceit common to writers, from the belief that one must await inspiration to the conviction that memorable poetry overcomes mortality.[19] Clearly, the speaker wishes to communicate what is involved in writing poetry, including "that by being both here and beyond / I am becoming a horizon" (CP, 91). Two things are in play here. The first is that by imaginatively stretching so far, he becomes a horizon for someone else, his friends perhaps. One encounters objects, events, and persons only within a horizon; yet here we are told that the speaker is becoming the very means whereby objects, events, and persons can be perceived from a given point. He is, if you like, becoming a poem. And the second is that by using his imagination, he is able to reach the very limit of his possible experiences, becoming his own horizon.

The Romantic rhetoric, with surrealist highlights, of the opening two quatrains is suddenly brought up short with a further injunction of something else to communicate: "that as the sun rises and sets I know my place" (CP, 91). Strand's quasi-biblical litanies are signature pieces of Darker (1970), and when reading "Breath" we would be right to recall Ecclesiastes 1:4–6:

> 1:4: One generation passeth away, and another generation cometh:
> but the earth abideth for ever.

1:5: The sun also ariseth, and the sun goeth down, and hasteth to
his place where he arose.
1:6: The wind goeth toward the south, and turneth about unto the
north; it whirleth about continually, and the wind returneth again
according to his circuits.[20]

"I know my place" despite the Romantic "lies" that he tells himself, and what saves
him, he says, is "breath." Far from being divine or semi-divine afflatus, breath is
found even in uninspired writing, "the forced syllables of decline," and is contained
in the body, seen in a Platonic manner (*soma sema*) as a "coffin," and yet also "a
closet of breath," where "breath" begins to stand for the spirit (*ruaḥ, pneuma*).[21]
If we feel that we are now on familiar philosophical and religious terrain, we
would be mistaken. The poem swivels in another direction in an image that pegs
Strand's idiom: "breath is a mirror clouded by words" (91).

We might think at first that the image suggests that breath is a mirror, that
it would represent one's spirit were it not for language preventing a full recovery of
self. A stronger reading, however, is that our words appear only in breath, and that
we can see ourselves—our spirits, if you wish—in that cloud. One's own creativity is
essential to self-recovery, and at best we see through a glass darkly. Hence "the cry
for help" to the stranger; the one speaking might come to self-knowledge in and
through intersubjectivity, although no assurance is given that any aid is forthcoming.
Here as elsewhere, Strand has a low estimate of the compassion of human beings;
only love humanizes. As with the faint blooms of breath in "The Accident," breath
here is powerful, and "all resistance falls away" from it. Three things are said, the
second two building on the first. Life irrepressibly asserts itself, not requiring that
it acquire "meaning." Life is light, and in its ascension, it overcomes darkness. And
at the end we learn that it is also love, life charged with meaning.

By now, following the furious pace of the speaker's instructions, we have
almost forgotten those who are away and who you and I are to meet; yet in the
poem's final words they return, hailed as beloved. Breath, then, is not merely
a blind drive of the body; it responds to an act of the will: it can be withheld,
slowed, or quickened. Finally, we learn that the deep inwardness that dominates
the poem is divided; there is a place for others in the subjectivity of the speaker.
In knowing that one is loved, one has the strength also to begin again, if need
be. It is not the stranger who can help us find self-knowledge, at least not in this
poem; it is those we already love. For self-knowledge requires an emptying of the
self before another person, and this self-emptying is less informed by the ethics
called forth by the neighbor than by the affection called forth by the friend. As
Strand will later testify, at the beginning of *The Late Hour* (1978), with the "coming of love [. . .] tomorrow's dust flares into breath" (*CP*, 183). Where Genesis
has God breathing life into Adam, Strand has human love furiously overcoming
the inexorable power of time, if only for a moment.

∽

"I feel the turning of breath / around what we are going to say," says the speaker of "The Room," a poem of pure anticipation of communication between a man and a woman (*CP*, 147). The phrasing inevitably recalls Paul Celan (who is included in *Another Republic*): "Poetry is perhaps this: an *Atemwende*, a turning of our breath" (*Dichtung: das kann eine Atemwende bedeuten*), though I choose not to enter into the labyrinth of meanings that Celan constructs in this one sentence.[22] What is to be said in this room, if Strand follows Celan, will be "a word against the grain" (*ein Gegenwort*) (*CP*, 40), a turning away from what is expected, and a breath of fresh air. If we follow Celan, it will be poetry (*Dichtung*) only if it cuts its figure against art (*Kunst*). Yet Strand's poem ends with no word being exchanged between the man and the woman; their entire conversation is telescoped and elided in the final two lines: "The beginning is about to occur. / The end is in sight" (*CP*, 148). "The Room" leads up to poetry but does not embody any, it would seem. And yet if poetry is language that counters convention, offering a new way of being in the world, "The Room" might well be a contender for poetry of a high level. Without meter or rhyme, the poem is nonetheless haunting in its repetitions of simple statements that slowly establish a mystery, frustrating our standard ways of understanding the world: "I stand at the back of a room," "you have just entered," and "I cannot remember." Throughout, we expect something to happen, and throughout we are disappointed. Clearly, the man and woman have met before, and we expect that they will see one another in the room and then speak. Yet that does not happen. Indeed, we are told that when they do meet (outside the space of the poem), "Your name will no longer be known, / nor will mine" (*CP*, 148). The human contact will fall short of or exceed what individualizes them and keeps them in the space of social convention.

When reading "The Room" and other poems by Strand that are like it, we might wonder what is actually thought in his poetry and how this takes place. There is no single answer. Yet, to begin, we might observe that very little of his poetry, if any, is mental action conveyed by transparent, ordered language. What there is may be found in some of Strand's earliest and later poems. Especially in the arc from *Reasons for Moving* to *The Story of our Lives*, there is little or no duality of meaning and sign; and if one seeks to explicate his poems (as I have been doing), one mostly finds that very little has been gained from the exercise. The poems are mysteries, not mystifications, and therefore are not illumined by attempts to expose a frame of mind or recover a secret. They are also alive; no critical procedures can turn them into objects. "The Room," we might say, is a realized movement of anticipation that has remained anticipation.

If we return for a moment to "The Accident," we can see how much "The Room" differs from it. Blanchot's remarks on the extraordinary bring to light our experience of reading the earlier poem:

The reader who reads tales of the extraordinary wants to be carried away in a headlong flight during which he repeatedly asks, "And then? And then?" while asking this other question under his breath: "But why? Why?" For him, the tearing pace of the story briefly stands in for verisimilitude. The story is justified because his attention has sped from the beginning to the end without openly requiring any other justification than that repeated "and then?" But this justification is merely provisional. The mystery retains all of its power only because it makes its presence felt for reasons other than the skillful ordering of the narrative, and regardless of whether such narrative adroitness is absolutely authentic and necessary. A cause must be found which is not an explanation (for the explanation of a mystery lies solely in the development of its obscurities it is never a revelation of its secret); it requires a reply which nonetheless does not cause the question to disappear, which rather makes it more pressing, even opaque, more able to turn the mind away from those expressions that guarantee it peace and contentment.[23]

Yet when we read "The Room," there is no narrative, no fantasy; a sense of mystery impinges on us because our accepted concepts and categories seem to have been disabled by what is experienced. Part of this mystery is that the poem takes place, it seems, in only a moment, though the moment is stretched so that it seems much time is passing. In one sense, a great deal is thought, including the feeling of dust falling, the coldness of the sunlight, a memory of sorrow, and the size of the room. Yet in another sense, the poem thinks nothing at all; it sidesteps or transcends the very conditions that thinking needs.

Perhaps the word "uncanny" is closer to one's experience of reading "The Room" than the word "mystery." Here, what is uncanny is the sheer strangeness that intrudes between two ordinary people; they seem to occupy a peculiar topological space that frustrates any easy passage from the one to the other. The effect is achieved with the simplest of words and the most straightforward of declarative sentences, and while the poem may well seem absolutely inward, taking place deep within one's self as well as within Strand's self, something in it shatters narcissism. The uncanny is what a human psyche cannot process because its very appearance, however fleeting it may be, indicates the reality of some hidden thing outside the self. In Strand's work, this sense of the uncanny is at its most intense in *The Story of Our Lives*. Thereafter, there is a discernable shift in his habits of perception. If he begins to allow Stevens to shine through him, and even at times for Whitman or Wordsworth to do the same, he never quite sets aside the uncanny. He will, however, no longer disdain using a closed form to open himself and his readers to what we prefer to repress. Think, for example, of those villanelles, "Two de Chiricos," in *Blizzard of One* (1998).

∽

Sometimes breath is hidden in Strand's poems; it withdraws to become a condition of possibility for poetry itself, and when this happens its most potent figure is Orpheus. In the later poetry, we no longer find a dramatization of the emptying of self; instead, we see another person who is anterior to the self, and this is the primal poet, inspiration itself. European and South American models tend to slip away in the later poetry, leaving Strand to contend with his local forebears.

Strand's Orpheus is the author of three sublime poems, and in "Orpheus Alone," from *The Continuous Life* (1990), he details them. First, there is the well-known lament for his wife Eurydice, bitten by a viper when running away from Aristaeus, that is sung before the powers of Hades; it makes even the Furies weep and has his wife overcome death, if only for a brief time, so that she may "step through the image of herself" (*CP*, 273). It would be hard to compete with Rilke's treatment of this theme in "Orpheus. Euyrdike. Hermes," and Strand does not attend to the poet's return to the sweet light and the second death of Eurydice. His lament draws its force from the beauty of his beloved while she was alive. The god of the underworld was hardly immune to female beauty, as his abduction of Persephone shows, and Strand's Orpheus plays upon his weakness. Unlike the speech given to Orpheus by Ovid, the one that Strand has him deliver is gorgeously erotic. He describes his wife when alive to the lord of death, dwelling lovingly on "her eyes, / Her forehead where the golden light of evening spread, / The curve of her neck, the slope of her shoulders, everything / Down to her thighs and calves" (*CP*, 273). It is sufficient to release his wife from death: poetry of the first circle has a fire that cannot be forgotten or slighted.

Second, Stand evokes that, with the definitive loss of Eurydice, Orpheus seeks solitude in the hills and there sings again, tuning the world to his desire. It is the poetry of magic, of miracle, and it stretches to another circle:

> [T]rees suddenly appeared in the bare place
> Where he spoke and lifted their limbs and swept
> The tender grass with the gowns of their shade,
> And stones, weightless for once, came and set themselves there,
> And small animals lay in the miraculous fields of grain
> And aisles of corn, and slept. (*CP*, 274)

In the *Georgics* and the *Metamorphoses*, Virgil and Ovid imagine trees coming to hear Orpheus as he sings, but Strand exceeds his classical sources and the desire for an earthly paradise in order to hear a third, more modern poem sung by the fabled poet.[24] The third poem is the great lyric of mortality; it does not come with Orpheus's forbidden gaze at Eurydice but is called forth only with the primal poet's own death by dismemberment: "it came in a language / Untouched by pity, in lines, lavish and dark, / Where death is reborn and sent into the world as a gift" (*CP*, 274). Strand's Orpheus is a figure of inspiration, to be sure, but also a reminder that expiration is not without value; it adds to the intensity of life and it bequeaths us the poetry of mourning. We think of the speaker of "Breath" who is becoming a horizon, touching his outermost limit, and surely, we also think of Stevens's "Sunday Morning" where the heavenly paradise is set aside in favor of mortal beauty. Yet Strand does not stretch himself into the gaiety of language, as Stevens does in *Harmonium* (1923) and later, but concentrates his energies on the poetry of mourning. His Orpheus, his inspiration, is the singer of the third poem.

If there is a defining moment, however, when Strand finds Orpheus in Stevens it is surely in *Dark Harbor* (1993). The proem to this long poem in forty-five cantos depicts the poet in the third person leaving his town, going into the woods, and approaching the sea. Whitman, even more than Stevens, is now the poet's Muse, even though the poet testifies that it will be "The burning / Will of weather, blowing overhead" (*CP*, 319). The poem ends with him having "but-toned / His coat, and turned up his collar, and began to breathe" (*CP*, 319). He enters more fully into the life of poetry beside the sea; it is a sharp turn from the resignation of "Poor North" in *The Late Hour* (1978) where a couple, working a "failing store" near St Margaret's Bay on the Atlantic coast of Nova Scotia, go out for a walk. Out in the wind, they "turn up their collars / and the small puffs of their breath are carried away" (*CP*, 213). In the later book, breath is anticipation of freedom and potency, not restriction and fleetingness. The poet will set off across this sea in search of a tranquil harbor; Cicero and Augustine made much use of the figure in commending the philosophical life to their readers, and their influence can be felt in the middle ages.[25] Yet Strand's safe harbor will be in the land of the dead, far from the storms of life.

I turn to consider the twenty-eighth canto, where Strand once again evokes Orpheus. It begins with a tribute to the power of song:

> There is a luminousness, a convergence of enchantments,
> And the world is altered for the better as trees
> Rivers, mountains, animals, all find their true place,
>
> But only while Orpheus sings. When the song is over
> The world resumes its old flaws, and things are again
> Mismatched and misplaced . . . (*CP*, 348)

Poetry does not breathe life into the things of the world but it creates a second world from what it is given. It does so not by divine fiat but by offering enchanting music and verse. (We are likely to recall the girl singing in Stevens's "The Idea of Order at Key West.") It is the second great poem, as evoked in "Orpheus Alone," though somewhat chastened. With poetry mere place becomes "true place," a proper configuration of nature where truth can manifest itself in things said there, believed there, acted out there. Song uncovers truth or, rather, is itself that very uncovering, and it depends on breath. For breath supports the voice by being released slowly, judiciously and in full awareness of the length of a musical phrase. Yet once the breath has expired, and once the song is over, the world returns to its former state, and the poet resigns himself to diminishment:

> Still, we feel better for trying,

> And there is always a glass of wine to restore us
> To our former majesty, to the well of our wishes
> In which we are mirrored, but darkly as though

> A shadowed glass held within its frozen calm an image
> Of abundance, a bloom of humanness, a hymn in which
> The shapes and sounds of Paradise are buried. (*CP*, 348)

Stevens consoles himself in "The Auroras of Autumn" that although there never was a place for innocence there certainly was a time, childhood.[26] Strand responds that although paradise is never to be found on earth, it may be discovered in poetry, in the time of a few breaths.

Dark Harbor ends with the poet finally reaching a haven, a misty shore, "with lots of stone cottages badly needing repair." It is the land of dead souls, "oblivious to their bodies, which the wind passes through" (*CP*, 366). As when Dante enters Limbo in the *Inferno* and speaks with Homer, Ovid, Lucan, and Horace, so Strand on the other shore hears of "many poets / Wandering around who wished to be alive again" (*CP*, 366). Their wish is not simply for more life but for the poetry that they could not write while alive: "They were ready to say the words they had been unable to say" (*CP*, 366). Their longing to say those words is to give voice to love, pain, and pleasure, to what these things mean on the other side of life. The poem concludes with the prospect of one of the dead poets, figured as an angel, about to sing; but it is forbidden for us to hear the sublime poetry of the dead, of those without breath. We must content ourselves with the poetry of mortality. Such is one lesson of Strand's *Collected Poems*.

Abbreviation

CP   Strand, Mark. *Collected Poems*. New York: Knopf, 2014. All references to poems by Strand are to this edition.

Notes

1. See Thomas Gray and William Collins, *Poetical Works*, ed. Roger Lonsdale (Oxford: Oxford University Press, 1977), 51.

2. See Plato, *Apology*, 22b. Martin Heidegger proposes, however, that poetry is a "wholesome danger" for thinking. See his *Poetry, Language, Thought*, trans. Albert Hofstadter (New York: Harper & Row, 1971), 8.

3. See "Partage formel," in René Char, *Oeuvres complètes*, introduction. Jean Roudaut, Bibliothèque de la Pléiade (Paris: Gallimard, 1995), 162.

4. See Eckart Schutrumpf, ed., *Heraclides of Pontus: Texts and Translations*, trans. Peter Stork, Jan van Ophuijsen, and Susan Prince (Piscataway, NJ: Rutgers University Press, 2008), 169.

5. Mark Strand, *Collected Poems* (New York: Knopf, 2014). All references to poems by Strand will be to this edition.

6. See Rimbaud's "À Georges Izambard," in Arthur Rimbaud, *Oeuvres complètes*, ed. André Guyaux and Aurélia Cervoni, Bibliothèque de la Pléiade (Paris: Gallimard, 2009), 340.

7. See, for example, "The Circular Ruins" and "Borges and I," in Jorge Luis Borges, *Collected Fictions*, trans. Andrew Hurley (New York: Viking, 1998), 96–100, 324.

8. See Franz Kafka, "The Burrow," in *The Penguin Complete Short Stories of Franz Kafka*, ed. Nahum N. Glatzer (Harmondsworth: Penguin, 1983), 325–59.

9. See Martin Heidegger, *Bremen and Freiburg Lectures: Insight into That Which Is and Basic Principles of Thinking*, trans. Andrew J. Mitchell (Bloomington: Indiana University Press, 2012), 4.

10. See Maurice Blanchot, *Thomas l'obscur*, pref. Pierre Madaule (reprint, Paris: Gallimard, 2005).

11. See Federico García Lorca, *Poesía completa* (Barcelona: Galaxia Gutenberg, 2013), 569–576.

12. See Charles Simic and Mark Strand, eds., *Another Republic: 17 European and South American Writers* (New York: The Ecco Press, 1976).

13. See Elizabeth Bishop, *Poems, Prose, and Letters* (New York: Library of America, 2008), 281–298.

14. See Rafael Alberti, *The Owl's Insomnia*, trans. Mark Strand (New York: Atheneum, 1973). With regard to Donald Justice, I am thinking of poems such as "The Thin Man" and "The Missing Person," which resonate with the poet of *Reasons for Moving*, in particular. See his *Collected Poems* (New York: Knopf, 2004), 88–90. (The influence of Justice is perhaps felt also in some of the weaker poems of *Sleeping with One Eye Open*, Iowa City: Stone Wall Press, 1964). With regard to Louis Simpson I have in mind his *Searching for the Ox* (New York: Morrow, 1976), and with respect to Bishop I refer to poems such as "The Map," "The Man-Moth," and "The Unbeliever," *Poems, Prose, and Letters*, 3, 10–11, 17.

15. See Søren Kierkegaard, *The Sickness unto Death: A Christian Psychological Exposition for Upbuilding and Awakening*, Kierkegaard's Writings XIX (Princeton, NJ: Princeton University Press, 1983), 114.

16. I allude of course to Harold Bloom's *The Anxiety of Influence: A Theory of Poetry* (New York: Oxford University Press, 1973).

17. See Carlos Drummond de Andrade, *Souvenir of the Ancient World*, trans. Mark Strand (New York: Antaeus Editions, 1976). It should be noted that in this col-

lection Strand does not use the words "after Carlos Drummond de Andrade." That expression is restricted to when he includes the translations in his own books of poetry.

18. See Drummond de Andrade, *Multitudinous Heart: Selected Poems*, trans. Richard Zenith (New York: Farrar, Straus, Giroux, 2015), 49.

19. Shakespeare, *As You Like It*, III. iii. 17–18.

20. *The Holy Bible* (King's James Version).

21. See Plato, *Cratylus*, 483a. Also see *Gorgias* 400b.

22. Paul Celan, "The Meridian," in *Collected Prose*, trans. Rosemary Waldrop (Manchester: Carcanet, 1986), 47.

23. Maurice Blanchot, "Ghost Story," in *Desperate Clarity: Chronicles of Intellectual Life, 1942*, trans. Michael Holland (New York: Fordham University Press, 2014), 108.

24. See Ovid, *Metamorphoses*, trans. Arthur Golding, ed. and introduction. Madeleine Forey (Baltimore, MD: Johns Hopkins University Press, 2002), X: 94–116. Also see Virgil's fourth Eclogue in C. Day Lewis, trans., *The Ecologues, Georgics and Aeneid of Virgil* (London: Oxford University Press, 1966), 126, and Shakespeare, *Henry VIII*, III: i, 3–14.

25. See, for instance, Cicero, *Brutus* 2.8, *De oratore* 1.60, 255, and Augustine, *De beata vita* 1.4. St Gregory the Great uses the figure in his "Letter to Leander," in *Moral Reflection on the Book of Job*, vol. 1, trans. Brian Kerns, introduction. Mark DelCogliano (Collegeville, MN: Liturgical Press, 2014), 47–48.

26. See Wallace Stevens, *Collected Poetry and Prose*, ed. Frank Kermode and Joan Richardson (New York: The Library of America, 1997), 360.

Bibliography

Alberti, Rafael. *The Owl's Insomnia*. Translated by Mark Strand. New York: Atheneum, 1973.

Andrade, Carlos Drummond de. *Souvenir of the Ancient World*. Translated by Mark Strand. New York: Antaeus Editions, 1976.

Andrade, Drummond de. *Multitudinous Heart: Selected Poems*. Translated by Richard Zenith. New York: Farrar, Straus, Giroux, 2015.

Bishop, Elizabeth. *Poems, Prose, and Letters*. New York: Library of America, 2008.

Blanchot, Maurice. "Ghost Story." In *Desperate Clarity: Chronicles of Intellectual Life, 1942*, translated by Michael Holland, 106–113. New York: Fordham University Press, 2014.

Blanchot, Maurice. *Thomas l'obscur*. Preface by Pierre Madaule. Reprint, Paris: Gallimard, 2005.

Bloom, Harold. *The Anxiety of Influence: A Theory of Poetry*. New York: Oxford University Press, 1973.

Borges, Jorge Luis. *Collected Fictions*. Translated by Andrew Hurley. New York: Viking, 1998.

Celan, Paul. "The Meridian." In *Collected Prose*, translated by Rosemary Waldrop, 37–55. Manchester: Carcanet, 1986.

Char, René. *Oeuvres complètes*. Introduction by Jean Roudaut. Bibliothèque de la Pléiade. Paris: Gallimard, 1995.

Gray, Thomas, and William Collins. *Poetical Works*. Edited by Roger Lonsdale. Oxford: Oxford University Press, 1977.

Gregory the Great, St. *Moral Reflection on the Book of Job*, vol. 1. Translated by Brian Kerns. Introduction by Mark DelCogliano. Collegeville: Liturgical Press, 2014.

Heidegger, Martin. *Bremen and Freiburg Lectures: Insight into That Which Is and Basic Principles of Thinking*. Translated by Andrew J. Mitchell. Bloomington: Indiana University Press, 2012.

Heidegger, Martin. *Poetry, Language, Thought*. Translated by Albert Hofstadter. New York: Harper & Row, 1971.

Justice, Donald. *Collected Poems*. New York: Knopf, 2004.

Kafka, Franz. "The Burrow." In *The Penguin Complete Short Stories of Franz Kafka*, edited by Nahum N. Glatzer, 325–359. Harmondsworth: Penguin, 1983.

Kierkegaard, Søren. *The Sickness unto Death: A Christian Psychological Exposition for Upbuilding and Awakening*. Kierkegaard's Writings XIX. Princeton, NJ: Princeton University Press, 1983.

Lewis, C. Day, trans. *The Eclogues, Georgics and Aeneid of Virgil*. London: Oxford University Press, 1966.

Lorca, Federico García. *Poesía completa*. Barcelona: Galaxia Gutenberg, 2013.

Ovid. *Metamorphoses*. Translated by Arthur Golding. Edited and introduced by Madelein Forey. Baltimore, MD: Johns Hopkins University Press, 2002.

Rimbaud, Arthur. *Oeuvres complètes*. Edited by André Guyaux and Aurélia Cervoni. Bibliothèque de la Pléiade. Paris: Gallimard, 2009.

Schutrumpf, Eckart, ed. *Heraclides of Pontus: Texts and Translations*. Translated by Peter Stork, Jan van Ophuijsen, and Susan Prince. Piscataway, NJ: Rutgers University Press, 2008.

Simic, Charles, and Mark Strand, eds. *Another Republic: 17 European and South American Writers*. New York: Ecco Press, 1976.

Simpson, Louis. *Searching for the Ox*. New York: Morrow, 1976.

Strand, Mark. *Collected Poems*. New York: Knopf, 2014.

Stevens, Wallace. *Collected Poetry and Prose*. Edited by Frank Kermode and Joan Richardson. New York: The Library of America, 1997.

11

Theater of Breath

An Artaud-Derrida Existential Conflict

JONES IRWIN

Introduction

Although Jacques Derrida's early work is often associated with phenomenology, with his readings of Husserl most especially, it can be argued that there is a greater emphasis on themes from the French *avant-garde* and literature in Derrida's early critique of philosophy as such. Thus, while preoccupied with phenomenology as an object of investigation, Derrida's own radical approach to a critique of phenomenology, and philosophy more generally, owes a great debt to a different countertradition of writers.[1]

This countertradition is somewhat eclectic in Derrida's employment of ideas, but nonetheless certain paradigmatic intellectual figures come to the foreground. Amongst these, perhaps Georges Bataille and Antonin Artaud[2] manifest the most explicit influence on deconstruction, not simply in the early work but also as a return to related thematics in Derrida's later texts (for example, in *On Touching* from 2000).[3] In this chapter, I will explore the specificity of Derrida's encounter with the thought of Artaud, a wild and enigmatic *oeuvre* brought together somewhat problematically under the title "The Theatre of Cruelty." Derrida's early encounter with Artaud is most powerful in his collection *Writing and Difference* (from 1967), where he devotes two essays to his reading.[4] In Derrida's later work, there is also a strong return to a focus on Artaud, in, for example, the essay "To UnSense the Subjectile."[5] These texts offer a multifaceted conception of the complexity and irreducibility of Artaud's thinking and artistic-philosophical practice, but in this

chapter I will especially refer to Derrida's understanding of Artaudian "breath."
I will present this encounter in the form of an existential conflict between the
two, which also involves significant affinities in both philosophy and application
to practice. It is certainly arguable nonetheless that Derrida presents a version of
Artaud to suit his own purposes and, in the first instance, we should thus begin
with a reading of Artaud's primary texts.

Artaud and Breath

Looking back on the intellectual life of 1930s France from the perspective of later
so-called "Continental philosophy," it is convenient to view much of the writings
and writers of this period as at odds with later developments. For example, we
can locate a distinct tendency within later thinkers such as Foucault and Deleuze
to present a paradigm shift taking place in post-1950s philosophy. Foucault's
preface to *Anti-Oedipus*, for example, locates the shift in the late 1960s.[6] Similarly,
Derrida's work castigates most especially what he sees as a humanist emphasis
in existential thought, for example in Sartre's thinking. Despite these critiques, a
different reading of the 1930s French philosophy is also possible, an interpretation that posits both an emergence of a very distinctive philosophical tendency
at this time and second, which sees a much stronger continuity between this
period and the later work.

   Artaud's texts are a particular case study in this regard, as we see both of
the positive and negative interpretations evident. Derrida's critique of Artaud, to
be discussed below, simultaneously affirms and distances itself from the "Theatre
of Cruelty." Here, I will offer a reading of Artaud that presents his work as radi-
calizing an existential perspective, with particular focus on the body, breath, and
expression. As Victor Corti has noted in his Introduction to the *Collected Works*,
"what Artaud proposed was a fundamental reconstruction in thought; he called
for destruction of our present social thought patterns and social judgement and
their replacement by the unformulated, the intuitive, by individual creation."[7]
In this latter sense, there is a clear line of continuity with the anti-Hegelianism
of Kierkegaard and the thinkers who follow the Danish existential philosopher
in the view that "subjectivity is truth." However, Artaud's conception of self or
individual is distinct; on his terms, there is a "mortal combat" between "mind
and flesh." We can trace this thematic in Artaud's early work in specific texts,
such as "The Situation of the Flesh."[8]

   The sense of a living, existential individual is here foregrounded by Artaud
as the focus of his philosophical concern. "I am reflecting on life. All the systems
I could devise would never equal these cries by a man occupied in rebuilding
his life."[9] He also emphasizes a break with a hegemonic kind of dualism; "I can
conceive a system in which the whole man would be involved, man with his

physical body and the summits, the intellectual projection of his mind."[10] We can associate this dualism with paradigmatically Platonism and Cartesianism in the tradition, but it remains a residual influence on succeeding philosophical thought. The kind of abstraction that this dualism is grounded in is traced by Artaud in the most contemporary manifestations of theater and philosophy. In contrast, and vehemently, he opposes what he refers to as "lifeforce" or "Flesh": "this is what I personally call the Flesh; I do not separate my thought from my life; with each of my tongue's vibrations I retrace all the paths of my thought through my flesh."[11] Significantly, he also refers explicitly to this reference as "Existence," drawing him close to the work of Sartre and going back to Kierkegaard, as mentioned above.

In a different essay, also from this earlier period, entitled "Umbilical Limbo," Artaud articulates the teleology of his philosophical intervention: "I suffer because the Mind is not in life and life is not Mind. We must get rid of the Mind [. . .] I would like to make a Book to disturb people like an open door leading them where they would never have gone of their own free will; simply a door communicating with reality."[12] Here we have the identified problem and crisis as well as the projected solution—if mind and dualism are at the root of the crisis, the solution must instead emphasize Flesh, Existence, and an intense reintegration of Mind and Reality. We can refer to this Artaudian approach as "a return to reality" if we understand that it involves a wholehearted critique of traditional realism (it reminds one of Pasolini's phrase "a reality which has nothing to do with realism)."[13]

It is here that Artaud's *Theatre of Cruelty* emerges, in the projected return to a rawness of "reality." This *Theatre of Cruelty* calls for a re-inspiration of "breath"—"the question of breathing is of prime importance."[14] Derrida's title for one of his essays on Artaud in *Writing and Difference*, "La Parole Soufflée,"[15] captures the ambiguity of either a "stolen speech" or "inspired speech," or both. The authentic self has been displaced, according to Artaud, by the machinations of Western metaphysics and its infiltrating influence on all art and social forms. Our breathing has been suffocated by overconceptualization and overtextualization. But here, Artaud also holds out for a different reality, a breathing (inspiration) that can be said to exist, or at least reexist, if his own project of a *Theatre of Cruelty* can be brought to fruition. What Artaud calls Cruelty signifies a new rigor and consciousness of the tragic theft of our very breath and "lifeforce," by metaphysics. It also seeks to reinstantiate what Artaud calls the "body without organs," in effect the authentic self who breathes for him- or herself, and who can inspire cultural and social revolution. One notable casualty here is the theological tradition and its hegemony on culture and human socialization. Artaud is unsparing: "do you know anything more outrageously fecal/than the history of God."[16]

While singular in its perspective, nonetheless Artaud's earlier work can be seen as aligned to a significant extent with the Surrealist movement. We will see below that Derrida's philosophical work also maintains connections with the surrealist inheritance. But with regard to such affinities, it is clear that this connection is much stronger in case of what we might refer to as a "dissident surrealism," a kind of offshoot group of artists and thinkers often at odds with Breton and the more official wing. Thus Artaud's work (as Derrida's) more easily aligns with Bataille, Klossowski, and Masson than with Breton. As Derrida puts it in "To Unsense the Subjectile," it is a question of "force before form."[17] Indeed, it is arguable that this declaration draws Derrida, Artaud, and the painter André Masson together. It is not for nothing that André Masson is Artaud's favorite painter, the "greatest painter in the world."[18] Thévenin also shows how Artaud's early texts especially were produced under the strong influence of Masson, while painting and drawing (as well as a "writing within drawing") are crucial for Artaud, early to late. Masson's art is also produced in the same conflict between force and form. As Kahnweiler has observed, Masson's universe "was not a world of forms, like that of the Cubists, but one of forces [. . .] This tragic art, which remains a stranger to nothing that is human, is truly the art of a generation which, even as it aspires to the Dionysian exaltation of Nietzsche, trembles before the prevailing *Weltangst*."[19] This description would also serve as an accurate evocation of Artaud's vision.

Derrida and Artaud: Deconstructing Breath

Derrida's encounter with Artaud remains characteristically double-edged. Here, I will be concerned primarily with the essay "La Parole Soufflée" (originally published in *Tel Quel* in 1965) or "The Breathed Speech" (or "The Stolen Breath") in which Derrida brilliantly aligns deconstruction with Artaud's reinvocation of "breath" while also cautioning about the complicity between Artaud's theater and the very metaphysics that he seeks to transgress. Derrida's interest in Artaud extends across the chronological breadth of his work, and to conclude this chapter I will look at Derrida's return to Artaud and specific questions of *avant-garde* poetics in his later writing. As we discussed above, Artaud's early work called, instead of words, for a physical theater and a physical language, of shouts, gestures, expressions; "we could listen more closely to life" and return to sonority, intonation, intensity. Derrida commends Artaud's work for overcoming the "naivete" of traditional metaphysics but also that of contemporary "critical and clinical discourse," where Derrida is referring to psychoanalysis and the work of philosophers such as Foucault and Blanchot. Despite the subtlety of the latter theorists, in effect they get Artaud wrong. Artaud's work presents more of a challenge to critical and philosophical discourse, and its conceptualizations, than has previously been allowed. Here, Artaud's central notion of "breath" is crucial for Derrida. Paradoxically, this must be reinforced by writing itself, but a nonphonetic, "hieroglyphic" *writing of the body*, to bring about "*the alienation of alienation*."[20] What must be overcome is what Derrida refers to in "La parole soufflée" as "the naivete of the discourse."[21] According to Derrida, Artaud's designation of the theatre of cruelty as "life" or "breath," for all its apparent utopianism, "absolutely resists—as was never done before—clinical or critical exegeses; he does so by virtue of his adventure; attempting to destroy the history of dualist metaphysics."[22] According to Derrida, Artaud "exhumes" the "ground of the clinic": "what his howls promise us, articulating themselves under the headings of existence, flesh, life, theatre, cruelty, is the meaning of an art prior to madness and the work; an artist's existence."[23]

The very title of Derrida's essay captures the pivotal and indispensable tension at the heart of Artaud's project; "spirited [soufflée] let us understand stolen by a possible commentator [. . .] at the same time let us understand inspired by an other voice."[24] Our bodies, and our very breath, our very sources of "lifeforce" are both poison and cure. Poison in the sense that they allow our identities to be lost, or "spirited away" in the alienation of everyday existence. Nonetheless, these bodies can also be "inspired" or "spiritualized." For Derrida, when Artaud refers to "my Body, my Life," these expressions must be understood "beyond any metaphysical determinations and beyond the limitations of being."[25] This would be a body that would overcome alienation through taking possession of itself in "a place where property would not yet be theft." But this vocation to propriety, to re-establish a proper body and life-existence, is constantly deferred in the quest for and consolidation of form. This, for Artaud, is the great tragedy of contemporary existence and constitutes a crisis in society, a truly political crisis: "if there is still one hellish, truly accursed thing in our time, it is our artistic dallying with forms, instead of being like victims burnt at the stake, signaling through the flames."[26]

It is this radicality of Artaud's project that Derrida considers so important, and also so uniquely effective in attempting to transgress the limits of Western philosophical thinking about life. "Artaud keeps himself at the limit, and we have attempted to read him at the limit. Artaud fulfils the most profound ambition of western metaphysics; but also affirms the law of difference; no longer experienced within metaphysical naivete but within consciousness."[27] Artaud thus achieves a "consciousness" that goes beyond traditional philosophical understanding while also remaining enigmatically dependent on philosophy. As Derrida observes in conclusion: "the transgression of metaphysics always risks returning to metaphysics; such is the question in which we are posed."[28] There is thus no final answer for Derrida here, but "a question in which we are posed." Artaud remains an "enigma of flesh."[29] As Artaud observes searingly in another early text, "Nerve Scales," "nothing, except fine Nerve Scales. A sort of impenetrable stop in the midst of everything in our minds."[30]

Derrida on Later Artaud

In "To Unsense the Subjectile," Derrida takes up the theme of an obscure, improper, or nongrammatical word ("subjectile") that Artaud uses three times in his texts (at Derrida's counting). Both thinkers, Derrida and Artaud, can be seen to "transform the relationship between art and the body."[31] Rather than being a localized or internalist aesthetic critique, Artaud's *Theatre of Cruelty* is rather profoundly political, "cruelty" being another name for life or desire, "the theatre of cruelty is life itself; the space it inhabits is that of original representation, the *archi*-manifestation of force or of life."[32]

A little like the Derridean notion of *différance*, the concept of the "subjectile" comes to take on a generalized significance for Derrida's reading, both with regard to Artaud's thought but also to the more overall relationship of philosophy to desire. The scene of the "subjectile" in Artaud constitutes a "dramaturgy," according to Derrida.[33] Even the word itself, which can be said to have no definitive meaning, designates a mini-drama: "between the beginning and the end of the word (sub/tile); the subjective and the projectile."[34] The term "subjectile" would mean neither/nor the subjective or the projectile, but it would carry resonances of both. With regard to the traditional notion of the subjective, Artaud would be declaring that "the body must be reborn,"[35] and calling for a new "bodily writing."[36] This would also relate to the question of "beingness": as Derrida notes, "the way Artaud treats the question of beingness; being starts with movement and not the inverse."[37] This would be a new philosophy of *becoming*, again showing the connections between Artaud and Nietzsche (as well as with Derrida). It would also constitute a liberation, a "delivery from a domination."[38] This would be the "projectile" aspect of the subjectile, a "force before form"[39] and an emphasis on radical *expression*.[40] And there would also be, Derrida tells us, a great consistency here in Artaud's work: "the machinery of the breath has always been at work."[41] From *The Theatre and its Double* right up until Artaud's last work, there would be an emphasis on breathing, on the sustaining expression of *breath*:

> Ten years ago language left,
> and in its place there came
> this atmospheric thunder,
>   this lightning
>
> . . .
>
> I say then that language distanced is a lightning that I brought on now in
>   the human fact of breathing, sanctioned by my pencil strokes upon
>   the paper.[42]

Of course, this is no neutral reading by Derrida. As the enigmatic title suggests, the "subjectile" is being "*unsensed*." Mary Ann Caws seeks to explicate the term as follows: "forcené/for-sené—unsensed by genius but not senseless; for unsense has in it the peculiar echo of an incense . . . something is consecrated here. Sense is not simply lost, it is gravely undone. There is a serious difference."[43] Derrida looks to Heidegger on Georg Trakl for some help: "the demented person dreams and he dreams as no one else could. . . . He is gifted with another sense."[44] But ultimately Derrida would not simply be talking of or on Artaud as intellectual object. He would also be speaking, in relation to the "unsense" and to the "subjectile," of deconstruction, and indeed of desire, more generally. Here, in "To Unsense the Subjectile," we would have conclusive evidence of Artaud's influence on the very "trajectory" of Derrida's work as a whole: "The *trajectory* (as well as the spurt or the -ject of a projectile), in other words the path (*sent, set*) of the *forcènement*."[45]

It would be a matter once more, as always, of "force before form": "Will I have been forcing things? [. . .] But first of all, no reading, no interpretation could ever prove its efficacy and its necessity without a certain forcing. *You have to force things*"[46] (Derrida's emphasis). This would then be precisely the performative dimension of Derrida's work, which would be more than merely a strategic adjunct. In *performing* philosophy in this way, Derrida would put the whole identity and self-understanding of the discipline into question each time he undertakes a deconstructive reading. And in this radicality and iconoclasm, this "force before form," Derrida would be precisely following (with significant digression and drift, by definition) an Artaudian trajectory.

An Existential Deconstruction between Artaud and Derrida

Artaud (and Derrida's) emphasis on existence here demonstrates a key (but underestimated) connection between deconstruction and existentialism. As Herman Rapaport has noted, Artaud (and Bataille) can be seen as "existentialists of a different feather."[47] As Bruce Baugh has observed, "Derrida is more existentialist than existentialism."[48] Such a view implies the need for a rewrite of the meta-level understanding of twentieth-century French philosophy, which tends to marginalize the existentialist emphasis as a minor aberration.

Much has been made of Derrida's disavowals of Sartre and of a certain "existentialist humanism (after the War)" (in, for example, the essay "Ends of Man,"[49] but it is clear that, even in his radical critique of *Existentialism and Humanism*,[50] Derrida still cites Sartre's *Nausea* as a key anti-humanist text. As he states in his later text, *A Taste for the Secret*:

> my intention was certainly not to draw away from the concern for existence itself, for concrete personal commitment, or for the existential pathos that, in a sense, I have never lost. Rather, what I did stemmed from my critical reflections on the reading of Husserl and Heidegger advanced by certain French existentialists such as Sartre and Marcel; and my dissent did not mean of course that I turned my back on existential questions. In some way, a philosopher without this ethico-existential pathos does not interest me very much.[51]

Derrida revisits these themes of existence and "the body" in one of his most significant later texts, *On Touching: Jean-Luc Nancy*. Again, Artaud's Theatre of Cruelty is a key point of reference for his interpretation here. Derrida first invokes Artaud, citing his project of the "proper body" and referring to Artaud's conception of "nerve-scales" or "nerve-meters" (*Pèse-nerfs*).[52] There would, nonetheless, need to be a certain ambivalence here, Derrida warns, toward any notion of a "body proper." We have seen in the Artaud essays in *Writing and Difference* that Derrida also sounds a note of caution with regard to a certain kind of residual metaphysics in Artaud, despite the fact that Artaud is said to resist clinical and critical exegeses "like no one before." So Derrida is foregrounding an emphasis on "sense" through Jean-Luc Nancy (which also reminds one of Artaud's "theatre of the senses"), but the metaphysical danger would loom large. Therefore it must be, as it is for Bataille and Nancy, "sense without an ontology of presence."[53]

In *On Touching*, he foregrounds a different but related problematic of "plasticity and technicity" (*en compte de la plasticité et de la technicité*).[54] Derrida seems to be arguing against the notion that one can draw the boundaries of touch at the organic limits of bodies. Rather we now have to consider a whole new dimension of "touch" and "sense," which has evolved from "the intertwining of techne and the body [*Verflechtung*]."[55] The term *Verflechtung* is a Merleau-Pontian term from *The Visible and the Invisible* (originally Husserlian), but here Derrida is using it precisely and explicitly to extend beyond the limits of what he sees as an anthropological boundary in phenomenology. We should also note that this "intertwining" (*Verflechtung*) looks back to Derrida's discussion of the "between" (*l'entre*) in *Dissemination* (the French here is *l'entrelacement*). *L'écriture du corps*, the writing of the body, would also be a kind of *l'entrelacement*, of intertwining.

If we are going to talk of "intertwining," with Jean-Luc Nancy we need to engage the philosophical significance of the virtual, or *techne*, of plasticity and technicity, of "machine-bodies" (*ce corps-machine*).[56] Derrida speaks of "amorous bodies, wrestling in the sheets of the Internet's webs" (*corps amoureux dans les draps du Web*)[57] and the whole image of virtual sexuality (or what Luciana Parisi has called "abstract sex"[58]) looms large. This revolutionizes what we mean by touching, beyond an anthropological limit: "the sense of touch is the sense of the electronic age" (*le sense de l'âge électronique*). This is "distance touching" (*toucher à distance érogène*).[59]

Our senses would now become "spaced out" into an "areality"; "sight becomes distended" (*la vue elle-même s'y distend*),[60] and this would be something to affirm for Derrida: "the oui that jouit" (*le oui qui jouit*).[61] This is a reference to the "yes that plays" in Cixous's discourse,[62] and it would all come back to the deconstructed I: "as in je/jeu."[63] This is the "I" that plays or the self that is also a "game," or "in the game," "*en jeu*," in Artaud's sense of "on stage."

Nancy goes on: "*salut* to the vision that did not cling to forms or ideas, but let itself be touched by forces."[64] Here, again, we see how central the whole *avant-garde* project of Artaudian "force before form" has been for Derrida, as recognized by Nancy. And there would be a "touching" here, and a being-touched, but beyond anthropology and with a certain postmodern virtuality. This would not lead to any greater sense but to a "clarity that only obscurity possesses [. . .] the manifest secret of life and death."[65]

Like Bataille, Nancy would be recognizing, through Derrida, the ultimate aporia of life and death, the gaping chasms between desire and fulfilment. And yet also this would be a joyous recognition of fundamental aporia, "the oui that jouit," as in "je/jeu."[66] This joyous (and somewhat raucous) element in deconstruction also reminds one of Foucault. There is, it seems to me, a strong affinity in the spirit of their work, if not always in the exact letter. Significantly, in his "A Preface to Transgression" essay on Bataille,[67] Foucault also returns in conclusion to the thematics of touch. Again, it is a matter of transgression, of a transgressive act, and here Foucault is referring to Bataille's infamous novel *L'Histoire de L'Oeil*: "the act that crosses the limit *touches* absence itself."[68]

From Bataille and Artaud through to Cixous, Derrida, and Nancy—what is being traced is a movement, a drift without any nodal "arche" or ground, but rather a process that is also a "lifeforce," an "Existence" and a fragile embodied breathing. In this chapter, we have sought to give expression to this Theater of Breath.

Notes

1. See Jones Irwin, *Derrida and the Writing of the Body* (Surrey: Ashgate, 2010).

2. Antonin Artaud, *Collected Works*, vol. 1 (London: Calder, 1968) and Georges Bataille, *Visions of Excess: Selected Writings 1927–1939*, ed. Allan Stoekl (Minneapolis: University of Minnesota Press, 1985).

3. Jacques Derrida, *On Touching: Jean-Luc Nancy* (Stanford, CA: Stanford University Press, 2005).

4. Jacques Derrida, *L'Écriture et la Différence* (Paris: Éditions du Seuil, 1967).

5. Jacques Derrida, "To Unsense the Subjectile," in *The Secret Art of Antonin Artaud*, Jacques Derrida and Paule Thévenin, trans. Mary Ann Caws (Cambridge: MIT Press. 1998).

6. Irwin, *Derrida and the Writing of the Body*, ivff.

7. Victor Corti, introduction to *Collected Works: Volume 1*, by Antonin Artaud (London: Calder, 1968), 9.

8. Antonin Artaud, "The Situation of the Flesh," in *Collected Works*, vol. 1, trans. Victor Corti (London: Calder, 1968), 164–166.

9. Artaud, *Collected Works*, 164.

10. Ibid.

11. Ibid.

12. Ibid., 49.

13. Quoted in Naomi Greene, *Cinema as Heresy* (London: Duckworth, 1974), 140. See also Pier Paulo Pasolini, *Heretical Empiricism*, trans. Ben Lawton and Louise K. Barnett (Washington, DC: New Academia, 2005).

14. Artaud, *Collected Works*, 84.

15. Jacques Derrida, "La Parole Soufflée," in *Writing and Difference* (Chicago: University of Chicago Press, 1978), 169–195.

16. Quoted in Derrida, *Writing and Difference*, 121.

17. Derrida, "To Unsense the Subjectile," 76.

18. Quoted in Derrida and Thévenin, *The Secret Art of Antonin Artaud*, 10.

19. Quoted in Rubin, *André Masson* (New York: Center for Contemporary Arts, 1984), 16.

20. Derrida, *Writing and Difference*, 230.

21. Ibid., 169.

22. Ibid., 174.

23. Ibid.

24. Ibid.

25. Ibid., 176.

26. Ibid., 178.

27. Ibid., 194.

28. Ibid.

29. Ibid.

30. Artaud, *Collected Works*, 75.

31. John Brannigan, "We have nothing to do with literature: Derrida and Surrealist Writing," in *The French Connections of Jacques Derrida*, ed. John Brannigan et al. (Albany: State University of New York Press, 1999), 56.

32. Brannigan, "We have nothing to do with literature," 59.

33. Derrida, "To Unsense the Subjectile," 62.

34. Ibid.

35. Ibid., 99.

36. Ibid., 85.

37. Ibid., 75.

38. Ibid., 69

39. Ibid., 76.

40. Ibid., 102–103.

41. Ibid., 120.

42. Ibid., 113.

43. Mary-Ann Caws, "Preface: Derrida's Maddening Text: AR-TAU," in *The Secret Art of Antonin Artaud*, Jacques Derrida and Paule Thévenin, trans. Mary Ann Caws (Cambridge: MIT Press, 1998), xiii.

44. Quoted in Derrida, "To Unsense the Subjectile," 70.

45. Ibid., 150.

46. Ibid., 156.

47. Herman Rapaport, *Later Derrida: Reading the Recent Work* (London: Routledge, 2002), 138.

48. Bruce Baugh, *French Hegel: From Surrealism to Postmodernism* (London: Routledge, 2005), 76.

49. Jacques Derrida, "The Ends of Man," in *Margins of Philosophy* (Chicago: University of Chicago Press, 1982), 109–136.

50. Jean Paul Sartre, *Existentialism and Humanism* (London: Metheun, 1980).

51. Jacques Derrida and Maurizio Ferraris, *A Taste for the Secret* (London: Polity, 2001), 60.

52. Derrida, *On Touching*, 61.

53. Ibid., 130.

54. Ibid., 220.

55. Ibid., 237.

56. Ibid., 237.

57. Ibid., 301.

58. Cf. Luciana Parisi, *Abstract Sex: Philosophy, Biotechnology, and the Mutation of Desire* (London: Continuum, 2004).

59. Ibid.

60. Ibid., 347.

61. Ibid., 34.

62. Hélène Cixous, *The Hélène Cixous Reader*, ed. Susan Sellars (London: Routledge, 1994), xviii.

63. Ibid., xviii.

64. Quoted Derrida, *On Touching*, 310.

65. Ibid.

66. Cixous, *Hélène Cixous Reader*, xviii.

67. Michel Foucault, "A Preface to Transgression," in *Aesthetics, Method, and Epistemology: Essential Works of Foucault 1954–1984*, vol. 2, ed. James D. Faubion (London: Penguin, 1998), 69–88.

68. Ibid., 86. My emphasis.

Bibliography

Artaud, Antonin. *Collected Works*. Vol. 1. Translated by Victor Corti. London: Calder, 1968.

Artaud, Antonin. "Nerve Scales." In *Collected Works*, vol. 1, translated by Victor Corti, 67–86. London: Calder, 1968.

Artaud, Antonin. "The Situation of the Flesh." In *Collected Works*, vol. 1, translated by Victor Corti, 164–166. London: Calder, 1968.

Artaud, Antonin. "Umbilical Limbo." In *Collected Works*, vol. 1, translated by Victor Corti, 47–65. London: Calder, 1968.

Bataille, Georges. *Visions of Excess: Selected Writings 1927–1939*. Edited by Allan Stoekl. Minneapolis: University of Minnesota Press, 1985.

Baugh, Bruce. *French Hegel: From Surrealism to Postmodernism*. London: Routledge, 2005.

Brannigan, John. "We have nothing to do with literature: Derrida and Surrealist Writing." In *The French Connections of Jacques Derrida*, edited by John Brannigan, Julian Wolfreys, and Ruth Robbins, 145–167. Albany: State University of New York Press, 1999.

Caws, Mary Ann. "Preface: Derrida's Maddening Text: AR-TAU." In *The Secret Art of Antonin Artaud*, Jacques Derrida and Paule Thévenin, translated by Mary Ann Caws, ix–xiv. Cambridge: MIT Press, 1998.

Cixous, Hélène. *The Hélène Cixous Reader*. Edited by Susan Sellars. London: Routledge, 1994.

Corti, Victor. Introduction to *Collected Works*, vol. 1, by Antonin Artaud, 9–15. London: Calder, 1968.

Derrida, Jacques. *L'Écriture et la Différence*. Paris: Éditions du Seuil, 1967.

Derrida, Jacques. "The Ends of Man." In *Margins of Philosophy*, 109–136. Chicago: University of Chicago Press, 1982.

Derrida, Jacques. "La Parole Soufflée." In *Writing and Difference*, 169–195. Chicago: University of Chicago Press, 1978.

Derrida, Jacques. *On Touching: Jean-Luc Nancy*. Stanford, CA: Stanford University Press, 2000.

Derrida, Jacques. "To Unsense the Subjectile." In *The Secret Art of Antonin Artaud*, Jacques Derrida and Paule Thévenin, translated by Mary Ann Caws, 59–148. Cambridge: MIT Press, 1998.

Derrida, Jacques. *Writing and Difference*. Translated by Alan Bass. Chicago: University of Chicago Press, 1978.

Derrida, Jacques, and Maurizio Ferraris. *A Taste for the Secret*. London: Polity, 2001.

Derrida, Jacques, and Paule Thévenin. *The Secret Art of Antonin Artaud*. Translated by Mary Ann Caws. Cambridge: MIT Press, 1998.

Foucault, Michel. "A Preface to Transgression." In *Aesthetics, Method, and Epistemology: Essential Works of Foucault 1954–1984*. Vol. 2. Edited by James D. Faubion, 69–88. London: Penguin, 1998.

Greene, Naomi. *Cinema as Heresy*. London: Duckworth, 1974.

Irwin, Jones. *Derrida and the Writing of the Body*. Surrey, UK: Ashgate, 2010.

Parisi, Luciana. *Abstract Sex: Philosophy, Biotechnology, and the Mutation of Desire*. London: Continuum, 2004.

Pasolini, Pier Paulo. *Heretical Empiricism*. Translated by Ben Lawton and Louise K. Barnett. Washington, DC: New Academia, 2005.

Rapaport, Herman. *Later Derrida: Reading the Recent Work*. London: Routledge, 2002.

Rubin, Andrew. *André Masson*. New York: Center for Contemporary Arts, 1984.

Sartre, Jean Paul. *Existentialism and Humanism*. London: Metheun, 1980.

12

The Media of Breathing

JOHN DURHAM PETERS

Alpha and Omega

Breathing is the alpha and omega of our time on earth. We breathe first at birth, and death is quite literally breath-taking. To speak with the King James Bible, in dying we "give up the ghost," an expression taken from the Greek verb *ekpneo* (to expire). But breathing's existential meaning is not found only at the beginning and end of life's alphabet, at the alpha and the omega, but also throughout the middle, in the L, M, N, or what we could call the elements (L-M-N) of existence. Things that are found in the middle, in what the ancient Greeks called the *metaxu* or "in between," in what the Romans called the *medius locus* (middle place) and later became the word "milieu," can be considered as media in the broadest sense.[1]

In this chapter I consider the media of breathing. Breath is everywhere in our culture at the moment—as a spiritual practice, as a medical urgency, as a record to be broken, as a biological need put into peril by climate change or industrial pollution. Breath implies life, respiration, as mere air does not, as in the haunting title of Paul Kalanithi's beautiful memoir of his own dying from lung cancer, *When Breath Becomes Air*.[2] But breathing is often considered to be something pure or natural and thereby removed from technical devices, that is, from media. In this chapter, I mean to rethink this assumption and show how an expanded conception of media actually illuminates much of what is most interesting about breath.

The field of media studies as I understand it not only concerns broadcasting, cinema, and the press but also the means of creating worlds and habitats, means that include cultural practices and body techniques on the one hand and material technologies and apparatuses on the other.[3] Media are often defined as content-distributing institutions such as radio, television, cinema, and the press, but here I will call those "mass media." "Media" as I use the term include both techniques and technologies. Techniques need not take any lasting material form (e.g., swimming technique), while technologies, in my definition, always require a physical tool or device (e.g., scuba gear). The concept of media is useful for the study of breath and breathing because media always put *techne* (art) and *physis* (nature) into mutual play, a relation that is particularly prominent in breathing. Techniques and technologies interact with and bring natural elements or organisms into the light. In this chapter, I understand media of breathing both as techniques (bodily practices such as yoga, singing, playing the flute, or giving birth) and as technologies (devices such as oxygen tanks, air conditioners, iron lungs, and spirometers).

It is one of the central claims of philosophical phenomenology and its many branches that the normal or natural or unnoticed background becomes visible only in a time of crisis or breakdown. Media usually stay in the middle or the background until they are disturbed, at times by analysis, in which case they become objects of theory and practice. Breathing, as one of the most basic and apparently automatic of all human activities, lends itself particularly well to a media analysis: it is an absolutely essential condition of life as we know it, almost always stays in the unconscious background, and yet it has been the subject of enormous technical elaboration. Breathing becomes theoretical or technical only when its usual functioning goes awry, as in a coughing fit or asthma attack, or when the natural breathing milieu is disturbed, such as when humans venture into such hostile environments as mines under the earth, dives into the sea, and flights into the air, or are exposed to severe air pollution or chemical warfare. When a newborn comes out of the womb into the air, when a human being—a land-animal par excellence—goes swimming, or when a miner in a mine shaft or a passenger in an airplane has difficulty breathing due to lack of oxygen, breath can no longer be taken for granted. When the natural or normal media fail, artificial media must step in to fill the gap, and natural ones rise to a new level of self-consciousness. Breathing techniques have arisen in practices, disciplines, and arts such as giving birth, singing, yoga, swimming, and deep-sea diving, all of which require the shepherding and conservation of breath and necessarily raise breathing to the level of conscious reflection, often, however, with the purpose of moving breath to a higher level of unconsciousness. Indeed, Marcel Mauss concludes his classic piece on body techniques with a discussion of "la technique des souffles" found in ancient China and India, a breathing practice whose various forms he considers to be widespread among diverse cultures.[4] Such breathing techniques are ancient, but breathing technologies—which either modify a hostile atmosphere or supplement a lacking body with apparatuses—are relatively recent and belong to modernity.

Martin Heidegger argued that made objects, especially works of art, can disclose truth processes, but he rarely extended this idea beyond paintings and chalices to ordinary, inconspicuous technical objects, even though his thinking has a distinctive feel for the meaning of instruments. But the idea that everyday objects are just as worthy of philosophical consideration as treasured works of art and items of religious ritual is absolutely constitutive for media theory in the wake of such figures as Harold Innis, Marshall McLuhan, and Friedrich Kittler, with their interests in such media as fisheries, linear type, and circuits. "Technology is a mode of revealing" (is eine Weis des Entbergens), according to Heidegger. Technology reveals nature, by unfolding potentials and awareness nature would never possess without intervention. Technology reveals nature as technical, as a storehouse of possibilities for use. In the twenty-first century the technosphere encompasses the biosphere, such that nature must be understood as technical, as something in need of human stewardship and steering.[5] In the classical understanding of elements, water, earth, air, fire, and the quintessence were the fundamental media of life on earth; current conditions call for a revival of such thinking.[6]

Romantic Breath (Kittler)

The analysis of breath is a venerable theme in German media studies, which like work by Innis and McLuhan, takes us beyond mass media as the main focus of interest. Take the famous opening line from Friedrich Kittler's *Aufschreibesysteme 1800–1900* (1985), a book foundational for the new field of media studies and later translated into English as *Discourse Networks*: "German literature begins with a sigh."[7] Kittler delights in showing how the obsession with breath and wind during Goethe's era, an era he calls "discourse network 1800," was officially a quest to find a common continuum between nature and humanity, but in fact a symptom of an educational system and gender-based division of labor that sought to convert texts into oral language via the mother's mouth. Texts were as it were ventilated by being read aloud, so that the breathing of the reading mother was the background accompaniment to all reading. (Here we might recognize phonetic writing, as a device for encrypting oral speech, as a breath technology.) The sigh Kittler referred to was the "Ach" uttered by Goethe's Faust, a sound also uttered by E.T.A. Hoffmann's mechanical doll Olympia and many other soulful yearners moved by *Sehnsucht* in the time of Goethe.[8] As Kittler noted, "ach" was a morpheme hidden within the German word *Sprache* (language) and the sound of a timeless and worldless soul that joined in one Nature and Spirit, human and nonhuman.[9]

Of course Kittler could be highly critical, even cynical, about this romantic breath-fetishism, especially in his early campaign to expel the spirit from the human sciences ("den Geist aus den Geisteswissenschaften auszutreiben"). But he could also treat the subject of breathing with remarkable subtlety. In his essay on Richard Wagner's operas called "World Breath," for instance, Kittler says that the media of Bayreuth were "optics and acoustics, lighting and wafts of breath [*Atemwehen*]." Wagner, who for Kittler was not only a poet and composer but also the first mass media impresario, joined Thomas Edison, inventor of the phonograph, in his willingness to transcend what Jacques Lacan calls "the symbolic" as the source of meaning. That is, both Wagner and Edison were acousticians interested in sound as such, including white noise, whether or not it had a linguistic meaning; both flattened the distinctions among such sounds as "wind and breath, the sounds of nature and human voices." Kittler's Wagner had what Lacan called a "respiratory erotics" centered on breathing as the sign of living human embodiment; Wagner called music "the breath" (*Athem*) of language. In his music dramas, breath served as a sign of life and death, and the ultimate breathing apparatus, sounding the world-breath itself, was the orchestra. Singing was not the privileged form but one among many arts of breathing distinguished for its "intensity of life in the diaphragm, lungs, throat, and mouth."[10] Here Kittler treats breath not only critically, but as the source of music, an undeniable sign of life, and raw material for media experiments.

The same is true in Kittler's recently published youthful essays written in a style reminiscent of Walter Benjamin, in which he ponders, in an almost ecstatic tone, how psychoanalysis might take up a theory of breathing. In contrast to orality and anality, he claims, breathing plays a relatively minor role in the psychoanalytic history of individuals, but breath remains nonetheless at the heart of our social, sexual, and musical lives. Of course Kittler, an inveterate chain smoker, brings smoking into his analysis as one of the many ways that breathing can be made into a cultural technique.[11]

The Natural History of Oxygen

Kittler's reflections on breath were exclusively about how techniques and technologies affect the breathing body. But there are also media that affect the atmospheric milieu. Let us consider the deep history of breathing, far back into its fascinating natural history. In the evolutionary history of life on earth oxygen was first a toxin. Oxygen is now the most widespread element in the lithosphere and the sea, as well as the atmosphere and biosphere, but this was not always the case. Oxygen has a volatile geological history and interacts crucially with both lithosphere and oceans. During the first three billion years the earth was a "giant oxygen vacuum."[12] The natural sinks of the planet quickly sucked up any available freestanding oxygen. (Mars remains in this state: any free oxygen is tied up in the lithosphere as rust, one reason Mars appears to be a red planet to us.) Oxygen remains a sociable element, ready to enter into relations with other elements, and represents the principal element in the air and the earth's crust today.[13] But it started to fill up the atmosphere when there were no mates left in land or sea. The oxygen vacuum could not last.

The first archaic wave of life on earth was anaerobic, consisting of organisms whose metabolism did not depend on oxygen. Cyanobacteria (blue algae) produced an overabundance of oxygen as a byproduct of photosynthesis that could no longer be absorbed by natural sinks such as the oceans or the lithosphere. (The earth, inasmuch as it participates in the exchange of oxygen and other elements, could even be said to breathe. Mountains, oceans, and forests are sometimes seen as planetary lungs, as they carry out the exchange of oxygen and carbon dioxide). Around 2.3 billion years ago, the so-called Great Oxidation Event took place, with catastrophic consequences that mark it still as the biggest extinction in earth's history. If carbon in the atmosphere now threatens life as we know it, oxygen once did the same. Some anaerobic life forms survived the catastrophe and live on, for instance, in our intestines and contribute to making wine and vinegar, but they are no longer the dominant species on earth. This catastrophic toxin, freestanding oxygen, eventually became the basis for respiration as organisms adapted evolutionarily to the new habitat, eventually becoming the dominant organisms on earth. But oxygen is still toxic: too much of it can lead to blindness or brain damage for newborns, and scuba divers must take care to avoid an overdose of it from their oxygen tanks.

Breathing is thus not in the least invariant or purely natural; rather, it has a decisively historical character. And respiration is not a condition for all forms of life. The equation that breathing air is life itself holds for only one part—though a very important once—of life on earth. Respiration, which produces carbon dioxide and water while burning sugars by means of oxygen, is the counterpart of photosynthesis, the transformation of light energy into chemical energy. When we breathe in, we unravel the work done by some plant remote in time and space. Respiration is the consumption of energy, photosynthesis its storage. Breathing is thus connected to the total circulation of life on our planet. Though every person has a unique respiratory signature, all of us are unified in our ecological dependence on photosynthesis for every drop of energy.

Comparative Phenomenology

The origin of life is in the water, and the assimilation of oxygen by organisms first took place in the oceans. As in the human fetus, so in biological history: breathing organs were first filled with fluid. The respiratory systems of land animals had to undergo a fundamental metamorphosis to be able to slurp the fuel of oxygen directly from the air instead of as diffused in an aqueous medium. Cetaceans, a family of mammals that include whales, porpoises, and dolphins, turned back to the sea from the land around fifty million years ago, and thus show the enormous plasticity of breathing organs and the creative diversity of evolution's natural laboratory. They retain lungs, rather than gills like fish, and thus can only breathe directly from the air. Their ear-nose-and-throat complex differs radically from ours. Dolphins speak (or rather "phonate") with their nose (or blowhole), hear with their jaw, and lack the musculature to move their faces expressively. As an organ of acoustic production, the cetacean blowhole appears to be just as versatile an instrument as the human voice, but dolphin hearing and phonation far exceeds ours in range and sensitivity, giving many species sonar powers.

During fifteen to fifty million years of ongoing evolution, among some cetacean species the two nostrils made a long journey to the top of the head where they converged into a single rather cyclops-like hole. Since cetacean breathing takes place through the blowhole and not the throat, breathing and swallowing, phonating and eating are completely separate; in contrast to humans, the dolphin nose and mouth are completely differentiated. Cetaceans cannot breathe or produce sound through their mouths; the evolutionary distinction of nose for breathing/phonating and mouth for feeding spares them the multitasking of the human throat for speech, breath, and food. A dolphin could never choke on its food. Humans, in contrast, have a single pass-through point by which we satisfy our needs for solid, liquid, and gaseous substances. (Cetaceans, by the way, cannot directly drink seawater, due to its high salinity, and hydrate indirectly from the organisms that they consume as food.) We breathe through our mouth or our nose, and normally direct traffic for the windpipe and the esophagus quite successfully, but these organs share precious real estate in the human body in a sometimes dangerous way unknown to our mammalian cousins in the oceans. Dolphins would never need to learn the Heimlich maneuver, a first-aid technique to save a person from choking.

If you will allow me a bit of speculation about comparative animal phenomenology, we could imagine one cetacean art that is essential to their existence: breathing technique. Human beings, of course, have developed a stunning array of diverse breathing arts and cultures, but these are rarely incontestable necessities for survival. John Cunningham Lilly, the American neurologist who launched the popular and ever proliferating story of communicating dolphins in the 1960s, began his first surgical experiments on dolphin brains in the mid 1950s with anaesthesia in order to numb the pain that his direct drilling into their skulls would cause. His research team swiftly killed five dolphins in a row before they realized that dolphins do not have autonomic breathing. With conscious control of breath taken away, the drugged animals suffocated to death.[14] Breathing among dolphins seems to be necessarily under conscious control. The blithe assumption that all animals necessarily breathe in the same way that we do can obviously be fatal. And when human autonomic breathing is interrupted—as in sleep apnea—the results can also be fatal.

If their breathing is always under conscious control, how do cetaceans sleep? Some experimentally observed dolphins can remain awake for five days in a row without showing symptoms of sleep deprivation. It appears that their brains sleep one hemisphere at a time, even shutting the corresponding eye, in what is known as "unihemispheric sleep."[15] Among humans, conscious breathing is an exception, but among cetaceans it seems to be the norm. Every cetacean seems to be a kind of yogi, a respiratory artist who puts breathing in the foreground of consciousness. Human breath, at rest, consists of more or less uniformitarian pulses unless interrupted by snoring or apnea, but cetacean breathing, especially among deep divers, involves huge cataclysmic intakes. A sperm whale at rest will breathe three to five times a minute, but in preparation for deep dives will hyperventilate, storing up oxygen in its blood, a saturating technique that has been inspirational for recent human freedivers. The staple in sperm whale diets is squid, which they hunt in forbiddingly cold and dark ocean depths, up to three kilometers below the surface of the ocean, holding their breath the entire time, and putting themselves at risk of the bends (nitrogen narcosis). Humans are thus not the only species to suffer occupational hazards! Emmanuel Levinas was thus perhaps wrong when he declared among all animals that humans were the ones capable of the longest breathing, though he was obviously not making a point about comparative zoology, but rather pneumatology.[16] Sperm whales can stay under for an hour on a single breath. One wonders what existential depths reflections on breathing might take among whale philosophers.

Exhalation also seems to be a cultivated technique among cetaceans. Some whales can blow circles of air bubbles into the water to herd fish together, and air bubbles also serve as an expression of breathing capacity and thus indirectly as a signal of bodily size, an important bit of information to share in the dark ocean. Bubbles may also build temporary shields of impermeability to sonar. Our lungs and breathing organs evolved in a world in which we could take environmental access to oxygen for granted, but marine mammals can breathe only at the ocean's surface (a fact that whale hunters have long exploited, "there she blows" being the classic call of a spotter on a whaling ship). Since they cannot survive outside the ocean—beaching is fatal—cetaceans must know how to modulate breathing at every point in time.

Breathing Technique

Perhaps breathing to cetaceans is more like singing to us, a craft in which breathing can never be left to its own devices; our habit could be their art. "A good voice teacher spends most of her time teaching people how to breathe."[17] The same is true for many other musical and athletic disciplines. Humpback whales can "sing" (if this is the right word for a practice humans have only known about since the mid-twentieth century) for up to twenty minutes without emitting air bubbles, and it seems that they are somehow recycling the air, perhaps like the circular breathing used by wind instrumentalists (the saxophonist Kenny G has held a continuous note for over 45 minutes). What would the art of singing be like without the suspension of the urgent need to draw breath? Kittler called singing the "final and most important transformation of breathing."[18] Human song creates art in the space where desire is hemmed in, where the body disappears into voice and air. When a person sings, every phrase is a battle against the desire to inhale. When a choir sings, they learn to breathe in concert. Song is one aspect of what Hegel beautifully called "gehemmte Begierde, aufgehaltenes Verschwinden"—"arrested desire, disappearance delayed," and thus sublimated into lasting work.[19] Might not cetacean song, if its phrases can extend into multiple-minute lines, have a completely different relation to breathing, and thus to finitude, desire, and embodiment?[20]

It is unclear what function whale song serves, but it is evidence that breathing techniques are found among cetaceans (though they lack breathing technologies). Breathing techniques as a rule emerge in hostile environments in which breath is strained or scarce. Among humans, some kinds of musical performance are a chief domain of breath control, such as the playing of woodwind and brass instruments. We get some interesting hints about the preciousness of breath to the performer from a classic treatise on flute playing from 1752 by Johann Joachim Quantz, a court composer and flautist who gave daily lessons to Frederick the Great. His book still counts as a canonical work in wind pedagogy and was recommended to me recently by two friends who play bassoon and oboe professionally. Its seventh chapter concerns the taking of breath in playing the flute. "Taking breath at the right time," says Quantz, "is an essential matter when playing wind instruments and in singing." When performers do not properly save up breath, melodies can be broken and notes that belong together can be separated. A composer could, in theory, write endless passages, but for a performer breath implies finitude. "To play long passages it is necessary to draw in a good supply of breath." In this flute-players might be compared to sperm whales before they dive into the depths. Quantz's book provides specific instructions about when to draw breath and at which notes. Stringed instruments, he notes, have a great advantage over wind instruments because playing them is relatively independent of physical need.[21] Quantz ties breathing directly to time and rhythm, as it always is.

The art of playing a woodwind instrument makes clear a fact obvious to anyone who has run too hard or held their breath: breath is a scarce resource and highly desired commodity. You can never get enough of it but always must. Some forms of music are stolen from and constitute a temporary denial of our primal desire to take breath, the first act we did after being born. Breath was our personal declaration of independence. Breathing is not just a background to everything we do, but the field in which fundamental questions such as time, being, embodiment, desire, and rhythm play out.

Technologies of Breathing

Oxygen, cetacean anatomy, and breath technique are not media in a traditional sense, though each one discloses in a different way a creative connection of nature and craft. Nature is not an unchangeable given, but is plastic and historical, full of almost technical adaptations to new circumstances; there is a media history to nature as well as culture. This is one crucial lesson of the evolutionary philosophies developed by figures such as Charles Sanders Peirce and Niklas Luhmann. But there are breathing media in a stricter sense such as material devices that aid breathing by either extending the body or modifying the environment. Such technologies—as distinct from techniques—are abundant in modernity, an epoch in which breathing increasingly is the object of technical, medical, military, and artistic manipulation. To speak with Heidegger, technology (*Technik*) has "revealed" (*entborgen*) breath and breathing. The two main forms are (1) apparatuses that directly affect the body's breathing, such as scuba gear, iron lungs, gas masks, or CPAP (Continuous Positive Airway Pressure) masks, and (2) forms of direct intervention into the breathing milieu, that is, of "air conditioning" that allows more or less normal breathing by creating atmosphere-like conditions in otherwise alien habitats such as aircraft or mines.

Mining was the primal source of modern breath technologies, as Lewis Mumford showed in his classic book *Technics and Civilization*.[22] The underground environment is alien and hostile—it is dark, wet, dangerous, often too hot or too cold, and can lack fresh air and abound in hazardous gazes, sometimes fatally so. Mumford argued that the mine was the first completely artificial environment inhabited by humans, and a seedbed of such inventions as 24/7 work, lighting, and, above all, ventilation. Mumford draws heavily on the massive twelve-volume work *De re metallica* (1556), a treasury of medieval technique by Agricola (Georg Bauer). Agricola, now regarded as a founding figure in geology, metallurgy, and mineralogy, was very familiar with the mining techniques and technologies of the sixteenth century thanks to his many visits to the mining region of the Erz Mountains in Saxony. The desire for salt, coal, and precious metals called forth numerous innovations in mining, both apparatuses such as primitive gasmasks that helped miners breathe in a harsh environment, and air conditioning and ventilation ducts, which modified the atmosphere enough to allow miners to more or less breathe normally. In mining, breathing was always dangerous, and miners ran both long-term health risks such as black lung as well as immediate ones such as suffocation. This explains the practice of bringing canaries into coalmines as indicators of air quality (they were an early warning system of toxic atmospheres because their smaller bodies showed the effects of bad air more quickly). In Mumford's view, the mine was a kind of hell, the primal scene of capitalist exploitation and the birthplace of modern physics, that is, an abstract world of quantity without color, air, and life. The mine for Mumford foreshadowed the trenches of World War I.

Air-Quake

And it is in the trenches that Peter Sloterdijk begins his analysis of breathing in the twentieth century. In his dramatically exaggerated claim, the century was born on 22 April 1915 with the first application of poison gas as a military weapon. Modernity appears in the sky, as Hans Blumenberg showed in his studies of early modern cosmology in Copernicus and Galileo, but Sloterdijk shows that historical upheavals can be seen in the lower atmosphere as well as the celestial vault. Mustard gas was the opening salvo of what he calls "atmoterrorism." In gas warfare, the breathing environment could not remain in the unnoticed background but had to become a manifest operation.[23] His thesis is that modernity is a "history of atmospheric explication." By *explication* he doesn't mean conceptual clarification, as that term normally does in English, but rather a historical process in which implicit assumptions about life and the environment are forced to become explicit objects of representation and management.

Poison gas suddenly and dramatically demonstrated the hitherto unconsidered fragility of the atmosphere. Chemical warfare abruptly brings what was once in the neglected, anciently buried, forgotten, unknown, never-known, or never-noticed background to a new level of excruciating clarity.[24] (Here Sloterdijk builds on the phenomenological idea that technology arises where habit is interrupted.) Modern men and women are "condemned to punctilious [*förmlichen*] climate anxiety and atmospheric design." After the cloud attacks of the first world war and the fire and atom bombs of the second, which showed the radiophysical dimension of the atmosphere with wickedly unprecedented clarity, we have lost forever an "unquestionably given, worry-free, taken-for-granted air milieu." Once to exist in the world was to exist in the breathable air without a second thought, but with what Sloterdijk calls the "air-quake" (*Luftbeben*) of the past one hundred years, we have lost the once unreflective character of breathing and have thus undergone a fundamental change in the nature of our existence.

Sloterdijk's narrative of the breathing milieu being broken once and for all by poison gas on 22 April 1915 is dramatic, but there have always been environments, as noted earlier, that make it hard for humans to breathe, such as underground, underwater, smoke, the arctic, high altitudes, and outer space. Media sprout up in harsh environments. Diverse breath media directly modify the atmosphere so that we can inhale and exhale more or less naturally (i.e., without artificial devices) in artificial environments. Housing, heating, and clothing allow us to breathe in the winter. Windows and other forms of ventilation allow for fresh air, and air conditioning (here taken in the usual sense) allows people to breathe (or even exist) in the summer season in places such as Saudi Arabia or Arizona. Oxygen tents provide higher concentrations of that gas to medical patients whose lungs are weak. Crazy ideas of geoengineering imagine altering the chemistry of the entire atmosphere in efforts at habitat maintenance and climate control.

Bodily Breathing Machines

Sloterdijk's analysis of modern atmospheric alteration rests overwhelmingly on military evidence (as is true also with Kittler), although there is plenty of industrial disturbance as well. War, of course, is an essential source of technical innovation (as Marx, Sombart, Mumford, and others have noted), but allied areas such as medicine and exploration have also inspired breathing media that alter the body's capacity for breathing rather than the atmosphere itself. My adult son, who was born ten weeks premature in 1986, survived the first four months of his life thanks to an endotracheal intubation that delivered oxygen directly to his immature lungs via an apparatus lodged in his windpipe. This intubation, as it happened, caused iatrogenic damage to his lungs, and he required supplemental oxygen for an additional year via a nasal cannula. For his first-year home, we had oxygen tanks in our house and tubes that connected him to them—a big tank for normal use at home, a small one for when he went out. (Thankfully, his lungs have since fully matured.) My wife can sleep much better thanks to her CPAP machine, which protects her against the risk of sleep apnea (spontaneous cessation of breathing) by providing a steady stream of air. Asthma patients benefit from inhalers that open up the pulmonary tubes and ease breathing. When breathing via mouth or nose is obstructed, doctors can install a tracheotomy tube, which allows for breathing directly from the trachea. Iron lungs are an early form of a branching family of apparatus designed to aid the breathing of patients whose muscles cannot manage respiration on their own.

All the previous media enable the body to cope with breathing requirements. But some recent innovations are hybrid between techniques and technologies— between bodily regimens and mechanical devices. Extreme athletes who take part in the sport of freediving and the related sport called, almost comically, "competitive apnea" can reach astonishing depths underwater on a single intake of air; the current world record, held by the Austrian Herbert Nitsch, is 214 meters deep, using fins and weights, but no oxygen. The world record for "static apnea," or holding one's breath underwater without movement after having hyperventilated with concentrated oxygen, has almost doubled from twelve minutes and thirty-four seconds in 2002 to twenty-four minutes and three seconds in 2016. Much of this recent acceleration has been aided by medical research and by comparative studies of cetaceans; some practitioners are themselves medical doctors. Such long spans without breathing mix bodily techniques (the system must be trained) and technologies (oxygen tanks do not occur in nature). Here is another example where technique steps in where the unaided body comes up short.

Clearly no human in the history of the world could ever go twenty-four minutes without inhaling unless he or she had help from a developed technical and technological apparatus. Such radical stretching of the possibilities of breathing is possible only in a rare historical moment: our own. It is indeed perhaps one of the chief marks of our time that breathing has become so pliable and so urgent. We measure lung capacity with spirometers and police measure the blood alcohol level of motorists with "breathalyzers" at the same time that breathing techniques spread abroad as therapies for the soul. The enveloping source of life in the air has taken on an increasingly artificial and self-conscious character as its manipulability and fragility have been "explicated" as Sloterdijk says.

With the technologization of the atmosphere also comes the atmospheriza-tion of technology, a historical development that culminates in the metaphor of so-called cloud computing. It is remarkable how automatically the word "cloud" in English has come to stand for online computing. This metaphor is one more sign of the long-term fall of the air from its taken-for-granted, natural status, and of the ways our time confounds atmospheric and technical facts.[25]

Media of Breathing: A Rough Classification

In this chapter, I have contrasted techniques as practices and technologies as material devices as well as the organism as a breather and the atmosphere as the enabling environment for breath. These four basic categories, I believe, account for the media of breathing. Let us divide them into four groups: (1) techniques that affect the breather and (2) the atmosphere, and (3) technologies that affect the breather and (4) the atmosphere.

Table 1. Outline of Breathing Media

	Organism	Environment
Techniques	1	2
Technologies	3	4

Quadrant 1 is one of the oldest domains of bodily techniques, certainly among humans and perhaps also other animals such as cetaceans. Humans have played with holding and modulating the breath in singing, sport, and spiritual practice. Birthing is one of the most important domains of breath technique as well, and midwives among other tasks coach mothers in breathing. Other authors in this collection and elsewhere explore the vast and fascinating arrays of human breathing techniques. I recommend especially the work of Maria José de Abreu.[26]

Quadrant 2 is equally ancient, though perhaps less effectual in producing reliable results. Humans have sought to manipulate the atmosphere for millennia through rain dances, animal sacrifices, holy fires, and other ritual techniques of propitiating the gods. The biblical prophet Elijah collaborated with YHWH to control the rain in order to teach the people a lesson, and Aeolus, the son of Poseidon, was the controller of the winds for the ancient Greeks, the friend/enemy of sailors. Chinese emperors sought the mandate of heaven, and bells, feng shui, and musical instruments have all sought to call forth good wind and weather or appease bad weather (though perhaps these belong in quadrant 4, due to the material devices involved). Television weather forecasters often take on the persona of shamans as they claim to bring the weather and take personal responsibility for it. As Kittler quipped, "we can never separate weather from the gods."[27] Though largely pushed aside by modern science, techniques of atmospheric manipulation are certainly a long-lasting part of human cultural practices.

Quadrant 3 designates medical and other enhancements of physiologi-cal or anatomical breathing capacities such as CPAP machines, nasal cannulas, intubation, iron lungs, and tracheostomies. There are also pharmaceuticals such as bronchodilators that enlarge pulmonary pathways when inhaled. Scuba (self-contained underwater breathing apparatus) and other kinds of diving gear belong here as well, though of course there is rarely a technology without a technique (one reason some recent theorists prefer the middle term *techne*): divers have to learn how to use and interact with these devices.

Expanding our definition of technologies that shape the breath, we might also include devices that measure or train the breath. I spent the summer of 1976 reading spirograms (this was before digital spirometry), which are graphic depictions of people's lung capacity. It was a menial task, and a way for a college undergraduate to contribute to a public-health research project, but I learned a lot about medical graphic methods. We might also include sound-recording or more specifically voice-recording devices here. The phonograph is one of a family of media that allow the spoken or sung breath, or at least its acoustic effects, to be played back at a later time. The technical origin of the phonograph, like that of the telephone and the cinema, is closely tied to a range of physiological devices.

An even more interesting and ancient technology of breathing is the art of writing. Several languages, such as ancient Greek, carry diacritical marks as instructions for aspiration. More fundamentally, the written vowels of the alphabet—as thinkers such as Spinoza and Herder pointed out—are markers of the breathed part of language. Spinoza compared the consonants and vowels to playing a flute: the constants were like the fingers on the holes on the flute, and vowels were the breath that flowed through it.[28] Herder thought Hebrew had no need of written vowels because language was voiced by the breath of God.[29] A consonant is an unvoiced abstraction, an asymptote marking a vocal sound's point or manner of articulation, but a vowel marks the flow of breath through the lungs, larynx, and vocal tract. A vowel is a vocal, and as a graphic mark, it is a technology shaping bodily performance.[30] Key among technologies of breathing are those that register and record.

Quadrant 4 is largely the domain of war and industry, of systematic and intentional or unintentional alteration of the atmosphere through such technolo-gies as architecture, ventilation, poison gas, cloud-seeding, or the burning of coal and gas, which has dumped enormous amounts of carbon and other particulates into the atmosphere. Every time we turn on a lightbulb or start a car, we add to atmospheric carbon. Every character on this page has a carbon cost. Such atmospheric effects are typically unintended side effects, but it is now possible to manipulate rainfall directly by dispersing chemicals into clouds around which crystals may form. Airports also practice weather modification by controlling fog or rain. Some technologies try to, but clearly do not, act directly on the atmosphere, such as psychoanalyst Wilhelm Reich's "cloudbusters," which he thought he could use to alter the atmosphere's "orgone energy." To me it is not clear if Reich's "cosmic orgone engineering" is any crazier than recent schemes for geoengineering that would dump sulfur compounds into the atmosphere in the hopes of blocking the sun to cool the planet! As we have seen in the natural history of oxygen, the atmosphere has a long and volatile history; remarkable about our moment is the way that human causes have entered into that history on an unprecedented geological level.

In addition to modification of the atmosphere in general, we should include in quadrant 4 technologies that build microhabitats such as ventilated mine shifts, cabin pressure in aircraft or underwater craft in which people can breathe without the need for a bodily supplement. A gas mask would belong in quadrant 3, and a regulated, breathable aircraft in quadrant 4. Scuba gear would belong in quadrant 3, but a submersible craft in which one could breathe normally in quadrant 4. Thus we see how the media of breathing cut across some of the main domains of human endeavor: art, religion, medicine, and warfare. Obviously—and fortunately for our ongoing inquiries—there are many counterexamples and hybrid cases for further research. Breathing turns out, again, not to be only the alpha and omega of our existence, but also in the very middle of it! It is the medium of our lives in every sense.

Table 2. Media of Breathing

	Organism	Environment
Techniques	Art, Athletics	Religion, Ritual
Technologies	Medicine, Registration	Warfare, Industry

Notes

1. Wolfgang Hagen, "Metaxy. Eine historiosemantische Fußnote zum Medienbegriff," in *Was ist ein Medium?*, ed. Stefan Münker and Alexander Roesler (Frankfurt: Suhrkamp, 2008), 13–29.

2. Paul Kalanithi, *When Breath Becomes Air* (New York: Random House, 2016).

3. I agree with those who argue that body techniques should be included within cultural techniques, such as Bernhard Siegert, *Cultural Techniques: Grids, Filters,*

Doors, and Other Articulations of the Real, trans. Geoffrey Winthrop-Young (New York: Fordham University Press, 2015) and Erhard Schüttpelz, "Körpertechniken," *Zeitschrift für Medien und Kulturforschung* 1 (2010): 101–120.

4. Marcel Mauss, "Les techniques du corps," *Journal de psychologie* 32 (1935): 293.

5. See Peter K. Haff, "Humans and Technology in the Anthropocene: Six rules," *The Anthropocene Review* 1 (2014): 1–11.

6. See my *The Marvelous Clouds: Toward a Philosophy of Elemental Media* (Chicago: University of Chicago Press, 2015).

7. Friedrich Kittler, *Aufschreibesysteme 1800–1900,* 3rd ed. (München: Fink, 1995), 11. "Die deutsche Dichtung fängt an mit einem Seufzer."

8. E.T.A. Hoffmann, *Der Sandmann* (Stuttgart: Reclam, 2015; first published 1816).

9. Kittler, *Aufschreibesysteme,* 55. See also Geoffrey Winthrop-Young, *Friedrich Kittler zur Einführung* (Hamburg: Junius Verlag, 2005), 23ff.

10. Friedrich Kittler, "Weltatem. Über Wagners Medientechnologie," in *Die Wahrheit der technischen Welt,* ed. Hans Ulrich Gumbrecht (Frankfurt: Suhrkamp, 2013), 160–180.

11. Friedrich Kittler, "Atmen," in *Baggersee: Frühe Schriften aus dem Nachlass,* ed. Tania Hron and Sandrina Khaled (Paderborn: Wilhelm Fink, 2015), 17–19.

12. Carl Zimmer, "The Mystery of Earth's Oxygen," *New York Times,* October 3, 2013.

13. See Nick Lane, *Oxygen: The Molecule that Made the World* (Oxford: Oxford University Press, 2004) and Donald E. Canfield, *Oxygen: A Four Billion Year History* (Princeton, NJ: Princeton University Press, 2014).

14. John C. Lilly, *Man and Dolphin: Adventures on a New Scientific Frontier* (Garden City, NY: Doubleday, 1961), chap. 3.

15. Sam Ridgway et al., "Dolphin Continuous Auditory Vigilance for Five Days," *Journal of Experimental Biology* 209 (2006): 3621–3628.

16. See Lenart Škof, *Breath of Proximity: Intersubjectivity, Ethics, and Peace* (Dordrecht: Springer, 2015), 138.

17. Judith Pascoe, *The Sarah Siddons Audio Files* (Ann Arbor: University of Michigan Press, 2011), 37.

18. "die letzte und wichtigste Verwandlung des Atmens." Kittler, "Weltatem," 164.

19. Georg Wilhelm Friedric Hegel, *Phänomenologie des Geistes* (Hamburg: Felix Meiner, 1952; first published 1807), chap. 22.

20. See Mladen Dolar, *A Voice and Nothing More* (Cambridge, MA: MIT Press, 2006).

21. Johann Joachim Quantz, *Versuch einer Anweisung die Flöte traversiere zu spielen* (Berlin: Johann Friedrich Voss, 1752), 73–76. Original quotations: "Dem Athem zu rechter Zeit zu nehmen, ist bey Blasinstrumenten, so wie beym Singen, eine sehr nöthige Sache." "Um lange Passagien zu spielen, ist nöthig, dass man einen guten Vorrath von Atem langsam in sich ziehe."

22. Lewis Mumford, *Technics and Civilization* (New York: Harcourt, Brace, 1934), chap. 2.

23. Peter Sloterdijk, *Schäume* (Frankfurt: Suhrkamp, 2004), 89.

24. Sloterdijk, *Schäume*, 140–141.

25. See my essay, "Cloud," in *Digital Keywords: A Vocabulary of Information Society and Culture*, ed. Benjamin Peters (Princeton, NJ: Princeton University Press, 2016), 54–62.

26. For instance, see Maria José de Abreu, "TV St. Claire," in *Deus ex Machina*, ed. Jeremy Stolow (New York: Fordham University Press, 2013), 261–280; and Maria José de Abreu, "Breath, Technology, and the Making of Community Cancão Nova in Brazil," in *Aesthetic Formations*, ed. Birgit Meyer (New York: Palgrave Macmillan, 2009), 161–182.

27. Friedrich Kittler, *Musik und Mathematik,* vol. 1, part 1 (Munich: Fink, 2006), 79. For more on the theme of atmospheric divination, see Peters, *Marvelous Clouds*, 243–248.

28. Benedictus de Spinoza, *Compendium Grammatices Linguae Hebraeae* (Amsterdam: Jan Rieuwertsz, 1677), chap. 1.

29. Johann Gottfried Herder, *Abhandlung über den Ursprung der Sprache* (Stuttgart: Reclam, 1966; first published 1772), chap. 3.

30. See my essay, "A Short History of Vowels" (manuscript in progress).

Bibliography

Abreu, Maria José de. "Breath, Technology, and the Making of Community Cancão Nova in Brazil." In *Aesthetic Formations*, edited by Birgit Meyer, 161–182. New York: Palgrave Macmillan, 2009.

Abreu, Maria José de. "TV St. Claire." In *Deus ex Machina*, edited by Jeremy Stolow, 261–280. New York: Fordham University Press, 2013.

Canfield, Donald E. *Oxygen: A Four Billion Year History*. Princeton, NJ: Princeton University Press, 2014.

Dolar, Mladen. *A Voice and Nothing More*. Cambridge, MA: MIT Press, 2006.

Haff, Peter K. "Humans and technology in the Anthropocene: Six rules." *The Anthropocene Review* 1 (2014): 1–11.

Hagen, Wolfgang. "Metaxy. Eine historiosemantische Fußnote zum Medienbegriff." In *Was ist ein Medium?*, edited by Stefan Münker and Alexander Roesler, 13–29. Frankfurt: Suhrkamp, 2008.

Hegel, Georg Wilhelm Friedrich. *Phänomenologie des Geistes*. Hamburg: Felix Meiner, 1952. First published 1807.

Herder, Johann Gottfried. *Abhandlung über den Ursprung der Sprache*. Stuttgart: Reclam, 1966. First published 1772.

Hoffmann, E.T.A. *Der Sandmann*. Stuttgart: Reclam, 2015. First published 1816.

Kalanithi, Paul. *When Breath Becomes Air*. New York: Random House, 2016.

Kittler, Friedrich. "Atmen." In *Baggersee: Frühe Schriften aus dem Nachlass*, edited by Tania Hron and Sandrina Khaled, 17–19. Paderborn: Wilhelm Fink, 2015.

Kittler, Friedrich. *Aufschreibesysteme 1800–1900*. 3rd edition. München: Fink, 1995.

Kittler, Friedrich. *Musik und Mathematik*. Vol. 1, part 1. Munich: Fink, 2006.

Kittler, Friedrich. "Weltatem. Über Wagners Medientechnologie." In *Die Wahrheit der technischen Welt*, edited by Hans Ulrich Gumbrecht, 160–180. Frankfurt: Suhrkamp, 2013.

Lane, Nick. *Oxygen: The Molecule that Made the World*. Oxford: Oxford University Press, 2004.

Lilly, John C. *Man and Dolphin: Adventures on a New Scientific Frontier*. Garden City, NY: Doubleday, 1961.

Mauss, Marcel. "Les techniques du corps." *Journal de psychologie* 32 (1935): 271–293.

Mumford, Lewis. *Technics and Civilization*. New York: Harcourt, Brace, 1934.

Pascoe, Judith. *The Sarah Siddons Audio Files*. Ann Arbor: University of Michigan Press, 2011.

Peters, John Durham. "Cloud." In *Digital Keywords: A Vocabulary of Information Society and Culture*, edited by Benjamin Peters, 54–62. Princeton, NJ: Princeton University Press, 2016.

Peters, John Durham. *The Marvelous Clouds: Toward a Philosophy of Elemental Media*. Chicago: University of Chicago Press, 2015.

Peters, John Durham. "A Short History of Vowels." (Manuscript in progress.)

Quantz, Johann Joachim. *Versuch einer Anweisung die Flöte traversiere zu spielen*. Berlin: Johann Friedrich Voss, 1752.

Ridgway, Sam, Don Carder, James Finneran, Mandy Keogh, Tricia Kamolnick, Mark Todd, and Allen Goldblatt. "Dolphin Continuous Auditory Vigilance for Five Days." *Journal of Experimental Biology* 209 (2006): 3621–3628.

Schüttpelz, Erhard. "Körpertechniken." *Zeitschrift für Medien und Kulturforschung* 1 (2010): 101–120.

Siegert, Bernhard. *Cultural Techniques: Grids, Filters, Doors, and Other Articulations of the Real*. Translated by Geoffrey Winthrop-Young. New York: Fordham University Press, 2015.

Sloterdijk, Peter. *Schäume*. Frankfurt: Suhrkamp, 2004.

Spinoza, Benedictus de. *Compendium Grammatices Linguae Hebraeae*. Amsterdam: Jan Rieuwertsz, 1677.

Škof, Lenart. *Breath of Proximity: Intersubjectivity, Ethics, and Peace*. Dordrecht: Springer, 2015.

Winthrop-Young, Geoffrey. *Friedrich Kittler zur Einführung*. Hamburg: Junius Verlag, 2005.

Winthrop-Young, Geoffrey. *Kittler and the Media*. Cambridge: Polity, 2011.

Zimmer, Carl. "The Mystery of Earth's Oxygen." *New York Times*, October 3, 2013.

IV

Breathful and Breathless Worlds

13

The Politics of Breathing

Knowledge on Air and Respiration

MARIJN NIEUWENHUIS

Alle Lebewesen besitzen angeborenes Pneuma, in ihm wurzelt ihre Lebenskraft.

—Jaeger[1]

Introduction

The Western tradition of thought instils a hidden and, for the most part, untold history of breathing. It is true that the meaning of breathing has preoccupied the minds of Ionian scholars, natural philosophers, idealists, and more recently, phenomenologists, but it would be equally correct to admit that only few of the moderns have engaged directly with the mystery of respiration. Irigaray[2] famously defined this odd historical lacuna in the tradition of Western thought as the "forgetting of air." Too preoccupied with inventing "ideologies, gods and hierarchies," Lenart Škof[3] writes, "[i]t was only with Heidegger's and Irigaray's theories that [the West] started to be fully and radically aware of the meaning of [its] being oblivious to the notions of being and breath in [its] history." Thought and representation have more often than not come before breathing and touching in epistemologies of knowledge. Perhaps this is a problem of the historical trajectory of Western philosophy, which over time came to imagine itself as separate from air and atmosphere.

This does not mean, however, that knowledge of the body's respiratory dependency did not develop in other fields. Philosophers in the "West" might (for a short time) have forgotten to think about breathing, but this does not mean that other fields of knowledge have done so as well. Rather than offering an attractive exposé of different philosophies and ways of thinking about breathing, which is perhaps the theme of some of the other contributions in this volume, I would like to demonstrate how knowledge of breathing has historically come to serve as a specific political technology.

This chapter provides a genealogical account of how knowledge of the air and its relationship to the body has informed processes of governance. My analysis does so by engaging with fields of knowledge not commonly associated with political or even the social sciences. I start my exploration into the science of breathing and air in ancient Greece but will end with and spend most of my time discussing the relevance of thinking about breathing on a much more inter-disciplinary plane of knowledge. My objective is to start a project of unfolding a story of breath as an *inspiring* medium for metaphysicians, alchemists, chemists, physicians, military commanders, and contemporary law enforcers. Every body of knowledge has to an extent contributed to how we today value, relate to, and think about the practice of breathing. Such a rich anthropology of breathing, admittedly unsatisfactory short and unfortunately restricted to experiences and ideas of breathing in the West, revolves around issues and questions of life, health, and biopolitics but also death, killing, and thanatopolitics.

As John Durham Peters noted in the previous chapter, the German thinker Sloterdijk[4] recently argued that the twentieth century began on April 22, 1915, when a German regiment launched chlorine attack in a Ypres front against French troops.[5] However, I find such a crude historical periodization as problematic as saying that we have forgotten about the air. The use of a toxic atmospheric against the breathing body of the enemy in World War I, the so-called "Chemists' War," would not have been possible without earlier discoveries of and speculations about the air. I consider an historical exploration into knowledge of breathing also of timely importance given the significance of breathing at a time of widespread aerial pollution and the increasingly prominent practice of police gassing. The subject of breathing is as central a question today as it was 2,500 years ago in Greece, and it urgently requires to be reclaimed by social scientists.

From Pneuma to Gas in One Short Breath

The relationship between air and the respiratory system was in ancient Greece a topic of intense debate, with the illusive notion of *pneuma* at its heart. The meaning and functioning of *pneuma* cannot simply be reduced to air or vital energy but is a concept that for the Greeks constituted a metaphysical question. Famous is Anaximenes's[6] only extant sentence: "Just as our soul [*psyche*], being air [*aer*] holds us together, so do breath [*pneuma*] and air [*aer*] encompass the whole world." Benso[7] adds that "*psyche* is *aer*; and *pneuma* are synonyms; therefore, the *psyche* is also *pneuma*." Breathing was said to separate the living from both the nonliving and the no-longer-living. All living entities were comprised of air, but it is in breathing that humans find their specific subjectivity. "When we stop breathing not only do we die but also our body decomposes. Thus, the air which is our soul maintains us in existence; it 'holds us together.' "[8]

The pre-Socratic metaphysical values attributed to breathing, not too dissimilar from contemporaneous attitudes to the air in Chinese (*qi*) and Indian (*prāṇa*) traditions, altered with the introduction of Aristotelian medical theory. The *De spiritu*, a text recently accredited, by some, to Aristotle, focuses not on innate *pneuma* but instead on innate heat, suggesting that it is not the respiratory system but, as Aristotle argued, the heart that is the "origin of heat [and] the citadel of the body."[9] What this meant was that *pneuma* was gradually no longer seen as a purely immanent field of energy but, rather, gradually transformed into a medium that transferred heat but also served as the bearer of the soul. The synthesizing of Aristotle's physiology with the Platonic notion of "the vehicle of the soul" [*ochema*] meant that pneuma could neither refer to breath, because it did not follow the development of a respiratory system, nor to birth, as it was considered a primary condition for life.[10]

Pneuma was by Neo-Platonists speculated to comprise star dust (ether) and seen as "less material than the physical body but more material than the soul."[11] It was only later that the soul and pneuma merged into one. Culianu[12] explains that "[w]hereas, for Aristotle, the pneuma was just a thin casing around the soul, for the Stoics, as well as for the doctors [from the Sicilian Medical School (among them Diocles)], the pneuma is the soul itself, which penetrates the whole body, controlling all its activities—movement, the five senses, excretion, and the secretion of sperm."

Agamben[13] explains that later Neo-Platonic and Stoic pneumatology converged into the idea of "in-spiration" (*phantastikon pneuma* or *spiritus phantasticus*), which finds its contemporary meaning in our "image-making" faculty, *imagination*. It should be remembered that the verb "to inspire" refers to both a practice of inhalation and enthusing, while "to expire" connotes a process of exhalation and lethal termination.[14] Writing on Levinas, Škof[15] writes that "in-spiration is the thing awakening my physical breathing: now my breath has become spiritual, pneumatic." Agamben[16] and others[17] have adopted the term *pneumophantasmology*, "which circumscribes at once a cosmology, a physiology, a psychology, and a soteriology," to explain how the convergence between physiology and medieval theology productively helped shape late medieval European poetry, art, and philosophy.[18]

Discussions and speculation on the breath did not stop in the Renaissance. Descartes's *Treatise of Man* (1633), a posthumous work on human physiology and anatomy, commences the project of the gradual de-spiritualization of *pneuma*. Descartes—who arguably was among the last of the traditional philosophers (before the phenomenologists) to take on breathing as a serious philosophical question—retained elements of Galen's theory of psychic *pneuma* in his mechanistic theory of animal spirits (*esprits animaux* [from *anima* and *anemos*, or breath]) but annulled the idea of *pneuma* in humans and replaced it with the concept of the mind (*cogito*). Breathing was as a consequence of the decision to prefer the *ratio* over respiration relegated to a lesser ontological order,[19] while air was gradually "materialised, drawn in to the world of weight, measure and mechanicity."[20]

The "secularization" of pneuma and the modern onset of the materialization of air resonated in popular and scientific imaginations of breathing. Especially alchemists found themselves well positioned between the emerging realm of modern science and the changing attitude to breathing. They seemed particularly keen to finally reveal the secrets of *pneuma* and the body's relationship to air.[21]

A key figure to mention in the evolution of knowledge about the air, situated between Cartesian mechanism and mythical vitalism, is Jan Baptist van Helmont (1580–1644), a Belgian contemporary of Descartes who was among the first to commence the unlocking of the chemistry of the air and the inventor of the word "gas" (borrowed from the Greek word *chaos*). He left the term largely ambiguous, but it is clear that it "covers a much larger range of phenomena than our chemical term 'gas' does."[22] His pneumatic chemistry supplanted both the concept of innate heat and pneumatic astral matter while instead focusing on Paracelsian principles of the chemical combustion (or "seminal interaction") of substances. Although van Helmont retained much of the vitalism of earlier thought, referring to Paracelsus's notion of *Archeus*,[23] his philosophy helped transform the concept of *pneuma* (or *spiritus*) into a more chemical category. The self-acclaimed "inventor of gas" fragmented the air into differentiated materialities and spirits (*Archei insiti*). This move paved the path forward to the gradual naturalization of the air in Robert Boyle's mechanical "pneumatical engine" (or air pump)[24] and in the indebted writings of Antoine Lavoisier (1743–1794), Joseph Priestley (1733–1804), Carl Wilhelm Scheele (1742–1786), among many of the other, sometimes forgotten, early discovers of gaseous compounds.

A Biopolitics of Breathing

The "discovery" of oxygen was modernity's "scientific" answer to the philosophical question of *pneuma*. Skinner,[25] writing respectively, notes that "pneuma was an attempt to explain the role of oxygen in living processes." Lavoisier adopted the term "oxygen" in 1789 to refer to "the basic breathable part of air [. . .], deriving it from oxys, *acid* [acide], ginomae [*sic*], *I produce* [*J'engendre*]."[26] The "discovery" of oxygen led to immediate speculations over its medical potential. Priestly was among the first to inhale what he called "dephlogisticated air"[27] (an air with a higher than normal percentage of oxygen), and the practice of "oxygen therapy" was soon adopted by physicians in France.[28] Oxygen therapy was promoted widely in academic papers, while "compressed air baths" and expensive "oxygen bars" soon made their appearances in places such as Berlin, London, Paris, and New York.[29] This was the start but certainly *not* the end of the attempt to commodify the air.

Oxygen was seen not only as a remedy against medical but also social ills. A Victorian epoch of respiration was proclaimed to purify society medically, morally, and spiritually. Connor[30] notes that "air-thinking" at the time "exhibited a characteristic compounding of omnipotence and anxiety, which is nowhere more marked than in the superstitious Victorian fear of draughts and specifically the belief that exposure to small currents of air will cause illness, a mild and magical delusion that remains almost universal." The American painter George Catlin[31] ran a popular campaign against the imagined Western tradition of breathing through the mouth, which he condemned as unnatural.

> We are told that "the breath of life was breathed into man's nostrils"—then why should he not continue to live by breathing in the same manner? [. . .] The atmosphere is nowhere pure enough for man's breathing until it has passed this mysterious refining process [of the nose].[32]

Knowledge of the air also translated into a regulatory framework to control, administer, and monitor atmospheric pollution levels in the urban areas in France[33] and Britain.[34] Florence Nightingale,[35] the foremother of modern hospital nursing, campaigned for ventilation against "foul air" in hospitals and prescribed the enlargement of wardens to allow for more "air space." It can generally be acknowledged that in both Britain and France there existed a widespread consensus that the air needed to be securitized to protect the breathing population. Whitehead's detailed account of the state's controlling and monitoring of air quality in nineteenth-century Britain explores the link between governance and science that respiration facilitated. He describes a historical development toward a "government with science," which he refers to as the "construction of a scientific apparatus of and for government."[36] It is of little surprise that much of Whitehead's discussion is placed in the context of Foucault's birth of social medicine which, as Whitehead shows, "identifies the regulation of the air as one of the central priorities of the new biopolitical regime of power [. . .] As the most immediate requirement for human life, the quality and availability of breathable air has clearly been a crucial environmental medium in and through which biopower has been expressed."[37]

Breathing had always been something of medical interest but, with the materialization of the air, was in the process of becoming an immediate interest of governance. A *Pneumatic Institution for Relieving Diseases by Medical Airs* in Bristol was set up as early as 1798.[38] It declared to "[administer] oxygen free of charge to 'out-patients [. . .] in consumption, asthma, palsy, dropsy, obstinate venereal complaints, scrophula or King's Evil and other diseases, which ordinary means have failed to remove.' "[39] The short-lived, yet historically influential, institute was founded by James Watt, Thomas Beddoes, and Humphry Davy. The first designed so-called "breathing apparatuses," many of which remain in use in hospitals today, while the latter two were especially known for their therapeutic experiments with nitrous oxide, which they named "laughing gas," and other gaseous compounds. Davy was especially renowned for his experimentation with laughing gas, which at times he was not afraid to inhale himself. Some of these experiments were collected as letters written by patients from the institution:

> I had never heard of the effects of the nitrous oxide, when I breathed the fix quarts of it. I felt a delicious tremor of nerve, which was rapidly propagated over the whole nervous system. As the action of inhaling proceeds, an irrespirable appetite to repeat is excited.[40]

Laughing gas was particularly popular among the wealthier classes. It would take more than half a century before the dentist Horace Wells finally started using it as a medium of anesthesia in dental surgeries. Unfortunately for him, Wells did not live long enough to receive recognition for his discovery of anesthesia. He died after cutting his femoral artery while under the influence of chloroform.

A Thanatopolitics of Gas

Pneumatic research moved quickly into other gaseous compounds with less pleasurable effects. It was soon realized that the air was a medium that could sustain breathing bodies but could also poison them. Of particular historical relevance are chlorine and phosgene, which served as primary agents in twentieth-century gas warfare. The inhalation of chlorine, which had been discovered earlier by Scheele in 1774, was initially hailed and promoted in medical journals as a disinfecting weapon that could be used against respiratory and tubercular diseases.[41] Some of the works published at the time enjoyed peculiar-sounding titles such as *Researches Respecting the Medical Powers of Chlorine, Particularly in Diseases of the Liver*.[42]

Investigations into the nature and functions of chlorine led to the discovery of a number of other gases, including phosgene. Phosgene is a mixture of carbon monoxide and chlorine, a chemical compound that is gaseous at room temperature. The invisible and odorless substance was discovered by Davy[43] (1812), but the first victim of what in World War I came to be named "Green Cross" [*Grünkreuz*] was probably the highly influential, albeit largely forgotten, English chemist William Cruickshank. Cruickshank's[44] experiments with phosgene and what then was known as "*heavy*, inflammable air," which today we call carbon monoxide, might have led to the earliest lethal gaseous intoxication.

The advent of World War I brought together many of modernity's new fields and developments in the science of air and respiration. The gaseous attack on breathing bodies propelled respiratory physicians and physiologists to operate at the forefront of developing gas masks, oxygen therapies, and medicine.[45] Gas, as a medicine and as weapon, brought science into direct contact with the state. Central to this development, however, remained the expertise and role of chemical engineers, which is also why the war popularly has been dubbed the "Chemists' War."[46] Freemantle[47] writes that the "chemistry of the First World War was not just confined to poison gases and explosives, but also to the development and production of numerous other chemical products used by the military either direct or indirectly." He[48] quotes Richard Pilcher, an eminent chemical adviser to the British government during World War I, who observed that "[m]any regard the war as largely a conflict between the men of science of the countries engaged."

The country best positioned in World War I was the country that was industrially most advanced in its chemistry. Before their usage as so-called pulmonary agents (*Lungenkampfstoff*) in the infamous battle of Ypres in 1915, which saw the German deployment of 150 tons of chlorine, both chlorine and the more damaging phosgene gas, introduced in December that year, had primarily served as dyeing and bleaching materials. Ryan and colleagues[49] write that phosgene before World War I was used in "moderately large quantities" for the "production of synthetic dyes" in the factories of Bayer, BASF, and other chemical plants in Germany. The advanced state of the country's production of phosgene was, as Coleman[50] argues, a significant factor in the state's ability to produce enormous quantities of poison gas in World War I.[51] Another factor that led to the decision to deploy chemical weapons was the influence the newly unified German state had in the development and direction of science as a means for industry but also the military.[52] The rapidly industrializing German state was interested and eager to engage science and industry in realizing the military potential of gas.[53]

The original intent of using gas was to attack an entrenched enemy who "was comparatively safe from projectiles but vulnerable to airborne poisons."[54] Cowell and colleagues[55] explain that "[d]uring this period, when the tank was in its infancy and the airplane had little direct impact on the ground, gas was the only weapon with the potential to break trench deadlock and solve 'the problem of the [deadlocked] Western Front.'" Besides its strategic purpose of forcing the enemy to move out of position, the attacking of breathing bodies also had strong psychological and physiological effect. The aim of gassing was not so much to kill the enemy but, as pulmonary agents are designed to do, to take away their breath. The suffocation of the air did not necessarily intend to kill as much to terrorize the enemy physiologically as much as psychologically.

For this reason, chemists saw themselves not as torturous murders but as humanitarians. The "father of modern chemical warfare" and Nobel Laureate Fritz Haber (1868–1918)[56] regarded chemical gases "as a means to break the stalemate of trench warfare, shorten the war, and therefore preclude the slaughter of millions by artillery and machine gun fire."[57] The same moral sentiment was shared by contemporaries of Haber, among them the Scottish politician and scientist Lyon Playfair (1818–1898).

Lyon Playfair[58] entertained and promoted the idea of deploying shells filled with cyanide (another discovery of Scheele) or phosphorus (developed for the first time by seventeenth-century alchemists) against Russian troops at the time of the Crimean War.[59] The British War Office morally condemned the plan, arguing it was "as bad as poisoning the enemy's water supply."[60] The response of Playfair was as profound as it was prophetic:

> There was no sense in this objection. It is considered a legitimate mode of warfare to fill shells with molten metal which scatters among the enemy, and produces the most frightful modes of death. Why a poisonous vapour which would kill men without suffering is to be considered illegitimate warfare is incomprehensible. War is destruction, and the more destructive it can be made with the least suffering the sooner will be ended that barbarous method of protecting national rights. No doubt in time chemistry will be used to lessen the sufferings of combatants, and even of criminals condemned to death.[61]

The idea that gassing is somehow morally superior over other forms of state violence is still prominent in the domestic deployment of so-called "nonlethal" lachrymators (or "tear gas") by contemporary law-enforcement officers. It is the fear of atmospheric violence rather than the consequences that still drives much of today's discourse on the use of gas in situations of interstate conflict and domestic law enforcement.

British casualties from gas warfare in World War I constituted only 1 percent of total deaths but haunted popular imaginations. Connor[62] writes that it is "not just the fact, but also the idea of gas, that tends towards a condition of saturation." I would go one step further and argue that the taking-away of breath is always more than "just" a physiological or even psychological practice. Watson[63] argues in his study on troop morale among German and British soldiers "that gas created uncertainty: unlike shrapnel, it killed from the inside, eroding a soldier's sense of control, while raising the terrifying fear of being suffocated." Brown[64]—at the time of writing, a U.S. soldier during the Vietnam War—quotes the experience of a Chemical Warfare Service officer: "Nothing breaks a soldier's will to fight so quickly as being gassed, even slightly. His imagination magnifies his real injury 100-fold." There are more than hints of metaphysical traces in these accounts of breathing.

Sloterdijk[65] uses the term "atmoterrorism" to describe how gassing propels the body's vital respiratory mechanism to turn against itself. This form of "terrorism of the *atmosphere* is to be understood as a human-made form of quake that turns the enemy's environment into a weapon against them."[66] "[I]t comprises a form of violence against the very human-ambient 'things' without which people cannot remain people."[67] The ramifications of this argument, however, can fully be grasped only by considering the long historical anthropological trajectory of what the breath metaphysically means in Western (but certainly also in other) traditions and cultures of knowledge. This history of thought, of which admittedly I barely scratch the surface here, is impregnated with a yet-to-be-accounted-for political obsession with the breath.

A Final Puff

The deployment of air as a weapon against the body's own breath is physiologically, psychologically, and even metaphysically a stroke of evil genius. The events of World War I were, despite the Geneva Protocol and earlier treaties,[68] not the end but merely the beginning of modern atmospheric governance. One need only recall the Nazi hydrogen cyanide genocide, the death by hydrocyanic acid in American death chambers, or the more recent sarin attacks in Halabja and Syria to understand the importance of gas killings in the last hundred years. Few forms of violence in the twentieth century have been feared as much as the intoxication of the air the body inhales. Its fearful disciplining effect also helps explain its current popularity among police enforcement.

The ongoing discovery of the potential of the air as a medium and means to discipline and punish gives the state an extraordinary new weapon to govern populations. Over the course of a century, gassing has transformed from an illegal means to wage war into a legitimate governmental technology to suppress and disrupt the movement of protesting bodies.[69] With the help of chemists, police officials, and physicians, lachrymators, hailed as the "most humane weapon ever invented,"[70] have in rapid time become the accepted norm in quelling urban protests and strikes across the world.[71]

The historical popularity of these now-called "Anti-Riots Controls" (RCAs), their societal normalization and general effectiveness of turning a terrifying atmosphere against the breathing body has led gas to become synonymous with law and order. The "moral effect produced by it on crowds"[72] allowed tear gas to transform itself into the preferred weapon in colonial oppression.[73] Tear gas, first deployed by the British Forces in Palestine, was said to offer "a humanitarian alternative to policemen's bullets [. . .] Britain's colonial police needed to keep up with the time."[74] A British police officer[75] in Delhi recounts the tear gassing of Sikh protestors against colonial rule in 1941:

> It was a memorable experience, on this day when tear gas was first used, to find that when the smoke had drifted away one could walk along a silent, deserted street which a minute earlier had been packed

by an angry, howling mob. The debris of flight was the only evidence
of their passing, the litter of shoes and garments bore witness to
their haste. They made no attempt to reassemble; they retired from
the fray, not to lick their wounds, but to dry their streaming eyes.

Many of the colonial experiences with gas would only much later come to inform
policing practices in the West.[76] Events such as the Ferguson protests, the ongoing political instability in many parts of the Middle East, and the border crisis
in Europe would suggest that the demand for purposes of airborne chemicals
will continue to grow exponentially in the years to come. Indeed, the policing
and securitization industry is predicted to grow by 30 percent over the next four
years.[77] Industry research[78] anticipates that demand will remain particularly high
in states facing popular unrest. The trend toward greater atmospheric policing is
an episode in a longer historical trajectory of the breath.

What Is in a Breath?

Knowledge of the body's relationship to the air has played a formative role in the
development of Greek metaphysics, medieval Christianity, and alchemy, but also
the modern sciences. Historical forms of pneumatic knowledge speak to deeply
personal issues related to the vital yet undefined relationships between one's body
and the atmospheric environment, but also take on a more collective and explicit
political dimension in which the atmosphere is used *against* the body. Breathing
is many things. Breathing was for the Greeks that which distinguishes life from
nonlife, for the Stoics, it was that which inspirits; the Christian Desert Fathers
spoke about breathing as a constant reminder of divine humility, while Levinas
and Irigaray[79] write about it as "the atmosphere of alterity," but it is with the emergence of the modern sciences that breathing becomes something else, something
secular, vulnerable, modifiable and, ultimately, of immediate interest to the state.

I do not believe that the air was "forgotten," as Irigaray[80] seems to suggest,
but rather that attention for the air has over the last couple of centuries shifted in
other directions. This also means that we need to historicize beyond Sloterdijk's
thesis presented at the beginning of the chapter.[81] The responsibility for an ethics of breathing has moved from the field of philosophy and theology into the
domain of natural scientists, chemists, and utilitarian experts in international law
for whom breathing has already long lost its original pneumatic meaning. Respiration has over the centuries become a preoccupation of an uncaring politics, while
knowledge of it has become appropriated to serve biopolitical and thanatopolital
purposes. The problem of politics, then, is perhaps not a lack of breathing space
but a general and more profound loss of the meaning of breathing itself.

Notes

1. Jaeger [1913] writing on Aristotle's theory of *pneuma* in Abraham Paulus Bos and Rein Ferwerda. "Introduction," in *Aristotle, On the Life-Bearing Spirit (De spiritu): A Discussion with Plato and His Predecessors on Pneuma as the Instrumental Body of the Soul*, ed. Abraham Paulus Bos and Rein Ferwerda (Leiden: Brill, 2008), 4.

2. Luce Irigaray, *The Forgetting of Air in Martin Heidegger* (London: The Athlone Press, 1999).

3. Lenart Škof, *Breath of Proximity: Intersubjectivity, Ethics and Peace* (Dordrecht: Springer, 2015), 3.

4. Peter Sloterdijk, *Terror from the Air* (Cambridge: MIT Press, 2009).

5. This was actually not the first time gas was used in World War I. Harry Salem, Andrew L. Ternay, and Jeffery K. Smart ("Brief History and Use of Chemical Warfare Agents in Warfare and Terrorism," in *Chemical Warfare Agents: Chemistry, Pharmacology, Toxicology, and Therapeutics*, ed. James A. Romano, Brian J. Lukey, and Harry Salem [Boca Raton: CRC Press, 2008], 6) and Jeffery K. Smart ("History of Chemical and Biological Warfare: An American Perspective," in *Medical Aspects of Chemical and Biological Warfare*, ed. Frederick R. Sidell, Ernest T. Takafuji, and David R. Franz [Washington, DC: Borden Institute, 1997], 14) note that "Germany's use of chemical weapons on the battlefield began on October 27, 1914, when they fired shells loaded with dianisidine chlorosulfonate, a tear gas, at the British near Neuve Chapelle." However, this and the subsequent attempt to deploy cylinders of xylyl bromide in November 1914 were unsuccessful.

6. Anaximenes in Silvia Benso, "The Breathing of the Air: Pre-Socratic Echoes in Levinas" (chapter 5 of this volume).

7. Ibid.

8. Richard D. McKirahan, *Philosophy before Socrates: An Introduction with Texts & Commentary* (Indianapolis, IN: Hackett Publishing House, 2010), 53.

9. Aristotle, *On the Life-Bearing Spirit (De spiritu): A Discussion with Plato and his Predecessors on Pneuma as the Instrumental Body of the Soul*, ed. Abraham Paulus Bos and Rein Ferwerda (Leiden: Brill, 2008), 138.

10. Ibid., 148.

11. Crystal Jade Addey, "In the Light of the Sphere: The 'Vehicle of the Soul' and Subtle-Body Practices in Neoplatonism," in *Religion and the Subtle Body in Asia and the West: Between Mind and Body*, ed. Geoffrey Samuel and Jay Johnston (Abingdon and New York: Routledge, 2013), 149.

12. Ioan P. Culianu, *Eros and Magic in the Renaissance* (Chicago and London: University of Chicago Press, 1987), 9.

13. Giorgio Agamben, *Stanzas: Word and Phantasm in Western Culture* (Minneapolis and London: University of Minnesota Press, 1993).

14. On this subject, see especially: Timothy Clark, *The Theory of Inspiration: Composition as a Crisis of Subjectivity in Romantic and Post-romantic Writing* (Manchester: Manchester University Press, 1997).

15. Škof, *Breath of Proximity*, 136.

16. Agamben, *Stanzas*, 94.

17. See, for instance, Culianu, *Eros and Magic*.

18. Charles Dempsey (*Inventing the Renaissance Putto* [Chapel Hill and London: University of North Carolina Press, 2001], 94) writes that for both Dante and Guido Cavalcanti "the workings of imagination derive, in part from the notion of pneuma as the vehicle of the soul, and in part from medical theories of the influxes of spirit into the body"

19. Cf. Jacques Derrida, *The Animal That Therefore I Am* (New York: Fordham University Press, 2008), 86.

20. Steven Connor, *The Matter of Air: Science and Art of the Ethereal* (London: Reaktion Books, 2010), 74.

21. For instance, see Nick Lane, *Oxygen: The Molecule That Made the World* (Oxford: Oxford University Press, 2003), especially chap. 1.

22. Delia Georgiana Hedesan, "'Christian Philosophy': Medical Alchemy and Christian Thought in the Work of Jan Baptista Van Helmont (1579–1644)" (PhD diss., University of Exeter, 2012), 240.

23. There exist links between *Archeus* and Severinus's *Spiritus* and even Aristotle's *Pneuma*. On these links see, for instance, Ibid., 229, 234. Toulmin and Goodfield quote van Helmont when he refers to " 'a certain vitall [*sic*] Air.' This might seem [they argue] like one more reincarnation of the Breath of Life, if it were not for one thing: that van Helmont refuses to identify it with *any* familiar inanimate substance. On the contrary, he insists, every different object contains in its seed an Archeus characteristic of its species, which turns it into (say) a beach-tree, a mackerel [. . .] [etc.]; and under suitable circumstances, when the organic form is deliberately destroyed, the Archeus can be released. With this doctrine as his foundation, he goes on to draw an unexpected conclusion: namely, that the world contains many distinct kinds of *gases*"; see Stephen Toulmin and June Goodfield, *The Architecture of Matter* (London and Chicago: University of Chicago Press and Goodfield, 1982), 152; original emphases.

24. Boyle (in Steven Shapin and Simon Schaffer, *Leviathan and the Air-Pump* [Princeton, NJ: Princeton University Press, 1985], 32), himself an ardent admirer of van Helmont, argued that "[i]t is the operation of the pneumatic engine, among all the scientific apparatus displayed in the engraving, that is going to enable the philosopher to approach God's knowledge."

25. Skinner in Daniel L. Gilbert, "Perspectives on the History of Oxygen and Life," in *Oxygen and Living Processes: An Interdisciplinary Approach*, ed. Daniel L. Gilbert (Heidelberg and Berlin: Springer-Verlag, 1981), 2.

26. Ibid., 14.

27. Priestley (in Chris Grainge, "Breath of Life: The Evolution of Oxygen Therapy," *Journal of the Royal Society of Medicine* 97 [October 2004]: 489) describes the experience in detail in his *Experiments and Observations on Different Kinds of Air* (1774): "The feeling of it to my lungs was not sensibly different from that of common air; but I fancied that my breast felt peculiarly light and easy for some time afterwards. Who

can tell but that, in time, this pure air may become a fashionable article in luxury. Hitherto only two mice and myself have had the privilege of breathing it."

28. Ibid.

29. Charles Alfred Lee, "The Physiological and Therapeutical Effects of Compressed Air Baths: A Lecture Delivered to the Students in the Medical Department in the University of Buffalo, Session of 1866-7" (Buffalo: James S. Leavitt, 1868).

30. Connor, *The Matter of Air*, 106.

31. George Catlin, *Shut Your Mouth and Save Your Life* (London: N. Trubner & Co., 1870), 27–28.

32. The myth that particle pollution could be prevented through mere nasal breathing would remain intact for at least another fifty years; see Mark Whitehead, *State, Science and the Skies: Governmentalities of the British Atmosphere* (Chichester: Wiley-Blackwell, 2011), 122.

33. See, for example, Laurence Lestel, "Pollution atmosphérique en milieu urbain: de sa régulation à sa surveillance," Vertigo (Hors-série) 15 (February 2013).

34. Whitehead, *State, Science and the Skies*.

35. Lynn McDonald, ed., Florence Nightingale and Hospital Reform: *Collected Works of Florence* (Ontario: Wilfrid Laurier University Press, 2012).

36. Whitehead, *State, Science and the Skies*, 15.

37. Ibid., 21.

38. It is somewhat ironic that many chemists experimenting with the medical prospects of gases were among the first to suffer from the lethal consequences of gas.

39. Grainge, "Breath of Life," 489.

40. "Patient" George Burnet in Humphry Davy, "Details of the Effects Produced by the Respiration of Nitrous Oxide upon Different Individuals, Furnished by Themselves," in *The Collected Works of Sir Humphry Davy*, ed. John Davy (London: Smith, Elder and Co. Cornhill, 1839), 308.

41. The medical use of chlorine did not end in the nineteenth century. David Nader and Spasoje Marčinko ("The Rise and Fall of 'Chlorine Chambers' Against Cold and Flu," in *An Element of Controversy: The Life of Chlorine in Science, Medicine, Technology and War*, ed. Hasok Chang and Catherine Jackson [London: British Society for the History of Science, 2007], 296–323) describe in an insightful edited volume, on the history of the substance, how chlorine was used in the United States in the 1920s as a medicine against influenza in designated so-called "chlorine chambers."

42. William Wallace, *Researches Respecting the Medical Powers of Chlorine, particularly in Diseases of the Liver; with an account of a new mode of applying this agent, by which its influence on the system can be secured* (London: Longman, Hurst, Rees, Orme, and Brown, 1822).

43. John Davy and Humphry Davy, "On a Gaseous Compound of Carbonic Oxide and Chlorine," *Philosophical Transactions of the Royal Society of London* 102 (1812): 144–151.

44. Cruickshank in Guy H. Neild, "William Cruickshank (FRS-1802): Clinical chemist," *Nephrology Dialysis Transplantation* 11 (1996), 1888; original emphasis.

45. See, for instance, Steve Sturdy, "War as Experiment: Physiological Innovation and Administration in Britain, 1914–1918: The Case of Chemical Warfare," in *War, Medicine and Modernity*, ed. Roger Cooter et al. (Stroud: Sutton Publishers, 1998), 65–84.

46. Michael Freemantle, *The Chemists' War: 1914–1918* (Cambridge: The Royal Society of Chemistry, 2015).

47. Michael Freemantle, *Gas! Gas! Quick Boys! How Chemistry Changed the First World War* (Stroud: The History Press, 2015), 14.

48. Ibid.

49. T. Anthony Ryan et al., eds., *Phosgene and Related Carbonyl Halides* (Amsterdam: Elsevier Science, 1996), 13.

50. Kim Coleman, *A History of Chemical Warfare* (Basingstoke and New York: Palgrave, 2005).

51. Kim Coleman (*A History of Chemical Warfare*, 15) writes that companies such as Bayer and BASF held a "virtual world monopoly not only in dyestuffs, but also in the majority of organic chemicals." Robert J.T. Joy ("Historical Aspects of Medical Defense against Chemical Warfare," in *Medical Aspects of Chemical and Biological Warfare*, ed. Frederick R. Sidell, Ernest T. Takafuji, and David R. Franz [Washington, DC: Borden Institute, 1997], 89) writes that "ninety percent of the dyes used around the world were produced in Germany."

52. Claudius Gellert ("The German Model of Research and Advanced Education," in *The Research Foundations of Graduate Education: Germany, Britain, France, United States, Japan*, ed. Burton R. Clark [Berkeley and London: University of California Press, 1993], 10) writes that "[s]tate expenditure on military research comprised two-thirds of all Imperial expenditure for scientific purposes after 1871."

53. The eminent Fritz Haber (in Pierce Watson O'Dell, *Air War: Its Psychological, Technical and Social Implications* [New York: Modern Age Books, 1939], 181), who in 1915 was proudly promoted captain, warned his superiors of the consequences of engaging in gas warfare. "I feel it my duty to warn you against adopting my schemes, or any scheme for gas warfare, if you think the war likely to continue for as much as three or four months longer [. . .] If you [. . .] believe that there is the slightest possibility of the war lasting longer than until the early summer of 1915, then you should on no account begin gas warfare. [. . .] Our enemies have a hundred times as much raw material as we, and, should the war last beyond the summer 1915, they will have time to overtake us in our stride, and to drench us with quantities of gas enormously greater than we shall ever be able to produce."

54. Coleman, *A History of Chemical Warfare*, 15.

55. Frederick Cowell et al., "Chlorine as the First Major Chemical Weapon," in *An Element of Controversy: The Life of Chlorine in Science, Medicine, Technology and War*, ed. Hasok Chang and Catherine Jackson (London: British Society for the History of Science, 2007), 241.

56. Fritz Haber, together with Carl Bosch, later would become world famous for converting atmospheric nitrogen to ammonia. The so-called Haber–Bosch process enabled modern agricultural food production and helped make atmospheric nitrogen an industrial commodity. While Haber used nitrogen to produce ammonia, physicians

still experimented with the use of nitrogen for medical purposes reasons. The inhalation of nitrogen gas, today discussed for capital punishment and euthanasia, was in the 1930s still used as a remedy against schizophrenia. An Indian physician, under British colonial supervision, reports his findings in 1939. "When 'given to highly excited patients for five minutes the patients not only quieted down in their excitement but were also able to sleep for hours [. . .] [and some were] quiet after this treatment for some days'"; Dhunjibhoy (1939) in Waltraud Ernst, *Colonialism and Transnational Psychiatry: The Development of an Indian Mental Hospital in British India, c. 1925–1940* (London: Anthem Press, 2014), 187.

57. Friedrich in Freemantle, *The Chemists' War*, 159; In a biography of Haber, Dietrich Stoltzenberg (*Fritz Haber: Chemist, Nobel Laureate, German, Jew* [Philadelphia, PA: Chemical Heritage Press, 2004], 133) writes that "[t]here is no question that Fritz Haber was the initiator and organizer of chemical warfare in Germany. He never denied this. Instead, even after the war, he continued to defend the use of chemical weapons as a feasible means of warfare and to support work in this area."

58. It needs pointing out that Playfair was the mentor of Frederick Guthrie (1833–1886), who was credited for having identified mustard gas (*Gelbkreuz*, "Yellow Cross").

59. Some of the discoveries made in twentieth-century gas warfare were later used for entirely opposite purposes. The positive effects of mustard gas on decreasing levels of lymphocytes, for example, inspired chemists to develop a nitrogen mustard compound that would later become the first chemotherapy drug mechlorethamine.

60. Miles in Joy, "Historical Aspects of Medical Defense against Chemical Warfare," 88.

61. Playfair in C.A. Browne, "Early References Pertaining to Chemical Warfare," *The Journal of Industrial and Engineering Chemistry* 14, no. 7 (1906): 646.

62. Connor, *The Matter of Air*, 252.

63. Watson in Edgar Jones, "Terror Weapons: The British Experience of Gas and Its Treatment in the First World War," *War in History* 21, no. 3 (2014): 357.

64. Prentiss in Frederic Joseph Brown, *Chemical Warfare: A Study in Restraints* (London and New Brunswick: Transactions Publishers, 2009; first published in 1968), 153.

65. Sloterdijk, *Terror from the Air*.

66. Peter Sloterdijk, "Airquakes," *Environment and Planning D: Society and Space* 27 (2009): 41.

67. Sloterdijk, *Terror from the Air*, 25.

68. The Lieber Code (1863), signed by President Lincoln at the time of the American Civil War, was among the first attempts to regulate the deployment of gas during war. It would form the basis for later international laws on chemical weapons and the Geneva Protocol that followed World War I. Jeffery K. Smart ("History of Chemical and Biological Warfare") argues that the American Civil War also was the first in which plans were developed to use chlorine and hydrochloric and sulphuric acid mixes as chemical warfare agents. The United States, however, did not sign to support the ban on the use of asphyxiating and deleterious gases in the subsequent 1899

Hague Convention (IV, 2), nor did it ratify the Geneva Protocol until after the Vietnam War, in which it was accused of using herbicides and defoliants as weapons of war.

69. See, for instance, Marijn Nieuwenhuis, "Breathing Materiality: Aerial Violence at a Time of Atmospheric Politics," *Critical Studies on Terrorism* 9, no. 3 (2016).

70. As the famous and polemic scientist J.B.S. Haldane wrote as early aş 1925 in Marion Girard, *A Strange and Formidable Weapon: British Responses to World War I Poison Gas* (London: University of Nebraska Press, 2008), 166.

71. See, for instance, Daniel P. Jones's ("From Military to Civilian Technology: The Introduction of Tear Gas for Civil Riot Control," *Technology and Culture* 19, no. 2 (1978): 151–168) very detailed account of the legal and political discussions around the introduction of police gassing in the United States in the 1920s. Research on the use of tear gas for policing was already underway in France before the start of World War I; see especially Arnaud Lejaille, "Introduction: Prelude a la Grande Guerre Chimique," accessed July 1, 2016, http://www.guerredesgaz.fr/these/Introduction/introduction.htm. The first recorded use of a lachrymator (ethyl bromoacetate), however, actually stems from the infamous 1912 arrest of the anarchist Bonnot Gang. Lejaille describes in detail how a second committee responsible for developing gas was comprised of members from the Pasteur Institute, the Academy of Medicine, police officials, and several chemists. The first committee, *La Commission d'Etudes du Génie*, was set up in 1909 and succeeded the more secretive *Commission des substances* (1905). British chemists optimized the French bromoacetate formula, adopted in the French military in 1913, and in January 1915 developed its own ethyl iodoacetate (or "SK," named after the South Kensington location of the Imperial College London laboratory where the substance was first synthesized). International law, public opinion, and the ethics of gassing seemed to have prevented the British Government from using gas in the early stages of the Great War. The German Chlorine attack changed British sentiment, but it would last until the Battle of Loos (1915) before British forces launched their first (chlorine) gas campaign.

72. Radley [1928] in Stephen Legg, *Spaces of Colonialism: Delhi's Urban Governmentalities* (Oxford: Blackwell, 2007), 106.

73. I deem it important to historicize and politicize the deployment of gas in Europe's twenty-first century. The story of gas must be contextualized as having been constitutive of a specific atmospheric politics. Few today seem to remember the precursors (*Enfumades*) of the Nazi gas chamber during the French colonial project in Algeria. In 1845, roughly a thousand women, men, and children are estimated to have been killed within merely two days as a result of asphyxiation (see, for instance, Chems Eddine Chitour, "Algérie, 1845, un jour de mai: Il était une fois les enfumades," *Le Grand Soir*, May 12, 2011, accessed August 3, 2016, http://www.legrandsoir.info/Algerie-1845-un-jour-de-mai-Il-etait-une-fois-les-enfumades.html). The French Governor-General of Algeria at the time argued that this "cruel extremity" was necessary to set a "horrifying example" that could "strike terror among these turbulent and fanatical montagnards" (Bugeaud in Benjamin Claude Brower, *A Desert Named Peace: The Violence of France's Empire in the Algerian Sahara, 1844–1902* [Chichester: Columbia University Press, 2009], 23). The events are narrated in Assia Djebar's novel

L'amour, la fantasia (*Fantasia: An Algerian Cavalcade*). Despite legal attempts to prevent the deployment of chemical warfare, gas continued to be used in many colonial settings (e.g., the Rif War [1921–1926], the Italian invasion of Ethiopia in 1935, and the French repression in its colonies throughout the 1920s). A serious historical account of atmospheric politics is long overdue.

74. Thomas [1936] in Martin Thomas, " 'Paying the Butcher's Bill': Policing British Colonial Protest after 1918," *Crime, histoire & sociétés* 15, no. 2 (2011): 72.

75. McLintic [1941] in Legg, *Spaces of Colonialism*, 145.

76. On what Foucault called the "boomerang effect" of Western colonization, see the following works of Stephen Graham, "Foucault's Boomerang: The New Military Urbanism," *OpenDemocracy*, February 14, 2013, accessed December 1, 2016, https://www.opendemocracy.net/opensecurity/stephen-graham/foucault%E2%80%99s-boomerang-new-military-urbanism; and Miguel de Larrinaga, "(Non)-lethality and War: Tear Gas as a Weapon of Governmental Intervention," *Critical Studies on Terrorism* 9, no. 3 (2016): 522–540.

77. Markets and Markets, "Non-Lethal Weapons Market worth $1,146.2 Million by 2018," accessed February 1, 2016, http://www.marketsandmarkets.com/PressReleases/non-lethal-weapons.asp.

78. Ibid.

79. In Škof, *Breath of Proximity*, 137.

80. Irigaray, *The Forgetting of Air*.

81. Sloterdijk, *Terror from the Air*.

Bibliography

Addey, Crystal Jade. "In the Light of the Sphere: The 'Vehicle of the Soul' and Subtle-Body Practices in Neoplatonism." In *Religion and the Subtle Body in Asia and the West: Between Mind and Body*, edited by Geoffrey Samuel and Jay Johnston, 149–167. Abingdon and New York: Routledge, 2013.

Agamben, Giorgio. *Stanzas: Word and Phantasm in Western Culture*. Minneapolis and London: University of Minnesota Press, 1993.

Aristotle. *On the Life-Bearing Spirit (De spiritu): A Discussion with Plato and his Predecessors on Pneuma as the Instrumental Body of the Soul*. Edited and translated by Abraham Paulus Bos and Rein Ferwerda. Leiden: Brill, 2008.

Benso, Silvia. "The Breathing of the Air: Pre-Socratic Echoes in Levinas." [Chapter 5 of this volume.] Originally published in *Levinas and the Ancients*, edited by Brian Schroeder and Silvia Benso, 9–23. Bloomington: Indiana University Press, 2008.

Bos, Abraham Paulus, and Rein Ferwerda. "Introduction." In *Aristotle, On the Life-Bearing Spirit (De spiritu): A Discussion with Plato and his Predecessors on Pneuma as the Instrumental Body of the Soul*, edited by Abraham Paulus Bos and Rein Ferwerda, 1–28. Leiden: Brill, 2008.

Brower, Benjamin Claude. *A Desert Named Peace: The Violence of France's Empire in the Algerian Sahara, 1844–1902*. Chichester: Columbia University Press, 2009.

Brown, Frederic Joseph. *Chemical Warfare: A Study in Restraints.* London and New Brunswick, NJ: Transactions Publishers, 2009. First published in 1968.

Browne, C.A. "Early References Pertaining to Chemical Warfare." *The Journal of Industrial and Engineering Chemistry* 14, no. 7 (1906): 646.

Catlin, George. *Shut Your Mouth and Save Your Life.* London: N. Trubner & Co., 1870.

Chitour, Chems Eddine. "Algérie, 1845, un jour de mai: Il était une fois les enfumades." *Le Grand Soir*, May 12, 2011. Accessed August 2, 2016. http://www.legrandsoir.info/Algerie-1845-un-jour-de-mai-Il-etait-une-fois-les-enfumades.html.

Clark, Timothy. *The Theory of Inspiration: Composition as a Crisis of Subjectivity in Romantic and Post-romantic Writing.* Manchester: Manchester University Press, 1997.

Coleman, Kim. *A History of Chemical Warfare.* Basingstoke and New York: Palgrave, 2005.

Connor, Steven. *The Matter of Air: Science and Art of the Ethereal.* London: Reaktion Books, 2010.

Cowell, Frederick, Xuan Goh, James Cambrook, and David Bulley. "Chlorine as the First Major Chemical Weapon." In *An Element of Controversy: The Life of Chlorine in Science, Medicine, Technology and War*, edited by Hasok Chang and Catherine Jackson, 220–254. London: British Society for the History of Science, 2007.

Culianu, Ioan P. *Eros and Magic in the Renaissance.* Chicago and London: University of Chicago Press, 1987.

Davy, Humphry. "Details of the Effects Produced by the Respiration of Nitrous Oxide upon Different Individuals, Furnished by Themselves." In *The Collected Works of Sir Humphry Davy*, edited by John Davy, 294–315. London: Smith, Elder and Co. Cornhill: 1839.

Davy, John, and Davy, Humphry. "On a Gaseous Compound of Carbonic Oxide and Chlorine." *Philosophical Transactions of the Royal Society of London* 102 (1812): 144–151.

Dempsey, Charles. *Inventing the Renaissance Putto.* Chapel Hill and London: University of North Carolina Press, 2001.

Derrida, Jacques. *The Animal That Therefore I Am.* New York: Fordham University Press, 2008.

Ernst, Waltraud. *Colonialism and Transnational Psychiatry: The Development of an Indian Mental Hospital in British India, c. 1925–1940.* London: Anthem Press, 2014.

Freemantle, Michael. *The Chemists' War: 1914–1918.* Cambridge: The Royal Society of Chemistry, 2015.

Freemantle, Michael. *Gas! Gas! Quick Boys! How Chemistry Changed the First World War.* Stroud: The History Press, 2015.

Gellert, Claudius. "The German Model of Research and Advanced Education." In *The Research Foundations of Graduate Education: Germany, Britain, France, United States, Japan*, edited by Burton R. Clark, 5–45. Berkeley and London: University of California Press, 1993.

Gilbert, Daniel L. "Perspectives on the History of Oxygen and Life." In *Oxygen and Living Processes: An Interdisciplinary Approach*, edited by Daniel L. Gilbert, 1–43. Heidelberg and Berlin: Springer-Verlag, 1981.

Girard, Marion. *A Strange and Formidable Weapon: British Responses to World War I Poison Gas*. London: University of Nebraska Press, 2008.

Graham, Stephen. "Foucault's Boomerang: The New Military Urbanism." *Open-Democracy*, February 14, 2013. Accessed December 1, 2016. https://www.opendemocracy.net/opensecurity/stephen-graham/foucault%E2%80%99s-boomerang-new-military-urbanism.

Grainge, Chris. "Breath of Life: The Evolution of Oxygen Therapy." *Journal of the Royal Society of Medicine* 97 (October 2004): 489–493.

Hedesan, Delia Georgiana. "'Christian Philosophy': Medical Alchemy and Christian Thought in the Work of Jan Baptista Van Helmont (1579–1644)." PhD diss., University of Exeter, 2012.

Irigaray, Luce. *The Forgetting of Air in Martin Heidegger*. London: The Athlone Press, 1999.

Jones, Daniel P. "From Military to Civilian Technology: The Introduction of Tear Gas for Civil Riot Control." *Technology and Culture* 19, no. 2 (1978): 151–168.

Jones, Edgar. "Terror Weapons: The British Experience of Gas and Its Treatment in the First World War." *War in History* 21, no. 3 (2014): 355–375.

Joy, Robert J. T. "Historical Aspects of Medical Defense against Chemical Warfare." In *Medical Aspects of Chemical and Biological Warfare*, edited by Frederick R. Sidell, Ernest T. Takafuji, and David R. Franz, 87–110. Washington, DC: Borden Institute, 1997.

Lane, Nick. *Oxygen: The Molecule That Made the World*. Oxford: Oxford University Press, 2003.

Larrinaga, Miguel de. "(Non)-lethality and War: Tear Gas as a Weapon of Governmental Intervention." *Critical Studies on Terrorism* 9, no. 3 (2016): 522–540.

Lee, Charles Alfred. "The Physiological and Therapeutical Effects of Compressed Air Baths: A Lecture Delivered to the Students in the Medical Department in the University of Buffalo, Session of 1866–7." Buffalo: James S Leavitt, 1868.

Legg, Stephen. *Spaces of Colonialism: Delhi's Urban Governmentalities*. Oxford: Blackwell, 2007.

Lejaille, Arnaud. "Introduction: Prelude a la Grande Guerre Chimique." 2015. Accessed July 1, 2016. http://www.guerredesgaz.fr/these/Introduction/introduction.htm.

Lestel, Laurence. "Pollution atmosphérique en milieu urbain: de sa régulation à sa surveillance." *Vertigo* (Hors-série) 15 (Février 2013).

Markets and Markets. "Non-Lethal Weapons Market worth $1,146.2 Million by 2018." 2014. Accessed February 1, 2016. http://www.marketsandmarkets.com/PressReleases/non-lethal-weapons.asp.

McDonald, Lynn, ed. *Florence Nightingale and Hospital Reform: Collected Works of Florence*. Ontario: Wilfrid Laurier University Press, 2012.

McKirahan, Richard D. *Philosophy before Socrates: An Introduction with Texts & Commentary*. Indianapolis, IN: Hackett Publishing House, 2010.

Nader, David, and Spasoje Marčinko. "The Rise and Fall of 'Chlorine Chambers' against Cold and Flu." In *An Element of Controversy: The Life of Chlorine in Science, Medicine, Technology and War*, edited by Hasok Chang and Catherine Jackson, 296–323. London: British Society for the History of Science, 2007.

Neild, Guy H. "William Cruickshank (FRS-1802): Clinical Chemist." *Nephrology Dialysis Transplantation* 11 (1996): 1885–1889.

Nieuwenhuis, Marijn. "Breathing Materiality: Aerial Violence at a Time of Atmospheric Politics." *Critical Studies on Terrorism* 9, no. 3 (2016): 499–521.

Ryan, T. Anthony, Christine Ryan, Elaine A. Seddon, and Kenneth R. Seddon, eds. *Phosgene and Related Carbonyl Halides.* Amsterdam: Elsevier Science, 1996.

Salem, Harry, Andrew L. Ternay, and Jeffery K. Smart. "Brief History and Use of Chemical Warfare Agents in Warfare and Terrorism." In *Chemical Warfare Agents: Chemistry, Pharmacology, Toxicology, and Therapeutics,* edited by James A. Romano, Brian J. Lukey, and Harry Salem, 1–20. Boca Raton, FL: CRC Press, 2008.

Shapin, Steven, and Simon Schaffer. *Leviathan and the Air-Pump.* Princeton, NJ: Princeton University Press, 1985.

Sloterdijk, Peter. "Airquakes." *Environment and Planning D: Society and Space* 27 (2009): 41–57.

Sloterdijk, Peter. *Terror from the Air.* Cambridge: MIT Press, 2009.

Smart, Jeffery K. "History of Chemical and Biological Warfare: An American perspective." In *Medical Aspects of Chemical and Biological Warfare,* edited by F.R. Sidell, E.T. Takafuji, and D.R. Franz, 9–86. Washington, DC: Borden Institute, 1997.

Stoltzenberg, Dietrich. *Fritz Haber: Chemist, Nobel Laureate, German, Jew.* Philadelphia, PA: Chemical Heritage Press, 2004.

Sturdy, Steve. "War as Experiment: Physiological Innovation and Administration in Britain, 1914–1918: The Case of Chemical Warfare." In *War, Medicine and Modernity,* edited by Roger Cooter, Mark Harrison, and Steve Sturdy, 65–84. Stroud: Sutton Publishers, 1998.

Škof, Lenart. *Breath of Proximity: Intersubjectivity, Ethics and Peace.* Dordrecht: Springer, 2015.

Thomas, Martin. "'Paying the Butcher's Bill': Policing British Colonial Protest after 1918." *Crime, histoire & sociétés* 15, no. 2 (2011): 55–76.

Toulmin, Stephen, and June Goodfield. *The Architecture of Matter.* London and Chicago: University of Chicago Press, 1982.

Wallace, William. *Researches Respecting the Medical Powers of Chlorine, particularly in Diseases of the Liver; with an account of a new mode of applying this agent, by which its influence on the system can be secured.* London: Longman, Hurst, Rees, Orme, and Brown, 1822.

Watson O'Dell, Pierce. *Air War: Its Psychological, Technical and Social Implications.* New York: Modern Age Books, 1939.

Whitehead, Mark. *State, Science and the Skies: Governmentalities of the British Atmosphere.* Chichester: Wiley-Blackwell, 2011.

14

Breath as the Hinge of Dis-ease and Healing

DREW LEDER

This chapter addresses breath as a theater for the play of health and illness. I will use a phenomenological approach focusing on the *lived body* as analyzed by figures such as Husserl,[1] Merleau-Ponty,[2] Straus[3] and others. The lived body, they contend is not co-identical with the *body-as-object*, the latter a thing in the world with material parts and functions. While one's lived body is installed within the spatiotemporal world, it is also the way in which *one has a world* to begin with through one's embodied powers of perception, desire, speech, movement . . . and breathing.

As such, I will not primarily take a conventional medical perspective on the body's respiratory functions and its role in diseases and treatments. This would constitute a textbook unto itself. We would also confront a relative lack of research concerning the efficacy of specific breathing techniques. Most clinical trials are funded in search of profitable treatments such as costly pharmaceuticals and surgeries. Much less research is done on low-cost, low-profit treatments such as the use of the breath for disease prevention and symptom reduction. (And the more effective breath techniques prove to be, the less profit is to be made from drug sales.) Moreover, what research there is on breath often employs it as but one component of a larger program, for example involving hatha yoga or Buddhist mindfulness protocols. This makes it difficult to tease out the efficacy of breath *per se*. And of course there is no single "breath treatment" that is being consistently evaluated, or compared with others. Hatha yoga's *prāṇāyāma*, for example, and by itself, includes a multitude of ways of modulating the breath.[4]

So although I will often use the Western biological and medical perspective as a frame of reference, my focus is on a fuller phenomenology of the lived body. I will suggest that breath is best understood as a *hinge*—between many embodied levels, organs, and functions, and between the body and its lifeworld. This is why breath can act as a hinge between trajectories of personal health, illness, and treatment.

A "hinge" is defined as something like a joint or flexible surface that holds together two parts, allowing them to swing relative to one another. For example, a door hinge both connects the door to a wall and allows separation, permitting the relative movement known as opening and shutting. The breath, as I will trace out, serves as a living hinge interfacing between the conscious and unconscious body; the voluntary and involuntary; physical dualities (such as left and right nostril, nose and mouth, chest and abdomen); the local and expansive act; movement and stillness; the flow of receiving and returning (inspiration, expiration); and, finally, the visible and invisible (material and immaterial) realms.

As a hinge, properly employed, the breath can create psychophysical flexibility, openness, and wholeness accompanied by a sense of ease. However, illness can result from a frozen or defective hinge, or states in which we become patently *unhinged*. Deficient breathing manifests in forms of physiological dysfunction, both acute and chronic, experiences of elevated stress, anxiety, or depression, and modes of existential suffering. Collectively, I will refer to such as forms of "*dis-ease*." The hyphen signifies that the word refers not only to physical diseases as conventionally understood, but also to a broader lack or loss (*dis*) of *ease*—comfort, flow, well-being. The phenomenology of the living breath, and its relation to dis-ease and healing, includes, connects, and in a certain sense transcends, traditional divisions between "body," "mind," and "spirit."

The Conscious and Unconscious

A first thing to notice about breath is the way we usually *don't* notice it—it hovers on the edge, a kind of hinge between the conscious and unconscious realms. We take some fifteen thousand breaths a day, but most of these spring to life and die away without really entering into our awareness. Even as I write on this theme my breath is proceeding silently, autonomously, at most a kind of subliminal background to my focused work. Scientists tell us the respiratory act is triggered by physiological events—for example, the buildup of carbon dioxide and acidosis—and controlled by brain centers—as in the brainstem's medulla oblongata and pons—that operate without the need for reflexive awareness. Instead of saying "I breathe," we might say "it breathes," freeing the "I," the ego-self, to focus on its outward tasks.

But pause for a moment and become aware of your breath. You can sense the air entering through nose and/or throat with accompanying tickling or sucking sensations. Also easily apprehensible is the lift and fall of the chest, the swelling of the belly. (Science tells us that this is the result of contractions of intercostal, diaphragmatic, and abdominal muscles, along with secondary respiratory muscles, creating volume-pressure changes.)[5] With some work, this awareness can be rendered more subtle, as a chef trains to notice flavors a novice would miss. For example, practitioners of Buddhist *vipassanā* (awareness) meditation grow adept at experiencing the slight coolness in the nostrils on inhalation, whereas exhaled air feels slightly warmer as a result of its travels through the body. This is not just a neat attentional trick. Cultivating breath awareness is a key spiritual practice used in the Buddhist eightfold path, Hindu method of *rājayoga*, Daoist energy-based methods, and many other religious traditions. (In this chapter I mostly use examples from Eastern traditions because this dovetails with my own practices and studies.) Breath is ideal as a meditative focus: ever available, repetitive, intimately connected with our energy, mood, and thoughts, and with the universe around us. The breath can thus be used to gain one-pointed focus; calm the restless mind and body; promote energy flow; and investigate and experience the deep sources of life and our interconnection with the All.

Yet breathing also retreats from awareness in a recessive pattern typical of visceral functions.[6] Certain of the body's inner organs—those of the liver or spleen, for example—disappear so fully from consciousness that it is only at times of severe dysfunction—such as the "liver pain" of hepatitis (actually caused by a swelling of surrounding tissues)—that the organ can be sensed at all. Similarly, some dimensions of respiration are buried in an unperceived interiority. We are not consciously aware of our seventy million microscopic alveoli, which together have the surface area of a football field, though this is the place where the "business" of respiration is accomplished—oxygen and carbon dioxide diffuse to and from blood-carrying capillaries.

Furthermore, during sleep, breath in its totality slips beneath awareness. As a hinge function, breath can form our passage from wakeful consciousness into a dormant, unconscious state. Many an insomnia specialist counsels breath awareness and modulation as a way to tune out the busy mind and world, and relax, or simply bore, ourselves into sleep.

Again, though, dysfunction can seize our attention. Perhaps our partner complains about middle-of-the-night snoring. (We may feel *unjustly* accused—why blame me for my unconscious acts?) Or we might suffer from sleep apnea, which can create fifty or more arousals (micro-awakenings) an hour, setting the stage for potential long-term health problems. Through the night, the sufferer (and I have been one) hovers on the restless borderline of conscious/unconscious states. The hinge of breath has become unhinged, provoking experiential as well as functional dis-ease. Diagnosis of the condition often involves undergoing a sleep study: the body is wired up to laboratory electrodes, while the patient under observation is counseled to "just go to sleep" while being monitored and observed. Good luck! A sleep lab was the site of perhaps my most sleepless night ever. I simply was too conscious of trying to fall asleep to be able to do so, the fate of many insomniacs.

The Voluntary and the Involuntary

Breathing is a hinge not only between conscious and unconscious levels, but the volitional and involuntary. Scientists tell us that as an action triggered by neural, chemical, and hormonal signals to subcortical brain centers, respiration is largely driven by the "autonomic" nervous system, from the Greek *auto-nomos*, meaning "self-ruled," or "run by its own laws." *It* does not need *my* intervention, and in fact the latter can be counterproductive. Try to "breathe correctly." Try it right now. The likelihood is that this conscious act disrupts your breath's natural flow, introducing slight bodily confusion and discomfort. For Daoists, the breath is a prime example of the principle that *wu-wei*, a kind of "action/nonaction" characterized by effortless spontaneity, is the best way to navigate through life.[7]

Yet simply leaving our breathing patterns as they are may leave problems unaddressed. In our modern high-pressured, multitasking world, bodies often manifest unhealthy patterns of constricted, shallow respiration. This is particularly associated with certain postures (slumped over, or wearing tight clothes over clenched tummies) and with "chest breathing," which develops as we age and is associated with sympathetic nervous system (fight-or-flight) activation. Rapid, shallow respiration, with insufficient oxygenation and unnecessary hormonal release, has been correlated with a number of stress-related disease patterns, both acute and chronic. Sometimes disordered breathing also constitutes a primary disease state, as with chronic obstructive pulmonary disease (COPD)—often involving chronic bronchitis and/or emphysema—making it difficult to access air.

Learning to deepen and direct the breath can thus be essential to disease control and prevention. For example, sufferers of COPD can train in techniques to improve breathing efficiency, such as pursed-lips and diaphragmatic breathing. More broadly, Herbert Benson, an advocate for the use of the "relaxation response" incorporating the breath along with the use of calming words and images, advocates this as a no-cost, noninvasive treatment for a wide range of diseases, including cardiovascular chest pain, anxiety and depression, hypertension, infertility, hot flashes, migraines, and chronic pain.[8] In the words of James Gordon, Professor of Psychiatry at George Washington University, "Slow, deep breathing is probably the single best anti-stress medicine we have [. . .] heart rate slows, blood pressure decreases, muscles relax, anxiety eases and the mind calms."[9] Andrew Weil, Professor of Medicine at the University of Arizona, and a leader in the field of integrative medicine, calls breathing "the simplest and most powerful technique you can use for protecting your health. I have seen breath control alone achieve remarkable results: lowering blood pressure, ending heart arrhythmias, improving long-standing patterns of poor digestion, increasing blood circulation throughout the body, decreasing anxiety [. . .] and improving sleep and energy cycles."[10] If such statements are to be believed, we have free and immediate access to a powerful health restorative, though many of us fail to use it. Again, our breathing patterns tend toward the unconscious and involuntary—unless we use this hinge to open the door to change.

Directions on how to work with the breath vary according to teacher and practice. Benson counsels simply breathing "slowly and naturally" to evoke the relaxation response.[11] This may be easier said than done. For Western adults, habitual breathing patterns may be far from "natural," if this refers to the abdominal breathing characteristic of a small child.

"Mindfulness" approaches (often rooted in Buddhist *vipassanā* practice) favor cultivating an awareness of the breath without trying to judge or alter it in any way.[12] Awareness itself often brings about gentle transformation. The breath may begin to calm and deepen, as if by itself. Again, this is reminiscent of the Daoist principle of *wu wei*, an "action/nonaction" more effective for letting things be.

There are other spiritual practices, though, that emphasize a variety of voluntary interventions, including ones that render the inhalation and exhalation even in length; prolong one or the other, or the pause between them; emphasize diaphragmatic, or a three-part, or "essential" or "full-body" breath; direct breath-energy up and down the spinal *cakras*, or follow it out of the body on exhalation; emphasize nasal breathing, either deliberately balanced or unbalanced; and/or associate the breath with mantra, chanting, or imagery. Sometimes these are designed as a time-limited meditation practices, but may also serve to re-pattern our habit-body.

Yet this is no easy matter. Practicing a breath-control technique for twenty minutes a day may be ineffective in changing long-term unconscious habits. In fact, such techniques can even do harm, instituting artificial patterns (holding your breath, forcing your breath) that take us farther away from any "natural" rhythm. As yoga teacher Donna Farhi writes:

> At one end of the spectrum is the unconscious, involuntary breath; at the other end is breathing that is controlled and regulated by the will, such as the classic breathing exercises done by yogis. Between these two extremes lies the "essential" breath, a conscious flow that arises out of the depth of our being and dissolves effortlessly back into our core [. . .] To access this essential breath, we must first be able to focus on and perceive our own breathing process; that is we must make the unconscious conscious.[13]

As the quote suggests, the two hinges we have been exploring—that between the breath as conscious/unconscious, and voluntary/involuntary—are related to one another, but can be used differently in different practices.

Physical Dialectics: The "Where" of Breath

Due to its centrality in sustaining life and an assortment of bodily functions, breath operates through a number of often paired, in some ways redundant, but also complementary, systems. Here too we see hinge structures at play. For example, one can inhale primarily through the nose or the mouth; and with an emphasis on the chest muscles or the diaphragm. (The mechanics of breathing are of course far more complex, but we have space only for a simplified treatment.) In a certain sense, either pair member "can get the job done," but not all usage-patterns are created equal. The nose has certain particle filters for dust and allergens that the mouth lacks. The large diaphragm can open up greater lower lung capacity, and more efficient oxygenation, than when breath is mostly reliant on chest muscle contractions. And nasal/abdominal deep breathing tends to trigger the vagus nerve and parasympathetic nervous system, slowing the heart rate, relaxing sphincters, increasing intestinal and glandular activity, and often calming the mind. The yogic tradition also focuses on another dialectic—that between the two nostrils. These are believed to be the terminus point for paired energy channels (iḍā in the left, piṅgalā in the right), each with its different properties that together need harmonizing and rebalancing. Hence the practice of Nāḍī Śodhana,[14] alternate nostril breathing.

Thus, the development and healing of dis-ease is related to the physical dialectics of respiration, though these are recruited differently by various medical and spiritual systems. The emphasis might be on swinging breath more toward one pole than another (e.g., practicing diaphragmatic rather than chest breathing); incorporating the fullness of the spectrum (as in the yogic "three-part" breath, with a progressive abdominal, chest, and clavicular component);[15] or in establishing balance, as in Daoist yin/yang, or yogic alternate nostril, practices.

While speaking of the physical dialectics of respiration, it is ultimately the *lived body* that breathes, not simply an objectified correlate. There is thus first-person experience of where breath takes place, which may differ from a third-person scientific analysis of respiration. In some cultures this borderline is porous. We see this, for example, in the Indian accounts of prāṇā, and the Chinese focus on qi: these life energies associated with the breath follow pathways through a "subtle body" that can be mapped from outside, but also felt and guided from within.

More generally, breathing can be performed, and experienced, virtually anywhere. One can experience breathing from, or to, any part of one's body—for example, directing healing energy into an injured leg. A meditation practice I employ involves following the breath upward on inhalation, and on exhalation, down into the sacrum, or lower body—though this seems to reverse the Western account of respiratory physiology.

Breath can be experienced as highly *localized*: I mentioned earlier the *vipassanā* technique of focusing on the air right where it enters the nostrils. But breath can also manifest as that which is naturally *expansive*. It fills our lungs, distributes its goods through the entirety of the body, and connects us to the limitless world beyond. One can learn a full-bodied breath that seems to flood one's entire form, even reaching deep into the earth and up to the sky.

Where then does breath take place? One might say *nowhere* in particular—it eludes capture—and *very particular places* that can be learned about and/or felt; and, finally, *everywhere*, having the healing power to access and harmonize left and right, up and down, self and other, heaven and earth.

Receiving and Returning

This issue of where breath takes place has brought us to a consideration of breath as a hinge between inner and outer. We might have begun there. Breath, after all, relies on a two-part structure of breathing in and out, receiving and returning. This constant exchange is at the heart of our organic survival. Deprived of it even for a few minutes and we will die.

Much else that is human rides along with this movement of air.[16] Like our animal cousins we can sniff in, noting scents of potential predator and prey, terrain and weather—or in the modern world, of alluring foods, or toxic gas fumes. On the out-breath, we use our mouth to shape air into meaningful sounds—words that label the things of our world, communicate with others, voice our prayers, even sing forth in melody. Our words, subvocalized, become one of the primary bases for our sense of an "inner mind" engaged in private monologue.[17] And the sounds we make, when transcribed into written signs, become reproducible and transmittable across space and time, fostering the development of complex human science and culture. Yet all begins with breathing in and breathing out.

This balance of in and out is central to many healing practices. As modern Westerners, we are often told to breathe more deeply, yet *trying to* can have a paradoxically opposite effect, as we constrict muscles in the effort to suck in more air.[18] Some teachers thus emphasize extending the out-breath. Through emptying the lungs more fully, and enjoying the relaxation that accompanies exhaling, the following inhalation naturally deepens. But this hardly touches on the variety of techniques taught by ancient and contemporary traditions, playing with the in-out hinge. For example, in yogic *prāṇāyāma* (breath control) practices, *Kāpālabhāti*, or "skull brightener breath" employs fast, vigorous exhalations to cleanse the sinuses and respiratory passages, improve circulation, tone muscles and visceral organs, and calm the mind. In "against-the-grain-breath" (*Viloma Prāṇāyāma* method), both inhalations and exhalations are broken into a series of brief steps and pauses, intensifying breath awareness and control. Various kinds of "ratio breathing" teach one to maintain inhalations and exhalations for specific counts, either to deliberately equalize their length (*sāma-vṛtti*) or to establish unequal ratios (*viśama-vṛtti*), each with its own benefits.[19]

Such techniques focus on the movement of breath within the body. But the cycle of inhalation and exhalation reminds us that breath, and our lived body, are ever self-transcending, thoroughly interdependent with the universe as a whole. Moment to moment we are sustained by breathing in the oxygen created by plant life, then exhaling carbon dioxide, an essential nutrient for plants. *Receiving and returning*. In a broader sense, "health," a word that shares the same root as "holy" and "wholeness," implies the maintenance of proper harmony with the whole. Lewis writes, "For the Daoist, breathing, when it is natural, helps open us to the vast scales of heaven and earth—to the cosmic alchemy that takes place when the radiations of the sun interact with the substances of the earth to produce the energies of life."[20] Breathing well is not just a personal but a planetary affair.

Of course, one cannot be healthy when the very air one breathes is filled with toxic and carcinogenic waste. Zen teacher Thich Nhat Hahn recognizes the ecological implications of this body–world reciprocity. He writes of the Sun as "the great heart outside of our body," pumping energy to all life, and the forests as "our lungs outside of our bodies"[21]—when we cut them down, or poison them with acid rain, it is as if we are cutting our own body.

Through the practice of *Tonglen*, Tibetan Buddhists use the in/out hinge of the breath as an instrument for the development and expression of compassion. One imagines oneself as breathing in the suffering of specific others (sometimes visualized as a dark or hot smoke), then breathing out to them a sense of spaciousness, positive energy, or specific gifts that would bring relief.[22] This well-wishing breath can gradually be expanded to all suffering sentient creatures. Paradoxically, this also helps relieve our own suffering. In giving we receive.

For Buddhists (I will linger a moment further in this tradition) the fundamental way to relieve suffering, our own and others, is to awaken from the delusion of the separate self. Zen emphasizes simple awareness of breath flow as a tool for realization. In attending to the hinge of the in-breath and out-breath, we see that all is in flux, impermanent and interconnected. There is no solid and separate self. In the words of Shunryu Suzuki:

> When we practice zazen [seated meditation] our mind always follows
> our breathing. When we inhale, the air comes into the inner world.
> When we exhale, the air goes out to the outer world. The inner world
> is limitless, and the outer world is also limitless. We say "inner world"

or "outer world," but actually there is just one whole world. In this limitless world, our throat is like a swinging door. The air comes in and goes out like someone passing through a swinging door. If you think, "I breathe," the "I" is extra. There is no you to say "I." What we call "I" is just a swinging door which moves when we inhale and when we exhale.[23]

Movement and Stillness

There is the flow of air on inhalation and exhalation, yes . . . but between them there is a pause, a rest . . . a moment that can be infinitesimal . . . or deliberately extended to great length . . . where the breath becomes *still*. Two moments really: the pause after inhalation has peaked, but before exhalation—the midpoint of a breath—and that at the end of exhalation, before the next breath. Certain spiritual traditions work deeply not only with the movement of breath but with these places of rest.

This can be used for health purposes—lengthening the breath pauses can facilitate relaxation and a deeper breath. (One has to be careful, though, not to overforce it.) But certain meditation practices also use these pauses as portals to awakening. In Buddhist terms, the "form" of breath movement is seen to arise from and disappear into the still and empty "formless," *śūnyatā*. In the Hindu tradition, this gap, suspending movement and thought, provides a gateway to a deep *samādhi* state. Swami Muktananda teaches the ancient Upanishadic use of the mantra *haṃsa*, which is said to be the sound the breath itself makes, and therefore a natural mantra repeated within us since birth thousands of times every day. But, he writes:

> When the breath comes in with the sound *haṃ*, and merges inside, there is a fraction of a moment that is completely still and free of thought. This is the *madhyadeśa*, the space between the breaths. This is where you have to focus in meditation. To focus on that space is the highest meditation and the highest knowledge. That still space between the breaths, that space where no thoughts exist, is the true goal of the mantra. It is a miraculous space. [. . .] the space of God, of Supreme Consciousness, of the Self.[24]

In the West, focused on action and purpose, we may view the breath as the constant movement of goods coming in and waste products going out. Efficiency, productivity, is key for the body factory. We thus model breathing as ceaseless activity. Yet we forget the moments of stillness from which the breath arises, and to which it returns as to its natural home.

The Visible and Invisible

There is yet another, and in this chapter, a final hinge, that like the previous is key to spiritual traditions: that between the visible and invisible. The breath seems to hover in a liminal space. We can feel the breath, even see it, if we blow on a piece of paper or feather and witness it waving in our wind. Yet the breath in and of itself remains invisible (unless it's particularly cold). It has no weight, no color, no measurable size, unlike the rest of our fleshy body. *Almost disembodied in its thin materiality, it is yet the active principle that keeps the body alive.* When breath departs, vitality goes with it, and we are left with an inert corpse.

The Greek word *psyche*, and the Latin *anima* and *spiritus*, all mean "breath" but can also be translated as "soul" or "spirit." The ancient words hinge across many meanings. This vital soul has been interpreted in diverse ways, as by Aristotle in *De Anima*, or Plato in the *Phaedo* and *The Republic*. Any detailed analysis of such is beyond the bounds of this chapter. Suffice it to say that this breath/soul can be conceptualized as the living principle that animates a body, but also as what we might call "mind" or "spirit," potentially separable from the body and eternal. From whence comes this sense of a soul-body split? It is reasonable to infer that *respiration*—so integral to life, and yet invisible, almost immaterial—was one phenomenological *inspiration* leading to Greco-Christian, and then Cartesian, modes of dualism—the notion of a soul that animates, but is also separable from, the body.

The invisible breath thus can be associated not only with corporeal life but also, paradoxically, with a disincarnate realm. The breath appears/disappears, seems material/immaterial, of this world/otherworldly in its invisible comings and goings. This chapter has a focus on health and dis-ease. But a certain kind of otherworldly dualism can imply that dis-ease is endemic to life, that which plunges the soul into limitation and suffering. This is Nietzsche's interpretation of Socrates's last words in the *Phaedo*, a call to offer a cock (a sacrifice) to Asclepius, the Greek god of healing.[25] Nietzsche writes, "This ridiculous and terrible 'last word' means for those who have ears: 'O, Crito, *life is a disease*' [. . .] Socrates, Socrates *suffered life*."[26] We thus come full circle. We have examined the many ways in which breath can be used to prevent or relieve dis-ease. But what if life is the true dis-ease and our cure is the *cessation* of breath?

Conclusions

All this complexity and ambiguity flows out of the many ways breath operates as a hinge, a flexible interface, swinging back and forth. Between what? Again, between the conscious and unconscious; voluntary and involuntary; physical dialectics, as of the nose and mouth, chest and abdomen, even left and right nostrils; receiving and returning through the in-breath and out-breath; movement and stillness; and finally, the visible and invisible. Each hinge offers a place for interpretation and intervention, for swinging the door one way or another, or utilizing and harmonizing both sides of a dialectic. At times, the focus is on physical health. A particular sort of breath may be recommended—deep and diaphragmatic, for example, developed through conscious effort, but perhaps reshaping unconscious habits, lessening stress and its related maladies. At times, the focus is treating dis-ease of an existential and spiritual nature. Then aspects of the breath—its flow of receiving and returning, its moments of stillness, its invisible, ethereal nature—serve as portals to transcendence. Such may allow for a heightened experience of life, and/or a grateful passage to death. It's all there when you take a breath—and it's breathtaking.

Notes

1. Edmund Husserl, *Ideas Pertaining to a Pure Phenomenology and to a Phenomenological Philosophy*, bk. 2, *Studies in the Phenomenology of Constitution*, trans. Richard Rojcewicz and André Schuwer (Dordrecht, Boston, and London: Kluwer Academic Publishers, 1989).

2. Maurice Merleau-Ponty, *Phenomenology of Perception*, trans. Colin Smith (London: Routledge and Kegan Paul, 1962).

3. Erwin Straus, *The Primary World of Senses: A Vindication of Sensory Experience*, trans. Jacob Needleman (New York: The Free Press of Glencoe, 1963).

4. Richard Rosen, *The Yoga of Breath: A Step-by-Step Guide to Pranayama* (Boston: Shambhala Press, 2002).

5. For an overview of the functional anatomy of breathing, see Donna Farhi, *The Breathing Book: Good Health and Vitality through Essential Breath Work* (New York: Henry Holt, 1996), 47–68.

6. Drew Leder, *The Absent Body* (Chicago: University of Chicago Press, 1990), 36–68.

7. Huston Smith, *The World's Religions* (New York: HarperCollins, 1991), 207–211.

8. Herbert Benson and William Proctor, *Relaxation Revolution: Enhancing Your Personal Health through the Science and Genetics of Mind Body Healing* (New York: Scribner, 2010). For an overview of research on the beneficial effects of breathing practices vis-à-vis specific conditions, see also Farhi, *Breathing Book*, 6; and Richard P. Brown and Patricia L. Gerbarg, "Yoga Breathing, Meditation, and Longevity," *Longevity, Regeneration, and Optimal Health: Annals of the New York Academy of Sciences* 1172 (2009): 54–62.

9. Carol Krucoff, "Breathe," *Washington Post*, May 2, 2000, 14.

10. Ibid., 15.

11. Benson and Proctor, *Relaxation Revolution*, 9.

12. Jack Kornfield, *A Path with Heart: A Guide Through the Perils and Promises of Spiritual Life* (New York: Bantam Books, 1993), 60–63.

13. Farhi, *Breathing Book*, 9.

14. Georg Feuerstein, *The Shambhala Encyclopedia of Yoga* (Boston: Shambhala, 1997), 127, 194–195, 219–220.

15. Carol Krucoff, *Yoga Sparks: 108 Practices for Stress Relief in a Minute or Less* (Oakland, CA: New Harbinger Publications, 2013), 42–43. Also see Dennis Lewis, *The Tao of Natural Breathing: For Health, Well-Being and Inner Growth* (San Francisco: Mountain Wind Publishing, 1997), 33.

16. Erwin W. Straus, "The Sigh: An Introduction to a Theory of Expression," *Tijdschrift voor Philosophie* 14, no. 4 (1952): 674–695.

17. Leder, *Absent Body*, 121–125.

18. Lewis, *Tao of Natural Breathing*, 41.

19. Rosen, *Yoga of Breath*, 227–253.

20. Lewis, *Tao of Natural Breathing*, 9.

21. Thich Nhat Hanh, *Peace is Every Step: The Path of Mindfulness in Everyday Life* (New York: Bantam Books, 1991), 103–106.

22. Pema Chödrön, *Start Where You Are: A Guide to Compassionate Living* (Boston: Shambhala, 1994), 38–39.

23. Shunryu Suzuki, *Zen Mind, Beginner's Mind* (New York: Weatherhill, 1970), 29.

24. Swami Muktananda, *I Am That: The Science of Hamsa from the Vijnana Bhairava* (South Fallsburg, NY: Siddha Yoga Publications, 1992), 38.

25. Plato, *The Last Days of Socrates* (London: Penguin, 1993), 185.

26. Friedrich Nietzsche, *The Gay Science* (New York: Vintage Books, 1974), 272.

Bibliography

Benson, Herbert, and William Proctor. *Relaxation Revolution: Enhancing Your Personal Health through the Science and Genetics of Mind Body Healing.* New York: Scribner, 2010.

Brown, Richard P., and Patricia L. Gerbarg. "Yoga Breathing, Meditation, and Longevity." *Longevity, Regeneration, and Optimal Health: Annals of the New York Academy of Sciences* 1172 (2009): 54–62.

Chödrön, Pema. *Start Where You Are: A Guide to Compassionate Living.* Boston: Shambhala, 1994.

Farhi, Donna. *The Breathing Book: Good Health and Vitality through Essential Breath Work.* New York: Henry Holt, 1996.

Feuerstein, Georg. *The Shambhala Encyclopedia of Yoga.* Boston: Shambhala, 1997.

Husserl, Edmund. *Ideas Pertaining to a Pure Phenomenology and to a Phenomenological Philosophy.* Book 2. *Studies in the Phenomenology of Constitution.* Translated by Richard Rojcewicz and André Schuwer. Dordrecht, Boston, and London: Kluwer Academic Publishers, 1989.

Kornfield, Jack. *A Path with Heart: A Guide Through the Perils and Promises of Spiritual Life.* New York: Bantam Books, 1993.

Krucoff, Carol. "Breathe." *Washington Post*, May 2, 2000.

Krucoff, Carol. *Yoga Sparks: 108 Practices for Stress Relief in a Minute or Less*. Oakland, CA: New Harbinger Publications, 2013.

Leder, Drew. *The Absent Body*. Chicago: University of Chicago Press, 1990.

Lewis, Dennis. *The Tao of Natural Breathing: For Health, Well-Being and Inner Growth*. San Francisco: Mountain Wind Publishing, 1997.

Merleau-Ponty, Maurice. *Phenomenology of Perception*. Translated by Colin Smith. London: Routledge and Kegan Paul, 1962.

Muktananda, Swami. *I Am That: The Science of Hamsa from the Vijnana Bhairava*. South Fallsburg, NY: Siddha Yoga Publications, 1992.

Nietzsche, Friedrich. *The Gay Science*. New York: Vintage Books, 1974.

Plato. *The Last Days of Socrates*. London: Penguin, 1993.

Rosen, Richard. *The Yoga of Breath: A Step-by-Step Guide to Pranayama*. Boston: Shambhala Press, 2002.

Smith, Huston. *The World's Religions*. New York: Harper Collins, 1991.

Straus, Erwin. *The Primary World of Senses: A Vindication of Sensory Experience*. Translated by Jacob Needleman. New York: The Free Press of Glencoe, 1963.

Straus, Erwin. "The Sigh: An Introduction to a Theory of Expression." *Tijdschrift voor Philosophie* 14, no. 4 (1952): 674–695.

Suzuki, Shunryu. *Zen Mind, Beginner's Mind*. New York: Weatherhill, 1970.

Thich Nhat Hanh. *Peace is Every Step: The Path of Mindfulness in Everyday Life*. New York: Bantam Books, 1991.

15

Invisible Suffering

The Experience of Breathlessness

HAVI CAREL

This chapter presents a philosophical framework for the understanding of the experience of breathlessness. I suggest that the experience of breathlessness is total and overwhelming to the sufferer, but also largely invisible to the outsider. How does this tension play itself out for the respiratory patient? How does this tension affect respiratory medicine and clinical work? How could the first-person experience of breathlessness be better understood? Can it be usefully harnessed in the clinic? And what can a distinctively philosophical analysis offer this process? These questions are explored in the chapter, in the hope of providing a sketch of such a philosophical framework aimed at understanding this debilitating and common symptom.

The structure of the chapter is as follows. It begins with an overview of breathing and the symptom of breathlessness, and how breathlessness is interpreted in the clinic and outside it. The second section provides a phenomenological account of breathlessness, moving away from understanding it as a medical symptom to understanding it as a broader existential, social, personal, cultural, and psychological phenomenon. The final section examines how such a philosophical framework may be operationalized in a respiratory clinic, providing some examples of its possible clinical uses.

What Is Breathlessness?

Breathing is a basic physiological process but also has deep cultural, spiritual, and personal meaning. It connects our inner and outer physical realms via the air drawn into and expelled from the lungs. It is generally under autonomic control, but we also have some voluntary control over our breathing, and can override its "default settings" by holding our breath or otherwise consciously manipulating it. Breathing plays a central role in cultural and spiritual practices such as meditation and is also associated with our state of mind and in particular our well-being and emotional state. Breathing's pathological derivative, breathlessness, is a major symptom in both respiratory and cardiac disease, as well as in anxiety disorders and some disorders that affect the chest muscles. Whilst the physiology of breathlessness is well understood, the subjective experiences of breathing and breathlessness are understudied and our vocabulary and concepts with which to understand them are limited.

Breathing contains interesting tensions and juxtapositions. For example, it takes place continuously but mostly unconsciously. It is essential to life but can be artificially sustained despite the absence of consciousness. Much of the time we are unaware of it, but when it goes wrong (e.g., in respiratory disease), it takes up our entire attention. In some disorders, for example panic disorders, breathing itself can become the focus of pathological ideation and fears. When we exert ourselves physically, breathing becomes labored, eventually leading to breathlessness. In such situations, our breath becomes the focus of attention, and the experience can be uncomfortable. In cases in which breathlessness is pathological, experiencing it can be much more extreme and become debilitating, life limiting, and the focus of much anxiety.

Breathing is also intimately connected to emotion: surprise or horror make us gasp, hearty laughter leaves us gasping for breath, crying involves involuntary short, sharp inhalations. Breathing is richly modulated by emotional experience, be it pleasurable or painful. The lungs are the only bodily site (other than the skin) where interior and exterior spaces are in constant exchange. We breathe in the air and what it contains, extract the oxygen we need, and expel carbon dioxide. The air around us, with its pollutants, odors, humidity, and heat, becomes internalized briefly, connecting us to the environment and exposing our lungs to pollutants, irritants, and potential sources of infection. The lungs are thus vulnerable and open to the external environment in a way that does not occur with other internal organs.

The very idea of breath is suffused with metaphor. The German poet Rainer Maria Rilke described breath as "an invisible poem." Breath takes place in the chest, the center of our body; metaphorically, it is the core of life: our first and last breaths mark life's beginning and end, and breathing continuously happens throughout life. However, biomedicine does not acknowledge how everyday experience and its meanings are implicated in breathing, and thus neglects to incorporate this rich vein into its understanding of breathlessness. Metaphor, emotion, and the spiritual and existential dimensions are not part of the language of the clinic, yet they are a central part of the experience of breathing and of breathlessness. This tension between medical and cultural or intuitive understandings of breathing and breathlessness lies at the heart of this chapter.[1]

Turning to breathlessness, we can see that it is a major symptom that appears in a number of very common diseases with high morbidity and mortality rates. According to improving and integrating respiratory services, 25 percent of attendees to emergency departments, 62 percent of elderly people, and almost all people with chronic obstructive pulmonary disease (COPD) (around 95 percent) report breathlessness.[2] Breathlessness is a key symptom in a number of common and serious diseases, such as heart failure and lung cancer, as well as in COPD, a condition with an increasing global prevalence owing to its association with smoking. Air pollution has been an important cause of respiratory disease and breathlessness historically, and women in developing countries often develop COPD as a result of time spent by cooking fires.[3] The World Health Organization currently ranks COPD as the fourth most common cause of death in developed countries, and it is estimated that it will become the third largest global killer by 2020.[4] COPD affects an estimated 3.7 million people in the UK, but only 900,000 of them are aware of having the condition.[5]

Gysels and Higginson have described both the symptom of breathlessness, and the patients suffering from it, as invisible. This invisibility stems from the fact that breathlessness is a condition that usually has an insidious onset and is often attributed by those who experience it to aging, lack of exercise, or smoking.[6] The stigma associated with smoking is also a factor encouraging people to hide their condition or its severity. Clinicians, who are increasingly less likely to visit people in their own homes, are unaware of the complex needs, limitations, and adjustments required when living with breathlessness.[7] And of course either moderate or severe breathlessness has a dramatic impact on mobility and can cause people to go out less, socialize less, and hence be seen less. All of these factors contribute to the invisibility of breathlessness and breathless people.

The traditional clinical approach to dealing with a symptom is to find out what is causing it, treat it, and wait for the patient to improve. This rarely happens in chronic breathlessness. As Johnson and colleagues argue, chronic breathlessness frequently results from incurable, often long-term, progressive conditions, and the symptom persists despite treatment of the underlying condition.[8] They have termed such breathlessness "refractory" and suggest that the attitude of clinicians and patients toward it is one of helplessness, with clinicians holding the view that "nothing more can be done," and patients feeling more helpless and hopeless. This leads to hopelessness and lack of attention to the symptom from both parties. Patients may no longer report increasing distress to their doctors; clinicians may fail to ask about the problems caused by the breathlessness, as they feel unable to help. The problem of invisibility is compounded by a sense of helplessness.[9]

When we reflect on our breathing or try to describe the experience of breathing, we filter this reflection and experience through a rich set of influences that has a long cultural history. These influences can determine, in part, our reactions to a diagnosis of a respiratory illness, and how we might understand it. When this lay understanding approaches the clinic, it comes up against a biomedical view of breathing. The lay perspective is met by a particular series of prescribed questions (e.g., breathlessness questionnaires) against which patients must assess their breathlessness and through which their understanding begins to change. That change may be temporary, until they leave the clinic or hospital and return home. But the influence of the biomedical view may be more sustained. For example, as a result of listening to a clinical discourse, a patient might adopt a deficit approach to her breathlessness, having been shown through lung function tests what percentage of predicted lung function she has. She might begin to experience her breathlessness as more anomalous and shameful than before. She may feel alienated from the physiological body that has let her down. The ways in which the subjective experience is shaped by the clinical gaze is another aspect of the experience of breathlessness that phenomenology can usefully illuminate. I therefore now turn to a phenomenology of breathlessness.

A Phenomenological Account of Breathlessness

A phenomenology of breathlessness can reveal the nature of the experience and its qualia. It can also structure the experience using phenomenological concepts, as I do below. The first distinction I would like to make as the foundation of this phenomenological description is between pathological and normal breathlessness. Normal breathlessness is the kind of breathlessness a healthy person experiences upon exertion. It may involve heavier, deeper breathing that is also speeded up. But regardless of the level of exertion, in a healthy person oxygen saturation levels remain above 97 percent; such exertion is not dangerous and does not lead to loss of control, such as fainting. Experientially, healthy breathlessness does not lead to feelings of panic, anxiety, or fear. It is not a total experience and does not remove its bearer from the familiar everyday sense of her body and of herself. In fact, normal breathlessness can be associated with enjoyable bodily exertion as well as with a sense of challenge and joy (e.g., in exercise, running, or dancing).

Pathological breathlessness, of the kind experienced by people with impaired lung or heart function, is entirely different. It, too, involves heavier, faster breathing, but unlike healthy breathlessness, it does not deliver the required amount of oxygen to support bodily exertion. The gap between the amount of oxygen required for the activity and the amount available determines the level of incapacitation and the acuteness of the breathlessness. A person with severe respiratory disease might not be able to walk or bend down to pick up a pen from the floor. At its worst, pathological breathlessness is debilitating and causes severe disability.

In pathological breathlessness, blood oxygen levels can drop severely, leading to dizziness, fainting, shaking, excessive sweating, and a sense of doom. It is a total and overwhelming experience of loss of control and is acutely unpleasant. It removes the breathless person from the normal course of events and can cause deep anxiety, panic attack, and trauma.

Such pathological breathlessness is characterized by several core features: it is an acute and extremely unpleasant experience that can lead to severe distress, but not pain (although evidence from brain-imaging studies shows that the same neural pathways are activated in breathlessness and in pain.[10] It is an overwhelming, but as discussed above, invisible sensation. Unlike other, more dramatic, symptoms (e.g., bleeding, fainting, seizures) that can be easily observed, breathlessness is hard to see. This is in line with the characterization of breathlessness as an "invisible disability."[11] We can add a third layer to Gysels and Higginson's twofold view of breathlessness, saying that patients and disease are invisible. I suggest that the experience of breathlessness is also invisible. Although you might see a person standing and looking uncomfortable, often they are not panting, talking, or making any noise. It is therefore extremely hard to discern the extreme nature of this experience and how discomfiting and upsetting it is. In extreme cases, breathlessness and accompanying oxygen desaturation can lead to feelings of nausea, dizziness, faintness, and incontinence.

Some first-person articulations of pathological breathlessness include sufferers saying that they feel trapped, as if they are about to die, that they are suffocating or drowning, and that these feelings are intimately associated with feelings of panic and loss of control. Here is a first-person account of the experience of breathlessness:

> Trapped. That is what breathlessness feels like. Trapped in the web of
> uncertainty, bodily doubt, practical obstacles, and fear. The deepest fear
> you can think of. The fear of suffocation, of being unable to breathe,
> the fear of collapsing, desaturated to the point of respiratory failure.[12]

Let us now ground this experience in a phenomenological framework, in order to flesh it out more fully and to orientate the experience to a rich phenomenological description.[13] On a phenomenological account, embodiment determines possibilities. Merleau-Ponty famously draws on Heidegger's notion of existence as "being able to be" [Seinkönnen], and formulates this ability as grounded in motility and embodied action.[14] In breathlessness, these possibilities are truncated, curtailed, or altogether closed off. As a result, the world shrinks and becomes hostile, as the pathologically breathless person's ability to freely navigate it, move within it, and experience it shrinks. These truncated possibilities restrict choices and freedom and often dictate what is and is not possible, and what is and is not worth the considerable additional effort that carrying out the choice entails for a person with restricted mobility. As a result, projects that were previously open and executed with freedom become delimited by restriction.

For example, if I want to go for a walk after dinner to stretch my legs, I stroll until I am satisfied, and then I return home. In effect, I have walked without bounds. But for the respiratory patient, the walk must be carefully planned, with gradient, distance, and terrain considered, amount of ambulatory oxygen to be taken calculated, and frequent stops for rest built in. The very same activity—going for a walk—becomes restricted, narrowed, riddled with discomfort and worry, and of course this changes the nature of the experience. The shape of the walk has been entirely dictated by the illness, and is therefore not experienced as free.

As a result, a vicious cycle of self-limitation may ensure, leading to reduced fitness caused by deconditioning, which itself is caused by the reduced activity level. This cycle often leads to feelings of helplessness, despair, fear, anxiety, and depression. Any activity needs to be carefully planned, and during its execution, constant attention is paid to the breath: am I desaturating? Do I need to increase the oxygen flow? Will this walk be too exhausting for me? Will I be able to walk back? Will I have enough oxygen? The constant explicit consideration places the activity in the shadow of the breathing and the experience of breathlessness, and the way in which it is constantly managed and heeded changes the nature of any activity. It becomes secondary to the breath and the management of breathlessness.

In other words, the body loses the transparency it normally has in health. Thus, for example, Jean-Paul Sartre writes about the transparency of health; Drew Leder discusses the absent body in health; and Leriche speaks of health as a state lived in "the silence of the organs."[15] In respiratory illness, this putative transparency[16] disappears, while the body, as Leder would put it, "dys-appears," that is, it appears, but in a state of dysfunction, aberration, attracting negative attention and requiring treatment, strict regimentation, observation, and special measures.[17]

One way of characterizing the type of experiences that can occur in breathlessness is through the notion of bodily doubt.[18] Normally we have a tacit underlying sense of bodily certainty that characterizes everyday embodied experience. But in illness this certainty breaks down and is replaced by bodily doubt. This sense of bodily doubt is the breakdown of this tacit certainty, and leads to a radically modified embodied experience. It does this in three ways: loss of continuity, loss of transparency, and loss of faith in one's body.[19] Breathlessness is a core example of this breakdown. In cases of pathological breathlessness there is a break from past ability to exert oneself and to perform actions freely. The body loses its transparency, as discussed above. And finally, bodily doubt is characterized by a loss of faith in one's body. A body that has broken down, disappointed, or otherwise failed the ill person is likely to give rise to feelings of deep alienation, suspicion, and lack of trust.

Because of the breakdown of bodily trust, and the loss of certainty and transparency, in the presence of pathological breathlessness daily activities become *a problem*. The sense of "I can," which Husserl suggests characterizes our embodied stance toward the world, changes into a new stance, of "I no longer can," or "I was once able to but am no longer."[20] Our connection to the world "goes limp," as Merleau-Ponty puts it.[21]

There are a few further ways in which the transparency (or relative transparency) of the body changes in pathological breathlessness. First, there now is artificial and conscious engagement with breath. The modulation of breath (and of oxygen flow, if used) becomes explicit, and the natural, tacit, way in which breath is normally modulated is lost. The habitual body described by Merleau-Ponty becomes habitually breathless.[22] Habits are changed, bodily repertoires shrink, activities that were once enticing, even fun, are now passed over as too difficult or too tiring. Behavior is now modulated by both motor and psychological self-censorship: certain movements (e.g., bending) are avoided; exertion is carefully weighed and planned, so as to avoid overexertion; plans are made, then remade, changed, and often cancelled, if they require too much effort or lead to anxiety about keeping up, possible fatigue, and social embarrassment. This process takes place on both a motor and a conscious level. On the motor level, movements that were once easy and natural but have become difficult, challenging, or lead to severe breathlessness are avoided:

> Every time I tried—and failed—to do something that was too strenu-
> ous, my body stoically registered the failure and thereafter avoided
> that action. The change was subtle, because this happened by stealth.
> The miraculous result created by my body's adaptive abilities was
> that I stopped feeling so acutely all the things I could not do. They
> were quietly removed from my bodily repertoire, in a way so subtle
> I hardly noticed it.[23]

To summarize, in pathological breathlessness, explicitness of action becomes second nature on both a motor and a conscious level. This creates a new terrain, in which freedom and obliviousness are replaced by hesitation and limitation. In this terrain, distances increase: it is full of barriers, disruption, and unanticipated obstacles. This leads to the breathless person being excluded from shared norms; concepts like "nearby" and "easy" no longer tally with the concepts used by healthy people. In this way illness disrupts meaning structures and sufferers must rebuild meaning and regain their foothold on the everyday. Of course, in cases of progressive breathlessness, that everyday shifts as disease progresses. The lost opportunities and relinquished activities require a continuous reworking of the boundaries of the possible.

I said above that everyday activities become a problem, something requiring explicit attention, planning, and thought. In a similar way, the body itself also becomes a problem, an obstacle, a stranger, because embodied normality is disrupted. As philosopher S. Kay Toombs writes, illness is a series of losses. The losses she attributes to illness experiences in general are especially apt in the case of breathlessness, because breath is needed for any and all activities. So the loss of breath—being breath-less—results in the following losses: first, there is a loss of wholeness, a loss of bodily integrity, of a reflective sense of wellness. The awareness and anticipation of loss also cause distress. Second, there is a loss of certainty, which is pervasive and irreparable. Third, a loss of control. Breathlessness causes anxiety, dysautonomy, worry about and preoccupation with controlling one's body, one's breath, one's speech, and one's actions. Fourth, sufferers experience a loss of freedom to act; and fifth, a loss of the familiar world.[24]

Let us know turn to the final section, in which I consider the implications of this analysis for the clinic, and suggest several ways in which a phenomeno-logical analysis of breathlessness can be utilized in the clinic.

Phenomenology in the Clinic

There are several ways in which inviting the first-person phenomenological perspective into the clinic can be important and useful. I suggest that this is particularly the case for breathlessness, for several reasons. First, there is a noted discrepancy between objective and subjective measurements of lung function; this has been reported in the literature and causes physicians difficulties in predicting how patients will continue to cope with everyday living. Patients often over- or underperform, relative to their objective lung function measurement,[25] and this makes treatment and the allocation of resources such as social care difficult and inaccurate.

Second, as discussed above, breathlessness is an invisible symptom. Seeing someone stop to catch her breath tells you nothing of the internal turmoil, panic, and mounting discomfort she may be experiencing. Without patient reports about the experience, breathlessness will continue to be invisible and poorly understood. Making such accounts available and giving them prominence in public and patient fora, decision-making committees and other consultative process will contribute to reducing the invisibility of both symptom and patients, many of whom are housebound, or find leaving the house difficult, and are therefore less visible to both public and health professionals.

Another reason it is important to articulate the phenomenology of breathless-ness is because it gives an opportunity to demonstrate the breadth and diversity of experiences of breathlessness. In particular, there are compelling accounts of well-being experienced within the constraints of ill health, and this opens the door to viewing wellness despite breathlessness as both achievable and significant.[26] Barbara Paterson proposes the "shifting perspectives model," in which the illness (in this case the breathlessness) can shift from foreground to background during periods of stable disease, and back to the foreground during disease progression or symptom exacerbation.[27] The important thing is to note the possibility of the breathlessness receding into the background and no longer affecting the breathless person's well-being, although she still has limited mobility and other restrictions.

Another reason to promote the presence of first-person accounts of breathlessness is that, like all illnesses, breathlessness is experienced very differently from the inside (first-person perspective) and from the outside (second- or third-person perspective). Health professionals might have an intimate acquaintance with the causes and process of a particular disease, or treatment options and prognosis, and of the symptoms, but they still lack the first-person knowledge of what it is like to experience a particular disease. This experience can be transformative in two ways: it can reveal to you what it is like to suffer from pathological breathlessness, and it can also transform you in deep ways through the experience of a serious illness.[28] The "insider" perspective on breathlessness can be instructive and edifying for the health professional who does not have first-hand experience of the disease, and hence remains an "outsider" to that experience. This can also help with the discrepancy between the perceived ease of task (for the health professional) and the challenge it presents to a patient.

Finally, phenomenological reflection has a positive force. It can help sufferers to order and discern confusing experiences, and can provide a reflective stance from which to think about the bewildering, painful, and sad experiences of illness and of breathlessness. I have developed a "patient toolkit" that uses philosophical ideas to support patients in making sense of their illness. The toolkit has three steps: (1) stripping away the sociocultural understanding of illness to make room for individual interpretations; (2) viewing illness from different perspectives (thematizing) to enable patients to understand it as a multidimensional process. Thematizing reveals illness as it may appear to the ill person, carer/s and health professionals; and (3) considering how illness changes the ill person's way of being.[29]

To conclude, accounts of breathlessness can help overcome the gulf separating the healthy person's understanding of the term and the harsh reality of pathological breathlessness. As Elaine Scarry notes:

> [. . .] when one speaks about "one's own physical pain" and about "another person's physical pain," one might almost appear to be speaking about two distinct orders of events. For the person whose pain it is, it is "effortlessly" grasped; while for the person outside the sufferer's body, what is "effortless" is *not* grasping it.[30]

The unsharability of unique experiences such as extreme pain or pathological breathlessness undermines care and knowledge. Insofar as we do not attempt to reconcile the clinical perspective with that of the breathless patient, breathlessness remains opaque, invisible, and refractory. Health professionals are not exempt from holding both unconscious and conscious biases and stereotypes and from falling prey to stigmatization of disease and to certain diseases in particular.[31] Patients' invisibility and suffering can be exacerbated by this stigma and by their attempts to mask their symptoms, as they are trailed by tacit assumptions about their life and choices (e.g., that they were smokers, that they are contagious).

The feelings of pity, terror, and denial that many people experience when they encounter people with respiratory disease may also inflect health professionals' conduct and attitudes. Hence another reason for bringing them into close and sustained contact with sufferers' accounts of their experiences. The difficulties they experience are lived in the first person, and yet perceived by others via masking, miscommunication, and stigmatizing labeling. Patients' feelings of shame, self-consciousness, and objectification are common and often reported, and influence one's self-perception of oneself *as perceived by others*.[32]

To conclude, I suggest that a phenomenology of breathlessness can account for the richness and diversity of breathlessness experiences, and articulate the positive and unintended consequences of suffering. These consequences include the ways in which breathless patients adapt to their limitations, their increased resilience in the face of everyday adversity, and what Jonathan Haidt terms "post-traumatic growth."[33] Breathlessness is a juncture of physiological, psychological, existential, spiritual, and cultural dimensions. It cannot be studied solely as a symptom but requires a rich phenomenological account that makes room for the possibility of wellness within the constraints of breathlessness. As I hope to have shown here, a phenomenological framework can provide the conceptual tools required to fill this need.

Acknowledgments

I am grateful to the Wellcome Trust for awarding me a Senior Investigator Award (grant number 103340), which enabled me to write this chapter.

Notes

1. Jane Macnaughton and Havi Carel, "Breathing and Breathlessness in Clinic and Culture: Using Critical Medical Humanities to Bridge an Epistemic Gap," in *Edinburgh Companion to Critical Medical Humanities*, ed. A. Whitehead and A. Woods (Edinburgh: Edinburgh University Press, 2016), 294–330.

2. For figures from improving and integrating respiratory services see https://www.networks.nhs.uk/nhs-networks/impress-improving-and-integrating-respiratory (accessed March 28, 2017).

3. Charlotte A. Roberts, "A Bioarcheological Study of Maxillary Sinusitis," *American Journal of Physical Anthropology* 133 (2007): 792–807.

4. Peter J. Barnes and Sabine Kleinert, "COPD—A Neglected Disease," *The Lancet* 364 (2014): 564–565.

5. British Lung Foundation, "Invisible Lives: Chronic Obstructive Pulmonary Disease (COPD)—Finding the Missing Millions" (London: British Lung Foundation, 2007), 3.

6. Marjolein Gysels and Irene J. Higginson, "Access to Services for Patients with Chronic Obstructive Pulmonary Disease: The Invisibility of Breathlessness," *Journal of Pain and Symptom Management* 36, no. 5 (2008): 451–460.

7. Ibid.

8. Miriam J. Johnson, David C. Currow, and Sara Booth, "Prevalence and Assessment of Breathlessness in the Clinical Setting," *Expert Review of Respiratory Medicine* 8, no. 2 (2014): 151–161.

9. Macnaughton and Carel, "Breathing and Breathlessness."

10. Mari Herigstad, Anja Hayen, Katja Wiech, and Kyle T.S. Pattinson, "Dyspnoea and the Brain," *Respiratory Medicine* 105, no. 6 (2011): 809–817.

11. Gysels and Higginson, "Access to Services."

12. Havi Carel, *Phenomenology of Illness* (Oxford: Oxford University Press, 2016), 109.

13. See also ibid.

14. Martin Heidegger, *Being and Time,* trans. John Macquarrie and Edward Robinson (London: Blackwell, 1962; first published in 1927); Maurice Merleau-Ponty, *Phenomenology of Perception,* trans. Donald A. Landes (London: Routledge, 2012).

15. Jean-Paul Sartre, *Being and Nothingness,* trans. Hazel E. Barnes (London and New York: Routledge, 2003; first published in 1943); Drew Leder, *The Absent Body* (Chicago: University of Chicago Press, 1990); Leriche as cited in Georges Canguilhem, *The Normal and the Pathological,* trans. Carolyn R. Fawcett (New York: Zone Books, 1991).

16. Although see Carel, *Phenomenology of Illness,* for a critique.

17. Leder, *The Absent Body.*

18. Havi Carel, "Bodily Doubt," *Journal of Consciousness Studies* 20, no. 7–8 (2013): 178–197.

19. Ibid.

20. Amy Kesserling, "The Experienced Body, When Taken-for-Grantedness Falters: A Phenomenological Study of Living with Breast Cancer," PhD diss., available via UMI, 1990.

21. Merleau-Ponty, *Phenomenology of Perception.*

22. Ibid.

23. Carel, "Bodily Doubt," 40–41.

24. S. Kay Toombs, "The Meaning of Illness: A Phenomenological Approach to the Patient–Physician Relationship," *Journal of Medicine and Philosophy* 12 (1987): 219–240; S. Kay Toombs, *The Meaning of Illness: A Phenomenological Account of the Different Perspectives of Physician and Patient* (Amsterdam: Kluwer, 1993).

25. P.W. Jones, "Health Status Measurement in Chronic Obstructive Pulmonary Disease," *Thorax* 56 (2001): 880–887.

26. O. Lindqvist, A. Widmark, and B. Rasmussen, "Reclaiming Wellness—Living with Bodily Problems as Narrated by Men with Advanced Prostate Cancer," *Cancer*

Nursing 29, no. 4 (2006): 327–337; E. Lindsey, "Health within Illness: Experiences of Chronically Ill/Disabled People," *Journal of Advanced Nursing* 24 (1996): 465–472; M. Little, C. Jordens, K. Paul, K. Montgomery, and B. Philipson, "Liminality: A Major Category of the Experience of Cancer Illness," *Social Science & Medicine* 47, no. 10 (1998): 1485–1494.

27. Barbara Paterson, "The Shifting Perspectives Model of Chronic Illness," *Journal of Nursing Scholarship* 33, no. 1 (2001): 21–26.

28. Havi Carel, Ian James Kidd, and Richard Pettigrew, "Illness as Transformative Experience," *The Lancet* 388, no. 10050 (2016): 1152–1153. doi:http://dx.doi.org/10.1016/S0140-6736(16)31606-3.

29. For a full description of the toolkit, see Havi Carel, "Phenomenology as a Resource for Patients," *Journal of Medicine and Philosophy* 37, no. 2 (2012): 96–113. doi:10.1093/jmp/JHS008.

30. Elaine Scarry, *The Body in Pain* (Oxford: Oxford University Press, 1985), 4.

31. Ian James Kidd and Havi Carel, "Epistemic Injustice and Illness," *Journal of Applied Philosophy* 34, no. 2 (2016): 172–190. doi:10.1111/japp.12172.

32. Luna Dolezal, "The Phenomenology of Shame in the Clinical Encounter," *Medicine, Health Care and Philosophy*, 18, no. 4 (2015): 567–576.

33. Jonathan Haidt, *The Happiness Hypothesis* (London: William Heinemann, 2006).

Bibliography

Barnes, Peter J., and Sabine Kleinert. "COPD—A Neglected Disease." *The Lancet* 364 (2014): 564–565.

British Lung Foundation. "Invisible Lives: Chronic Obstructive Pulmonary Disease (COPD)—Finding the Missing Millions." London: British Lung Foundation, 2007.

Canguilhem, Georges. *The Normal and the Pathological*. Translated by Carolyn R. Fawcett. New York: Zone Books, 1991.

Carel, Havi. "Bodily Doubt." *Journal of Consciousness Studies* 2, no. 7–8 (2013): 178–197.

Carel, Havi. "Phenomenology as a Resource for Patients." *Journal of Medicine and Philosophy* 37, no. 2 (2012): 96–113. doi:10.1093/jmp/JHS008.

Carel, Havi. *Phenomenology of Illness*. Oxford: Oxford University Press, 2016.

Carel, Havi, Ian James Kidd, and Richard Pettigrew. "Illness as Transformative Experience." *The Lancet* 388, no. 10050 (2016): 1152–1153. doi:http://dx.doi.org/10.1016/S0140-6736(16)31606-3.

Dolezal, Luna. "The Phenomenology of Shame in the Clinical Encounter." *Medicine, Health Care and Philosophy* 18, no. 4 (2015): 567–576.

Gysels, Marjolein, and Irene J. Higginson. "Access to Services for Patients with Chronic Obstructive Pulmonary Disease: The Invisibility of Breathlessness." *Journal of Pain and Symptom Management* 36, no. 5 (2008): 451–460.

Heidegger, Martin. *Being and Time*. Translated by John Macquarrie and Edward Robinson. London: Blackwell, 1962. First published in 1927.

Haidt, Jonathan. *The Happiness Hypothesis*. London: William Heinemann, 2006.

Herigstad, Mari, Anja Hayen, Katja Wiech, and Kyle T.S. Pattinson. "Dyspnoea and the Brain." *Respiratory Medicine* 105, no. 6 (2011): 809–817.

Johnson, Miriam J., David C. Currow, and Sara Booth. "Prevalence and Assessment of Breathlessness in the Clinical Setting." *Expert Review of Respiratory Medicine* 8, no. 2 (2014): 151–161.

Jones, P.W. "Health Status Measurement in Chronic Obstructive Pulmonary Disease." *Thorax* 56 (2001): 880–887.

Kesserling, Amy. "The Experienced Body, When Taken-for-Grantedness Falters: A Phenomenological Study of Living with Breast Cancer." PhD diss. available via UMI, 1990.

Kidd, Ian James, and Havi Carel. "Epistemic Injustice and Illness." *Journal of Applied Philosophy* 34, no. 2 (2016): 172–190. doi:10.1111/japp.12172.

Leder, Drew. *The Absent Body*. Chicago: University of Chicago Press, 1990.

Lindqvist, O., A. Widmark, and B. Rasmussen. "Reclaiming Wellness—Living with Bodily Problems as Narrated by Men with Advanced Prostate Cancer." *Cancer Nursing* 29, no. 4 (2006): 327–337.

Lindsey, E. "Health within Illness: Experiences of Chronically Ill/Disabled People." *Journal of Advanced Nursing* 24 (1996): 465–472.

Little, M., C. Jordens, K. Paul, K. Montgomery, and B. Philipson. "Liminality: A Major Category of the Experience of Cancer Illness." *Social Science & Medicine* 47, no. 10 (1998): 1485–1494.

Macnaughton, Jane, and Havi Carel. "Breathing and Breathlessness in Clinic and Culture: Using Critical Medical Humanities to Bridge an Epistemic Gap." In *Edinburgh Companion to Critical Medical Humanities*, edited by A. Whitehead and A. Woods, 294–330. Edinburgh: Edinburgh University Press, 2016.

Merleau-Ponty, Maurice. *Phenomenology of Perception*. Translated by Donald A. Landes. London: Routledge, 2012.

Paterson, Barbara. "The Shifting Perspectives Model of Chronic Illness." *Journal of Nursing Scholarship* 33, no. 1 (2001): 21–26.

Roberts, Charlotte A. "A Bioarcheological Study of Maxillary Sinusitis." *American Journal of Physical Anthropology* 133 (2007): 792–807.

Sartre, Jean-Paul. *Being and Nothingness*. Translated by Hazel E. Barnes. London and New York: Routledge, 2003. First published 1943.

Scarry, Elaine. *The Body in Pain*. Oxford: Oxford University Press, 1985.

Toombs, S. Kay. *The Meaning of Illness: A Phenomenological Account of the Different Perspectives of Physician and Patient*. Amsterdam: Kluwer, 1993.

Toombs, S. Kay. "The Meaning of Illness: A Phenomenological Approach to the Patient–Physician Relationship." *Journal of Medicine and Philosophy* 12 (1987): 219–240.

16

Feminist Politics of Breathing

MAGDALENA GÓRSKA

Breathing and politics are not usually considered relevant to one another. Is it therefore possible to engage with breathing as a force of social justice? What kinds of atmospheres can corpomaterial dynamics of breathing help envision for the possibility for individuals and social groups to live breathable lives?

It is my aspiration here to argue that politics can take place not only in terms of governance, social movements, identity politics, and biopolitics but also in terms of quotidian bodily actions—such as breathing. By working with breath as a force that is common to all living and breathing (in this chapter, human) beings yet differential in its enactments, I propose a rethinking of politics in which corpomaterial actions matter—politics not based on universalizing, homogenizing, or essentializing understandings of embodiment or subjectivity but conceptualized and enacted intersectionally in their specific situatedness and dispersal in the individual and structural dynamics of power relations. This chapter of the volume, therefore, explores the possibility of such politics in relation to the quotidian practices of breathing.

Breathing as a Relational Enactment

Breathing is a process that is shared across (human and nonhuman) life forms. It is a force that brings beings to life and engages their existence in the ongoing metabolization of the atmospheric and material processes of living. As such, dynamic breathing is a matter of not only human-embodied subjects but also, for example, other animals, over- and underwater beings, plants, soil, and elements.

But even as a force that is shared by all breathing beings, breathing is not a homogenous phenomenon. For example, human breathing is enacted differently in relation to lung specificities such as those that are partially collapsed, with diverse materialities such as cancer or coal dust sediment, and with different sizes and respiratory capacities. Similarly, breathing also has different rhythms and flows across different bodies that—according to their age, constitution, and size—breathe at different rates and depths. Breath can also be enacted with diverse respiratory aids and technologies, such as respiratory ventilators; oxygen stations, which out of necessity started to appear in metropolises with severe air pollution, such as Beijing; or even as part of a privileged lifestyle, as newly appearing oxygen bars aspire to become part of the contemporary entertainment and well-being industry.

Breathing is also a differential phenomenon in terms of the diverse ways it is understood. In Western perspectives, breath is considered to be enacted through inhalation and exhalation. But in *Prāṇāyāma*, for example, breathing is considered to consist of four parts: inhalation, an air-full pause after inhalation, exhalation, and an air-empty pause after exhalation.[1] Breath also has different meanings within, for example, theories and practices of yoga; pain control; and philosophical, mystic, and religious thought in which breathing is associated predominantly with spirits, gods, and the immateriality of life. And even when it is considered material, the way breathing is described, bounded, and conceptualized also differs if it is approached from the perspective of physiology, anatomy, biochemistry, or physics—classifications through which it both escapes as well as becomes intelligible. And, as mentioned earlier, breathing also transforms depending on whether it is understood as a human or nonhuman activity, and depending on the breathing actors (e.g., oxygen, diaphragm, trees) one follows.

In its persistent commonality and constant differentiation, breathing can thus inspire diverse analyses of relational natural and cultural as well as material and social scapes that are dispersed across diverse spaces, times, geopolitical relations, ecosystems, industries, and urbanization while being situated in their phenomenal specificities. Considering such simultaneously common and differential enactments of breathing it is, hence, necessary to work with a nonreductive understanding of it—one that does not reduce breathing into one homogenized narrative, one particular enactment, or one form of politics or ethics.

In developing such an approach, I find the agential realist philosophy developed by feminist physicist and theorist Karen Barad[2] particularly helpful for working with breathing's dynamics of simultaneous commonality and differentiation. The approach Barad develops allows one to account for the simultaneous material and discursive, natural and cultural, human and nonhuman enactments of breathing as an ethico-onto-epistemological phenomenon. The concept of *phenomenon* mobilized here is of an agential realist character—the concept is understood not as an ontologically prior object with preexisting boundaries and properties but as one that comes into being through the ethico-onto-epistemological dynamism of its intra-active and differencing constitution.

The concepts *intra-action* and *ethico-onto-epistemology* are neologisms developed by Barad through her work in quantum physics to rearticulate contemporary notions of causality and the relation of knowledge, ethics, and reality. Barad, in developing the notion of intra-action, challenges interactive understandings of causal dynamics (which presuppose entities that preexist relational dynamics) and instead proposes thinking about the dynamics of relating as processes of a simultaneously ontological, epistemological, and ethical—or, as Barad puts it, an ethico-onto-epistemological—constitution.[3] In such an approach, phenomena do not preexist relations ethically, epistemologically, or ontologically but are enacted in processes of intra-active relating. Through intra-action, phenomena come into being in a way through which none of the "components" that materialize within the intra-active processes preexist these processes or have any pregiven essence. These components, or *relata* in Barad's[4] words, are always bound to the phenomena, and they come to exist and acquire boundaries and properties within specific intra-actions. While intra-activity is a causal dynamism of the ethico-onto-epistemological constitutiveness of phenomena, it is simultaneously a dynamism of *differentiation*—as I elaborate elsewhere[5]—in which phenomena obtain boundaries and properties through dynamics of "differential patterns of mattering."[6]

The intra-active (understood as mutually constitutive but without preexisting entities) while differential (i.e., not homogenizing or flattening) reconceptualization of causality, then, allows scholars to work with breathing as simultaneously situated and dispersed, in its particular enactments that are simultaneously common and differential. In such an approach, then, I understand breathing in its specific situatedness (e.g., breathing enacted in specific panic attacks or in a coal miner's dusty lungs)[7] while simultaneously common and dispersed dynamic to be enacted in the agential multiplicity of diverse relata that are constitutive of the phenomenon (e.g., the role of the diaphragm for breathing). Simultaneously, the relata are constituted themselves by the process of intra-active and differential ethico-onto-epistemological becoming. For example, organs such as the lungs, which are usually understood in a homogenized way, are enacted differently in relation to the ways individuals live within social power relations—living with anxieties transforms the ways one breathes, and living with dusty lungs syndrome transforms the lungs as an organ.

The intra-active, differential, and phenomenal approach therefore allows for an engagement with breathing as a relational enactment of the intra-active constitutiveness and differentiation of diverse substances, fluids, organs, and cultural, environmental, and affective practices as well as social power relations. Such a relational understanding of breathing opens up possibilities for interdisciplinary knowledge production practices and for developing politics through a posthumanist reconceptualization of contemporary understandings of human embodiment, subjectivity, and power.

Why Breathing Matters

For decades, feminist corporeal, postcolonial, Marxist, and queer scholarship has criticized the historical but persistent heritage of the notion of "the (cis-male, white, disembodied) human."[8] Despite this criticism and the alternative approaches that the feminist scholarship has been developing, contemporary Western main-stream humanism, in relation to which this chapter is situated, is still embedded in Cartesian logic, white male supremacy, disembodiment and rationalization of the privileged notion of subjectivity, and racialized and classed (to name a few power dynamics) embodiment of "the Other." Such an approach is clearly mani-fested in, for example, (white, Western, classed) human exceptionalist discourses mobilized in contemporary European right-wing politics and anti-immigration rhetoric that have dominated the European political landscape, leading to its transformation in the time of Brexit. In light of the persistence of such humanism and its terrifying political consequences, I believe that together with the critical approaches developed in feminist research and activism, breathing can be a force that articulates the necessity of rethinking contemporary understandings of the relationalities of humanism, human-embodied subjectivities, and power; and it also offers directionalities for doing so.

For example, in its diversity and in the flow of its worldly circulation, breath challenges binary logics that constitute contemporary notions of human subjectivity. It problematizes the distinction between concepts such as "inside" and "outside" by troubling notions of corpomaterial boundaries in the worldly metabolization of oxygen; it complicates notions of self, other, and environment in challenging individualistic concepts of humanness and articulating its transcorporeal[9] charac-ter that defies bodily and subjective boundaries of the self; it also problematizes human exceptionalism by embedding humans in the intra-actively[10] constitutive atmospheric, material, and social dynamics of living.

Breath is, therefore, a force that challenges conventional boundaries and opens up possibilities of reimagining what it means to be an embodied *posthu-manist* subject who is not *in* the world but is—as is articulated in a diversity of approaches by feminist scholars such as Donna Haraway,[11] Rosi Braidotti,[12] Mette Bryld and Nina Lykke,[13] Myra Hird,[14] Stacy Alaimo,[15] and Cecilia Åsberg[16]—*of* the world, as Barad[17] argues.

As I discuss elsewhere in relation to coal mining,[18] breathing articulates how social justice politics are simultaneously matters of environmental politics, as breathing polluted air enacts particular (geopolitically specific) intersectional forms of existence and resistance. For example, pursuing the diversity within the breathability of life and air quality can lead to researching the dynamics of geo-political economic and (neo)colonialist power relations. It can lead to questions about political, social, and economic distribution and the maintenance of privilege or lack thereof; it can lead to questions about the power that materializes not only in (un)breathable and (non)toxic air but also in political, social, and ethical matters such as whose lives are breathable and whose loss of breath is grievable.

A respiratory analysis can also provide insight into relationalities that accentuate contemporary trends in the development of neoliberalism and its consequences at both local and global levels. It can allow for an analysis of complex socioeconomic processes through which pollution-reducing technologies enable certain countries, or specific geopolitical areas in many parts of Europe, to enjoy cleaner and fresher air while other countries or areas suffocate in smog. The vast relationalities these breathing scapes unfold can offer respiratory interventions in the development of interdisciplinary social and environmental justice politics.

Moreover, as research concerned with the social element of environmental pollution and social deprivation shows,[19] breath and air matter in terms of social geographies in which intersectional positioning is related to how and what saturation of air pollution one breathes. According to a health geography study by Jamie Pearce and colleagues, for example,

> the unequal exposure to air pollution between advantaged and disadvantaged groups provides a direct causal explanation for the socioeconomic gradient in ill health, particularly for those diseases related to air pollution such as asthma and lung cancer. [. . .] [A]s well as suffering greater levels of exposure, disadvantaged populations are likely to be more susceptible to the effects of air pollution upon health. This inequity arises because communities with higher levels of relative disadvantage experience poorer provision of medical care, housing, and access to facilities such as grocery stores, and adverse psychosocial conditions. [. . .] [Also,] disadvantaged communities have a higher susceptibility to predisposing health conditions such as diabetes and asthma, because of socioeconomic differences including occupation, social support, and medical care, which renders them more sensitive to the effects of air pollution. Therefore, this combination of factors relating to environmental justice provides a set of interrelated mechanisms that help to illuminate some of the pathways that lead to inequalities in health.[20]

As Pearce and colleagues indicate, breathing is therefore a political matter that is natural, cultural, and social. As such, it is also an *intersectional* political matter. Working with a natural-cultural-intersectional understanding of breathing creates space for respiratory political questions: How do the environmental politics of air pollution matter as part of intersectional social justice politics? How can they articulate the differential ways in which the ability to take a breath and to breathe fresh air is a matter of intersectional situatedness in and enactment of local and global power relations? And what kind of implications and affinities are enacted when, for example, a light switch on the wall of every single living room (with electricity) enacts specific practices of privileging and deprivileging that are empowered by the mere possibility (which in many geopolitical areas is a matter of privilege) of turning it on? Or when some electricity users breathe fresh air while others live in areas polluted by coal mining, or breathe coal dust for a living?

It matters if and how one can breathe and if and how one's life is breathable. One of the crucial contributions of feminist studies—particularly of Black and Marxist feminism in their specifically different interventions[21]—is the discussion of the intersectional specificity of whose lives matter and how. And the intersectional understanding of embodiment and subjectivity, materiality and discursivity, and nature and culture is central for working with breathing as a transformative force of change that does not homogenize or universalize politics but works with the simultaneous specific situatedness and dispersal of social power relations. As an intersectional phenomenon, therefore, breathing is a matter of environmental and social justice politics that are intra-actively constitutive yet differential.

The politics of breathing can also, therefore, be developed through enactments of breath other than environmental ones, such as agential dynamics of affect. When living with anxieties or undergoing panic attacks, many people experience a change in breathing. Such transformations are usually explained merely physiologically, but an intra-active analysis of physiological processes allows for an engagement with breathing transformativity as a matter of corpo-affectivity[22]—a dynamic of the mutual constitutiveness of corpomateriality and affect.

Feminist affect studies—exemplified in the works of such scholars as Ann Cvetkovich,[23] Eve Kosofsky Sedgwick,[24] Sara Ahmed,[25] Sianne Ngai,[26] Heather Love,[27] Laurent Berlant,[28] and Jack Halberstam,[29] as well as groups such as Public Feelings and Feel Tank Chicago and art projects such as *The Alphabet of Feeling Bad*[30] and *An Unhappy Archive*[31]—have already recognized the role of affect as a response to the dynamics of social power relations. They have argued for the significance of affective dynamics such as depression, shame, trauma, and failure and problematized normative ideals of happiness and affective attachments. These affective processes are analyzed as part of the operation of social power relations that, as Ann Cvetkovich argues regarding depression, are "manifestation[s] of forms of biopower that produce life and death not only by targeting populations but also more insidiously by making people feel small, worthless, hopeless."[32]

Within feminist studies, affective dynamics became recognized as valuable responses to social power relations. They are also perceived as manifestations of intersectional oppressive structures such as racism, classism, colonialism, heteronormativity, gender normativity, sexism, and ableism.

But, additionally, as breathing in anxieties and panic attacks articulates, corpomaterial and corpo-affective dynamics are more than just responses to or manifestations of social conditions. As I argue elsewhere,[33] anxious and panicky breathing is also a material enactment of and challenge to contemporary power relations that are enacted individually and structurally. These kinds of breath transform dynamics of living by enacting a break and necessitating change. In this way, they enact specific materializations and productions as well as transformations and alternatives to the dominant social norms and power relations.

But as transformative forces, anxieties and panic attacks are also often painful and unbearable. They are not alternatives in the ideational sense of desired ways of being. And, simultaneously, in their painfulness they break norms apart. These breaks are terrifying, but they also open potentialities of being otherwise. The political potentialities of anxious and panicky breathing are, therefore, not only optimistic or happy in themselves, or for the sake of being alternatives, but enactments of different directionalities. They enact change in the form of radical disruption, immobility, and rejection of the normative pressure of being an intersectional embodied subject of the neoliberal political, social, and cultural economy. They claim what it means to be a human-embodied subject in a differential way. In their suffocating forcefulness, they are also articulations of the necessity to take space, to take a breath, and to live a breathable life.

I therefore understand breathing as a force that not only materializes, recognizes, and manifests social power relations but also forces social and environmental transformation. In this approach, breath in its trans-corporeal and lively and deadly operations becomes not only a symbolic but also a literal enactment of the struggle for breathable life—a struggle that, as I have argued above, takes place in quotidian practices of living and is inherently intersectional and posthumanist, in which the notion of humanness relies not on impermeable boundaries but rather on respiratory co-becoming.

Within such an approach, Sara Ahmed's words articulated in relation to queer and postcolonial scholarship and activism can become a motto for feminist politics for breathable lives:

> The struggle for a breathable life is the struggle for queers to have space to breathe. Having space to breathe, or being able to breathe freely is [. . .] an aspiration. With breath comes imagination. With breath comes possibility. If queer politics is about freedom, it might simply mean the freedom to breathe.[34]

Breath is, therefore, a lively and deadly force not only physiologically but also affectively and socially. As Ahmed points out, breathing can become a force of taking space for breathable existence, an aspiration for social transformations that challenge intersectional dynamics of privilegization and deprivilegization, and a request for freedom that is common to all while recognizing differential needs and accountabilities in relation to social power structures.

Feminist Politics of Breathing

In this chapter I have argued for a nonreductive understanding of breathing and for specific respiratory politics. I've argued for an understanding of politics in which embodiment, affect, and power are mutually constitutive—for politics that take place not only on the streets or in forms of organized governmentality but also in quotidian corpomaterial and corpo-affective practices, which are not joyful or acceptable, for the sake of creating an alternative, but ambivalent.

As Jack Halberstam points out, "alternatives dwell in the murky waters of a counterintuitive, often impossibly dark and negative realm of critique and refusal."[35] And although imagining lives otherwise through, for example, anxious and panicky breathing involves engaging with the ambivalence of the intra-active constitution of immobility and potentiality and of pain and empowerment, it is this ambivalence that I believe can enact ruptures, transformations, and negotiations of hegemonic norms of embodiment and subjectivity and of contemporary exceptionalist humanism.

The political potential of breathing for environmental and social justice, therefore, is not found in simply embracing living in polluted air or experiencing anxieties and panic attacks as phenomena of resistance. It is in the dynamics of the complex and ambivalent articulations those phenomena open up through breaking worlds apart and demanding change. The political interventions of breathing, for example, during panic attacks or with dusty lungs are not simply in their acceptance but in the recognition of the political power they enact in *calling out* individual and systemic intersectional operations of power relations and in *calling in*[36] (dynamic and temporary) affinities or separations through similarities and differences. Such politics call for social, cultural, geopolitical, and paradigmatic changes as well as for changes in daily life. They call for approaches in which politics and change do not idealize resistive phenomena but work with their simultaneous potentiality and unbearability, painfulness and undesirability.

Simultaneously, to come back to my earlier points, such politics cannot be generalized and unified. They are always situated in their particular intersectional enactments. Simultaneously, they are dispersed in the structural patterns of the operations of intersectional power relations.

What I have, therefore, strived to argue for is an articulation of politics that matter in a quotidian, individual, and structural manner—politics that are always provisional, under constant negotiation, and in which positions of privilege and lack thereof matter and shift as part of dynamic coalitional and separatist, geopolitically situated and dispersed social and environmental justice work. Such politics are about the intra-active constitution and differentiation of nature and culture as well as human and nonhuman and are inherently intersectional and posthumanist. In these politics, every breath one takes is a process of intra-active metabolization of power relations. This is the case in terms of not only air pollution and environmental toxicity but also breathing through the racist, gendered, classist, ableist, sexist, cis-, and heteronormative social norms of human subjectivity and struggling for nonhegemonic breathable life and existence.

Notes

1. Lenart Škof, *Breath of Proximity: Intersubjectivity, Ethics and Peace* (Dordrecht: Springer, 2015).

2. Karen Barad, "Posthumanist Performativity: Toward an Understanding of How Matter Comes to Matter," *Signs* 28, no. 3 (March 1, 2003): 801–831; Karen Barad, *Meeting the Universe Halfway: Quantum Physics and the Entanglement of Matter and Meaning* (Durham, NC: Duke University Press, 2007).

3. Barad, *Meeting the Universe Halfway*.

4. Ibid.

5. Magdalena Górska, "Breathing Matters: Feminist Intersectional Politics of Vulnerability" (PhD diss., Linköping University, 2016).

6. Barad, *Meeting the Universe Halfway*, 206.

7. Górska, "Breathing Matters."

8. Cf. Susan Bordo and Alison Jaggar, eds., *Gender/Body/Knowledge: Feminist Reconstructions of Being and Knowing* (New Brunswick and London: Rutgers University Press, 1989); Donna Haraway, *Simians, Cyborgs, and Women: The Reinvention of Nature* (New York: Routledge, 1991); Judith Butler, *Bodies That Matter: On The Discursive Limits of "Sex"* (New York: Routledge, 1993); Rosi Braidotti, *Nomadic Subjects* (New York: Columbia University Press, 1994); Elizabeth Grosz, *Volatile Bodies: Toward a Corporeal Feminism* (Bloomington: Indiana University Press, 1994); Kathy Davis, ed., *Embodied Practices: Feminist Perspectives on the Body* (London: Sage, 1997); Katie Conboy, Nadia Medina, and Sarah Stanbury, eds., *Writing on the Body: Female Embodiment and Feminist Theory* (New York: Columbia University Press, 1997); Lynda Birke, *Feminism and the Biological Body* (New Brunswick, NJ: Rutgers University Press, 2000); Margrit Shildrick, *Embodying the Monster: Encounters with the Vulnerable Self* (London and Thousand Oaks: Sage Publications, 2002); Margrit Shildrick, *Dangerous Discourses of Disability, Subjectivity and Sexuality* (Basingstok and New York: Palgrave Macmillan, 2009); Ketu Katrak, *The Politics of the Female Body: Postcolonial Women Writers* (New Brunswick, NJ: Rutgers University Press, 2006).

9. Stacy Alaimo, "Trans-Corporeal Feminisms and the Ethical Space of Nature," in *Material Feminisms*, ed. Stacy Alaimo and Susan Hekman (Bloomington: Indiana University Press, 2008), 237–264.

10. Barad, "Posthumanist Performativity"; Barad, *Meeting the Universe Halfway*.

11. Haraway, *Simians, Cyborgs, and Women*; Donna Haraway, "Otherworldly Conversations; Terran Topics; Local Terms," in *The Haraway Reader* (New York:

Routledge, 2004), 125–150; Donna Haraway, "When Species Meet: Staying with the Trouble," *Environment and Planning D: Society and Space* 28, no. 1 (2010): 53–55.

12. Braidotti, *Nomadic Subjects*; Rosi Braidotti, *The Posthuman* (Cambridge and Malden: Polity Press, 2013).

13. Mette Bryld and Nina Lykke, *Cosmodolphins: Feminist Cultural Studies of Technology, Animals and the Sacred* (London and New York: Zed Books, 2000).

14. Myra Hird, *The Origins of Sociable Life: Evolution After Science Studies* (New York: Palgrave Macmillan, 2009).

15. Stacy Alaimo, *Bodily Natures: Science, Environment and the Material Self* (Bloomington: Indiana University Press, 2010).

16. Cecilia Åsberg, "The Timely Ethics of Posthumanist Gender Studies," *Feministische Studien: Zeitschrift für interdisziplinäre Frauen- und Geschlechtforschung* 1 (2013): 7–12.

17. Barad, *Meeting the Universe Halfway*.

18. Górska, "Breathing Matters."

19. Cf. Benedict Wheeler, "Health-Related Environmental Indices and Environmental Equity in England and Wales," *Environment and Planning A* 36, no. 5 (May 1, 2004): 803–822; Anna Germani, Piergiuseppe Morone, and Giuseppina Testa, "Environmental Justice and Air Pollution: A Case Study on Italian Provinces," *Ecological Economics* 106 (2014): 69–82; Cindy Padilla et al., "Air Quality and Social Deprivation in Four French Metropolitan Areas—A Localized Spatio-Temporal Environmental Inequality Analysis," *Environmental Research* 134 (2014): 315–324.

20. Jamie Pearce, Simon Kingham, and Peyman Zawar-Reza, "Every Breath You Take? Environmental Justice and Air Pollution in Christchurch, New Zealand," *Environment and Planning A* 38, no. 5 (May 1, 2006): 934.

21. Cf. Sojourner Truth's speech from 1851 "Woman's Rights," in *Words of Fire: An Anthology of African-American Feminist Thought*, ed. Beverly Guy-Sheftall (New York: The New Press, 1995), 36; Sign Arnfred et al., *Staekkede Vinger: Om Alexandra Kollontajs Samtid Og Ideer* (Copenhagen: Tiderne skifter, 1978); Combahee River Collective, "A Black Feminist Statement," in *This Bridge Called My Back: Writings by Radical Women of Colour*, ed. Cherrié Moraga and Gloria Anzaldúa (Watertown, MA: Persephone Press, 1981), 210–218; bell hooks, *Ain't I a Woman: Black Women and Feminism* (Boston: South End Press, 1981).

22. Gór ska, "Breathing Matters."

23. Ann Cvetkovich, *An Archive of Feelings: Trauma, Sexuality, and Lesbian Public Cultures* (Durham, NC: Duke University Press, 2003); Ann Cvetkovich, *Depression: A Public Feeling* (Durham, NC: Duke University Press Books, 2012).

24. Eve Kosofsky Sedgwick, *Touching Feeling: Affect, Pedagogy, Performativity* (Durham, NC: Duke University Press, 2003).

25. Sara Ahmed, *The Cultural Politics of Emotion* (Edinburgh: Edinburgh University Press, 2004); Sara Ahmed, *The Promise of Happiness* (Durham and London: Duke University Press, 2010).

26. Sianne Ngai, *Ugly Feelings* (Cambridge, MA: Harvard University Press, 2007).

27. Heat her Love, *Feeling Backward: Loss and the Politics of Queer History* (Cambridge, MA: Harvard University Press, 2009).

28. Lauren Berlant, *Cruel Optimism* (Durham, NC: Duke University Press, 2011).

29. Judith Halberstam, *The Queer Art of Failure* (Durham, NC: Duke University Press, 2011).

30. Karin Michalski, *The Alphabet of Feeling B* (Berlin, 2012).

31. Karin Michalski and Sebastian Baumann, "An Unhappy Archive" (Exhibition project, Karlsruhe, 2014).

32. Cvetkovich, *Depression*, 13.

33. Górska, "Breathing Matters."

34. Ahmed, *Promise of Happiness*, 120.

35. Halberstam, *Queer Art of Failure*, 2.

36. Ngọc Loan Trần, "Calling IN: A Less Disposable Way of Holding Each Other Accountable," accessed January 4, 2015, http://www.blackgirldangerous.org/2013/12/calling-less-disposable-way-holding-accountable.

Bibliography

Ahmed, Sara. *The Cultural Politics of Emotion*. Edinburgh: Edinburgh University Press, 2004.

Ahmed, Sara. *The Promise of Happiness*. Durham, NC: Duke University Press, 2010.

Alaimo, Stacy. *Bodily Natures: Science, Environment and the Material Self*. Bloomington: Indiana University Press, 2010.

Alaimo, Stacy. "Trans-Corporeal Feminisms and the Ethical Space of Nature." In *Material Feminisms*, edited by Stacy Alaimo and Susan Hekman, 237–264. Bloomington: Indiana University Press, 2008.

Arnfred, Sign, Maj Skibstrup, Mette Bryld, and Nina Lykke. *Staekkede Vinger: Om Alexandra Kollontajs Samtid Og Ideer*. Copenhagen: Tiderne skifter, 1978.

Åsberg, Cecilia. "The Timely Ethics of Posthumanist Gender Studies." *Feministische Studien: Zeitschrift für interdisziplinäre Frauen- und Geschlechtforschung* 1 (2013): 7–12.

Barad, Karen. *Meeting the Universe Halfway: Quantum Physics and the Entanglement of Matter and Meaning*. Durham, NC: Duke University Press, 2007.

Barad, Karen. "Posthumanist Performativity: Toward an Understanding of How Matter Comes to Matter." *Signs* 28, no. 3 (2003): 801–831.

Berlant, Lauren. *Cruel Optimism*. Durham, NC: Duke University Press, 2011.

Birke, Lynda. *Feminism and the Biological Body*. New Brunswick, NJ: Rutgers University Press, 2000.

Bordo, Susan, and Alison Jaggar, eds. *Gender/Body/Knowledge: Feminist Reconstructions of Being and Knowing*. New Brunswick and London: Rutgers University Press, 1989.

Braidotti, Rosi. *Nomadic Subjects*. New York: Columbia University Press, 1994.

Braidotti, Rosi. *The Posthuman*. Cambridge and Malden: Polity Press, 2013.

Bryld, Mette, and Nina Lykke. *Cosmodolphins: Feminist Cultural Studies of Technology, Animals and the Sacred*. London: Zed Books, 2000.

Butler, Judith. *Bodies That Matter: On the Discursive Limits of "Sex."* New York: Routledge, 1993.

Combahee River Collective. "A Black Feminist Statement." In *This Bridge Called My Back: Writings by Radical Women of Colour*, edited by Cherrié Moraga and Gloria Anzaldúa, 210–218. Watertown, MA: Persephone Press, 1981.

Conboy, Katie, Nadia Medina, and Sarah Stanbury, eds. *Writing on the Body: Female Embodiment and Feminist Theory*. New York: Columbia University Press, 1997.

Cvetkovich, Ann. *An Archive of Feelings: Trauma, Sexuality, and Lesbian Public Cultures*. Durham, NC: Duke University Press, 2003.

Cvetkovich, Ann. *Depression: A Public Feeling*. Durham, NC: Duke University Press Books, 2012.

Davis, Kathy, ed. *Embodied Practices: Feminist Perspectives on the Body*. London: Sage, 1997.

Germani, Anna, Piergiuseppe Morone, and Giuseppina Testa. "Environmental Justice and Air Pollution: A Case Study on Italian Provinces." *Ecological Economics* 106 (2014): 69–82.

Górska, Magdalena. "Breathing Matters: Feminist Intersectional Politics of Vulnerability." PhD diss., Linköping University, 2016.

Grosz, Elizabeth. *Volatile Bodies: Toward a Corporeal Feminism*. Bloomington: Indiana University Press, 1994.

Halberstam, Judith. *The Queer Art of Failure*. Durham, NC: Duke University Press, 2011.

Haraway, Donna. "Otherworldly Conversations; Terran Topics; Local Terms." In *The Haraway Reader*, 125–150. New York: Routledge, 2004.

Haraway, Donna. *Simians, Cyborgs, and Women: The Reinvention of Nature*. New York: Routledge, 1991.

Haraway, Donna. "When Species Meet: Staying with the Trouble." *Environment and Planning D: Society and Space* 28, no. 1 (2010): 53–55.

Hird, Myra. *The Origins of Sociable Life: Evolution after Science Studies*. New York: Palgrave Macmillan, 2009.

hooks, bell. *Ain't I a Woman: Black Women and Feminism*. Boston: South End Press, 1981.

Katrak, Ketu. *The Politics of the Female Body: Postcolonial Women Writers*. New Brunswick, NJ: Rutgers University Press, 2006.

Love, Heather. *Feeling Backward: Loss and the Politics of Queer History*. Cambridge, MA: Harvard University Press, 2009.

Michalski, Karin. *The Alphabet of Feeling Bad*. Berlin, 2012.

Michalski, Karin, and Sebastian Baumann. "An Unhappy Archive." Exhibition project, Karlsruhe, 2014.

Ngai, Sianne. *Ugly Feelings*. Cambridge, MA: Harvard University Press, 2007.

Padilla, Cindy, Wahida Kihal-Talantikite, Verónica Vieira, Philippe Rossello, Geraldine Le Nir, Denis Zmirou-Navier, and Severine Deguen. "Air Quality and Social

Deprivation in Four French Metropolitan Areas—A Localized Spatio-Temporal Environmental Inequality Analysis." *Environmental Research* 134 (2014): 315–324.

Pearce, Jamie, Simon Kingham, and Peyman Zawar-Reza. "Every Breath You Take? Environmental Justice and Air Pollution in Christchurch, New Zealand." *Environment and Planning A* 38, no. 5 (May 1, 2006): 919–938.

Sedgwick, Eve Kosofsky. *Touching Feeling: Affect, Pedagogy, Performativity*. Durham, NC: Duke University Press, 2003.

Shildrick, Margrit. *Dangerous Discourses of Disability, Subjectivity and Sexuality*. Basingstoke and New York: Palgrave Macmillan, 2009.

Shildrick, Margrit. *Embodying the Monster: Encounters with the Vulnerable Self*. London and Thousand Oaks: Sage Publications, 2002.

Škof, Lenart. *Breath of Proximity: Intersubjectivity, Ethics and Peace*. Dordrecht: Springer, 2015.

Trân, Ngọc Loan. "Calling IN: A Less Disposable Way of Holding Each Other Accountable." Accessed January 4, 2015. http://www.blackgirldangerous.org/2013/12/calling-less-disposable-way-holding-accountable.

Truth, Sojourner. "Woman's Rights." In *Words of Fire: An Anthology of African-American Feminist Thought*, edited by Beverly Guy-Sheftall, 36. New York: The New Press, 1995.

Wheeler, Benedict. "Health-Related Environmental Indices and Environmental Equity in England and Wales." *Environment and Planning A* 36, no. 5 (May 1, 2004): 803–822.

Postface

17

The Commonwealth of Breath

DAVID ABRAM

Gusting the tops of small waves, a wind carrying salt spray collides with another thick with tree pollen; edges of both merge with a breeze plucking lichen spores from the surface of rocks as it rides up the hill where I sit, high above the coast, gazing at a far-off tanker filled with tar sands crude. Behind me, another breeze lingers at the forest edge, spiced by truck exhaust and the reek from two oyster shells broken open by a raven. I breathe in, and all those unseen currents converge, pollen and petrol fumes flooding up through my nostrils (tweaking dendrites and spreading twangs of sensation along my scalp) and then down into my chest, charging my blood and feeding the vigor in my limbs. I stretch, shoulder muscles cracking, and exhale. The feelings sparked by the sight of that tanker lend their tremor to the breath pouring out through my lips: wonder and worry texture the small vortices in front of me and the eddying flows that rush past me, informing the interference patterns between my exhalations and those of the tall cedars and the mist rising from the Salish Sea.

∾

What is climate change if not a consequence of failing to respect or even to notice the elemental medium in which we're immersed? Is not global warming, or global weirding, a simple consequence of taking the air for granted?

It is easy, you might say, to overlook something that's invisible. We don't commonly notice our breathing, although it enables all that we do notice. And we don't commonly see the air, since it's that through which we see everything else. The atmosphere is ungraspable, unmappable, and hopelessly unpredictable—an ever-shifting flux we're generally unable to lay eyes on. The unseen quality of the air is what prompted so many traditional peoples to pay surpassing respect to this medium, acknowledging the breath and the gusting wind as aspects of an especially sacred power, a ubiquitous and meaning-filled plenum in which they found themselves immersed.

Yet in the modern era, it's that same invisibility that leads us to take the air for granted; since we can't see it, perhaps there's nothing of consequence there. We have ceased speaking to the unseen spirits that gathered near rivers or lingered near certain herbs. We have stopped feeling for the invisible qualities that reside in particular places. We have quit tasting the breeze, stopped noticing the steady gift of our breath, and generally forgotten the air. Today, we rarely acknowledge the atmosphere as it swirls between two persons. We don't speak of the air between our body and a nearby tree, but rather the empty space between us. It's empty. Just an absence of stuff, without feeling or meaning. A void.

And hence, a perfect place to throw whatever we hope to a-void. The perfect dump site for the unwanted byproducts of our industries, for the noxious brew of chemicals exhaled from the stacks of our factories and power plants and refineries, and the stinging exhaust belching forth from our fossil-fueled vehicles—spewing from automobiles and airplanes, cruise ships and tug boats and giant tankers lugging thick tar sands oil to be processed in foreign ports. Even the most opaque, acrid smoke billowing out of the pipes will dissipate and disperse, always and ultimately dissolving into the invisible. It's gone. Out of sight, out of mind.

Mind—or consciousness, or awareness[1]—is a hopelessly amorphous and ephemeral phenomenon, one that's mighty tough to pin down. Gobs of scientific papers and books have been published in recent years trying to account for the emergence of awareness, or to explain how consciousness is constituted within the brain. Many of these works are dramatically at odds with one another, for there exists no clear agreement as to just what this enigma that we call "consciousness" actually *is*.

Part of the difficulty stems from the intransigence of old notions, in particular our age-old assumption that mind is a uniquely human property, an utterly intangible substance that resides somewhere "inside" each of us. A problematic assumption. Given the blithe obliviousness with which we shove other species over the brink of extinction, and our ready capacity to wreak havoc upon ecosystems utterly essential to our own flourishing, it might be that a bit of humility is in order. We may not be quite as conscious as we've thought. At this broken moment in the human story, when the continued survival not only of our kind but of much of our world is in question, it may be that a fresh conception, or image, of mind is in order. An image that has a sort of wisdom built right into it.

Curiously, our experience of awareness—this amorphous and ephemeral power—has much in common with our felt experience of earth's atmosphere.

Consider the air, the light-filled and fluid element in which you're now immersed, with its agitations and its calms, its storms and its subsidences. Consider the unseen currents drifting between the soils and the scudding clouds and circulating among us wherever we find ourselves, pouring in through the door and eddying along the walls, streaming in at your nostrils and circulating within you as well. Like the quality of awareness, the fluid air constantly informs us, and yet it's exceedingly difficult to catch sight of. We glimpse the air only indirectly, as it bends the branches of a birch tree, or slants the rain, or steals a page from our fingers and sends it flapping down the street. We drink the air ceaselessly, alchemizing it within our flesh and replenishing it with every outbreath, yet seem unable to fully bring it to our attention. Itself invisible, the atmosphere is that *through which* we see everything else—much as consciousness, which we cannot see or grasp, is that *through which* we encounter all other phenomena. We are unable to step apart from consciousness, in order to examine it objectively, for wherever we step it is already there.

Mind, in this sense, is very much like a medium in which we're corporeally situated, and from which we're simply unable to extricate ourselves without ceasing to exist. Everything we know or sense of ourselves is conditioned by this atmosphere. We are intimately acquainted with its character, endlessly transformed by its influence upon us. And yet we're unable to characterize this medium from outside. We are composed of this curious element, permeated by it, and hence can take no real distance from it.

To acknowledge this affinity between air and awareness is to allow this curious possibility: that the awareness that stirs within each of us is continuous with the wider awareness that moves around us, twisting the grasses and lofting the crows. Each organism partakes of this awareness from its own unique angle or situation within it, imbibing it through our nostrils or through the stomata in our leaves, altering its chemistry and quality within us before we breathe it back into the surrounding world.

Is consciousness really the special possession of our species? Or is it, rather, a property of the breathing biosphere—a quality in which we, along with the woodpeckers and the spreading weeds, all participate? Perhaps the apparent "interiority" we ascribe to the mind has less to do with a separate consciousness located somewhere *inside me* and another entirely separate and distinct consciousness that sits *inside you*, and more to do with the intuition that we are both situated *within it*—a recognition that we are carnally immersed in an awareness that is not, properly speaking, ours, but is rather the earth's.[2]

∾

Among the Inuit and Yupik peoples inhabiting the circumpolar arctic, the enigma is named *Sila*. There are variants in local dialects: *Hila, Hla, Shla, Sla, Tla*. All voice the same mystery, most commonly called *Sila:* the wind-mind of the world, source of all breath. *Sila* is the elemental wonder of the air, and of the winds that stir and sometimes surge within it, of storm and mist and every other kind of weather, but also: *awareness, consciousness.*

Silarjuaq: that which has no creator; constant flux and change; mind at large. *Silatuniq:* wisdom. Both from *Sila:* the intelligence of the air, the mind of the cycling seasons and the weather.[3] The great indweller in the air, *Sila* is the source of all breath, of all life, of all awareness. Awairness. Wind-mind.

In the early 1920s, an old Inuit *angakoq* (or shaman) named Najagneq spoke in conversation with the Danish explorer, Knud Rasmussen. His words were translated by Rasmussen into Danish, and then by others into English. Najagneq spoke of

> [. . .] a power that we call *Sila*, that cannot be explained in simple words. A great spirit sustaining the world and the weather and all life on earth, a spirit so mighty that its speech to humankind is not through common words, but through storms and snow and rainfall and the fury of the sea; all the forces of nature that men fear. But it has also another means of utterance, through sunlight and calm seas and through small children innocently at play, understanding nothing. Children hear a soft and gentle voice, almost like that of a woman. It comes to them in a mysterious way, but so gently that they are not afraid; they only hear that some danger threatens [. . .] When times are good, *Sila* has nothing to say to humankind, but withdraws into its endless nothingness, where it remains as long as people do not abuse life and act with respect toward the animals that are their food. No one has ever seen *Sila;* its place is a mystery, at once intimately among us and unspeakably far away.[4]

Rasmussen's written records and many more recent ethnographies make evident the importance, for the Inuit, of another, more intimate power: the "breath-soul," or *inua*, that indwells each living being, providing life and awareness to humans, animals, and plants. A person's breath-soul, however, is simply her part of the wider mind of the wind, since *Sila*, the sensibility in the air, subsumes all individual *inua*, or breath-souls, within itself.

> *Sila* is the life-giving element, which enfolds all the world and invests all living organisms [. . .] *Sila* is the word for air, without air there is no life; air is in all people and all creatures [. . .] Every individual is said to have as part of his soul the life force, the life-giving spirit, which is part of the whole animating force *Silap Inua* [the Indweller in the Wind]. This is of course something which never dies, air and

the life-giving force go on indefinitely, and so then does the soul of man. When the air passes out of the body at the moment of physical death, it is simply the passing of the soul back into its original matrix.[5]

This old, circumpolar understanding neatly unties the modern philosophical knot conventionally known as "the mind–body problem"—the puzzle of how a purely immaterial mind, or consciousness, interacts with (or is generated by) a thoroughly material body. To the Inuit, consciousness may be invisible and ineffable, but it is hardly immaterial; it is, rather, the sentience of the unseen but nonetheless palpable element *in which we participate with the whole of our breathing bodies.* The sun-infused air is our common medium, a broad intelligence that we share with the other animals and the plants and the forested mountains, yet each of us engages it with the particularities of our own flesh. And since your body is different from mine in many ways, so your experience of awareness—your interface with the common medium—is necessarily richly different from mine. The still more contrasting experience of a praying mantis or a pileated woodpecker—or of a field of wild lupines, for that matter—are as curiously different from our experience as their bodies are different from ours. Each being's awareness is unique, to be sure, yet this is not because an autonomous mind is held inside its particular body or brain. Rather, each engages the common awareness from its own extraordinary angle, through its particular senses, according to the capacities of its flesh.

∾

Such an elegant conception, if taken seriously, opens a range of previously unsuspected insights into the contemporary climate predicament. Yet this perspective, at once strangely new and startlingly old, is hardly unique to the indigenous traditions of the far north. After a long summer spent teaching, and learning, on the northwest coast of North America, I have just this week returned to my home in the southwest desert, reacquainting myself with the sunset hues of sandstone and the scents of juniper and sage. Here in this land there flourish an array of native cultures, speaking languages from at least five unrelated language families, each of which practices its own intensely respectful relation to the unseen atmosphere.

Among the Dineh (or Navajo) people, the encompassing and fluid power that grants all beings life, movement, and awareness is called *Nilch'i*, the Holy Wind. *Nilch'i* is the whole body of the air, or atmosphere, including those parts of the air in motion and those at rest; it is the medium through which all beings (mountains, coyotes, cottonwood trees, owls) communicate with one another. The sacred nature of the Holy Wind resides not merely in our thorough dependence upon it, but in its subtlety and invisibility: we witness it only by means of the visible things that it animates. There exist innumerable local winds, breezes, storms, gusts, and whiffs that stir within the broad body of the Holy Wind, including the winds that dwell and circulate within each of us. The individual "wind within one" was long misunderstood by anthropologists, who assumed that it referred to an autonomous spirit, or soul, akin to the personal soul of Christian belief. These interpreters failed to recognize that, for the Navajo, the "wind within one" was continuous with the enveloping wind at large—that the wind circulating within each person was informed by the wider wind that sweeps the desert grasses. Similarly, the two little winds, called "wind's children," that linger in the spiraling folds of a person's ears, often whispering worded insights to her as she goes about her days: these, as well, are just a part of the expansive body of Holy Wind. For the Navajo, in other words, the very thoughts that we hear churning within our heads are spoken by small whirlwinds, or eddies, within the vast transparence of *nilch'i*, the fluid wind-mind of the world.[6]

Within this rich cosmology, the different qualities of the various gusts, gales, whirlwinds, crosscurrents, blasts, and breezes that roll across the desert are recognized in the diverse names by which they are invoked: Dawn Man, Sky Blue Woman, Twilight Man, Dark Wind, Wind's Child, Revolving Wind, Glossy Wind, Rolling Darkness Wind, and many others. The Navajo distinguish unpredictable winds and steady winds, harmful winds and helpful winds. Each person must navigate among these invisible influences with great care, striving to bring her life into *hozho*—dynamic balance—with these immersive powers.

Nor are humans purely passive with respect to the Holy Wind. Like the mountains in the four directions, like the plants and the other animals, human persons are one of the Wind's dwelling places, one of its many centers; just as we are nourished and influenced by the air at large, so our thoughts and our actions affect the air in turn. Human intentions can most effectively alter the world around us through the power of spoken utterance, through oral prayer and chanted song, which resonate and transform the very texture of the surrounding winds. Hence, among the Navajo, abundant energy and artistry are given to ceremonies like the Blessingway, wherein persons invoke and project *hozho* into the enveloping atmosphere through a ritual cycle of songs. At the conclusion of any such ceremony, the participants breathe the renewed *hozho* back into their lungs, making themselves a part of the harmony, order, and beauty that they have just established in the ambient medium through the power of the chant.[7] The relation between the Navajo people and the animate cosmos that enfolds and includes them is participatory and reciprocal; they are not just passive recipients of Wind's influence, but instead are both passive and active, inhaling and exhaling, receiving the nourishment of the myriad beings and actively nourishing them in turn.

Meanwhile, among the many pueblo cultures (including the Hopi, the Zuni, and the various pueblos villages of northern New Mexico) another emphasis predominates: the preciousness of life-giving rain within this high desert realm. Whenever a person from the pueblo dies, her vapor-essence is felt to journey across the land to the dwelling place of the *kachinas*—the spirit ancestors. The *kachinas* are regularly "fed" by the respectful actions of those who are alive, and by the seasonal ceremonies, the resplendent dances and prayer offerings undertaken throughout the yearly cycle by the villagers. The spirit ancestors, feeling thus honored, return to their respective pueblos whenever they choose: they gather and thicken within the sky's transparence, materializing as clouds carrying and bodying-forth the rain essential for the corn and the other crops upon which the people depend. In the pueblo cosmologies, death brings into existence the ancestors, who return as rain-bearing clouds fertilizing the soil with water. The moisture feeds the corn that, in turn, nourishes the living. Human life and human death are here an integral part of the hydrological cycle. As the people depend on the climate so, reciprocally, the climate depends on the people for its continued flourishing.

I shudder to speak of matters held so sacred to these oral traditions, and even more so to *write* of these understandings, which were never meant to be written down. Much as I tremble to speak aloud the most sacred name of the Holy in my own tribal, Jewish tradition, the four-letter name that—rightly spoken—is not other than the inhale and the exhale, the living breath of awareness. And so I ask the blessing of my ancestors, feeling them in the unseen *ruaḥ* (Hebrew for the divine wind, or "rushing spirit") that surrounds me, here, as I write. I bow to the various peoples indigenous to this region where I dwell, as well as to the animals, plants, and spirits of this parched terrain, asking their permission that I may write, here, of these things. Because these storied knowings, of which I comprehend so little, nonetheless need to be heard once again, and what is common among them needs to be felt, acknowledged, and replenished if life is to flourish.

Oral cultures are cultures of story. Spoken and chanted stories were the living encyclopedias of our oral ancestors, dynamic and lyrical compendiums of practical knowledge. Preserved among the many layers of these tales (tucked within the complex adventures of their characters) were precise instructions for the gathering of specific plants and how to prepare them as foods and as medicines, for tracking bear or hunting caribou, and for enacting the proper rituals of gratitude when a hunt was successful. The stories carried instructions about how to fend for one's family when a prolonged drought dried up the local streams, or—more generally—how to live well in a specific land without destroying the land's wild vitality.

Such practical intelligence, intimately related to a particular place, is the hallmark of any deeply oral culture. Continually tested in interaction with the living land, altering in tandem with subtle changes in the local earth, even today such living knowledge resists the fixity and permanence of the printed page. Nor does it come across when printed or displayed on the electronic screen, whose disembodying sheen and glide ensure that the place-based secrets hidden within each tale will be lost in the digital tide, as the story loses its analog grip on a particular soil. Since it is specific to the way things happen *here*, in this high desert—or coastal estuary, or mountain valley—this kind of intimate intelligence loses much of its meaning when abstracted from its terrain, and from the particular animals, plants, and practices that are a part of its life. Such intelligence, properly speaking, is an attribute of the living land itself; it thrives only in the direct, face-to-face interchange between those who dwell and work in that place.

The primacy of breath in oral traditions—the identification of awareness with the unseen air, and the consequent sacredness accorded to the invisible medium in which we and the other creatures are bodily immersed—has been for most human cultures a simple and obvious intuition, although interpreted, storied, and ritualized in divergent ways by different peoples in different bioregions. The intuition is empowered by the centrality of the spoken (rather than written) word in indigenous lifeways; for traditionally oral cultures, verbal language is not, primarily, a visible set of static marks, but rather an utterance carried on the exhaled breath. *Words, here, are nothing other than shaped breath.* Hence the fluid air is the implicit intermediary in all communication, the very medium of meaning.[8]

∾

"The media" is the phrase we use, today, to name our various forms of widespread communication. Yet all of our many media—whether written, electronic, or digital—derive from the original *medium* of communication: the unseen air that once transmitted all our songs and spoken stories as it carried the whistling of blackbirds and the gurgled utterances of frogs, bearing lichen spores and bee swarms and the exhalations of humpback whales.

Radio personnel still use the phrase "we are on air" or "we are off air" to indicate when they're broadcasting. Yet while contemporary media tacitly depend on the fluid atmosphere, the new media all contribute to the overlooking, or forgetting, of the original medium. In this regard, our newly invented media mimic a tendency endemic to the alphabet, the invention that made them all possible.

The earliest versions of the alphabet, which arose in the ancient near east in the second millennium BC, took care not to violate the primacy of the unseen medium that surrounds and animates all visible things. Like other early Semitic alphabets, the early Hebrew (or paleo-Hebrew) *aleph bait* avoided inscribing the vowels upon the parchment or papyrus; in these most ancient forms of the alphabet, only the consonants were written down. The consonants, of course, are the shapes by which we sculpt our sounded breath, forming words with the tongue, lips, and teeth as we exhale. The vowels, meanwhile, are the sounds made by the breath itself as it vibrates our vocal chords and flows out through the mouth. To the ancient Hebrews, the vowels—as sounded breath—were inseparable from the *ruah̠*, the divine wind, a mystery whose invisibility they dared not violate. For the *ruah* was the unseen but immanent presence of GD (the divine breath that the Holy One first blew into the nostrils of Adam, bringing the first human form to life). And so the Semitic scribes wrote only the consonants, the structure or skeleton of the words. Even today, the reader of a traditional Hebrew text must herself choose which vowels to pronounce between the written consonants, lending her own breath to those bones on the page in order to make them come alive and begin to speak.[9]

Phoenician traders carried the early *aleph bait* across the Mediterranean. When the ancient Greeks encountered and adapted this Semitic invention for their own tongue, they inserted written letters to represent the vowel sounds. For the first time, the breath sounds were rendered visible and explicit on the written page. By this simple move, making a visible representation of the invisible breath, the Greek scribes effectively *desacralized* the unseen medium. They breached the older (Hebraic) taboo on imaging the invisible, effectively de-sanctifying the breath and the wind, making it possible for alphabetic readers to begin to overlook, or forget, the pervasive power of the air. Indeed, the sensuous interplay between the *visible* and *invisible* aspects of surrounding nature was soon replaced, in ancient Athens, by a new dichotomy between sensuous nature as a whole and another, wholly nonsensible world hidden entirely beyond the physical. The Greek philosopher Plato, developing his new conception of an immaterial heaven of pure ideas—a dimension not just invisible, but thoroughly intangible, and hence beyond all bodily ken—was, with this conception, sanctioning a new forgetfulness of the immanent mystery of the air itself, a forgetting first made possible by the very script in which he wrote his many dialogues.[10]

With the gradual spread of the new, vowelized alphabet, and—later—with the broad dissemination of alphabetic texts made possible by the printing press, the primacy of spoken phrases that sculpt and ride the fluid air was slowly displaced by our spreading fascination with the written word. Meaning drained out of the air and became fixed on the page. Fewer and fewer people sensed their ancestors in the winds, or in the quiet stirring of leaves in a forest, since now the ancestors seemed to speak much more clearly from the *bound* leaves of books. The surrounding air, divested of awareness or psyche, lost its felt reality; it came to be felt mostly as a kind of absence, merely the hurrying of molecules, endlessly, meaninglessly.[11] And soon was hardly felt, or noticed, at all.

∾

Like the air, the "new media" are ubiquitous, pervasive, and ever present. With the advent of the Internet and the emergence of wireless computing, the new media permeate our workspaces and our homes, suffusing the space of our cities and towns. As cellular, GPS, and now smart phones proliferate, digital media inform the electromagnetic spectrum throughout more and more of the countryside, infiltrating woodlands and swamps, glancing off mountain ridges, washing through even the wild backcountry. They saturate our lives. We may power off the iPhone or shut the lid on our laptop, but the information's still churning all around and even through us, ready to display itself as soon as we open whatever new handheld gadget, whatever screen-fitted thingamajig currently accompanies us.

Omnipresent as air, seemingly *omniscient* as well, the new media perfectly deflect the atmosphere from our attention. Unlike the bothersome subjection of our animal flesh to whatever weather's brewing, we feel we have control over *these* media, able to conjure whatever data we wish onto the screen (in whatever interface we have chosen). Humans alone are online here; no other species clutter the frequencies or muddle the field with their pheromones. There's no ambiguity, nor the bother of having to expose our pimples, or render ourselves vulnerable by meeting others in the palpable world of flesh and blood. The tangible earth's getting way too weird anyway, with its fires and famines and floods, its flaring riots and refugees: better to hang out online, adrift in the cloud.

The new media grab our focus and hold our fascination, and they keep our kids occupied, too, granting us a ready vacation from the perplexity of the real, or helping us avoid it altogether.

Sooner or later, though, the media trance leaves us gasping for air. Because the ubiquitous data's all so instantaneous, so much of it instantly accessible, answers to any question right here at our fingertips and right now in our face, though we have not had a moment to digest or even chew the last meal or morsel. There is too much of it, a superfluity of information, a glut, a flood. Info on pretty much anything and everything we can think of, and mostly what we cannot, but now here it is anyway: a paragraph that's mildly relevant to the problem that my kids and I are puzzling out this afternoon, yet halfway down that paragraph a highlighted word links to another nugget of interesting knowledge attached to a video clip; the first few seconds of the segment abruptly call to mind another video I had wanted to glance at last week but forgot, regarding the luscious mating ritual of hermaphroditic leopard slugs, so I try to find it now on *Youtube* or *Vimeo* but get snagged by someone's TED talk about a new app for mapping gender inequality across countries and cultures. All these images, all this text, all this digital data churning past thick as flies, dense as fog, viscous as syrup laced with corn starch and captions, mucilaginous, and we are in the thick of it, mouths wide open, glugging.

Hence the need for air. For a bit of breathing space. For a chance to breathe.

A filter would be useful, some way of standing and taking our bearings in the midst of this tide that keeps rising. A way of remembering what is primary, and catching our breath, letting our digital encounters dissolve back into the spacious quietude, an open silence broken only now and then by the sigh of the wind through the tall grasses. There is a need for depth, for possibilities that beckon from afar, for enigmas that reside in the distance. Or rather for some things that are close by and accessible while others wait in the far-off hills, and still others roam the middle space between these, foraging among the stones at the edge of the creek. There is a need for distances that we feel and sometimes commit ourselves to crossing—giving our muscles to the slow, patient craft of making our way through the palpable depths of the sensuous.

The oncoming storms of climate change, the never-before-seen winds tossing down power lines and ripping out trees by their roots, the thudding torrents of rain in some regions and the unbroken heat cracking the soil in others, all are a consequence of our long forgetfulness. Of our forgetting the invisible, taking for granted what we could not see. We overlooked that element held most holy by our oral ancestors, the unseen flux long assumed to be the very source of all awareness, wind-mind of the world: the Commonwealth of Breath.

The swelling storms are a simple consequence of treating the atmosphere as an open sewer, a magic dump site for whatever we wished to avoid. *Out of sight, out of mind . . .* or so we thought.

But for our oral elders and ancestors, that which dissipates as smoke or dissolves into the unseen air is by that very process slipping *into* the mind, *binding itself back into the encompassing awareness from which our bodies steadily drink, the wild sentience of the world, moody with weather . . .*

We renew our participation in the more-than-human community—in the breathing commons—by telling stories. Not, however, stories that we print in books or post on glowing screens, or send out as podcasts. Stories, rather, that we tell *aloud*, face to face, sharing the same air with those who listen and offer a tale in return. Not just tales that have been written, or recorded, and hence abstracted from the whisper and sing-song and push-pull of the local earth where they once drew their relevance. Stories, rather, that hold sway in particular places, carrying in their textures and rhythms something of the relation between humans and the other animals, herbs, waters, woodlands, and weather patterns that compose the cycling life of the land where we dwell.

Scholars, philosophers, and authors attentive to what has been called "the new materialism," and the other emerging discourses in which the vibrancy and eloquence of material things are re-asserting themselves, have much necessary work to do, disclosing the manifold ways that ostensibly human narratives arise from our ongoing corporeal interchange with various other bodies and fluid trajectories—with other material agencies that express themselves to, and often through, our own bodily materiality, speaking through our actions, our technologies, our creative endeavors. But material ecocritics should consider resisting the instinctive academic impulse to write down and record every single one of their findings; they should consider withholding a few of their crucial discoveries from the page and the glowing screen, in order to let those insights dwell in their particular places, in order to shape them on the breath between their body and breathing terrain. Writing is an astonishing magic, but one that's best used judiciously, since it tends to shut out other beings that do not speak in words. As long as we humans communicate mostly via these more mediated modes of interchange, as long as face-to-face oral culture remains dormant, then the human collective will likely stay somewhat impervious to the full presence of these palpable others.

Writing matters down easily interrupts our felt rapport with other earthly beings, since it involves transcribing our ongoing exchange with the many-voiced cosmos into an almost exclusively human register. We translate our dialogues with wind and pelting rain, with petrochemicals, genetically altered insects, and melting glaciers into a discursive space that nonetheless remains largely closed to other species, impenetrable to other shapes of sentience. We maintain the pretense that humans alone can make sense of what's happening; even as we critique it, we re-inscribe our aloofness from the animate, expressive earth.

Of course, our body remains participant in countless conversations that cannot be translated into words. Such corporeal exchanges *can*, however, find their way into tales and tellings that involve our whole speaking and gesturing organism; when we engage in such oral storytelling, the other beings in the sensorial vicinity—whether humans or flapping crows, whether the termite-riddled trunk of an old oak or the collapsed ruin of an old factory—can readily register (and perhaps even *feel*) something of what's being said, since our speaking has its own material rhythm and pulse, since our creaturely body's caught up in the awkward dance of the thing we're saying. And so other expressive bodies—coyotes howling, a squeaking bicycle, streamwater gushing through culverts or rolling over the guttural stones—can enter into and alter the story in the present moment of its telling.

By listening for such tales, and beginning to tell them aloud out in the terrain, in the very place where those events might have happened (whether in a backcountry stand of tall pines or among the toxic slurry ponds left by an abandoned mine), we begin to rejuvenate oral culture. By sharing such tales as we replant a clearcut forest, by spinning a fresh song out of the struggle to block a tar sands pipeline, or to halt the spread of hydraulic fracking, we bring our sounding bodies back into resonance with the other beings that surround. And as we weave such stories, aloud, into the craft of gathering herbs or raising kids in that land, we begin to bind human language back into a much wider conversation. By turning off our screens, now and then, to come together in the flesh, by camping beneath the buzzing streetlights on a city square exposed to the weather, by gathering along a river to honor the cyclical return of the salmon, or telling a tale of the migrating cranes as they flap their way north above our upturned faces, we bring our spinning minds back into alignment with the broad intelligence of the biosphere.

The feathered wings of those cranes paddle *through* the invisible, as their echoing cries stutter down through the vast silence. Our animal senses awaken; we remember the primacy of the sensuous cosmos that reigns underneath all our abstractions. The breathing earth articulates itself not in statistics but in seedpods

and storms and spoken stories. Listening, shaping a phrase on the wind, falling
silent . . . in this way we reacquaint ourselves with our real community, and
orient ourselves to meet the clouds massing in the distance. The land's awareness slides easily in and out of our nostrils. We reclaim our membership in the
commonwealth of breath.

Notes

1. I use these terms, here, in their broadest or most inclusive sense, including
within their meaning not just focused awareness (or full *waking* consciousness), but
simple sensibility or sentience.

2. Of course from the perspective of salmon, sea lions, and kelp fronds, or the
divergent angle of humpbacks trading their eerie glissando-cries across the fathoms,
it is not *air* but rather the fluid medium of *water* that carries the glimmering quality
of awareness, altering its modes and moods with the tides, hiding uncountable feeling
tones within its depths—sensations that sometimes blossom out of the thickness to
surround and seep into and become one's being for a time. Yet how uncannily different,
how oddly other is *water* from *air* when one inhabits it as one's element and medium!

3. Jaypeetee Arnakak, in Timothy Leduc, *Climate Culture Change: Inuit and
Western Dialogues with a Warming North* (Ottawa: University of Ottawa Press, 2010),
26–31.

4. Daniel Merkur, *Powers Which We Do Not Know: The Gods and Spirits of the
Inuit* (Moscow: University of Idaho Press, 1991), 46. See also Leduc, *Climate Culture
Change*, 21–22. The English translation of Rasmussen's notes, written in Danish, varies
slightly across these and other texts.

5. Robert G. Williamson, *Eskimo Underground: Socio-Cultural Change in the
Central Canadian Arctic* (Uppsala: Almqvist & Wiksell, 1974), 22–23.

6. James Kale McNeley, *Holy Wind in Navajo Philosophy* (Tucson: University of
Arizona Press, 1981). This book is the fruit of twenty years of close association with
the Navajo. McNeley is married to a Dineh woman; both of them taught for many
years at Shiprock on the Navajo Reservation in Arizona. See also David Abram, *The
Spell of the Sensuous: Perception and Language in a More than Human World* (New
York: Vintage Books, 1997), 230–237.

7. Gary Witherspoon, *Language and Art in the Navajo Universe* (Ann Arbor:
University of Michigan Press, 1977), 61.

8. If you doubt the ubiquity of this notion, ponder for a moment the etymology of the common English words "spirit" (from Latin *spiritus*: a breath, or a gust of
wind), or "psyche" (from the ancient Greek verb *psychein*: to breathe or to blow, as a
wind). Consider the Latin word for the soul, *anima* (from the older Greek *anemos*,
meaning wind) from whence derive such terms as "animal" (an ensouled being) and
"unanimous" (being of one mind). Or consider the term "atmosphere," itself cognate
with the Sanskrit word *ātman*, which signifies the soul or self (whether of the cosmos,
or of a person).

9. Traditional Hebraic spirituality was both literate and oral at the same time. The Hebrew scribes and priests were literate in their relation to the visible cosmos, insisting that GD could not be found in the visible things of the world. But by avoiding writing down the vowels, they preserved an intensely oral, animistic relation to the invisible air, wind and breath—to the unseen medium that moves between and binds all visible things.

10. For abundant and carefully documented evidence for this claim, see the chapters "Animism and the Alphabet" and "The Forgetting and Remembering of the Air," in Abram, *Spell of the Sensuous*, 93–135 and 225–260.

11. A paraphrase of Alfred North Whitehead, who described the scientific conception of nature at the end of the seventeenth century as "merely the hurrying of material, endlessly, meaninglessly." Alfred North Whitehead, *Science in the Modern World* (Cambridge: Cambridge University Press, 1953), 69.

Bibliography

Abram, David. *The Spell of the Sensuous: Perception and Language in a More-than-Human World*. New York: Vintage Books, 1997.

Leduc, Timothy. *Climate Culture Change: Inuit and Western Dialogues with a Warming North*. Ottawa: University of Ottawa Press, 2010.

McNeley, James Kale. *Holy Wind in Navajo Philosophy*. Tucson: University of Arizona Press, 1981.

Merkur, Daniel. *Powers Which We Do Not Know: The Gods and Spirits of the Inuit*. Moscow: University of Idaho Press, 1991.

Whitehead, Alfred North. *Science in the Modern World*. Cambridge: Cambridge University Press, 1953.

Williamson, Robert G. *Eskimo Underground: Socio-Cultural Change in the Central Canadian Arctic*. Uppsala: Almqvist & Wiksell, 1974.

Witherspoon, Gary. *Language and Art in the Navajo Universe*. Ann Arbor: University of Michigan Press, 1977.

Contributors

David Abram, Alliance for Wild Ethics, United States

Abram is a cultural ecologist and geophilosopher and the author of *The Spell of the Sensuous: Perception and Language in a More-than-Human World*, and *Becoming Animal: An Earthly Cosmology*. Hailed as "revolutionary" by the *Los Angeles Times*, as "daring" and "truly original" by *Science*, Dr. Abram's writings have catalyzed the emergence of several new disciplines, including the rapidly growing field of Ecopsychology. His essays on the cultural causes and consequences of environmental disarray are published in numerous magazines, scholarly journals, and anthologies. David is the co-founder and Director of the *Alliance for Wild Ethics* (AWE), a consortium of individuals and organizations working to ease the spreading devastation of the earth through a rapid transformation of culture. Widely sought after as a uniquely powerful educator and speaker, Dr. Abram recently held the international *Arne Naess Chair in Global Justice and the Environment* at the University of Oslo. A distinguished Fellow of Schumacher College, he is a recipient of the international *Lannan Literary Award* for Nonfiction, and of fellowships from the Rockefeller and the Watson Foundations. David lives with his two children in the foothills of the southern Rockies.

Silvia Benso, Rochester Institute of Technology, United States

Benso is Professor of Philosophy at the Rochester Institute of Technology, Rochester, New York. Among her areas of interest are ancient philosophy, contemporary European (especially Italian) philosophy, the history of philosophy, ethics, aesthetics, and feminist theories. Besides having published articles on Nietzsche, Heidegger, Levinas, and ancient philosophy (especially Plato), she is the author of *Thinking After Auschwitz: Philosophical Ethics and Jewish Theodicy* (in Italian), *The Face of Things: A Different Side of Ethics*, *Viva Voce: Interviews with Italian Philosophers*, and the co-author of the volume *Environmental Thinking: Between Philosophy and Ecology* (in Italian). She has also co-edited various volumes, including *Contemporary Italian Philosophy: Between Ethics, Politics and Religion*,

Levinas and the Ancients, and *Between Nihilism and Politics: The Hermeneutics of Gianni Vattimo*. She is the general co-editor for the series Contemporary Italian Philosophy published by SUNY Press.

Petri Berndtson, University of Jyväskylä, Finland

Berndtson is a PhD student in philosophy at the University of Jyväskylä (Jyväskylä, Finland). The topic of his PhD thesis is the phenomenological ontology of breathing. His main research interests and expertise lie in the experiential phenomenon of breathing, phenomenology (especially Merleau-Ponty), embodiment, the elemental poetics of air (Bachelard), and contemplative studies. Berndtson is a former full-time lecturer of philosophy at the Lahti University of Applied Sciences (Lahti, Finland). He has also been a guest lecturer at the Trondheim Academy of Fine Art (Trondheim, Norway). In addition, he has invented a method called *Philosophical Breathwork*, which is a philosophico-experiential way of working with breathing. More information can be found at his websites: www.philosophicalbreathwork. com and https://jyu.academia.edu/PetriBerndtson.

Havi Carel, University of Bristol, United Kingdom

Carel is Professor of Philosophy at the University of Bristol, where she also teaches medical students. She is currently a Wellcome Trust Senior Investigator, leading a five-year project, the Life of Breath (www.lifeofbreath.org). Her third monograph was published by Oxford University Press in 2016, entitled *Phenomenology of Illness*. Havi was voted by students as a "Best of Bristol" lecturer in 2016. She is the author of *Illness* (2008, 2013), shortlisted for the Wellcome Trust Book Prize, and of *Life and Death in Freud and Heidegger* (2006). She is the co-editor of *Health, Illness and Disease* (2012) and of *What Philosophy Is* (2004). She uses film in teaching and has co-edited a volume entitled *New Takes in Film-Philosophy* (2010). She also co-edited a special issue of *Philosophy* on "Human Experience and Nature" (2013). She previously published on the embodied experience of illness, epistemic injustice, well-being within illness, and the experience of respiratory illness in *The Lancet, BMJ, Journal of Medicine and Philosophy, Journal of Medical Ethics, Journal of Applied Philosophy, Theoretical Medicine and Bioethics, Medicine, Healthcare and Philosophy*, and in edited collections. In 2009–11 Havi led an AHRC-funded project on the concepts of health, illness, and disease. In 2011–12 she was awarded a Leverhulme Fellowship for a project entitled "The Lived Experience of Illness." In 2012–13 she held a British Academy Mid-Career Fellowship. For further information, see her websites: bristol.academia.edu/ HaviCarel and www.bristol.ac.uk/school-of-arts/people/havi-h-carel/index.html

Tamara Ditrich, University of Sydney, Australia

Ditrich has been researching and lecturing in Sanskrit and Pāli at a variety of sites, in academic subjects related to Asian religions and languages at several universities in Europe and Australia. Her research areas include Buddhist Studies (mainly in Pāli), Sanskrit Linguistics, and Vedic Philology.

John Durham Peters, Yale University, United States

Durham Peters is Professor of English & Film and Media Studies at Yale University. He is the author of the books *Speaking into the Air* (1999), *Courting the Abyss* (2005), and *The Marvelous Clouds* (2015). His interests lie in the history and theory of media and their connections with adjacent fields of knowledge.

Rolf Elberfeld, University of Hildesheim, Germany

Elberfeld is Full Professor of Philosophy at the University of Hildesheim. He studied Philosophy, Japanology, Sinology, and History of Religion in Würzburg, Bonn, and Kyoto, Japan. His fields of research are Intercultural Philosophy, Comparative Aethetics/Ethics, Phenomenology, Japanese Philosophy, Philosophy of Language, and the body. He is the author of *Kitaro Nishida (1870–1945): Moderne japanische Philosophie und die Frage nach der Interkulturalität* (1999); *Phänomenologie der Zeit im Buddhismus: Methoden interkulturellen Philosophierens* (2004); *Sprache und Sprache: Eine philosophische Grundorientierung* (2012); and *Philosophieren in einer globalisierten Welt: Auf dem Weg zu einer transformativen Phänomenologie* (2017).

Magdalena Górska, Utrecht University, Netherlands

Górska is Assistant Professor in Gender and Postcolonial Studies at the Graduate Gender Program, Department of Media and Culture Studies at Utrecht University. She holds a doctorate in philosophy from the Department of Thematic Studies–Gender Studies at Linköping University, and was a Visiting Scholar at the Department of Feminist Studies, University of California, Santa Cruz. Her initial research experiences were formed during her undergraduate studies at the Faculty of Humanities and at the Department of Gender Studies at Charles University. Her research develops a nonuniversalizing and politicized understanding of embodiment in which human bodies are conceptualized as agential actors of intersectional politics. Her work offers anthropo-situated while posthumanist discussions of human embodiment and agency and focuses on the quotidian corpomaterial and corpo-affective practices as political matters. She is the author of *Breathing Matters: Feminist Intersectional Politics of Vulnerability* and a founder of the Breathing Matters Network.

Kevin Hart, The University of Virginia, United States

Hart is the Edwin B. Kyle Professor of Christian Studies in the Department of Religious Studies at the University of Virginia, where he also holds professorships in the Department of English and the Department of French. His most recent books are *Kingdoms of God* and *Poetry and the Sacred*. His *Wild Track: New and Selected Poems* appeared in 2015.

Jones Irwin, Dublin City University, Ireland

Irwin is a Senior Lecturer in Philosophy and Education at the Institute of Education, St Patrick's Campus, Dublin City University, Republic of Ireland and Co-Chair of the EdD Doctoral program. He is also Subject Leader for Philosophy in Open Education, DCU. He studied philosophy at University College Dublin (BA/MA) and did his PhD at University of Warwick. Since 2014, he has also been seconded to develop a values and comparative religious education curriculum with the Irish state. His research interests are in aesthetics, ethics, philosophy of education, and existential philosophy. His main publications are three books, *Derrida and the Writing of The Body* (Surrey, Ashgate, 2010); *Paulo Freire's Philosophy of Education* (Bloomsbury/Continuum, London/New York, 2012), and [with Dr. Helena Motoh] *Zizek and His Contemporaries: On the Emergence of the Slovenian Lacan* (Bloomsbury, London, 2014). He is currently completing a monograph, *The Pursuit of Existentialism: From Sartre and Beauvoir to Contemporary Thought* (Acumen/Routledge, London, 2017).

David Michael Kleinberg-Levin, Professor Emeritus, Northwestern University, United States

Kleinberg-Levin is the author of many journal publications and has published books in phenomenology, philosophical psychology, moral philosophy, philosophy of art, aesthetics, and art criticism. His books include *Before the Voice of Reason: Echoes of Responsibility in Merleau-Ponty's Ecology and Levinas's Ethics* (2008); *Gestures of Ethical Life: Reading Hölderlin's Question of Measure After Heidegger*; and, most recently, a trilogy of books on the fate of the promise of happiness in the language of literature: Vol. I. *Redeeming Words and the Promise of Happiness: A Critical Theory Approach to Wallace Stevens and Vladimir Nabokov*, Vol. II. *Redeeming Words: Language and the Promise of Happiness in the Stories of Döblin and Sebald* (2013), and Vol. III. *Beckett's Words: The Promise of Happiness in a Time of Mourning*. For more information on Dr. Kleinberg-Levin's work, consult www.academia.edu.

Drew Leder, Loyola College, Maryland, United States

Leder is a phenomenological philosopher who writes often on the intersection of philosophy and medical issues. His new book, *The Distressed Body: Rethinking Illness, Imprisonment, and Healing* (University of Chicago, 2016) reflects on such issues, as well as work he has done over two decades with men incarcerated in maximum-security institutions. The latter was also the subject of another book, *The Soul Knows No Bars*, written in conjunction with incarcerated citizens. Dr. Leder is a Professor of Philosophy at Loyola University, Maryland, where he teaches Eastern as well as Western Philosophy. He also is the author of a series of books on cross-cultural spirituality, reaching out to a general audience. These include *Spiritual Passages*, *Games for the Soul*, and *Sparks of the Divine*.

James Morley, Ramapo College, New Jersey, United States

Morley received his doctorate in clinical psychology from Duquesne University in 1988. His publications and edited works have been in the area of the phenomenology of imagination, qualitative phenomenological methodology, and South Asian contemplative thought. His formal interest in yoga began in 1993, when he made the acquaintance of T.K.V. Desikachar, whose wife Menaka instructed him in *asana* and *pranayama* practice. Since then, he has been struck by the strong convergences between phenomenology and the Indian yoga tradition. In 1995, he spent a sabbatical leave in India, where he studied yoga therapy at the Krishnamacharya Yoga Mandiram and taught at the University of Madras. In the summer of 1997 he was a research Fellow at the National Institute of Advanced Studies, Bangalore. Morley is currently a Professor of Clinical Psychology at Ramapo College of New Jersey. He is a certified yoga instructor and the Director of the Krame Center for Contemplative Studies and Mindful Living. Since 2013, he has been the Editor-in-Chief of *The Journal of Phenomenological Psychology*.

Marijn Nieuwenhuis, University of Warwick, United Kingdom

Nieuwenhuis is Teaching Fellow in International Relations and East Asia at the University of Warwick. His research is at the intersection of Political Geography and International Relations. His current research focuses on the "politics of the air" and deals with questions of technology, pollution, security, territory, and governance.

Tadashi Ogawa, Professor Emeritus, Kyoto University, Japan

Ogawa was born in 1945 in Osaka Prefecture in Japan. He studied Philosophy at the University of Kyoto from 1965to 1974 and then became a lecturer in Philosophy and German at Kyoto Sangyo University in 1974, a professor at the Hiroshima University in 1978, and at the Kyoto University in 1991, and then a professor emeritus at Kyoto University in 2008. He was also the President at the University of Human Environments in Okazaki from 2008 to 2010 and then at the Koshien University in Hyogo from 2012 to 2014. He is currently an advisor for the section of Humanities at the Toyota Technological Institute in Nagoya.

Jana S. Rošker, University of Ljubljana, Slovenia

Rošker is one of the founders of the Department of Asian Studies at the University in Ljubljana (Slovenia). She obtained her PhD at Vienna University and carried out her post-doc research at the Beijing University, People's Republic of China, and the Center for Chinese studies in Taipei, Taiwan. She obtained numerous prestigious national and international grants and awards and is currently leader of three research projects in the field of Asian studies. Her main research interests include methodology of intercultural research, Chinese epistemology, Chinese logic, and Modern Confucianism in East Asia. In these research fields she has published eleven books and over one hundred academic articles. She is chief editor of the journal *Asian Studies*, which has been published by her department since 1998. Rošker is also the founder and first president of the *European Association of Chinese Philosophy* (EACP).

Lenart Škof, Science and Research Center, Slovenia

Škof is Professor of Philosophy and Head of the Institute for Philosophical Studies at the Science and Research Center (Koper, Slovenia) and Research Director at the Alma Mater Europaea (Maribor, Slovenia). He is also Visiting Professor of Religion at Faculty of Theology, University of Ljubljana. Škof received a KAAD grant (Universität Tübingen), Fulbright Grant (Stanford University, academic host: Richard Rorty), and Humboldt fellowship for experienced researchers (Max Weber Kolleg, Universität Erfurt, academic host: Hans Joas). His main research interests lie in ethics, religious studies with contemporary theology, and in intercultural and Indian philosophy (he translated Yajurvedic Upanishads into Slovene), the philosophy of American pragmatism, and the philosophy of Luce Irigaray. He recently co-edited *Breathing with Luce Irigaray* (2013) and *Poesis of Peace: Narratives, Cultures and Philosophies* (2017) and is an author of several books, among them *Pragmatist Variations on Ethical and Intercultural Life* (2012), *Breath of Proximity: Intersubjectivity, Ethics and Peace* (2015), and *Ethik des Atems* (2017). He is the president of the Slovenian Society for Comparative Religion. His current research project is dedicated to Antigone, feminist ethics, and questions of philosophy, religious justice, and peace. Visit his website at https://uni-lj.academia .edu/LenartŠkof.

Index

extrapolating.